Extra-Ordinary Men

Extra-Ordinary Men

White Heterosexual Masculinity in Contemporary Popular Cinema

NICOLA REHLING

LEXINGTON BOOKS

A division of
ROWMAN & LITTLEFIELD PUBLISHERS, INC.
Lanham • Boulder • New York • Toronto • Plymouth, UK

LEXINGTON BOOKS

A division of Rowman & Littlefield Publishers, Inc.
A wholly owned subsidiary of The Rowman & Littlefield Publishing Group, Inc.
4501 Forbes Boulevard, Suite 200
Lanham, MD 20706

Estover Road
Plymouth PL6 7PY
United Kingdom

British Library Cataloguing in Publication Information Available

Library of Congress Cataloging-in-Publication Data

Rehling, Nicola, 1970–
  Extra-ordinary men : white heterosexual masculinity in contemporary popular cinema /
Nicola Rehling.
    p. cm.
  Includes bibliographical references and index.
  ISBN-13: 978-0-7391-2482-6 (cloth : alk. paper)
  ISBN-10: 0-7391-2482-X (cloth : alk. paper)
  ISBN-13: 978-0-7391-3389-7 (electronic)
  ISBN-10: 0-7391-3389-6 (electronic)
  1. Masculinity in motion pictures. 2. Heterosexual men in motion pictures. 3. Whites
in motion pictures. I. Title.
  PN1995.9.M34R44 2009
  791.43'6526662
  [2 22]   2008042288

Printed in the United States of America

♾™ The paper used in this publication meets the minimum requirements of American
National Standard for Information Sciences—Permanence of Paper for Printed Library
Materials, ANSI/NISO Z39.48–1992.

To Yiannis

Contents

Contents

Acknowledgements

This book would not have been possible without the help, support, and encouragement of many people. However, most thanks must go to Ruth Parkin-Gounelas, who supervised the doctoral thesis on which this book is based. Her questioning mind, intellectual and theoretical rigour, and perceptive readings of my drafts never failed to inspire me. She has taught me the true meaning of being a scholar. I would also like to thank my co-advisors: Elsi Sakellaridou, for her scrupulous reading of my work, and Michalis Kokkonis, for his ongoing support throughout the writing of my thesis. The other members of my examining committee—Karin Lagopoulou, Alexandros Lagopoulos, Nick Kontos, and Effie Yiannopoulou—also offered incisive comments which were invaluable during the revision of my thesis.

There are also numerous people who have helped me throughout my academic career. In particular, I am deeply indebted to Steve Watts and Steve Xerri for believing in me at a crucial time and for kindling my interest in gender theory. Mandy Merck has also influenced my work in immeasurable ways, particularly in arousing my fascination with the complexities of popular cinema, gender, and sexuality. I look back on her stimulating and inspiring MA courses at Sussex University (1994-95) with great fondness. I would also like to thank Vicky Lebeau for her challenging MA seminars at Sussex University, and for her helpful comments on an early draft of this manuscript, comments which caused me to question assumptions that I had taken for granted. I am also grateful to Reynold Humphries for his perceptive and enthusiastic reading of this manuscript. Thanks also to my students at Aristotle University of Thessaloniki and City College of Thessaloniki (Affiliated Institution of Sheffield University) for their love of popular cinema, their lively and enthusiastic discussions, and their taxing questions, which have helped me develop my research.

A very early draft of part of chapter two appeared in *Gramma: Journal of Theory and Criticism* 9 (2001). A slightly modified version of chapter eight, "Everyman and No Man: White Masculinity in Contemporary Serial Killer Movies," appeared in *Jump Cut: A Review of Contemporary Media* 49 (2007), www.ejumpcut.org. I would like to thank both journals for granting permission to reprint versions of these articles.

These acknowledgments would not be complete without thanking friends and family who have encouraged me throughout this project. Warm thanks go to all my friends for their support, especially to Sara Hannam, Sean Homer, Aneta Karagiannidou, and Cleopatra Kondouli for their helpful comments and suggestions. I am also grateful to my sister, Clare, for keeping me grounded and for always being able to make me laugh. I am indebted more than I could ever say to my parents for their unflagging encouragement, ongoing emotional and financial support, and for instilling in me the confidence to realize my ambitions. I will also be eternally grateful to my parents-in-law for babysitting my son, Andreas, and helping make the writing of this book possible. Andreas has provided a constant source of laughter and inspiration, and has given me new insights into the workings of masculinity. Lastly, words cannot express my gratitude to my own white heterosexual male, Yiannis, for persuading me to embark on this project, for demonstrating unlimited reserves of patience when I shut myself in my study for hours at a time, and for always having faith in me. This book is dedicated to him, with love.

Introduction

One of my pleasures in watching popular films has always been that of watching the extraordinary Hollywood male stars that grace the big screen, from my childhood crush on John Travolta in *Grease* (1978) to my recent academic interest in filmic masculinities. The title of this book obviously refers to some of the remarkable men that have dominated popular cinema in the last two decades, be he Arnold Schwarzenegger's humanized but invincible cyborg in *Terminator 2: Judgment Day* (1991), Keanu Reeves's messianic console cowboy in *The Matrix* (1999), or Russell Crowe's unreconstructed, primal warrior in *Gladiator* (2000).

However, the title also works at another level of meaning. *Extra-Ordinary Men: White Heterosexual Masculinity in Contemporary Popular Cinema* explores popular cinematic representations of white heterosexual masculinity at a time when its neutrality has been challenged by the politics of identity. The title refers to this process of rendering "extra-ordinary" what has historically been considered the most "ordinary"—and therefore the most invisible—identity. In other words, *Extra-Ordinary Men* treats white heterosexual masculinity as a specifically gendered, raced, and sexual category rather than the dominant, structuring norm, and views its historical universal status as an ideological formation. It analyzes how the marking of the universal identity, primarily through the identity critiques that have dominated the political arena in the U.S. in the last four decades, has produced a host of anxieties, as well as desires, that are played out in popular films. One of my main contentions is that, while white heterosexual masculinity continues to be the dominant identity in terms of economic, social, political, and representational strength, its very ordinariness means that it is also haunted by the anxiety that it is a vacuous identity. Being "ordinary" might, after all, place one in the privileged position of embodying social norms, but "ordinary" is also synonymous with "unexceptional," "unremarkable," "average," even "boring." Anxiety concerning the potential sterility and emptiness of white heterosexual masculinity has, I argue, been compounded by the celebration of difference and the investment in minority identity that attends postmodernism and identity politics. This plays itself out in popular films in a myriad of ways. For instance, the ability of white heterosexual masculinity to stand as the universal identity is made manifest in films such as *Falling Down* (1993) and *Fight Club* (1999), the protagonists of which are not even named, with the directors of both films claiming that they were meant to function as "everyman" figures.[1] At the same time, as I will argue in the first two chapters of this book, both protagonists experience the sense of a profound *absence* of identity, articulating the need for an identity politics of their own. In both films, the protagonists' appeals to victim status work to rid them of the burden of their oppressive ordinariness. As we shall see in chapters 4 and 8, similar anxieties are evident in the images of hypernormative white heterosexual masculinity that abound in cyberfantasies, typified by the blank, uniform, depthless agents in *The Matrix*, and the serial killer movie, such as Kevin Spacey's affectless, two-dimensional killer, John Doe, in *Se7en* (1995).

As well as attempting to problematize normative masculinity, highlighting its internal contradictions and instabilities, this book also explores the recuperative strategies deployed in popular films to reassert white heterosexual male hegemony, strategies that often recenter white heterosexual masculinity in the very act of decentering it. Indeed, in many popular films, the "ordinary" straight white male protagonists prove to be "extra-ordinary" by narrative closure, often through the motifs of redemption and/or transcendence. The title also points to the fact that white heterosexual men continue to command an extra-ordinary amount of screen space, indicative of the representational power wielded by the normative identity in terms of the political economy of Hollywood production. For example, Allan G. Johnson has observed that, even though white heterosexual males make up less than twenty percent of the U.S. population, they represent ninety percent of the characters in films winning the Academy Award category for Best Picture from 1965 till 1999.[2] British films have also followed suit, with the alleged *renaissance* of '90s British cinema largely dependent on the host of films about "ordinary" white men either trying to come to terms with a restructured economy in films indebted to the social realist tradition, such as *Brassed Off* (1996), *The Full Monty* (1997), and *Billy Elliot* (2000), or else learning to overcome their commitment phobia in romantic comedies like *Four Weddings and a Funeral* (1994), *Fever Pitch* (1997), and *Notting Hill* (1999).

Most of the films that *Extra-Ordinary Men* analyzes are in self-conscious dialogue with the contemporary discourse of "masculinity in crisis," which, as Sharon Willis notes, "is really white heterosexual masculinity desperately seeking to reconstruct itself within a web of social differences, where its opposing terms include not only femininity, but black masculinity and male homosexuality."[3] What this underscores, of course, is that identity is always constructed in relation to its others. Those others, however, rarely provide the required stability, rendering identity a site of ongoing resignification and contestation. It is precisely this instability that the plethora of popular films which narrativize "(white) masculinity in crisis" screen.

However, the very phrase "masculinity in crisis" is intrinsically problematic in that it postulates a once stable, coherent, unified masculinity. Indeed, restoring this allegedly lost, primal masculinity is the fantasy articulated by the American men's movement of the '90s or films such as *Fight Club*, both of which I analyze in Part 1 of this book. This is not to underestimate the huge impact of social movements (most obviously feminism, the civil rights movement, and lesbian and gay activism), historical events such as the Vietnam and Iraqi wars, and, most importantly, the brutal effects of late capitalism and a downsized economy on many "ordinary" men who believe themselves to be disenfranchised (see chapter 1). But it is also the case that almost every period of rapid social change in modern Western civilization has witnessed outpourings of anxiety about the state of (white heterosexual) masculinity, with masculinity most often synonymous with nation. Rather than asserting that masculinity is *currently* in crisis, therefore, it is more productive to pay attention to which particular forms of male insecurities are made manifest at specific historical junctures.[4] Moreover, as Sally Robinson contends, discussion as to whether or not masculinity is really in crisis is moot, since "masculinity in crisis" is a performative discourse that enacts and produces what it seemingly names.[5]

Indeed, since the early '80s, the media on both sides of the Atlantic has become obsessed with the beleaguered white male, who has been represented as increasingly victimized as years progress, a trajectory that I chart in Part 1 of this book. The '80s also witnessed a burgeoning production of books on masculinity, both popular publications (from self-help manuals to popular psychology) and academic literature, particularly from the new discipline of Men's Studies that was established in the academy by the decade's end. At the same time, the sheer number of popular films that screen white heterosexual masculinity in crisis suggests that laying bare the insecurities of the normative identity need not necessarily rob it of its structuring and ideological force. As Tania Modleski puts it, "we need to consider the extent to which male power is actually consolidated through cycles of crisis and resolution."[6]

For this very reason, work on masculinity, including work that explores the instability of male identifications, was initially greeted with considerable suspicion by some feminist theorists, who expressed concern that this might be yet another phallic ruse, a means of refocusing attention on normative masculinity in an allegedly postfeminist era.[7] Other theorists expressed concern that academic research into masculinity by (female) feminists represents "significant digression from a feminist project that remains underdeveloped in its attention to differences *among women*."[8]

However, analyzing cinematic representations of straight white men is an important task, since it can shatter the illusion that normative masculinity is a seamless identity, revealing it instead to be a volatile category that can only be stabilized through reiteration. In other words, academic theorizing can serve to demonstrate that the hegemony of white heterosexual masculinity, and therefore white patriarchy, is never totalizing.[9] For example, as I will show in chapter 3, the hypermasculine bodies of Sylvester Stallone and Arnold Schwarzenegger have been read by many critics as an assertion of white phallic power, but also as indicative of straight white male insecurities—evidence of white heterosexual masculinity's continuous need of verification, as well as its performative nature. Moreover, the sheer excessiveness of these filmic masculinities has also been regarded as verging on parody and camp.[10]

Recent feminist-inflected inquiry has also asserted the political importance of exploring "masculinities"—that is, the differences within masculinity. As Robyn Wiegman notes, the linking of maleness, masculinity, and male supremacy was imperative in early second-wave feminism, facilitating the articulation of a politicized feminist identity and the forging of female solidarity in opposition to a common enemy. However, many feminists, particularly feminists of color and socialist feminists, whose allegiances crossed over into the axes of race and class, took second-wave feminism to task for its white, middle-class prejudices in its failure to theorize not only the differences between women, but also the differences between men. As Wiegman puts it, "[b]ecause all men do not share equal masculine rights and privileges—because some men are, in fact, oppressed by women of prevailing race and class—assumptions about power as uniformly based on sexual difference (men as oppressor, women as oppressed) have long been under pressure to give way."[11]

This book joins recent scholarship in arguing against viewing masculinity as a monolithic or static category, regarding it instead to be in constant flux, subject to historically contingent, cultural, social, economic, political, and psychic forces.[12] For instance, just some of the diverging representations of white heterosexual masculinity I discuss in *Extra-Ordinary Men* include Michael Douglas's "sexually harassed," "angry white male" in *Disclosure* (1994), Harrison Ford's reformed, child-like "New Man" in *Regarding Henry* (1991), Tom Hanks's goofy American hero in *Forrest Gump* (1994), Russell Crowe's fearless, laconic, avenging warrior in *Gladiator*, John Travolta's clumsy, garrulous gangster in *Pulp Fiction* (1994), Brad Pitt's erotically objectified, small-time crook in *Thelma and Louise* (1991), Kevin Spacey's evangelical, deadpan serial killer in *Se7en*, Eminem's "white trash" rapper in *8 Mile* (2002), Hilary Swank's embodiment of transgendered white masculinity in *Boys Don't Cry* (1999), and *The Full Monty's* unlikely bunch of British, working-class, male strippers. While popular cinema is certainly producing diverse, multiple images of masculinity, it is also the case that more sophisticated tools and theoretical paradigms are now available with which to explore and decode filmic masculinities—a point to which I will return.

The postmodern valorization of difference, which in itself must be understood as one of the underlying causes of the current discourse on "(white) masculinity in crisis," has also led to work exploring how identities are always traversed by other identities. Rather than simply adding the oft-cited mantra of "race, nation, sexuality, and class" to a discussion of an already given masculinity, this book attempts to explore how masculinity, whiteness, and heterosexuality are always articulated through each other, as well as through and against those other identity categories in opposition to which they define themselves.

Unlike many other studies of masculinity, where whiteness and heterosexuality are taken as default or neutral categories, the whiteness and heterosexuality of male characters in films are foregrounded, and the relationship between these different identities interrogated. I also place particular emphasis on how class, a sadly neglected category in many books on film and gender, always cuts across white heterosexual masculinity, problematizing the notion that it is a coherent, stable category, and pointing to the fact that white male power is always dependent on economic status—a fact that popular cinematic representations of "white trash" masculinity in films such as *Natural Born Killers* (1994) or *8 Mile* make all too clear. Nation is another such identity category that inflects representations of white heterosexual masculinity, and this book makes several references to British films, exploring the import of nation in constructions of normative masculinity.

Since identity is always constructed through "the relations to what it is not, to precisely what it lacks, to what has been called its *constitutive outside*,"[13] I will discuss those opposing categories that form white heterosexual masculinity's unstable borders. However, I have also been careful to analyze several films that do not obviously play the white heterosexual male characters off against their others—such as *Reservoir Dogs* (1992), which almost exclusively screens straight, white, urban males—so as to dispel the notion that white heterosexual masculinity is only a gendered, sexualized, and raced identity when seen in relation to bodies that carry a surplus of signification—in particular, the bodies of women and men of color. What is important to stress here is that the cinematic gaze is by no means neutral as regards the representation of raced and gendered bodies, but is rather complicit in the prevailing visual regime which inscribes certain identities, especially gender and race, indelibly on the flesh (though not always with epistemological certainty, as I hope to illustrate in chapters 5 and 6). In other words, all bodies that populate the cinematic screen are necessarily marked, even those belonging to "ordinary" white men. Throughout this book, therefore, I highlight the whiteness and maleness of white male characters in order to challenge the seeming neutrality and invisibility of the dominant identity.

Extra-Ordinary Men also probes into those gaps between and excesses within identity categories that render identification such a profoundly precarious affair. To do so, I draw on certain tenets of psychoanalysis in order to explore the "resistance to identity at the very heart of psychic life."[14] Building on the Freudian model of the unconscious, "the guarantee of non-closure in the practices of subjectivity,"[15] Jacques Lacan has famously theorized that all subjects are structured by lack, an insight that renders the Symbolic Order and its governing Law of the Father mutable and historically contingent. Particularly interesting for feminist inquiry, therefore, is the fact that the symbolic structure of patriarchal power "cannot take account of the contingencies of actual [male] experience."[16] Popular cinema obsessively dramatizes the gap between the phallic ideal and the individual male subject, often in a melodramatic mode, a tendency

I explore most fully in chapters 2 and 3. Fantasy, in the Lacanian paradigm, is precisely that which attempts to fill the subject's lack-in-being. Cinema is one such space in which fantasy is staged, hence the dominance of Lacanian psychoanalysis in contemporary film theory. Psychoanalysis, particularly Julia Kristeva's theory of abjection, also provides convincing explanations for male fears of the feminine, rooting them in the male subject's pre-Oedipal relationship with the mother.[17] These fears are narrativized in many of the films I discuss, from *Fight Club* to *The Matrix*.

However, I also agree with David Savran that, while providing a compelling discourse for explaining how identifications are always caught up in a circuit of fantasy, disavowal, and desire, we need to be aware that the categories of psychoanalysis are themselves complicit "with a particular history of the subject."[18] Moreover, while psychoanalysis is deeply bound up in the social and the political, the goals of this book also required a more historicizing paradigm. Consequently, while utilizing psychoanalytic theory, I have also firmly grounded representations of white heterosexual male identifications in their socio-historical context, and have considered films in terms of the political economy of production. I have also engaged in more detailed textual readings of films than those offered by certain strands of Lacanian film theory, particularly the influential work of Slavoj Žižek, who largely uses film texts to illustrate his reading of Lacan. While Lacanians such as Joan Copjec and Žižek have offered important revisions of concepts such as the "look" and the "gaze," *Extra-Ordinary Men* draws on, as well as problematizes, the notion of the "gaze" in order to address the question of spectator positioning via the cinematic apparatus.[19] It also pays scrupulous attention not only to sexual difference, but also other differences that are often deemed secondary in psychoanalytic discourse.

Throughout this book, but particularly in Part 2, I also aim to complicate the very identity categories that I will be using, in particular "masculinity" and "whiteness," in order to free them up from appeals to an ontological body, since "the excesses of the body always threaten whatever restrictions from the discursive practices may be placed on it."[20] Although I will be arguing that gendered and racial identities attached to the body are discursively produced, I also emphasize the importance of individual investment in those identities, as well as the very real material effects that the embodiment of a particular identity can bring.[21]

In this respect, I have drawn heavily on the work of Judith Butler, in particular her understanding of gender as a performative category, as set out in her groundbreaking book *Gender Trouble: Feminism and the Subversion of Identity* (1990).[22] My own work is greatly indebted to Butler's contention that gender is internally assumed by the subject through identifications—not volitionally, but rather through discursive, regulatory practices, themselves governed by hegemonic norms, which "perform," that is *produce*, the categories which they purport to describe. For Butler, gender categories are always inextricable from the social context that produced them. Since identifications are always radically unstable, heterosexist patriarchy is forced to adapt itself continually, opening up space for potential subversion. Butler's work is thus important in exploring how masculinity is a citational category that can therefore be cited differently in potentially transgressive (but equally potentially hegemonic) ways—an argument I explore in my queering of white heterosexual masculinity in chapter 5. By arguing that gender resides not in the body but in identifications, Butler's work has opened up discussions of alternative masculinities to include transgender masculinity, which I explore in my analysis of *Boys Don't Cry*, as well as what Judith Halberstam has termed "female masculinity" in her 1998 book of that name, a comprehensive study of biological women who identify as masculine or male.[23] This questioning of the ontology of gender obviously has implications for normative masculinity, which has secured its hegemony through appeals to essentialism.

Queer theory generally has also destabilized the heterosexual/homosexual binary of sexual identifications, often by reading texts "against the grain" to locate potentially "queer" readings in ostensibly "straight" texts. Eve Kosofsky Sedgwick's pioneering study *Between Men: English Literature and Male Homosocial Desire* (1985) forms part of this work, and has undergridded my discussions of homosocial bonding, homoerotic desire, and concomitant misogyny in contemporary films such as *Reservoir Dogs* and *Fight Club*.[24] Judith Butler's exploration of how heterosexual identifications are always dependent on the abjected homosexual other has also informed my queering of white heterosexual masculinity in chapter 5.[25] Queer theory has provided an important framework for exploring the fragility of heterosexual identifications, as well as for interrogating the heterosexist assumptions not only of the dominant culture, but also of established theoretical paradigms, in particular psychoanalysis, which queer theory both deploys and queers.

As I show in chapter 6, critical race theory has also questioned the biological basis of embodied identity by arguing that "race" is a social and discursive construct, though one that, like gender, entails concrete material and ideological effects. For the purposes of this book, I have drawn on what has become known, often rather pejoratively, as "whiteness studies," a school of thought which gained a foothold in the U.S. academy in the '90s. While it tends to refer to the work carried out by white theorists, it is important to note that the impetus to explore whiteness emanated from theorists of color. For instance, whiteness studies makes frequent reference to the work of theorists such as W. E. B. Du Bois and James Baldwin, and their comments on the damaging effects of people "becoming" or believing themselves to be "white." Feminists of color, such as Toni Morrison, have also been instrumental in critiquing white feminists for ignoring the racial privileges their whiteness affords them in a patriarchal order that is always racialized. Morrison's *Playing in the Dark: Whiteness and the Literary Imagination* (1992) is also a founding text of whiteness studies. It uncovers the crucial "black presence" in white-authored American national literature, and explores the surplus of meanings attached to blackness, while whiteness is often represented as "mute, meaningless, unfathomable, pointless, frozen, veiled, curtained, dreaded, senseless, implacable."[26] In a similar vein, bell hooks—who notes that, in the black imagination, far from being invisible, whiteness is associated with "the terrible, the terrifying, the terrorizing"—has called upon whites to examine the privileges of their racial identity, arguing that white supremacist attitudes can only be unlearned by "the destruction of the category 'whiteness.'"[27]

.   The most useful branches of whiteness studies aim at revealing whiteness to be a historically variable, socially constructed, ontologically empty, fundamentally unstable category, caught up in a dialectical tension with its polar other—blackness—upon which it depends for self-definition. Most theorists categori- cally state the need to make whiteness visible in order to rob it of its normative status. By drawing attention to the fact that whiteness is "the empty and therefore terrifying attempt to build an identity on what one isn't and on whom one can hold back,"[28] the best work in whiteness studies hopes to reveal that "whiteness is not just about bodies and skin color, but rather more about the discursive practices that, because of colonialism and neo-colonialism, privilege and sustain the global dominance of white imperial subjects and Eurocentric worldliness."[29] This book focuses on how whiteness is always open to potential "contamination," always traversed by socioeconomic and political factors, and often underwritten by fears of its ordinariness and sterility. Richard Dyer's work on whiteness in film has also been invaluable in this respect. As Dyer puts it, "[t]rying to think about the representation of whiteness as an ethnic category in mainstream film is difficult, partly because white power secures its dominance by seeming not to be about anything in particular but also because, when whiteness *qua* whiteness does come into focus, it is often revealed as emptiness, absence, de- nial, or even a kind of death."[30] It is my contention that North American, middle-class, heterosexual, male whites experience this sense of emptiness, disembodiment, and non-existence most acutely, since they have no other particularities of identity to which they can lay claim.

Like masculinity studies, whiteness studies is inevitably caught up in the institutional privileges that it attempts to dismantle, as its rapid establishment in the U.S. academy effectively demonstrates. It can also gesture at "me-too-ism" in staking out a distinct turf for white scholars to examine their own whiteness,[31] and has often been viewed by theorists of color as white academics muscling in on race. Moreover, in exploring how whiteness and blackness are locked in a mutually informing binary in the U.S. imagination, whiteness studies often marginalizes other racial identities, as well as rendering the discipline very much a North American affair, with little exploration of how whiteness varies across different cultural or national contexts. In this book, therefore, I have also attempted to explore whiteness in relation to non-black U.S. racial identities, in addition to referring to a few films with British subject matter, such as *The Full Monty* and *Ali G Indahouse* (2002), in order to explore the historical and social contingencies of white identifications. I have also combined the insights of whiteness studies with the work on race carried out by theorists of color, such as Frantz Fanon, whose seminal *Black Skin, White Masks* (1952) mapped the Lacanian paradigm onto a colonial context in order to form a theory of the racist imaginary (see chapter 6).[32] I have also attempted to address whiteness in relation to questions of racism, power, and hierarchy, rather than merely difference. In so doing, one branch of whiteness studies I have found useful is recent research into labor history, particularly the work of David Roediger and Eric Lott, which has been highly instructive in revealing the complex economic and political processes involved in racial formation.[33] I have also made substantial use of "white trash" scholarship. Annalee Newitz and Matthew Wray, the main proponents of this school of thought, focus on the racialized identity of America's white poor in order to "examine the differences within whiteness," and thereby destabilize essentialist appeals to "white identity as the primary locus of social privilege and power."[34] Newitz and Wray's work is useful in illuminating the inextricability of racial and class identities, as well as "[delineating] a separation between race and class" by revealing that class "cuts across race lines."[35]

Extra-Ordinary Men takes contemporary, popular Hollywood cinema as the source of its main texts. Partly this is because popular films are often far more complex than they tend to be given credit for, and frequently contain ruptures, gaps, tensions, and incoherencies that indicate collective anxieties and desires, as well as ideological conflict. Furthermore, popular cinema is not only a prime site in which identities are played out, produced, consumed, negotiated, and contested; some contemporary popular films have also recently shown themselves to be extremely self-conscious about politicized discourses of identity.[36] Throughout this book I have attempted to politicize the identities that, as Sharon Willis has observed, many popular films merely fetishize and aestheticize, "transform[ing] *only* the rhetoric of the dominant discourses without changing their structural effects."[37] At the same time, I go beyond the simple process of critiquing stereotypes, which often fails to take on board the ways in which cinema mobilizes unconscious desires and contradictory, unresolved identifications.

As with most contemporary popular culture theorists, I interrogate the ways in which "popular culture both reflects *and shapes* broader social forces," and forms part of an ongoing interaction between the processes of production and consumption.[38] This dialectical framework is essential if we are to interpret "a cinema that is always reading us—reading our social configurations of power and desire, pleasure, and violence." As Sharon Willis puts it, "[t]his is part of film's allure: as we read it, it also reads us."[39] I have thus explored the means by which the spectator is encouraged to respond to or identify with the given film texts in order to help me place my chosen films firmly in their political context and engage with the politics of representation. I also, though, locate the potential for spectators to engage in what Stuart Hall has termed "negotiated" and "oppositional" readings.[40]

As well as mainstream Hollywood texts, I also focus on some key crossover independent films that have tapped into collective cultural concerns, and therefore act as important barometers for exploring prevailing fantasies and anxieties about "ordinary" men. For example, both Quentin Tarantino's *Reservoir Dogs* and Neil Jordan's *The Crying Game* (1992) were independently produced, but were box-office as well as critical successes. I also refer to a few U.K. productions, primarily for the purposes of comparison, in order to explore the import of national context and representational codes on my object of study, and to illustrate that models of U.S. white heterosexual masculinity cannot simply be mapped onto other cultural and social realities. Furthermore, the globalization of filmmaking has rendered the notion of national cinema itself problematic. One of my key texts, for example, is *The Full Monty*, the subject matter, director, actors, and aesthetic of which are very much British, but which was funded and distributed entirely by Twentieth Century Fox. The fact it grossed over £250 million worldwide reveals that concerns about "(white) masculinity in crisis" are not limited to American soil, even if that "crisis" is presented in profoundly different ways (see chapter 1). Moreover, the cultural domination of Hollywood texts, particularly in Anglophone nations such as Britain, means that non-U.S. viewers are mediating their experiences through U.S. films even if they resist the ideologies they encode, a process that is reversed when foreign films fare well in the U.S.

Extra-Ordinary Men also recognizes that New Hollywood is characterized by its interaction with other media, most obviously television, but additionally those as diverse as literature, popular music, video clips, advertising, computer games, and, perhaps most importantly, the popular media, be it talk shows, journalism, or film reviews. Indeed, many of these media now make up essential ancillary markets as part of the New Hollywood impetus towards synergy. I thus, on occasion, refer to other media, and explore commonalities and divergences in their representations of white heterosexual masculinity. For instance, certain films are produced as vehicle pieces for already-established musical artists with their own star persona, thereby providing a ready-made audience, as well as allowing plenty of opportunities for joint advertising of both the film and its soundtrack. I explore this phenomenon in chapter 6 with my discussion of *8 Mile*, starring white rap artist Eminem, a film which reveals the huge influence that hip hop and African-American culture wield over constructions of U.S. white heterosexual masculinity. Moreover, while films have become an important arena for product placement, many contemporary popular films deploy some of the representational codes of advertisements, a transaction I explore in my analysis of the commodified white male body in chapter 3.

To this extent, then, *Extra-Ordinary Men* has attempted to break down the territorialism of academic disciplines and their defined objects of study. Taking my lead from cultural studies, I have adopted a rigorously interdisciplinary approach, responding not only to the hybridized nature of postmodern media, but also to the multi-faceted nature of my topic, which required a variety of interrelated theoretical frameworks.

As with all projects, this book is substantially indebted to existing research, not only on masculinity, such as Lynn Segal's *Slow Motion: Changing Masculinities, Changing Men* (1990) and Susan Faludi's *Stiffed: The Betrayal of Modern Man* (2000), but also work on masculinity and cinema, which developed throughout the late '80s and '90s.[41] At this time, feminist film theory was working through the seeming impasse of the rigid structuring male/female, active/passive binary instituted by Laura Mulvey in her seminal "Visual Pleasure and Narrative Cinema" (1975), in which masculinity was associated with mastery, activity, sadism, voyeurism, and fetishism (see chapter 3).[42] In the '80s theoretical inquiry into masculinity was aided by the resurgence of certain "male" Hollywood genres, such as the revisionist western, the establishment of the blockbuster as Hollywood's prime money-making enterprise, and the revival of British social realism with films which took working-class masculinity as their central problematic.[43] While some theorists turned their attention to non-hegemonic (namely gay and non-white) masculinities, Steve Neale inserted the male body into the Mulveyan schema in his *Screen* essay "Masculinity as Spectacle" (1983).[44] The importance of Neale's essay, as Claudia Yates notes, lies in his theorization of heterosexual masculinity and his recognition of the plurality of screen masculinities.[45] Neale's text has provided an important starting point for my own analysis of the commodification of the straight white male body, one main difference being that I directly address the import of race.

Other books on masculinity and film published in the last 20 years have been important influences. Susan Jeffords's *The Remasculinization of America: Gender and the Vietnam War* (1989), which analyzes Vietnam texts that function as ideological vehicles for screening the remasculinization of an allegedly feminized American nation, along with her later *Hard Bodies: Hollywood Masculinity in the Reagan Era* (1994), have influenced my analysis of wounded white males and the hypermuscular white male body in chapters 2 and 3.[46] Other critics turned their attention to the proliferation of sensitive white men, especially fathers, on the big screen, which has been read as a strategy of appropriation by Tania Modleski, Elizabeth Traube, and Fred Pfeil, whose arguments inform my own discussion of damaged white men and cross-dressing comedies.[47] Several anthologies were also published in the '90s which helped form this project. Steven Cohan and Ina Rae Hark's *Screening the Male: Exploring Masculinities in Hollywood Cinema* (1993) led the way in taking issue with earlier film theory working in the Mulveyan paradigm that "for the most part confidently equated the masculinity of the male subject with activity, voyeurism, sadism, fetishism, and story, and the femininity of the female subject with passivity, exhibitionism, masochism, narcissism, and spectacle."[48] In the same year, Constance Penley and Sharon Willis edited *Male Trouble*, based on a *Camera Obscura* special issue, which roughly shared the same premise, as did the two (superbly named) anthologies edited by Pat Kirkham and Janet Thumin—the male-authored *You Tarzan: Masculinity, Movies and Men* (1993) and female-authored *Me Jane: Masculinity, Movies and Women* (1995).[49] Other later anthologies include Harry Stecopoulos and Michael Uebel's *Race and the Subject of Mascu-*

linities (1997), Peter Lehman's *Masculinity: Bodies, Movies, Culture* (2001), and Phil Powrie, Ann Davies, and Bruce Babington's *The Trouble with Men* (2004).[50] Yvonne Tasker's *Spectacular Bodies: Gender, Genre and the Action Cinema* (1993) was also instrumental in kindling my own theoretical interest in popular filmic masculinities, as was Peter Lehman's *Running Scared: Masculinity and the Representation of the Male Body* (1993). Sharon Willis's *High Contrast: Race and Gender in Contemporary Hollywood Film* (1997), which subjects popular film texts to a politically-informed psychoanalytic reading, has also been instructive in shaping my own theoretical paradigm.[51]

Despite the proliferation of books on masculinity and film, *Extra-Ordinary Men* is the first book exclusively devoted to representations of white heterosexual masculinity in contemporary popular cinema. That said, this book is hugely indebted to several studies of white heterosexual masculinity that include cinema among their chosen texts. Perhaps the most influential work in this respect has been Thomas DiPiero's *Camera Obscura* article "White Men Aren't" (1992), in which he argues for the importance of theorizing "average white guys," despite the attendant risk of further normalizing them, "since the work that goes into obfuscating white men's gender and racial characteristics is also responsible for sustaining their political, cultural, and economic dominance." With reference to *Grand Canyon* (1991) and *White Men Can't Jump* (1992), DiPiero explores how "[t]he white male protagonists of these films continually appeal to other people—primarily to women and to black men, to reveal to them the secrets of their own identities." He contends that white heterosexual masculinity in these films "is not represented so much as an identity in our culture as what I will be calling a hysterical response to a perceived lack of identity."[52] This point has been essential in my exploration of images of sterility and vacuity that often inform popular cinematic representations of "ordinary" men. Fred Pfeil's *White Guys: Studies in Postmodern Domination and Difference* (1995) also analyzes white heterosexual masculinity, but in a variety of texts and media, including the "rampage film" and the "sensitive-guy film." Pfeil's importance lies in his consideration of the impact of economic class and corporate capitalism on constructions of normative masculinity, not to mention his insistence that white heterosexual masculinity is not monolithic.[53] Sally Robinson's *Marked Men: White Masculinity in Crisis* (2000) and David Savran's *Taking It Like a Man: White Masculinity, Masochism, and Contemporary American Culture* (1998) have both been essential in my analysis of the common motif of "wounded" men in contemporary cinema, and in my exploration of how male masochism can function to reaffirm white male hegemony in a postfeminist, post-civil rights America, though neither author focuses solely on cinema.[54]

In part, then, the contribution of my own project, as I perceive it, lies in developing many of the rich insights provided by these studies, and extending them to produce a comprehensive study of representations of white heterosexual masculinity in contemporary British and American popular cinema. In so doing, however, it also considerably updates and adds to existing research. Most obviously, it analyzes many contemporary popular texts that have yet to receive sub-stantial critical attention, such as *Ali G Indahouse*, *8 Mile*, and *Troy* (2004). Moreover, my focus on contemporary films, as well as my contextualization of filmic texts, has also necessitated reference to more recent cultural and social phenomena (such as the impact of virtual and electronic culture on constructions of normative masculinity, the increased commodification of the white male body, the appearance of transgendered subjects in popular media texts, the influ-ence of hip hop on U.S. and British white masculinities), as well as the impact of historical events, most notably 9/11. Furthermore, I also explore stylistic innova-tions in contemporary popular cinema, in particular the increased use of post-modern textual strategies such as parody, pastiche, and intertextuality in main-stream texts, and consider how these strategies impinge on filmic representations of normative masculinity, with particular attention placed on the influence of Quentin Tarantino's cinema. My focus on the intersectionality of whiteness, heterosexuality, and masculinity also brings new questions to bear on the image of masculinity than those posed in existing research. One such question has been how filmic representations of white heterosexual masculinity have responded to identity critiques, the answer being, I argue, not only the inscription of the "white male as victim" figure that critics such as Robinson and Savran have comprehensively outlined, but also the anxiety that normative masculinity is a vacuous, sterile identity. I also explore the transactional uses to which this image of "extra-ordinarily ordinary" masculinity is put in popular cinema, demonstrat-ing how it provides a vehicle with which to articulate concerns about not only "(white) masculinity in crisis," but also the increased technologization and virtu-alization of society and culture in postmodernity. Moreover, this book's decon-struction of three normative identities—masculinity, whiteness, and heterosexu-ality—has also necessitated the incorporation of new theoretical paradigms, such as queer theory and "whiteness studies," absent from many earlier studies, alongside the application of feminist and feminist-inflected theory. Its focus on the differences not only *within* masculinity, but also within *white heterosexual* masculinity, has also led to more emphasis being placed on the role of class and nation than in previous studies of filmic masculinities, with the exception of Fred Pfeil's *White Guys*.

The sheer predominance of white males on screen means that *Extra-Ordinary Men* cannot claim to offer a comprehensive, definitive account of popular cinematic representations of white heterosexual masculinity; rather, it traces some of the most interesting trends, exploring how white heterosexual masculinity currently straddles the poles of universality and specificity, ordi-nariness and extra-ordinariness.

This book is divided into three parts. Part 1, "The Politics of the 'White Male as Victim,'" focuses on the impact of identity politics on popular cinematic representations of "ordinary" white men. The structural logic of identity politics is such that it requires a dominant identity—white heterosexual masculinity—with access to the privileges to which minority groups aspire. In the process, white heterosexual masculinity has been emptied out of positive content, most often ascribed the role of oppressor. At the same time, identity critiques have rendered its traditional claims to universality and invisibility increasingly untenable. One response to this state of affairs has been the tendency of many white heterosexual men, both on and off screen, to represent themselves as victims, trading on the common correlation of victimhood and innocence, and thereby insulating themselves from "evil white guy" status. Chapter 1 explores the notion that white heterosexual men are the newest victims—having lost ground to women, people of color, and lesbian and homosexuals—in two Hollywood films, *Falling Down* and *Disclosure*. The chapter then looks at how the British comedy hit *The Full Monty* covers similar concerns, but largely avoids the backlash mode of its Hollywood equivalents, primarily due to its willingness to attribute blame for white male feelings of disenfranchisement where it truly belongs—on late capitalism and the economic insecurity, alienation, and social stratification that it produces. It ends by considering Spike Lee's more critical take on the "angry white male" with *25th Hour* (2004). Chapter 2 explores the impetus to literalize the wounds inflicted on the white male psyche, thereby rendering "ordinary" men "extra-ordinary" and, by extension, innocent, in the male melodramas *Regarding Henry* and *Forrest Gump*. It then analyzes the fin-de-millennium cult hit *Fight Club*, which takes the tendency to literalize white male wounds to its limit point in its parodic representation of (white) male hysteria and masochism. It also explores how *Fight Club*'s tongue-in-cheek, postmodern "both/and" stylistics legitimize its screening of the fantasy of white male rephallicization through masochistic endurance, as well as its concomitant exclusion of women and other minorities from the political sphere.

Part 2, "Coming Apart at the Seams? White Heterosexual Masculinity and the Body in Popular Cinema," explores how anxieties regarding shifting conceptions of normative white masculinity are inscribed in and through the body in popular cinematic texts. Chapter 3 traces the increased eroticization of the white male body in popular cinema of the last two decades, exploring how this disrupts the traditional economy of the gaze. It also analyzes films as diverse as *The Full Monty*, *The Real Blonde* (1988), and *American Psycho* (2000) which narrativize the damage that this process inflicts on "ordinary" white men, in particular in alienating them from a *productive* body. It also examines the self-reflexive parody that accompanied displays of white hypermasculine bodies in the '90s action genre, focusing on *Terminator 2*, but ends with a discussion of the recent resurgence of the epic genre, which offers a nostalgic return to images of primal, white male physicality. Chapter 4 unpacks the associations between historical discourses of white male disembodiment and the virtual bodies of '90s science fiction cinema, placing particular attention on *Strange Days* (1995) and *The Matrix*. It explores how the concomitant association of white heterosexual masculinity with disembodiment (evident in both Christian and Cartesian discourse) has been a source of ideological strength, but is also grounds for considerable anxiety—white heterosexual masculinity is not only unable to access the positive investment in the minoritized body that characterizes identity politics,[55] but also, by virtue of its very ordinariness, is often deemed a blank, depleted identity. I explore how the depthlessness and disembodiment of cyberculture and simulation technology are primarily represented by "ordinary" white men in contemporary cinematic cyberfantasies, while women and people of color often stand in for embodied subjectivity and the Baudrillardian "real."

Chapters 5 and 6 both highlight the internal contradictions and instabilities of white heterosexual masculinity, positing it as a performative construct that must continually reconsolidate itself through discursive practices. Both chapters are interested in the ramifications for "ordinary" white men when identity is seen as fictional, provisional, and potentially trangressable, since one way in which white heterosexual masculinity has historically secured its privileged position as structuring norm is through appeals to ontological and biological differences. Chapter 5 examines representations of the performativity of normative masculinity and the instability of heterosexual identifications in cross-dressing comedies and transgender passing narratives, focusing particularly on *The Crying Game* and *Boys Don't Cry*. Chapter 6 analyzes cinematic representations of white male "wiggers" (white emulators of black culture) in the films of Quentin Tarantino, *Bamboozled* (2000), *Ali G Indahouse*, and *8 Mile*. As well as interrogating the dependence of white heterosexual masculinity on black masculinity for self-definition, a relationship that is often undergridded by homoerotic desire, this chapter also explores how such racial crossovers point to anxieties about the sterility of white masculinity, with the appropriation of black culture rendering "wiggers" *extra-ordinarily* white. It also reveals how these racial crossovers often reiterate crude stereotypes of African-American masculinity manufactured in the white imagination, much like the minstrel tradition they inevitably rehearse.

Part 3, "Marking White Male Violence: The Gangster and the Serial Killer," focuses on two screen figures that have dominated popular cinema in recent years in order to gender and racialize the apparent neutrality of white male violence. Chapter 7 concentrates on Tarantino's impulse to deconstruct the screen gangster and foreground the performative structures of white heterosexual masculinity, even as his films simultaneously articulate the phallic model of masculinity that his white male gangsters fail to live up to. It also analyzes how Tarantino's white male characters are always marked by identity categories of gender, race, and sexuality, though this recognition is primarily referenced through paranoiac hate speech. Aggression, physical and verbal, erupts when white heterosexual masculinity is posited as a precariously unstable identity, with violence against its others providing a means of policing its inherently leaky borders. Chapter 8 focuses on the serial killer, who, both on and off screen, is statistically most likely to be a white male. However, the demonization of the screen serial killer through discourses of sexual deviance or class inferiority in films such as *The Silence of the Lambs* (1991), *Kalifornia* (1993), and *Natural Born Killers* is suggestive of attempts to render the serial killer "extra-ordinary," and thus dis-

616 Introduction

tance normative white masculinity from brutality and aggression. At the same time, I explore the difficulty many films face in insulating serial killing from more socially accepted, institutionalized forms of white male violence. In my analysis of films such as *Se7en* and *Copycat* (1995) I also interrogate the competing tendency in contemporary serial killer films to code the serial killer as "extra-ordinarily ordinary." While images of an affectless, depthless white masculinity certainly articulate concerns about white heterosexual masculinity, in particular the anxiety that it lacks specific content, they are also used to articulate concerns about virtual and postmodern culture, a deployment which underscores white heterosexual masculinity's ongoing ability to stand in for humanity.

Notes

1. Mark Salisbury, "Get Out of My Face," *Empire*, July 1993, 77; Gavin Smith, "Inside Out," *Film Comment*, September/October 1999, 61. I develop this point in my discussion of the films in chapters 1 and 2 respectively.
2. Allan G. Johnson, *Privilege, Power and Difference* (Mountain View, CA: Mayfield, 2001), 108, quoted in Hernan Vera and Andrew M. Gordon, *Screen Saviors: Hollywood Fictions of Whiteness* (New York: Rowman and Littlefield, 2003), 9.
3. Sharon Willis, *High Contrast: Race and Gender in Contemporary Hollywood Film* (Durham, NC: Duke University Press, 1997), 31.
4. Yvonne Tasker, *Spectacular Bodies: Gender, Genre and the Action Cinema* (London: Routledge, 1993), 119.
5. Sally Robinson, *Marked Men: White Masculinity in Crisis* (New York: Columbia University Press, 2000), 10.
6. Tania Modleski, *Feminism Without Women: Culture and Criticism in a "Postfeminist" Age* (New York: Routledge, 1991), 7.
7. See, for example, Modleski, *Feminism Without Women*, 1-15; Rosi Braidotti, with Judith Butler, "Feminism by Any Other Name," *Differences: A Journal of Feminist Cultural Studies* 6, no. 2-3 (1994): 43.
8. Constance Penley and Sharon Willis, introduction to *Male Trouble*, ed. Constance Penley and Sharon Willis (Minneapolis: University of Minnesota Press, 1993), vii.
9. Thomas DiPiero, "White Men Aren't," *Camera Obscura: A Journal of Feminism and Film Theory* 30 (1992): 115; Pat Kirkham and Janet Thumin, "Me Jane," introduction to *Me Jane: Masculinity, Movies and Women*, ed. Pat Kirkham and Janet Thumin (New York: St. Martin's Press, 1995), 13; Fred Pfeil, *White Guys: Studies in Postmodern Domination and Difference* (London: Verso, 1995), 33.
10. Barbara Creed, "From Here to Modernity: Feminism and Postmodernism," *Screen* 28, no. 2 (1987): 65; Mark Simpson, *Male Impersonators: Men Performing Masculinity* (London: Cassell, 1994), 25.
11. Robyn Wiegman, "Unmaking: Men and Masculinity in Feminist Theory," in *Masculinity Studies and Feminist Theory: New Directions*, ed. Judith Kegan Gardiner (New York: Columbia University Press, 2002), 34-35.
12. Pfeil, *White Guys*, ix; Candida Yates, *Masculine Jealousy and Contemporary Cinema* (Houndmills, Basingstoke: Palgrave Macmillan, 2007), 8; Lynn Segal, *Slow Motion: Changing Masculinities, Changing Men*, rev. ed. (London: Virago, 1997), xxxiv.

13. Stuart Hall, "Introduction: Who Needs Identity?" in *Questions of Cultural Identity*, ed. Stuart Hall and Paul du Gay (London: Sage, 1996), 4.

14. Jacqueline Rose, *Sexuality in the Field of Vision* (London: Verso, 1986), 91.

15. Rosi Braidotti, *Metamorphoses: Towards a Materialist Theory of Becoming* (Cambridge: Polity/Blackwell, 2002), 39.

16. Kirkham and Thumin, "Me Jane," 13.

17. Julia Kristeva, *Powers of Horror*, trans. Leon Roudiez (New York: Columbia University Press, 1982).

18. David Savran, *Taking It Like a Man: White Masculinity, Masochism, and Contemporary American Culture* (Princeton, NJ: Princeton University Press, 1998), 10.

19. Joan Copjec, "The Orthopsychic Subject: Film Theory and the Reception of Lacan," in *Film and Theory: An Anthology*, ed. Robert Stam and Toby Miller (Malden, MA: Blackwell, 2000), 437-55; Slavoj Žižek, *The Fright of Real Tears: Krzysztof Kieślowski between Theory and Post-Theory* (London: BFI, 2001), 33-35. Also see chap. 3, n. 6 of this book.

20. Patrick Fuery, *New Developments in Film Theory* (Houndmills, Basingstoke: Macmillan, 2000), 72.

21. Class, it should be added, is also an identity that remains unforgivingly material, though is less obviously inscribed on the body, but rather evoked in films through visual signifiers, such as costume, through dialogue, such as diction and accent, or through characters' performances of socially perceived class-bound behavior and experiences.

22. Judith Butler, *Gender Trouble: Feminism and the Subversion of Identity* (New York: Routledge, 1990).

23. Judith Halberstam, *Female Masculinity* (Durham, NC: Duke University Press, 1998).

24. Eve Kosofsky Sedgwick, *Between Men: English Literature and Male Homosocial Desire* (New York: Columbia University Press, 1985).

25. Butler, *Gender Trouble*, 57-65.

26. Toni Morrison, *Playing in the Dark: Whiteness and the Literary Imagination* (London: Picador, 1992), 5-6, 59.

27. bell hooks, *Black Looks: Race and Representation* (Boston: South End Press, 1992), 170, 12.

28. David Roediger, *Towards the Abolition of Whiteness* (London: Verso, 1994), 13.

29. Raka Shome, "Whiteness and the Politics of Location: Postcolonial Reflections," in *Whiteness: The Communication of Social Identity*, ed. Thomas K. Nakayama and Judith N. Martin (London: Sage, 1999), 108.

30. Richard Dyer, *The Matter of Images: Essays on Representation* (London: Routledge, 1993), 141.

31. Richard Dyer, *White* (London: Routledge, 1997), 10.

32. Frantz Fanon, *Black Skin, White Masks*, trans. Charles Lam Markmann (New York: Grove, 1967).

33. David Roediger, *The Wages of Whiteness: Race and the Making of the American Working Class* (London: Verso, 1991); Eric Lott, *Love and Theft: Blackface Minstrelsy and the American Working Class* (New York: Oxford University Press, 1993).

34. Annalee Newitz and Matthew Wray, "What Is 'White Trash'? Stereotypes and Economic Conditions of Poor Whites in the United States," in *Whiteness: A Critical Reader*, ed. Michael Hill (New York: New York University Press, 1997), 169.

35. Matthew Wray and Annalee Newitz, introduction to *White Trash: Race and Class in America*, ed. Matthew Wray and Annalee Newitz (New York: Routledge, 1997), 8.

36. Jude Davies and Carol R. Smith, *Gender, Ethnicity and Sexuality in Contemporary American Film* (Edinburgh: Keele University Press, 1997), 6.

37. Willis, *High Contrast*, 2.

38. C. Lee Harrington and Denise D. Bielby, "Constructing the Popular: Cultural Production and Consumption," in *Popular Culture: Production and Consumption*, ed. C. Lee Harrington and Denise D. Bielby (Malden, MA: Blackwell, 2001), 6, 9.

39. Sharon Willis, "Disputed Territories: Masculinity and Social Space," in *Male Trouble*, ed. Constance Penley and Sharon Willis (Minneapolis: University of Minnesota Press, 1993), 266.

40. Stuart Hall, "Encoding/Decoding," in *The Cultural Studies Reader*, ed. Simon During (London: Routledge, 1993), 90-103.

41. Segal, *Slow Motion*; Susan Faludi, *Stiffed: The Betrayal of Modern Man* (London: Vintage, 2000).

42. Laura Mulvey, "Visual Pleasure and Narrative Cinema," in *Visual and Other Pleasures* (Houndmills, Basingstoke: Macmillan, 1989), 14-26.

43. Phil Powrie, Ann Davies, and Bruce Babington, "Introduction: Turning the Male Inside Out," in *The Trouble with Men: Masculinities in European and Hollywood Cinema*, ed. Phil Powrie, Ann Davies, and Bruce Babington (London: Wallflower, 2004), 2-3.

44. Steve Neale, "Masculinity as Spectacle," in *The Sexual Subject: A Screen Reader in Sexuality*, ed. Mandy Merck (London: Routledge, 1992), 277-87.

45. Yates, *Masculine Jealousy and Contemporary Cinema*, 51.

46. Susan Jeffords, *The Remasculinization of America: Gender and the Vietnam War* (Bloomington: Indiana University Press, 1989); Susan Jeffords, *Hard Bodies: Hollywood Masculinity in the Reagan Era* (New Brunswick, NJ: Rutgers University Press, 1994).

47. Modleski, *Feminism Without Women*, 61-111; Pfeil, *White Guys*, 37-70; Elizabeth G. Traube, *Dreaming Identities: Class, Gender and Generation in 1980s Film* (Boulder, CO: Westview, 1992), 123-69.

48. Steve Cohan and Ina Rae Hark, introduction to *Screening the Male: Exploring Masculinities in Hollywood Cinema*, ed. Steve Cohan and Ina Rae Hark (London: Routledge, 1993), 2.

49. Constance Penley and Sharon Willis, eds., *Male Trouble* (Minneapolis: University of Minnesota Press, 1993); Pat Kirkham and Janet Thumin, eds., *Me Jane: Masculinity, Movies and Women* (New York: St. Martin's, 1995); Pat Kirkham and Janet Thumin, eds., *You Tarzan: Masculinity, Movies and Men* (London: Lawrence and Wishart, 1993).

50. Harry Stecopoulos and Michael Uebel, eds., *Race and the Subject of Masculinities* (Durham, NC: Duke University Press, 1997); Peter Lehman, ed., *Masculinity: Bodies, Movies, Culture* (New York: Routledge, 2001); Phil Powrie, Ann Davies, and Bruce Babington, eds., *The Trouble with Men: Masculinities in European and Hollywood Cinema* (London: Wallflower, 2004).

51. Tasker, *Spectacular Bodies*; Peter Lehman, *Running Scared: Masculinity and the Representation of the Male Body* (Philadelphia: Temple University Press, 1993); Willis, *High Contrast*.

52. Thomas DiPiero, "White Men Aren't," 115, 126, 117. DiPiero has since extended his discussion into a book with the same title, though his only reference to cinema

includes this original essay in a modified form. *White Men Aren't* (Durham, NC: Duke University Press, 2002).

53. Pfeil, *White Guys*. See espec. the intro.

54. Robinson, *Marked Men*; Savran, *Taking It Like a Man*.

55. Robyn Wiegman, *American Anatomies: Theorizing Race and Gender* (Durham, NC: Duke University Press, 1995), 50.

Part One

The Politics of the
"White Male as Victim"

Chapter One
Losing Ground: Representations of White Male Disenfranchisement in Anglo-American Popular Cinema

From Backlash to Betrayal: Historical Background

In 1991 Susan Faludi caused a storm with her polemical but influential *Backlash: The Undeclared War Against Women*, which, as the title implies, investigated the anti-feminist hostility "set off not by women's achievement of full equality," as the media had claimed, "but by the increased possibility that they might win it."[1] Nearly a decade later, Faludi followed up her success with *Stiffed: The Betrayal of Modern Man* (2000), in which she states that in *Backlash* she had been operating under an erroneous assumption: "that the male crisis in American society was caused by something men were *doing* unrelated to something being done to them."[2] The resulting interviews with hundreds of angst-ridden men, who considered themselves to be victims of feminism, affirmative action, immigrants, absent fathers, and government and federal authorities, to name but a few, provide important personal accompaniments to the more public discourses on white male disenfranchisement that flourished in the '90s. Faludi is careful to point out that the men interviewed were unable to understand that their problems were rooted in a downsized economy and/or unrealizable ideologies of American manhood, leading them to believe that they had lost ground to women, people of color, and immigrants. At the same time, Faludi's own shift from "backlash" to "betrayal" is highly symptomatic of the general popularization of discourses of "(white) masculinity in crisis" in the '90s media, both in the U.S. and, as we shall later see, Britain as well.

As Faludi points out, the U.S. media in the '90s was preoccupied with probing into beleaguered manhood, though "[t]he economic and social roots of young male pathology were largely overlooked by a media that preferred other culprits: testosterone, drugs, 'permissive' or neglectful working parents (which, either way, almost always meant Mom), or, increasingly by the decade's end, feminism."[3] This flurry of concern in the mainstream media largely focused on *straight white* male welfare, primarily because deeply entrenched racist and homophobic discourses deemed gay masculinities and masculinities of color to be in crisis as a matter of course. Problems faced almost exclusively by women, such as date rape and domestic violence, were sidelined for laments over male failings, confirming, as Lynn Segal notes, that "'manhood' still has a symbolic weight denied to 'womanhood.'" For this reason, "men appear to be emerging as the threatened sex; even as they remain, everywhere, the threatening sex, as well."[4]

Media concern was most fully stoked in the '90s by the development of the men's movement, an umbrella term used to define a series of diverse groups mobilized around discourses of male disenfranchisement. While in the '70s Britain had witnessed the socialist pro-feminist men's movement and the publication of the anti-sexist, male-authored magazine *Achilles Heel*, the '90s American men's movement was a different affair, attracting huge media interest, as well as netting vast profits for its founders through publications, conferences, and weekend retreats. The American men's movement encompasses a small pro-feminist and gay liberation faction, but more often refers to movements populated by men who, as Segal notes, want "to turn back time: to reclaim and reaffirm the imagined origins of true masculinity."[5] These organizations include overtly anti-feminist, right-wing groups and the Christian Promise Keepers. However, the men's movement tends to be synonymous with Robert Bly and his devout following, though he rapidly spawned numerous imitators.

Bly, a '60s peace activist and poet, hit the headlines with his best-seller *Iron John: A Book About Men* (1990), an eclectic mixture of myth, fairy stories, poetry, New Ageist biological essentialism, and naive historical analysis, all packaged up in a melodramatic yet highly defensive prose. Bly argues that male grief "has reached a depth now that cannot be ignored," placing the blame on his perceived large-scale feminization of society, a phenomenon which, he claims, began in the '70s, and has resulted in generations of "soft males."[6] The inescapably phallic title of his book stems from Bly's rendition of the Grimm Brothers' fairytale, in which a prince steals a key from his mother's pillow in order to release the wild man that is held captive in the palace; after symbolically wounding his finger, the boy is eventually helped by the wild man to win the hand of the princess. For Bly, this fairytale is a paradigmatic male myth that envisions a path to full manhood: young men must liberate themselves from the sway of their emasculating mothers, use the wounds they have received, especially from their father, in order to access the wild man within and restore rule to male elders. Though he is careful to state that he has no objection to feminism, he holds the absence of fathers and paternal authority responsible for male pain, noting that "[b]etween twenty and thirty percent of American boys now live in a house with no father present, and the demons there have full permission to rage."[7]

Bly's movement has now largely disbanded, though its decline might point to the widespread assimilation of its main tenets.[8] Certainly, its sentiments are endlessly circulated in Hollywood films, particularly in what Fred Pfeil refers to as the "sensitive-guy films" of the '90s, which I discuss in chapter 2.[9] In its heyday, it was also often ridiculed by the mainstream press, especially for its weekend retreats comprised of male rituals, such as drumming workshops, and its consciousness-raising style seminars in which men discussed anxieties, especially those relating to their fathers. Yet Bly acquired a loyal following, populated overwhelmingly by white, lower-middle-class, middle-aged, heterosexual males, who, as Michael S. Kimmel and Michael Kaufman point out, were the men hardest hit *psychologically* by the so-called "crisis in masculinity," caused, in part, by the gains won by feminism, lesbian and gay activism, and the civil rights movement—all of which challenged straight white men's assumptions of privilege at a time when, while among the most powerful sectors of American society, few in fact experienced any individual sense of empowerment.[10]

The movement's overwhelming whiteness, its appropriation of ethnic rituals (such as the use of the Native-American talking stick at meetings), its implicit indictment of women for feminizing the male population, its elision of differences between men, and its refusal to contemplate the privileges that inhere in white heterosexual masculinity have all resulted in accusations of misogyny, white supremacy, and heterosexism. However, Kimmel and Kaufman point out that there is a "progressive whisper" to the men's movement in that it opens up space for a redefinition of manhood.[11] Fred Pfeil follows suit. While critiquing the movement for its failure to recognize that the root causes of male suffering stem from corporate capitalism, job insecurity, and the erosion of wages in real terms, he argues that it at least acknowledges that "there is *something* wrong with normative white heterosexual masculinity"—a point he sees related to the fact that a large number of participants seek the help of the movement "in resolving the ongoing external and internal crisis flowing from their inevitable complicity with the evil of white masculinity, their membership in a bad tribe."[12]

While Bly and his followers tended to subsume all differences under the banner of the battle between the sexes, the '90s also witnessed sweeping hysteria in the U.S. media over the "angry white male," an iconic figure who soon became a repository for backlash anxieties that straight white men had lost out not only to women, but also other minority groups, particularly people of color. The "angry white male" discourse points to the difficulty of white heterosexual masculinity functioning as an unmarked, neutral category in the wake of the heated debates that raged in the U.S. in the '90s over multiculturalism, illegal and legal immigration, sexual harassment, feminist-inspired legislation, gays in the military, gay marriages, and numerous other issues that pointed to the increasingly hybridized nature of contemporary U.S. life—all of which were manipulated by the right to produce a rhetoric of white male victimization. As George Lipsitz argues, building on the Reagan administration's fusing of a "possessive investment in whiteness" with masculinity, patriarchy, and heterosexuality, current neo-conservative discourse encourages white men "to feel their losses as whites, as men, as heterosexuals, but not as workers or community members," channeling all resentment in the direction of minority groups rather than "transnational capital and the economic austerity and social disintegration it creates and sustains."[13] In a remarkable reversal, white men, who had once been the oppressors, or at best inhabited the ordinary, universal position, transmuted into a self-proclaimed, marginalized, extra-ordinary group.

While attacking a wide range of targets, from women to federal government, the "angry white male" was a particularly racially charged discourse. Key '90s media events involving African-Americans, such as the Thomas-Hill hearings, the Rodney King affair, and the televised O.J. Simpson trial, had resulted in race dominating the headlines in sensationalized accounts which failed to probe into institutionalized racial injustice.[14] The Rodney King verdict also triggered the Los Angeles uprisings in 1992. While the Los Angeles insurrections were in fact a multiethnic affair, with significant Latino and white participation, and a high percentage of Korean victims, the media chose to present it as a black "riot" with white victims. This robbed the insurgents of any political intent, shored up white paranoia of black bodies, and reinscribed a Manichean black/white racial binary that fails to reflect contemporary U.S. racial demographics.

Such media representations have helped fuel white male resentment at affirmative action policies, resentment which stems all the way back to the Bakke case (1974-78), but which reached a fever pitch in the '90s, with affirmative action commonly represented as a form of reverse discrimination rather than a righting of institutionalized wrongs.[15] White male anger over affirmative action is effectively illustrated in Paul Haggis's Oscar-winning, racial drama *Crash* (2004) when, in a heated exchange with a black female state employee, who refuses him medical help for his sick father, Matt Dillon's cop states, "I can't look at you without thinking about the five or six more qualified white men that didn't get your job." His racist attitude, evident throughout the film, is directly attributed to affirmative action when he explains that his father's janitor business collapsed when the state gave priority to minority-owned firms. While the film is critical of his racism, showing the devastating effect his behavior has on a black couple that he abuses in his role as law enforcer, it also shows him more sympathetically when it screens his struggle to look after his sick father, both practically and economically. The film thus explores the psychology of those white men that suffer from neo-liberal economies, but are unable to understand their alienation other than in racial/racist terms.[16] *American History X* (Tony Kaye 1998) also attributes racism in the son to suffering endured by the father. Derek (Edward Norton), an eventual recruiter for a neo-fascist movement, is highly influenced by his fireman father, who objects to affirmative action policies and the teaching of black authors at high school, and who is later killed putting out a fire in a black neighborhood. The strength of the film is that it charts how neo-conservative discourses can easily spiral into white supremacy, though, unlike *Crash*, it does not suggest how more mundane practices work to reconfigure white power, and thereby enables white audiences to distance themselves from the shocking behavior of white supremacist extremists.[17]

Certainly, claims that white men have lost ground to women and men of color do not fall on deaf ears at a time of profound economic insecurity. For instance, according to a nationwide poll carried out by the *Washington Post*, the Kaiser Foundation, and Harvard University in 1995, 58% of whites thought that the average African-American was as well or better off than the average white in terms of employment, and 41% thought this was true as regards income, while black unemployment at the time was actually double that of white, and black income 40% lower.[18] Indeed, it is still white men who head the earning tables. According to U.S. Statistical Abstracts (2003), black and Hispanic men earn about 70% of white male counterparts, white women still earn three-quarters that of white men, while women of color earn little more than half the median white male wage.[19] At the same time, it is also important to remember that in 2003 more than 24 million whites, including over 10 million white males, were living in poverty, along with nearly 9 million blacks, over 9 million Latinos, and 1.4 million Asians.[20] In other words, being a white male is no guarantee of financial security.

The "angry white male" figure took its most extreme form with the Patriot Movement, a diverse but popular alliance of right-wing, anti-federalist groups, ranging from Christian to white supremacist militias. Beliefs differ in degree, though many factions oppose feminism, abortion rights, affirmative action, homosexuality, and immigration; but the most reviled enemy is indubitably the federal government. Media hysteria about the militia movement peaked after the 1995 bombing of the Alfred P. Murrah Federal Building in Oklahoma by Timothy McVeigh and Terry Nichols. The Oklahoma bombing shocked white America partly because, as Michael Hill points out, McVeigh was the "all-American defendant," who implicated white subjectivity in his terror.[21] Only after the bombings did the media investigate the relationship between the rise of the paramilitary right and the figure of the "white male as victim."[22] Yet, in many ways, McVeigh had merely taken to extremes the discourses of white male paranoia that neo-conservatives had exploited so effectively in their attempt to convince their constituency of white heterosexual males of their disenfranchisement.

In using the term "paranoia," I am following Patrick O'Donnell's understanding of cultural paranoia; that is, paranoia denoting "the symptomatic condition of postmodernity," as opposed to a personal, pathological disorder.[23] However, the two are inextricably related. In Freud's famous case study, the paranoiac Judge Daniel Paul Schreber exhibited symptoms such as megalomania, a sense of impending doom, delusions of persecution, the sense of being under constant surveillance, an obsession with order, fantasies of being at the center of plots and conspiracies, and "racist, homophobic, or gynophobic fear and hatred of those marked as other deployed as a means of externalizing certain internal conflicts and desires."[24] The same narcissistic and masochistic structures, which articulate the desire for "absolute centeredness, immediacy, transparency, and control," also undergird cultural paranoia, which, O'Donnell argues, "must be looked at within the larger, global perspective provided by Jameson's understanding of the intersections of late capitalism and postmodernity."[25] For O'Donnell, cultural paranoia rearranges chaos into order, consolidates the borders of identity, and thus functions as a "compensatory fiction" in response to the "schizophrenias of postmodern identity, economy and aesthetics."[26] As Fredric Jameson himself puts it, "the possibility of conspiracy confirms the possibility of the very unity of the social order itself" so that paranoia forms "an attempt . . . to think a system so vast that it cannot be encompassed by the natural and historically developed categories of perception with which human beings normally orient themselves."[27] At the same time, while white male paranoia undoubtedly forms a defensive response to the uncertainties and fragmentation of the contemporary social reality, resentment is directed primarily at women and people of color, rather than corporate capitalism and the profound insecurities it generates. Since, as Martin Fradley notes, paranoia functions in "a cyclical double bind, staging various masochistic fantasies in order to master them . . . wherein anxiety and neurosis manifest themselves in (self-)aggrandizement and unambiguous certitude,"[28] the narcissistic and masochistic mode of paranoia allows average white guys to feel recentered and reempowered in a postfeminist, multicultural era. Indeed, O'Donnell suggests that all identity categories "reveal the work of paranoia as that which both polices the boundaries between self and other, and like the border patrol, has more to do the more susceptible those boundaries are to transgression and erasure."[29] Consequently, while white male paranoia might shore up normative masculinity as a category, it is also indicative of the inherent instabilities and fragilities of white heterosexual masculinity, which, like all identities, constructs itself in relation to its equally unstable others. As Martin Fradley, writing specifically of normative masculinity, asserts, paranoia "expose[s] the performativity of masculinity, the need to continually reassert and reiterate the centrality of that supposed normalcy and the fundamental conservatism it seeks to uphold."[30] White male paranoia, then, is symptomatic of white heterosexual masculinity's claims to ordinariness—a source of strength but also anxiety—as well as its desire to consolidate its power by claiming its victimized, marginalized status—that is, its extra-ordinariness—articulated through the notion that the dominant identity has lost ground to its gendered and raced others, and now requires an identity politics of its own.

In the rest of this chapter, I aim to explore representations of white men "losing ground" in two Hollywood films that screen white male paranoia—*Falling Down* (Joel Schumacher 1993) and *Disclosure* (Barry Levinson 1994)—before turning to the British comic hit *The Full Monty* (Peter Cattaneo 1997), primarily for comparative purposes, in order to elaborate the point that even in the highly globalized world of cinematic representations, white heterosexual masculinity is always culturally and historically bound. In all three films, anxie-

ties over white male disenfranchisement are spatially inscribed, with traditionally white- and male-controlled space occupied by women and/or people of
color. The conditions of late capitalism, namely high unemployment, job insecurity, the globalization of capital, dependence on poorly paid female or immigrant
labor, and the entry of women into management, have led to a massive restructuring of both public and private space wherein conventional gendered and racial encodings no longer necessarily apply. The white male protagonists of *Falling Down* and *Disclosure* (both played by the "angry white male" *par excellence* Michael Douglas) perceive themselves not only as having no space to call
their own, but also, in the wake of identity politics—from which white men, as
the dominant, structuring norm, are excluded—as having no place from which to
speak (except that of oppressor). They are thus forced to borrow the rhetoric of
minority groups. *The Full Monty* translates concerns similar to *Disclosure* onto a
British terrain, in particular in its self-conscious, often comic representation of
the reversals of gendered spaces and places in an era of large-scale deindustrialization and concomitant chronic male unemployment. However, it largely avoids
falling into the backlash discourses of *Falling Down* or *Disclosure* due to its
willingness to tackle class and right-wing economic policies.

Falling Down: The "Angry White Male" in a Reterritorialized America

Described by Martin Fradley as "perhaps *the* Ur-text in Hollywood's take on the
angsty, angry white male,"[31] *Falling Down* was singled out for attention in both
the popular media at the time of release and film criticism of the mid-'90s for its
portrayal of specifically white male grievances in a postfeminist, multicultural,
postindustrial America. *Newsweek* even ran the film as its cover story (March
29, 1993) with the headline "White Male Paranoia: Are They the Newest Victims—or Just Bad Sports?" As Jude Davies and Carol R. Smith point out, *Falling Down* is a prime example of a "talky," a film that overtly engages with debates of politicized identity and/or social issues, deliberately courting media
attention and controversy as part of its marketing strategy.[32]

Certainly, Michael Douglas, the protagonist, is no stranger to controversy,
which is now intrinsic to his star persona. This provocative edge was launched
with *Fatal Attraction* (1987), a staunch attack on feminism and a saccharine
reaffirmation of bourgeois family values, which laced Douglas's persona with
what would become his enduring trademark: the victimized white male. Capitalizing on this performance, *Basic Instinct* (1992) casts Douglas as a trigger-happy
cop at the mercy of his desires for Catherine Tramell (Sharon Stone), a wealthy,
sexually independent, bisexual author with a predilection for stabbing her male
lovers to death with an ice-pick while in the throes of orgasm. The film's analogies between sexual deviance and serial killing, not surprisingly, led to U.S.
cinemas being picketed by lesbian and gay activists. Released a year after *Falling Down*, *Disclosure* features Douglas accusing his female boss of sexual har-

assment, and amplified Douglas's persona of the belligerent white male, furious at being labeled everyone's oppressor, and single-mindedly intent on proving his own victimization. If, as Richard Dyer argues, the charisma of stars stems from their embodiment of the ideological contradictions of the culture to which they belong,[33] Douglas would seem to epitomize the instabilities of U.S. white heterosexual masculinity in the first half of the 1990s.

Director Joel Schumacher describes *Falling Down*'s protagonist, D-FENS, as "the seemingly ordinary man who snaps suddenly."[34] The desire to universalize Douglas's character is evident in the decision to use the name D-FENS in the film's final credits rather than Bill Foster, the name we only learn at the film's end. D-FENS is taken from Foster's personalized registration plate, showing him to be a man who defines himself through his job of "building important things to protect us from the communists," as his mother puts it—except that the Cold War is over, the defense industry massively downsized, and D-FENS left without a job and, we later learn, without a family or home. As both an everyman figure but also an "angry white male," whose whiteness and maleness are no longer beside the point, but whose injury can only be articulated from what Robyn Wiegman terms "an implicit and prior claim to the universal,"[35] D-FENS epitomizes the contested positioning of contemporary U.S. white heterosexual masculinity, particularly as regards its ordinary and/or extra-ordinary status.

The title of the film, itself a spatial metaphor, overtly proclaims the white male's perceived fall from privilege, a fall that, as numerous critics have noted, is mapped out in terms of space and territory.[36] The spatial inscription of white male angst is evident from the opening scene, which opens with a disorientating, claustrophobic, extreme close-up of the inside of D-FENS's mouth. Without cutting, the objective camera then pulls slightly back to reveal his upper-lip, beaded with sweat, and slowly pans up, still with the same uncomfortable proximity, to his nose and bespectacled eyes, at which point it pulls away to reveal D-FENS stuck in a traffic jam. Despite the film's suggestion that D-FENS has no space to call his own in an America that has been reterritorialized along race and gender lines,[37] D-FENS literally dominates the screen. Only *Fight Club* (1999), which opens inside its beleaguered white male protagonist's brain, has begun by placing its viewers so firmly inside the angst-ridden white male psyche. From the moment D-FENS abandons his car and begins his trek across LA on foot, he is pitted against an array of multicultural, multiracial, gendered, and sexual others. These encounters are punctuated by scenes of either Prendergast (Robert Duvall), the white police officer who eventually tracks him down, or D-FENS's ex-wife, Beth (Barbara Hershey), and her panicked reactions to his phone calls and threats to come home for his daughter's birthday. This narrative segmentation reflects the fragmentation of Los Angeles across class and race lines, as well as the battle of the sexes on the domestic front. In all these conflicts, even as D-FENS dispenses violence, he casts himself as a victim defending the "ordinary" male's ground.

This is apparent from his first encounter with difference, his confrontation with a Korean shopkeeper (Michael Paul Chan). The racial dynamics of this scene are initially masked through the depiction of commonly experienced frustrations, encouraging identification with D-FENS until he oversteps the mark and becomes verbally and physically abusive. D-FENS is refused change for the telephone, but when he takes a can of coke (that all-American product) to the counter, the Korean charges him eighty-five cents, a price D-FENS not only considers extortionate, but one which still leaves him without change for the telephone. This confrontation quickly slides into a racially charged verbal exchange when D-FENS criticizes the Korean's English accent ("Don't you have 'Vs' in China?"), and retorts, "You come to my country, you take my money, you don't even have the grace to learn how to speak my language." Here D-FENS posits America as the homestead of the white male, which has been invaded by otherness. However, the film makes it clear that the America that D-FENS consistently appeals to no longer exists, symbolized by a none-too-subtle cutaway shot of a pot of American flags upturned in the ensuing struggle. D-FENS's demand for linguistic uniformity (a sentiment shared by many characters in *Crash*) is also a demand for the preservation of white hegemonic control, evident in his later encounter with a Latino gang, whose territory he has inadvertently wandered into because he failed to read their "sign": "Maybe if you wrote it in fucking English, I could fucking understand it." When the Korean assumes that D-FENS wants to rob him, D-FENS expresses incredulous rage, presumably because, as an ordinary white male dressed in a suit and tie, he has never experienced the criminalizing gaze. It is at this point that he announces, "I'm rolling back prices to 1965," before smashing up the shop's wares with a baseball bat (another key American symbol) until the Korean starts suggesting lower prices. Obviously, this suggests a desire to roll back American life generally,[38] to a culturally uniform America he could make sense of, an America where white middle-class men were guaranteed the privileges, on both the public and private front, that traditionally accompanied their sex and skin color, a time before second wave feminism, the civil rights movement, the full-scale technologization of the workplace, Asian economic competition (as symbolized by the Korean), the defeat in Vietnam, and, importantly for D-FENS, an unemployed defense worker, a time when the Cold War was strongly entrenched in the American imagination. In other words, D-FENS's desire to go "home" is really a desire for things to go back to the way things were, a desire visually inscribed through his '50s "'buzz-cut' hairstyle, horn-rimmed, large-lensed glasses," white shirt, and tie.[39]

Los Angeles is the perfect geographical setting for a screening of white male grievances. California is "a traditional hotbed for identity politics,"[40] as recent debates over Proposition 209 and the scandal over gay marriages have shown, and thus a prime site for the contestation of politicized discourses of identity. Huge-scale downsizing, especially in the defense sector, and the collapse of the manufacturing industry have led to high unemployment among all sectors of the population and a shift to the badly paid service industry. In the last twenty-five years, new patterns of segregation have emerged as whites have moved to the suburbs, while newer immigrants from Mexico, Central America, and South East Asia have joined African-American inhabitants, resulting in decaying, neglected ghettoes with majority non-white populations. For example, whites in South Central Los Angeles comprised less than 5% of the population at the time of the film's release.[41] Moreover, according to the 2000 Census, whites make up only 31.1% of the population of Los Angeles, while Hispanics make up 44.6%, Blacks 9.5% and Asians 11.8%.[42] With Los Angeles often represented as a synecdoche for a future America, these demographics certainly destabilize the black-white paradigm which continues to inform the American racial imagination, as well as indicating that white centrality is certainly statistically—if not politically, economically, and culturally—under threat.

D-FENS informs Beth that the city is "sick," a point of view that the film would seem to confirm, as it presents exploitative and stereotypical images of inner-city poverty and suffering (the homeless, the unemployed, AIDS victims, immigrant fruit sellers, to name a few) through the prism of the beleaguered, paranoid, white male gaze. As Elana Zilberg points out, "[t]hese 'inner city folk,' . . . , serve as little more than a textured backdrop" to the tragic journey of the Anglo-American protagonist.[43] Los Angeles is painted as a city where, for the "average" white male, all urban spaces have become hostile, unreadable, and occupied by others.[44] When D-FENS passes through the territory of the Latino gang, they accuse him of trespassing on private property and demand a toll. D-FENS acknowledges, with great condescension, that they are having a "territory dispute," stating that he wouldn't want them in his backyard either—a staggering conflation of the privatized space of the bourgeois home and a run-down, urban wasteland. D-FENS is also labeled a trespasser by a homeless man in a public park and by rich golfers when he wanders into their exclusive golf club—reminders that D-FENS's "ordinary" status is evoked as much through class as through gender, sexuality, and race.

While urban space is overwhelmingly coded as male, Beth represents the domestic space to which D-FENS is also denied access: Beth has received a restraining order from a judge who wanted to make D-FENS an example, even though he had never become physically violent. D-FENS is thus posited as a victim of feminist-inspired legislation until the end of the film when Beth's intuition is finally validated. Forced to move back in with his neurotic mother, and with his father absent, presumably dead, it is suggested that "the demons" have had "full permission to rage," to use Robert Bly's expression. The loss of male control in the domestic sphere is also conveyed through Prendergast's relationship with his equally neurotic, demanding wife. Prendergast has become every inch Robert Bly's feminized "soft man," tolerating his wife's unreasonable demands and accepting a desk job to appease her, rendering himself the butt of office jokes. The film's representation of Prendergast's wife and D-FENS's mother are also indissociable from the billboard advertisement for sun lotion which enables Prendergast to track D-FENS down. The advertisement—which features a tanned woman in a bikini, with the added graffiti of a small cartoon man trapped in her cleavage crying out "Help me!"—connects D-FENS and Prendergast not only diegetically, but also thematically by spatially inscribing their shared fear of being suffocated by women. Sharon Willis also observes that the advertisement, which implies white people's desire to brown up, suggests that "a fear of engulfment by the feminine intersects with fears of being overrun by otherness."[45]

The doubling of D-FENS with Prendergast does not stop here.[46] Both men are fathers who have lost children, Prendergast through Sudden Infant Death Syndrome and D-FENS through the legal system. Furthermore, Prendergast's assumption that his Japanese colleague can understand Korean is obviously paralleled with D-FENS's assumption that the Korean shopkeeper was Chinese. Despite this slip, though, Prendergast, who maintains a close but politically correct relationship with his female Latina partner Sandra (Rachel Ticotin), is offered up as an example of how ordinary white men should manage difference. However, his heroic status is only confirmed after a trajectory of remasculinization, when the "soft man" finds the "wild man" within, to use Bly's mythopoetic terminology. By the end of the film, Prendergast silences his wife in sexist language, punches a colleague who insults his wife, swears at his police chief on national television, and decides not to retire despite the promises he had made to his wife. Most importantly, though, in the closing "show-down" between the "sheriff" and the "bad guy"—which brings to a logical conclusion the film's reworking of the Western genre, and its motif of the "lone white male in the wilderness"[47]—D-FENS draws a plastic water pistol, while Prendergast draws the real thing. Prendergast shoots D-FENS dead, screening the typical theme of "regeneration by violence" that Richard Slotkin has located in frontier literature and mythology.[48]

D-FENS is also played off against Nick (Frederic Forrest), the vicious, homophobic, sexist, fascist owner of the army surplus store, who assumes that D-FENS held up Whammy Burger because of "all the niggers working there," whereas in fact he held it up because it refused to serve him breakfast past the allotted time. As Carol Clover argues, Nick functions as an essential foil, allowing the film to "define D-FENS as your average short-tempered neighbour who just happened to break one day."[49] D-FENS also tries to enforce this distance, informing Nick, "We are not the same. I'm an American, you're a sick ass'ole." At the same time, the men are also paralleled through the visual codes deployed. For instance, when an infuriated Nick simulates being a black prisoner raping D-FENS, muttering "give it to me, give it to me" in a frenzy of homoerotophobic excitement, Nick's mouth fills the screen in an extreme close-up that self-consciously replicates the film's opening shot of D-FENS. This doubling is reinforced through the mirror that mediates shots between the two men; consequently, when D-FENS shoots at Nick, he also shoots at his own reflection, suggesting a moment of utter self-hatred, as well as pointing to the difficulty the film faces in separating D-FENS's white male paranoia from Nick's neo-fascism. Indeed, after killing Nick and reaching what he calls "the point of no return," D-FENS trades in his nerdy short-sleeved white shirt and tie for military fatigues from Nick's shop. This attire also plays on the sartorial codes of the Patriot Movement, as well as underscoring the film's reworking of the white male rampage genre, typified by the *Rambo* series, though the jungle, while equally foreign to the white male protagonist, is now the streets of LA.[50]

The fact that Nick chooses to humiliate D-FENS through a simulated bi-racial rape also screens white male fears of being invaded by otherness, both racial and sexual, as well as being suggestive of the instabilities of Nick's paranoid masculinity. Earlier, Nick had attacked two gay potential customers in malicious hate speech that confirmed his rampant homophobia. His rape fantasy thus renders him Freud's typical paranoid subject, who projects onto others, in this case black males, those repressed aspects of the self he finds repellent, namely homoerotic desire. As Paul Smith puts it, "[i]n paranoia, the libido is turned upon the ego itself so that, in a loose sense, the paranoiac's object choice is his/her own ego. Freud suggests that in such a case anything perceived as noxious within the ego (in the interior, as it were) is then projected onto external objects: the 'subject' thus endows the external world with what it takes to be its own worst tendencies and qualities."[51] As well as suggesting Nick's repressed homoerotic desires, his fantasy of inhabiting a sadistic black body not only highlights the paranoiac's assumption that the others it attempts to subjugate will respond with vengeful aggression, thereby justifying his/her paranoia in the first place, but also stages a masochistic scenario, wherein white men assume the victim function to a black aggressor. It is therefore important that, in a film seemingly determined to spare African-Americans from being one of those others against whom D-FENS is pitted, and equally determined to maintain D-FENS as an ordinary guy and potential figure of identification, the masochistic fantasy that the white man is being "fucked" by the black man is nonetheless articulated, albeit through a mediating secondary character.

The actual African-American male that D-FENS does encounter, who is rushed away by police for parading outside a bank carrying a placard stating "not economically viable" in protest at being denied a loan, has no obvious narrative function and his role is surprisingly limited in view of the fact that African-Americans are usually posited as a signifier of race and a repository for white paranoia in popular representations. In part, this can be attributed to the film's attempt to comment on the shifting racial dynamics of LA in the wake of new immigration patterns, as well as a desire to placate the African-American community, which has made significant gains in the politics of representation in Hollywood. However, despite the brevity of their encounter, D-FENS later borrows the protestor's words: "I've lost my job. Well, actually I didn't lose it. It lost me. I'm overeducated, under-skilled. Maybe it's the other way round, I forget. And I'm obsolete. I'm not economically viable." As Liam Kennedy argues, the homology established between the two men functions as a gesture of "historical amnesia" which "negates the alterity of the black subject" and elides the specificity of African-American social, cultural, and racial oppression.[52] At the same time, D-FENS's appropriation of the African-American's words suggests that while many white men experience similar economic insecurities to people of color under late capitalism, unlike minorities, they are bereft of a discourse and place from which to speak in "a culture that appears to organize itself around the visibility of differences and the symbolic currency of identity politics."[53] Lacking a discourse of class which might help him comprehend his predicament, and unable "to locate himself with respect to a history of oppression and its contestation, and/or to establish an identity with others in the same condition," D-FENS can only experience his losses as an "inexplicable victimisation."[54]

Falling Down is a landmark film for highlighting that white heterosexual masculinity can now function as a specific, extra-ordinary, politicized identity in the U.S. rather than just the invisible norm, albeit through the inscription of white male victimhood. At the same time, the terms of white patriarchal hegemony remain intact, with white heterosexual masculinity redeemed through the figure of Prendergast, while even D-FENS sacrifices his life so that his daughter can gain his life insurance, with fatherhood offering a racially innocent path of white male redemption. Moreover, the fact that *Falling Down* focuses relentlessly on the plight of two ordinary guys, and marginalizes the grievances of the straight white male's others, means that, as with *Disclosure*, despite the film's discursive suggestion that middle-class white men have lost ground, the disproportionate amount of screen space they continue to command tells a rather different story, at least as far as the politics of representation is concerned.

Disclosure: The Feminization of the Workplace

Released a year after *Falling Down*, *Disclosure* deployed Douglas's star persona of "angry white man" to full effect and was also marketed as a "talky," self-consciously mobilizing the discourses of sexual harassment that had fuelled countless talk shows in the wake of the Thomas-Hill affair. As Herman Beavers notes, the Thomas-Hill hearings "connoted the emergence of a new kind of public scrutiny: for men, as it pertained to how they treated women in the workplace, for women, as it pertained to how they 'threatened' male hegemony."[55] Meredith Johnson (Demi Moore) certainly threatens male authority at work by falsely accusing Douglas's character, Tom Sanders, of sexual harassment, a charge that Tom directs back at her. However, it later turns out that Tom's conniving boss, Bob Garvin (Donald Sutherland), had orchestrated the harassment accusations in order to fire Tom and blame him for the production line problems in Malaysia, thereby saving the merger of his computer firm, Digicom, with another American company. Tom is thus posited as the victim of not so much sexual harassment, but rather feminist-inspired anti-discriminatory legislation.[56] Sharon Willis has argued that often in popular representations "one difference is made to stand in for, to do the job of, to trivialize or eclipse, the others."[57] In the case of *Disclosure*, the overdetermined "battle of the sexes" plotline veils other concerns aside from white male victimization at the hands of feminism; more covertly, the sexual harassment narrative plays out anxieties over the perceived "feminization" of the workplace, along with the restructuring and regendering of public and private space, while at a further level of displacement, as Davies and Smith argue, it transcodes the threat of the U.S. economy losing ground to Asian others in the marketplace.[58]

Despite the fact that the plot of *Disclosure* is actually driven by the intrigues of corporate conspiracies, the film was marketed through its sexual harassment narrative. One of the advertising posters, which featured a picture of Demi Moore and Michael Douglas wrapped in each other's arms (neither seeming particularly harassed), accompanied by the slogan "sex is power," offered the promise of the illicit sex scenes that Douglas had delivered in *Basic Instinct*. The actual "non-sex sex" scene, to use the words of Tom's wife Susan (Caroline Goodall), eroticizes the sadomasochistic power dynamics of the workplace. On entering Meredith's office, Tom hears her on the phone flirtatiously telling an unnamed interlocutor in a spatially encoded metaphor, "I like all the boys under me to be happy." This power relation is reinvoked when Meredith actively seduces Tom, murmuring, "Don't worry. I'm not gonna bite," before performing oral sex on him in a scene that seems designed to screen the pleasures of male passivity. However, when she conflates professional and sexual power to the tune of "let me be the boss," an imperative which obviously touches a raw nerve, Tom aggressively assumes the active role, leaving Meredith to pant breathlessly, "Now you've got all the power. You've got something I want." The film self-consciously engages with the issue of consent that had driven discussions about female date rape at the time of release. Tom moans "no" thirty-one times before he eventually pulls away (with no difficulty, as Meredith points out in the mediation hearings) after catching sight of his reflection in the glass partition. In her defense, Meredith suggests that sometimes no means yes, a statement for which she is reprimanded by Tom's prominent feminist lawyer, Catherine Alvarez (Roma Maffia): "No means no. Isn't that what we tell women? Do men deserve less?" The incommensurate power differentials between men and women are thus deftly elided.

Catherine soon initiates Tom into feminist rhetoric: "Sexual harassment is not about sex. It's about power. She [Meredith] has it, and you don't." When his wife tells him he should just apologize, Tom appropriates Catherine's words: "Sexual harassment is about power. When did I have the power? When?" As with *Falling Down*, then, the film articulates anxieties that white men lack a place from which to speak their disenfranchisement, and are forced to borrow from the political discourses of their others. This enables Tom to claim a new minority identity—the oppressed white guy unjustly accused of being everyone else's oppressor: "Why don't I just admit it. Why don't I just be that guy, that white evil male you're all complaining about. I'd like it. Then I could fuck everyone." Then, parodying this evil white male role, he calls down his Asian maid so that he can satisfy a "patriarchal urge." His understanding of himself as per-secuted, though, has more than an ironic tinge in that it is undermined by the *mise-en-scène* of his luxurious home.[59] He also spares little thought for how his white patriarchal posturing might impact on his obviously intimidated Asian maid. Her reaction, however, is given no narrative space, as with the experiences of all the Asian women in the film, from the cleaner who is fired for witnessing Tom and Meredith's encounter, to the workers in the Malaysian plant, whose labor enables American companies to reap in huge profits.

As well as comprising a backlash response to pro-feminist legislation, the sexual harassment narrative also enables *Disclosure* to explore "[t]he sexualisa-tion of work," to use Yvonne Tasker's phrase, common to many neo-*noir* thrill-ers, such as *Fatal Attraction* and *The Last Seduction* (1994).[60] Meredith's first appearance is mediated through Tom's approving gaze, revealing her shapely legs as she walks up the stairs. Later, before their first meeting, the camera lin-gers on her stiletto shoes, a signifier of sexual as well as professional power, before cutting to reveal Demi Moore's face for the first time. This self-conscious fetishistic camerawork is an obvious intertextual reference to the film's *noir* heritage; however, this deployment of the traditional male gaze, whereby Tom is "bearer of the look" and Meredith its passive object,[61] is partially dislodged when it becomes apparent that Meredith is aggressive in both the bedroom and the boardroom. The film's visual economy, as with other neo-*noir* films, such as *The Last Seduction*, thus has it both ways: working women as eroticized sex objects rendered safe through fetishization, and working women as threats to male professional dominance. Moreover, in accordance with the traditional *noir* male point of view, Meredith is rendered opaque and unknowable, a blank screen onto whom concerns about white heterosexual masculinity are projected.

The sexualization of the workplace is represented as dangerous for Tom, since it jeopardizes not only his professional authority, but also his home life. Writing of neo-*noir* films generally, Sharon Willis notes, "[l]oading anxieties onto the question of sexual difference and sexuality, these films figure a private war of the sexes that foregrounds masculine anxieties about incompetence, weakness, and failure in a universe where the boundaries between the private and the public or professional are constantly shifting."[62] *Disclosure* seems intent on exploring the collapse of the public/private space distinction, traditionally gendered masculine/feminine, now that the division of labor has changed, along with the ramifications this has for normative masculinity. Tom's wife is not only a successful lawyer (albeit part-time), but also, according to the film's final credits, has kept her maiden name.[63] At the same time, the film takes pains to proclaim Tom's "New Man" credentials. The opening scene shows him arriving at work late on the day he was expecting to be promoted because he was helping Susan with the children. The toothpaste smeared on his tie, which attracts sev-eral comments throughout the day, and which Tom fruitlessly attempts to rub clean, reinforces his failure to keep the private and public spheres separate. Meredith, by contrast, has no truck with domesticity; on seeing a picture of

Susan, she observes, "She looks like she always has food in the refrigerator. . . . In my fridge back home I've got a couple of bottles of champagne and an orange." In fact, Meredith is shown to have little existence outside of the public space of work, even working out on her Stairmaster in her office whilst plotting maliciously with senior management.

Meredith is exemplary of the neo-*noir femme fatale*, who, according to Yvonne Tasker, combines elements of both the traditional *femme fatale* and the 1970s stereotype of the "independent woman," and whose "threat quite overtly lies in the context of work."[64] The traditional *femme fatale* has largely been explained as a complex ideological response to the shifting gender roles during the Second World War: played off against the good domestic woman, the *femme fatale* was criminalized in a representational strategy that attempted to facilitate the reassimilation of women, many of whom occupied professional positions in wartime, back into the home.[65] The *femme fatale* has proved to be a popular object of study within feminist theory because of the power her sexuality affords her, even if she is punished or seduced in narrative closure. Mary Anne Doane has argued that the traditional *femme fatale* is "not the subject of power but its carrier," but as Tasker notes, the postclassical/postmodern deadly women "know how to wield the power that they possess."[66] Indeed, while the traditional *femme fatale* represented fears of female entry into the workplace, in contemporary films, the fear is of women entering senior management. Bridget (Linda Fiorentino) in *The Last Seduction* even humiliates the men that work under her through taunts about their failures *as men*. Of course, as Frank Krutnik argues, traditional *noir* had always explored the "discrepancy between, on the one hand, the licit possibilities of masculine identity and desire required by the patriarchal cultural order, and, on the other hand, the psychosexual make-up of the male subject-hero."[67] Neo-*noir*, however, seems intent on developing the masochistic potential of the male protagonist, with the "hero" emerging as even more vulnerable and inept than his predecessors.[68] Indeed, Tom is only saved in the final instance by Stephanie (Rosemary Forsyth), one of the good, but desexualized women with whom Meredith is contrasted. However, the fact that Stephanie is finally given the promotion that Tom had been expecting allows the film to flaunt its "'liberal' credentials"[69] while suggesting that the fear of women taking over the workplace might well be justified.

The fear that men have lost ground to working women, a fear that assumes the workplace to be male territory by default, is indissociable from the specter of male redundancy that haunts *Disclosure*. This fear is largely evoked through an unnamed middle-aged man on the ferry, who functions as one of the "ghosts with a résumé" that Tom is so terrified of becoming. When Tom gives him the phone number of his secretary Cindy (Jacqueline Kim) in case a job opening crops up, the man bitterly retorts, "You used to have fun with girls. . . . Nowadays she probably wants your job." While Tom never utters such anti-feminist opinions (that are nonetheless articulated by means of this minor character), his masculinity is still very much tied up in traditionalist notions of the male as breadwinner. In fact, when Susan suggests that he should resign and that she should go back to work full-time, he indignantly replies, "I am perfectly capable of supporting my own family." The end of the film also amplifies the fear that women are more employable than men when the fired but unruffled Meredith informs Tom, "I've had calls from ten head-hunters with job offers in the last hour. Don't be surprised if I'm back in ten years to buy this place."

Meredith's occupation of traditional male territory also transcodes anxieties about the feminization of work *per se*. As Donna Haraway notes, "[t]o be feminized means to be made extremely vulnerable; able to be disassembled, reassembled, exploited as a reserve labor force seen less as workers than as servers; subjected to time arrangements on and off the paid job that make a mockery of a limited work day; leading an existence that always borders on being obscene, out of place, and reducible to sex."[70] Along with the loss of job security, the general shift from an industrial to a service economy has widely been regarded as a process of feminization, partly because no tangible product is made, but also because the skills demanded are traditionally coded as feminine.[71] Meredith's initial presentation at Digicom, with her use of flashy, electronic props, is all style and surface, causing Tom to state that she wouldn't know the difference between software and a cashmere sweater. In other words, the film articulates the anxiety that the postmodern workplace privileges appearance (gendered feminine) over production (gendered masculine). A similar emphasis on performativity is also inscribed through the firm's open-plan, glass-partition design, a spatial restructuring which functions much like the panoptica that Michel Foucault discusses in *Discipline and Punish* (1975), allowing senior management constant surveillance of employees—a design which, coupled with the roving objective camera, inserts Tom's paranoia firmly into the film's *mise-en-scène*. As B. Ruby Rich has observed, in neo-*noir*, the male protagonists "turn out to be the sole repositories of authenticity" with a mandate "to hold fast in a postmodern world of shifting significances, to reject dispersal and masquerade and therefore corruption, to be 'themselves' in the absence of any other comprehensive rules."[72] While Tom seems vulnerable to surveillance because of his authenticity, Meredith's rapid rise is attributed to her feminine ability to manipulate surfaces, including her immaculate appearance. Tom's scruffy attire, therefore, in a film where management is signified as feminized through its attention to dress (one manager even sinisterly files his nails as he schemes),[73] represents his self-conscious attempt to distance himself from performativity, representing himself as the "hands-on" productive type whose traditionalist masculinity is still firmly intact.

The fear that the workplace is being feminized is also compounded by the film's participation in discourses that code digital and virtual technologies as feminine due to their miniature, internalized, passivity-inducing qualities, a point I develop in chapter 4.[74] In her first presentation, Meredith extols the abilities of virtual technology to free us from race, gender, nationality, personality, place, and time, in a speech that deftly skirts around the physical labor and exploitation of the female workers in Malaysia, whose small hands produce the technology that makes transcendence over the body a possibility for a privileged few. It is thus interesting that in the special effects sequence that represents the virtual space where Digicom's files are stored, which Tom enters in order to learn about the plot that Meredith has been hatching against him, Tom appears in a naturalized human form while Meredith is denied a body. Meredith startles both Tom and the spectator as her figure darts from behind a file and hovers around him as a two-dimensional facial photograph perched on a fetishistic, metallic skeletal frame, explained by the narrative logic of her accessing the system from her office PC. On seeing this image, a horrified Tom cries out, "she's in the system!" His panic at being "invaded," though, reveals how the threat that digital and virtual technologies pose to the average professional white male *vis-à-vis* the specter of huge job losses and labor restructuring is actually conflated with the feminine through the monstrous figure of Meredith. In fact, if the film has left us in any doubt about this, the symbolic connotations are clear when Tom ends up being locked out of the system and saved by his use of more traditional technologies such as fax, e-mail, video, answer phone, and mobile phone.[75] In the film's representational strategies, therefore, Tom's unforgiving materiality, which connotes his authenticity, is juxtaposed to Meredith's two-dimensionality and concomitant duplicity. Moreover, this scene also expresses the anxiety that she has usurped the traditionally white male Cartesian prerogative of disembodiment (see chapter 4). The "white male as victim" discourse is further extended when it becomes apparent that women can have it both ways; that is, Meredith may well extol the joys of transcending the body, but can still appeal to embodied identity in order to mobilize anti-discrimination legislation to which white heterosexual men have no access.

The Malaysian women that Meredith forgets in her Western-centric, class-bound celebration of virtual disembodiment give another twist to the film's backlash anxieties, suggesting that the future workplace will be not only feminized, but also Asianized. In their perceptive reading of the film, Davies and Smith have argued that, by means of a "strategy of encoding, the threat of the female other in the workplace figures the threat of Asian others in the market-place." The threat posed by Pacific Rim economies to the U.S. economy is represented in a displaced form. "Actual Asians are screened out almost completely," and the Malaysian plant is only shown briefly in a mediated form, primarily through recorded TV footage of Meredith visiting the factory, though in order to disavow racism, the film adds the character of Cindy Chang to Michael Crichton's novel. Nobody in the film characterizes the merger with the American company as a protective move against a possible foreign take-over, but in the novel, the American company with which Digicom merges is called Conley-*White*. In short, the sexual harassment narrative allows a screening of a corporate takeover that "focuses anxieties over both internal and external challenges to the American economy: the economic and social effects of the switch away from domestic manufacturing on the one hand, and the globalization of capital and the emergence of Pacific Rim economies on the other."[76] To build on Davies and Smith's arguments, if Meredith is aligned with Asian competition, a displacement enabled through historical Western discourses that feminize the Orient, then once again, as with *Falling Down*, the victimized white male figure acts as a synecdoche for a threatened America, with both having ceded territory to their others.

The Full Monty: The Reversals of Gendered Spaces and Places

Anxieties about the feminization of the workplace are screened more sympathetically in the British comedy hit *The Full Monty*. *The Full Monty* avoids blaming individual women for male disenfranchisement by squarely placing the responsibility on the collapse of Sheffield's steel industry, although the film again retains a male perspective, with little exploration of how unemployment and/or social deprivation affect female characters, unlike Ken Loach's *Raining Stones* (1993), for example. In this respect, *The Full Monty* joins a host of contemporary British films, such as *Naked* (1993), *Brassed Off* (1996), *Trainspotting* (1996), *The Van* (1996), *Nil by Mouth* (1997), *Twin Town* (1997), *My Name Is Joe* (1998), *TwentyFourSeven* (1997), *Billy Elliot* (2000), and *The Football Factory* (2004), which take white working-class masculinity as their central problematic. Indeed, what with Hugh Grant's middle-class neurosis, commitment-phobia, self-effacing awkwardness, and verbal incontinence in romantic comedies such as *Four Weddings and a Funeral* (1994), *Notting Hill* (1999), *About a Boy* (2002), and *Love Actually* (2003), it would seem that British cinema's alleged renaissance in the '90s was highly dependent on representations of "(white) masculinity in crisis," which became its biggest cultural export, even though many of these films received American financial backing.

The popularity of these films in the U.S. is no doubt partly due to the fact that they tapped into the heated debates about alleged male failings and disempowerment that consumed both sides of the Atlantic.[77] The '90s British popular media also obsessed over boys' failure at school, the higher rate of depression, suicide, drug addiction, accidents, and cardiovascular disease among men, as well as shorter male life expectancy, in discussions which lacked substantial material analysis.[78] Pressure groups mobilized around fathers' rights also attracted, and continue to attract, sustained media attention, such as when, in 2004, a member of Fathers 4 Justice scaled the walls of Buckingham Palace dressed as Batman in order to protest his lack of access to his children. On the whole, though, the "angry white male" figure did not emerge in the same way in Britain as in the U.S. While anti-feminist sentiments were prevalent, there was not the equivalent resentment at affirmative action, since positive discrimination policies are rare (though are planned to be introduced). Moreover, the deeply entrenched class system in Britain means that white masculinity is always read through the lens of economic class, whereas in the U.S. class discourse is often eclipsed by discussions of race. Despite Britain's shameful colonial legacy and evidence of institutionalized racism,[79] it does not have 400 years of slavery on its own soil as part of its racial history—whereas dramas of race permeate every aspect of U.S. life. Nevertheless, racist hostility in Britain is routinely directed at ethnic minorities, asylum seekers, and immigrants, many of whom now come from former Eastern Europe, as well as British Muslims in the wake of 9/11 and the London bombings in 2005. As with the U.S., this hostility is articulated primarily through the more insidious discourses of nation, ethnicity, religion, and cultural uniformity rather than race or skin color, with the obvious exception of white supremacists, who have made massive inroads, as the performance of the British National Party in the 2002 and 2006 local elections has shown.

As well as representing a historically different model of white heterosexual masculinity than *Falling Down*, *The Full Monty* also partakes of a very different cinematic tradition, self-consciously positioning itself within the "angry young men" films of '50s and '60s British New Wave.[80] Shot on location, using realistic lighting and *mises-en-scène*, primarily set in the industrial north of England in order to comment on the British class system and rigid north-south divide, British New Wave films were often termed "kitchen sink" dramas because of their thematic concern with the nitty grittiness of everyday life. The use of realistic speech patterns, regional accents, and a non-star cast were all attempts to challenge the Hollywood model.[81] Importantly, though, a focus on the working-classes in fact meant a focus on the working class *man*, in particular anxieties that consumerism, suburbanization, and mass culture were assaulting traditional forms of working-class masculinity, as played out in films such as *Saturday Night and Sunday Morning* (1960), *The Loneliness of the Long Distance Runner* (1962), and *This Sporting Life* (1963).[82] However, the subject matter of an overwhelming majority of '90s films, such as *Brassed Off*, *The Full Monty*, *The Van* and *Billy Elliot*, is the *non*-working man, a symptom of large-scale deindustrialization, especially in the north. These films are often set during the time of Margaret Thatcher's Conservative government (1979-90), under whose aegis hundreds of thousands of jobs in the manufacturing industry were lost, resulting in an undermining of the givens upon which traditional notions of working-class masculinity were predicated. These films are all marked by nostalgia for a time when the working-class man was guaranteed employment, homosocial ties, the breadwinner role, and paternal authority.

Like *Disclosure*, *The Full Monty* insists on showing how women have moved into all traditionally male space, resulting in gender reversals that are a source of the film's often poignant humor. This is most strikingly played out when the protagonist, Gary (Robert Carlyle), and his friend, Dave (Mark Addy), discover that the traditional bastion of the working-class male, the working man's club (an ironic and obsolete term in this context), features a women-only night of male strippers. When Dave confesses that his wife Jean (Lesley Sharp) is among the audience, but that he cannot prevent her from going because "it's her money," Gary replies, "She's already got you hoovering, and I saw it, and I let it go. But this, no, no! You want to get her out of·there and tell her what's for." Gary's laddish response expresses concern that male unemployment feminizes men through enforced domestication, with Dave denied the role as head of the household because he no longer brings home the family wage. Barred from entering the club, Gary and Dave are reduced to breaking into the men's toilets in order to fetch Jean. However, at that moment Jean and her friends decide to use the men's toilets to avoid the queue, thus invading revered male space, leaving Gary to peer through a hole in the wall in a shot that self-consciously mirrors Norman Bates's (Anthony Perkins's) voyeuristic gaze in *Psycho* (1960). But instead of gaining an illicit glance at the female body, Gary is treated to the sight of a woman urinating like a man, accompanied by hoots of laughter from her friends. This ultimate usurpation of the male role is pondered over by the men at the job club (another redundant term) in one of the film's most self-conscious and amusing references to the battle of the sexes:

> Gary: When women start pissing like us, that's it. We're finished, Dave, extincto.
> Dave: I mean, how? . . . You know, how?
> Friend: Genetic mutation, innit? They're turning into us.
> Gary: The theory is men won't exist, except in zoo or somethin'. I mean, we're not needed no more, are we? Obsolete. Dinosaurs. Yesterday's news.

This rather masochistic discourse on male obsolescence is similar to a line in *Disclosure* when one of Tom's colleagues states of women, "They're stronger, they're smarter, they don't fight fair. It's the next step in human evolution. It's like the Amazons—keep a few of us around for sperm and kill off the rest." Unlike *Disclosure*, however, women in *The Full Monty* are not shown to be arrogating management positions; nor do they usurp skilled manual work, though the clip from *Flashdance* (1983) that Gary's crew study for dance moves does allow this fear to be articulated, with Dave commenting that he knows a lot more about welding than "some chuffin' woman." However, the job center is populated solely by men, as if unemployment were purely a male social problem. Moreover, women are represented as not only more employable than men, but also in a position to find jobs for their husbands or ex-husbands, albeit poorly paid work such as packers in the textile industry. What is in danger of being overlooked in the film, therefore, is the fact that women are more employable solely because they are prepared to accept low-paid, menial work that both Gary and Dave, as skilled workers, reject. When Dave tells Gary that Jean wants him to accept a job as a security guard in the supermarket she works for, Gary replies, "you're worth more than that," a point with which the film concurs by screening Dave's decision to walk out on the job as part of the film's feel-good conclusion.

On the one hand, then, *The Full Monty* excels at showing the humiliation experienced by skilled, working-class men who are forced to enter an unskilled labor market, humiliation that is conveyed through images not only of emasculation, most obviously through Dave's impotence, but also infantilization. This infantilization is also spatially inscribed, such as when the men sit at school-like desks at the job center, where they are patronized by staff who teach them how to write application letters, or when Gary's gang wait for Gerald (Tom Wilkinson) in a crèche, where Dave gets a child's hoop stuck on his wrist. The men's childish antics, such as the Punch and Judy show they act out with gnomes in front of a window while Gerald is having his first interview in months, are coded as signifiers of irresponsibility, but also escapist strategies for coping with the pressures of redundancy.

On the other hand, the film's suggestion that the only jobs available are "feminine" ones implies that women, unlike Dave, are not "worth more than that," an assumption that can only be arrived at through prefeminist notions of male entitlement. In this respect, Claire Monk is right to argue that preoccupation with the "underclass" in '90s British films enables other anxieties and resentments around gender to be displaced onto concerns about economic disempowerment.[83] For instance, although women are not held directly responsible for male unemployment, they still exacerbate the men's plight.[84] While Jean is represented sympathetically, Gerald's wife is an obsessive consumer, and with Gerald too ashamed to tell her that he has lost his job, "she's out there now, let loose on high street, with fucking Barclaycards, spending." Gary's ex-wife Mandy (Emily Woof) is also portrayed as heartless (except for the utopian final scene when she cheers Gary on), refusing Gary access to his son Nathan unless he can produce his maintenance arrears of £700.

Having lost their claim to traditional working-class male territory, the men are forced to inhabit pastures new, which, in this case, means the stage of the working-man's club when Gary puts together his troop of unlikely male strippers. The men also rehearse in "the very space where they had once performed in 'properly' masculine ways, as manual workers: the empty factory."[85] The humor produced by such reversals indicates that the trading of gendered spaces and places can never be symmetrical. Nonetheless, the film suggests that the occupation of traditionally female arenas, while ostensibly humiliating, can afford its own pleasures. Whereas *Billy Elliot* represents a male adolescent's journey into the world of ballet as liberation from the repressive, heterosexist masculinism of his working-class father and brother, *The Full Monty* posits stripping as a means of reestablishing the much-missed homosocial bonds that existed in the workplace. Somewhat paradoxically, Gary's stripping scheme also remasculinizes its participants, precisely because it renders them self-made men, though it is not without irony that this gestures at the same self-reliant and entrepreneurial spirit that the Conservative government claimed to want to nurture in its allegedly benefit-dependent, unemployed citizens. Gary's business venture also earns him the respect of his son—highlighting the importance awarded to fatherhood in constructions of white masculinity on both sides of the Atlantic.

As with *Fight Club* (see chapter 2), the film also suggests that, in the absence of women, homosocial bonds between men can transcend all differences. But unlike most Hollywood versions of beleaguered white masculinity, which are characterized by individualistic narratives, *The Full Monty* tells the story of a group of men of different ages, races, and sexualities, united by their shared experience of economic disempowerment. For instance, the middle-class Gerald was once a foreman but is now, Gary states, "scrap like the rest of us." Gary's crew also features two gay characters, Guy (Hugo Speer) and Lomper (Steve Huison), and one black character, Horse (Paul Barber). But while this can be interpreted as a self-conscious attempt to represent a diversity of working-class masculinities, most narrative space is allotted to the stories of Gary and Dave, examples of more "ordinary" working-class men. The romance between Guy and Lomper is devoted only a few seconds of screen time, and while it comes as rather a surprise, meaning that potential stereotypes can only be ascribed retrospectively (Guy is hugely endowed and Lomper still lives at home with his mother), their sexuality is given no narrative attention. This undeveloped storyline is indicative of the nominal inclusion of gay characters in British mainstream cultural representations, but with homophobia still rife, it is more than a little utopian to imagine that heterosexual males would express no concern about stripping with gay men, the sole acknowledgement of their sexuality being Dave's unwitting pun, "there's nowt so queer as folk."

Horse's race also attracts no comment, except through the film's self-conscious debunking of the mythical huge black penis (see chapter 3). As with other minor black characters in the film, Horse speaks with a broad Yorkshire accent, suggesting full assimilation into British life. On the one hand, as with other anti-heritage films such as *Brassed Off*, *Trainspotting*, and *Twin Town*, this self-consciously rearticulates new conceptions of nation in an age of multiculturalism, devolution, and the ever-widening north-south divide, incorporating those identities which are often excluded from the hegemonic notions of Britishness that the heritage film and its equivalents, such as *Notting Hill*, excel at representing.[86] On the other hand, though, race and racism, as with homophobia, are largely screened out as part of the film's desire to represent social disenfranchisement solely in terms of economic class and gender. The film thus suggests that bi-racial male bonding is only possible if race remains unspoken.

Some measure of this erasure is the fact that the film was based on an original script by Paul Buckner featuring a group of all black men from Coventry through which Buckner wished to explore the changing nature of black British masculinity and sexuality. Producer Umberto Pasolini at Twentieth Century Fox replaced this version with a more box-office friendly story about white men, with the introduction of Horse's family functioning as a token concession.[87] In other words, while the film suggests that regional differences are more important than racial differences, the idea of black men representing British regional masculinity was apparently unthinkable. Even as the film suggests that gender and class remain the dominant dividers of British society, this market-led decision shows the hegemonic power that inheres in whiteness, even if that power is unevenly distributed along the lines of class, gender, and sexuality. This remarkable displacement of a story about black masculinity literally exemplifies the central argument undergridding this chapter—that these films' suggestion that white heterosexual men have lost ground is sharply contradicted by the actual screen space that straight white men command in popular cinema. However marginalized or "extra-ordinary" white heterosexual masculinity might cast itself, it can still always rely on its "ordinariness," which, according to box-office logic, allows it to play into larger potential audiences, whereas a film focusing on a group of black men is a financial risk since it would immediately be considered a black film that would only attract a niche market. These films are thus exemplary of how narratives that screen the decentering of white heterosexual masculinity often work to recenter the dominant identity.

   The Full Monty also demonstrates that the American model of white masculinity cannot simply be mapped onto a British terrain. As well as having a different racial history, a point I discuss in more detail in chapter 6, Britain's rigid class system, combined with a labor movement that, while weakened under Conservative and New Labour governments, continues to make its presence felt, has resulted in cinematic representations of working-class male collectivism, though they are often articulated in a deeply nostalgic mode (*Brassed Off, Billy Elliot, The Full Monty*). While class is posited as the overriding difference between men in British social realist films of the '90s, often at the expense of other identity categories, in the U.S., on the other hand, class, which is most often represented indirectly in popular cinema but rarely overtly articulated, is often subsumed into discourses of race. The dominance of identity politics in the U.S., which has made notable inroads for women, people of color, lesbians, and gay men, as well as other minority groups, who were often responding to the failure of the left to embrace the politics of difference, has also resulted in white men of the middle- and working-classes, many of whom have only relatively recently suffered the devastating effects of job losses, bereft of a discourse with which to articulate their often very real disenfranchisement. The danger, already witnessed both on and off screen, is that white men direct their anger at feminism, multiculturalism, affirmative action, and political correctness, and, to paraphrase Annalee Newitz and Martin Wray, by painting themselves as the victims of victims, they can believe that they have the richest and most marginalized identities around.[88]

White Male Paranoia in a Post-9/11 World

It was left to Spike Lee to provide a corrective to the paranoid white male of *Falling Down* with *25th Hour* (2004), based on a novel by David Benioff. The film tells the story of the last day of freedom for Monty (Montgomery) Brogan (Edward Norton) before he begins a seven year prison sentence for dealing heroin. It stars Edward Norton, who, by the end of the '90s, replaced Michael Douglas as the archetypal "angry white male" due to his critically acclaimed performances in films such as *American History X* and *Fight Club*, a film I discuss at length in the following chapter. In *25th Hour*, Norton expands upon this role in a scene that attracted much attention in reviews: as he stares at himself in a mirror, his reflection begins a litany of abuse at a host of diverse New Yorkers—a scene in intertextual dialogue with Lee's famed series of monologues in *Do the Right Thing* (1989), each featuring a character directing a stream of racial abuse at a racial other in a direct address to the camera. The sequence, which lasts about five minutes, deploys parallel editing, switching from shots of Monty's reflection in medium close-up, set against a dark backdrop which isolates him from any social context, to intercutting, rapid shots of the diverse recipients of his abuse. New York is thus portrayed through Monty's straight white male perspective and is painted as being equally as fragmented and overrun by otherness as *Falling Down*'s Los Angeles. The targets of Monty's diatribe include squeegee men, Sikhs and Pakistanis ("terrorists in fuckin' training"), "Chelsea boys," overcharging Korean grocers, Russian gangsters, Wall Street brokers, Puerto Ricans ("twenty to a car"), uptown Brothers ("Slavery ended 137 years ago. Move the fuck on"), rich East Side wives, corrupt cops, child-molesting priests, and, finally, Osama Bin Laden ("You towel-headed camel jockeys can kiss my royal Irish ass!"). Initially, then, like D-FENS, Montgomery blames everyone else for his plight, making no attempt to disguise the racist, sexist, and homophobic edge of his discourse. However, his rant is abruptly undercut when his reflection suddenly states, "No, fuck you, Montgomery Brogan. You had it all and you threw it away, you dumb fuck!"—a textbook illustration of Freud's insight that paranoid hatred of others is most often a projection of loathed characteristics in the ego.

The fact that this scene is divorced from the film's main narrative renders identification with Monty's point of view difficult, unlike *Falling Down*, which elicits identification by screening commonly experienced urban frustrations through D-FENS's point of view, which goes some way to masking the gender and race implications of D-FENS's resentment.[89] Moreover, whereas D-FENS can only regard himself as a victim, Monty ultimately accepts some responsibility for his situation, although his regret focuses more on the fact that he let his greed get the better of him than it does on the fact that he made his money by preying on the misery of addicts. However, Spike Lee's typically polysemous film not only invites sympathy for Monty (the very first scene shows him rescuing an injured dog), but also screens criticisms of his chosen profession, most notably from his best friend, Francis (Barry Pepper), whose occupation in Wall Street, the film suggests, is equally as parasitical and morally dubious. Unlike *Falling Down*, *25th Hour* also offers the prospect of racial reconciliation for its white male protagonist: Not only is his girlfriend Puerto Rican, but also, as his distraught father drives him to prison and Monty stares out of the window, the reverse shots feature the same people of color who appeared as targets of his hysterical rant during the mirror sequence; this time, however, they stare back at him benignly and supportively, wishing him farewell, rather than figuring as signifiers of an invading otherness. In particular, a young black boy on a bus stares at him compassionately, and writes his own name on the bus window, leading Monty to respond with the same gesture. This scene invites comparison with a similar moment from the opening scene of *Falling Down*, when the sight of a bus draped in the U.S. flag and packed with screaming children from a variety of racial backgrounds (an obvious symbol of multicultural America) is one of the triggers that causes D-FENS to abandon his car and begin his fateful odyssey across Los Angeles.

As well as being a more self-aware and introspective protagonist than D-FENS, Monty is also an Irish-American, and has therefore lived his whiteness differently than the WASP characters that Michael Douglas played in *Falling Down* and *Disclosure*. Irish-Americans are an interesting example of what Theodore W. Allen terms "racial oppression without reference to skin color," and for this reason have become the focus of much recent scholarship on whiteness.[90] Monty's Irish roots are remarked upon on many occasions, suggesting that Monty possesses a white, ethnic identity—that is, an *extra-ordinary* whiteness—to which D-FENS cannot lay claim. Moreover, Monty does not experience the same sense of losing ground as D-FENS, since Monty's working-class status, urban background, and ethnically marked whiteness mean that he simply has less ground to lose. Monty is also aware that his predicament can be blamed on economic class, admitting that he took the easy way out in order to earn the money that would save his father's bar from debts and his father from loan sharks, as well as offering him the upwardly mobile lifestyle he craved. The fact that most of Monty's acquaintances in the drug scene are either people of color or immigrants, while his girlfriend is Puerto Rican, also suggests that Monty is familiar with racial diversity, unlike D-FENS, who has led a more sheltered life and regards the center of Los Angeles to be a foreign jungle occupied by otherness. For this reason, Monty also recognizes that his whiteness is not beside the point, aware that in prison he will be "a skinny little white boy with no friends."[91]

The fact that Monty lists Osama Bin Laden as one of the initial recipients of his hatred in his mirror scene rant also foregrounds how the "angry white male" figure dovetails with the paranoia that characterizes post-9/11 mainstream America. *25th Hour* has been heralded for being the first film to capture the mood of a post-9/11 New York, such as the poignant shots of ground zero, accompanied by Terence Blanchard's haunting musical soundtrack, that follow Francis's assertion that "it's all over" for Monty—an editing choice that inevitably links the tragic fate of the white male protagonist with the tragedy befalling New York, even if Spike Lee claims that was not his intention.[92] Neo-conservative discourse also parallels the fate of ordinary white men with the state of the nation, though in decidedly more reactionary ways than in Lee's film. White heterosexual masculinity is often given the job of standing in for the equally unstable sign of nation, and both are figured as being under attack in the masochistic, paranoiac fantasies that shape contemporary neo-conservative rhetoric. As Eric Lott has noted, "[t]he domination of international others has depended on mastering the other at home."[93] For this reason, "the scapegoating of otherness," which O'Donnell regards as "essential to the ongoing work of paranoia,"[94] shows little sign of abating and will no doubt continue to be effectively deployed to consolidate assertions that not only the U.S., but also "ordinary" white American men, have lost significant ground.

In the following chapter, I will continue to explore representations of white heterosexual male victimology, focusing on popular American films that literalize the wounds that, it is suggested, ordinary white men currently bear. The wounded white male body often allegorizes the ailing national body, but most of these films also narrativize male healing, thus offering the hope of the regeneration of both "ordinary" men and nation.

Notes

1. Susan Faludi, *Backlash: The Undeclared War Against Women* (London: Vintage, 1992), 14.

2. Susan Faludi, *Stiffed: The Betrayal of Modern Man* (London: Vintage, 2000), 7.

3. Faludi, *Stiffed*, 46.

4. Lynn Segal, *Slow Motion: Changing Masculinities, Changing Men*, rev. ed. (London: Virago, 1997), x, ix.

5. Segal, *Slow Motion*, xxi.

6. Robert Bly, *Iron John: A Book about Men* (Reading, MA: Addison-Wesley, 1990), x, 3.

7. Bly, *Iron John*, 8, 96.

8. Kenneth Clatterbaugh, "Literature of the U.S. Men's Movements," *Signs* 25, no. 3 (2000): 883-94.

9. Fred Pfeil, *White Guys: Studies in Postmodern Domination and Difference* (London: Verso, 1995), 38.

10. Michael S. Kimmel and Michael Kaufman, "Weekend Warriors: The New Men's Movement," in *Theorizing Masculinities*, ed. Harry Brod and Michael Kaufman (London: Sage, 1994), 262.

11. Kimmel and Kaufman, "Weekend Warriors," 283.

12. Pfeil, *White Guys*, 195, 217.

13. George Lipsitz, *The Possessive Investment in Whiteness: How White People Profit from Identity Politics* (Philadelphia: Temple University Press, 1998), 71, 97.

14. In 1991 Anita Hill accused fellow African-American Clarence Thomas of sexual harassment during his Supreme Court confirmation hearings. Rodney King was captured on video being viciously beaten by LAPD officers, who were acquitted when the court was moved to a predominately white community that was home to a large proportion of LAPD police officers. O.J. Simpson, a former premier footballer, shocked the nation when he was arrested for murdering his former white wife. The verdict of the televised trial (Oct. 1995), which found Simpson not guilty, was watched by 142 million viewers.

15. Allan Bakke became an iconic "white male victim" when, in 1974, he brought a lawsuit against the University of California for denying him entry into medical school, claiming that the university's quota system under affirmative action legislation constituted an infringement of his constitutional rights.

16. I am grateful to Reynold Humphries for alerting me to this point.

50 Chapter One

17. Both *Crash* and *American History X* deploy the trope of white male redemption that, as we shall see throughout this book, characterizes many Hollywood representations of "angry white men," often in rather didactic narratives.
18. Michael Hill, "Introduction: Vipers in Shangri-la: Whiteness, Writing, and Other Ordinary Terrors," in *Whiteness: A Critical Reader*, ed. Michael Hill (New York: New York University Press, 1997), 9.
19. "Table 684: Median Income of People in Constant (2003) Dollars by Sex, Race, and Hispanic Origin: 1980-2003," *The 2006 Statistical Abstract*, www.census.gov/compendia/statab/tables/06s0684.xls (accessed November 5, 2006).
20. "Table 696: Persons Below Poverty Level, By Selected Characteristics 2003," *The 2006 Statistical Abstract*, www.census.gov/compendia/statab/tables/06s0696.xls (accessed November 5, 2006).
21. Hill, "Introduction," 1; Michael Hill, "Can Whiteness Speak? Institutional Anomies, Ontological Disasters, and Three Hollywood Films," in *White Trash: Race and Class in America*, ed. Matthew Wray and Annalee Newitz (New York: Routledge, 1997), 172.
22. David Savran, *Taking It Like a Man: White Masculinity, Masochism, and Contemporary American Culture* (Princeton, NJ: Princeton University Press, 1998), 206.
23. Patrick O'Donnell, *Latent Destinies: Cultural Paranoia and Contemporary U.S. Narrative* (Durham, NC: Duke University Press, 2000), 5.
24. O'Donnell, *Latent Destinies*, 13; Sigmund Freud, "Psychoanalytic Notes on an Autobiographical Account of a Case of Paranoia (Dementia Paranoides) (1911 [1910])," in *Case Histories II: The "Rat Man," Schreber, The "Wolf Man," A Case of Female Homosexuality*, ed. Angela Richards, trans. James Strachey (London: Penguin, 1990), 129-223.
25. O'Donnell, *Latent Destinies*, 7, viii.
26. O'Donnell, *Latent Destinies*, 7, 16, 11.
27. Fredric Jameson, *The Geopolitical Aesthetic: Cinema and Space in the World System* (London: BFI, 1992), 79, 1-2.
28. Martin Fradley, "Maximus Melodramaticus: Masculinity, Masochism and White Male Paranoia in Contemporary Hollywood Cinema," in *Action and Adventure Cinema*, ed. Yvonne Tasker (London: Routledge, 2004), 238.
29. O'Donnell, *Latent Destinies*, 18-19.
30. Fradley, "Maximus Melodramaticus," 238.
31. Fradley, "Maximus Melodramaticus," 236.
32. Jude Davies and Carol R. Smith, *Gender, Ethnicity and Sexuality in Contemporary American Film* (Edinburgh: Keele University Press, 1997), 3.
33. Richard Dyer, "Charisma," in *Stardom: Industry of Desire*, ed. Christine Gledhill (London: Routledge, 1991), 58.
34. Mark Salisbury, "Get Out of My Face," *Empire*, July 1993, 77.
35. Robyn Wiegman, "'My Name Is Forrest Gump': Whiteness Studies and the Paradox of Particularity," in *Multiculturalism, PostColoniality and Transnational Media*, ed. Ella Shohat and Robert Stam (New Brunswick, NJ: Rutgers University Press, 2003), 239.
36. Carol Clover, "White Noise," *Sight and Sound*, May 1993, 7-9; Liam Kennedy, *Race and Urban Space in Contemporary American Culture* (Edinburgh: Edinburgh University Press, 2000), 33-42; Elisabeth Mahoney, "'The People in Parenthesis': Space Under Pressure in the Post-Modern City," in *The Cinematic City*, ed. David B. Clarke (London: Routledge, 1997); Elana Zilberg, "*Falling Down* in *El Norte*: A Cultural Poli-

tics and Spatial Poetics of the ReLatinization of Los Angeles," *Wide Angle* 20, no. 3 (1998): 182-209.

37. Clover, "White Noise," 9; Mahoney, "The People in Parenthesis," 174.

38. Jude Davies, "Gender, Ethnicity and Cultural Crisis in *Falling Down* and *Groundhog Day*," *Screen* 36, no. 3 (1995): 220-21.

39. Paul Gormley, *The New-Brutality Film: Race and Affect in Contemporary Hollywood Cinema* (Bristol: Intellect Books, 2005), 60.

40. Clover, "White Noise," 9.

41. Michael Omi and Howard Winant, "The Los Angeles 'Race Riot' and Contemporary U.S. Politics," in *Reading Rodney King, Reading Urban Uprising*, ed. Robert Gooding-Williams (New York: Routledge, 1993), 102.

42. "Racial/Ethnic Composition Los Angeles Country, 2000 Census," *Los Angeles Almanac*, October 21, 2003, http://www.laalmanac.com/population/po13.htm (accessed December 20, 2006).

43. Zilberg, "*Falling Down* in *El Norte*," 193. A contrast can be drawn with the more recent *Crash*, which deploys a multi-perspective point of view rather than privileging the white male gaze, its fragmentary, multiple narratives reflecting the multiracial tension and segregation of Los Angeles. Rather than viewing the city as "sick," an African-American cop in *Crash* suggests that people in LA miss touching each other so much that they "crash into each other just so [they] can feel something." The title, along with its narrative, thus offers the prospect of racial rapprochement, as well as conflict.

44. Mahoney, "People in Parenthesis," 174.

45. Sharon Willis, *High Contrast: Race and Gender in Contemporary Hollywood Film* (Durham, NC: Duke University Press, 1997), 16.

46. Several critics have picked up on this doubling. See, for example, Clover, "White Noise"; Richard Dyer, *White* (London: Routledge, 1997), 221-22; Kennedy, *Race and Urban Space in Contemporary American Culture*, 40-41; Willis, *High Contrast*, 4.

47. Kennedy, *Race and Urban Space in Contemporary American Culture*, 39.

48. Dyer, *White*, 34; Richard Slotkin, *Regeneration through Violence: The Mythology of the American Frontier, 1600-1860* (New York: HarperPerennial, 1996).

49. Clover, "White Noise," 8.

50. Davies, "Gender, Ethnicity and Cultural Crisis," 221-22.

51. Paul Smith, *Discerning the Subject* (Minneapolis: University of Minnesota Press, 1988), 95.

52. Kennedy, *Race and Urban Space in Contemporary American Culture*, 38-39.

53. Sally Robinson, *Marked Men: White Masculinity in Crisis* (New York: Columbia University Press, 2000), 3.

54. Davies and Smith, *Gender, Ethnicity and Sexuality*, 34.

55. Herman Beavers, "'The Cool Pose': Intersectionality, Masculinity, and Quiescence in the Comedy and Films of Richard Pryor and Eddie Murphy," in *Race and the Subject of Masculinities*, ed. Harry Stecopoulos and Michael Uebel (Durham, NC: Duke University Press, 1997), 272.

56. Davies and Smith, *Gender, Ethnicity and Sexuality*, 46.

57. Willis, *High Contrast*, 6.

58. Davies and Smith, *Gender, Ethnicity and Sexuality*, 39.

59. Yvonne Tasker, *Working Girls: Gender and Sexuality in Popular Cinema* (London: Routledge, 1998), 132.

60. Tasker, *Working Girls*, 132.

61. Laura Mulvey, "Visual Pleasure and Narrative Cinema," in *Visual and Other Pleasures* (Houndmills, Basingstoke: Macmillan, 1989).

62. Willis, *High Contrast*, 64.

63. Davies and Smith, *Gender, Ethnicity and Sexuality*, 45.

64. Tasker, *Working Girls*, 121.

65. Frank Krutnik, *In a Lonely Street: Film Noir, Genre, Masculinity* (London: Routledge, 1991), 57-65.

66. Mary Ann Doane, *Femmes Fatales: Feminism, Film Theory, Psychoanalysis* (New York: Routledge, 1991), 2; Tasker, *Working Girls*, 121.

67. Krutnik, *In a Lonely Street*, 85.

68. Tasker, *Working Girls*, 127.

69. Tasker, *Working Girls*, 132.

70. Donna Haraway, "A Manifesto for Cyborgs: Science, Technology, and Socialist Feminism in the 1980s," *Socialist Review* 15, no. 2 (1985): 86.

71. Segal, *Slow Motion*, xix.

72. B. Ruby Rich, "Dumb Lugs and Femme Fatales," *Sight and Sound*, November 1995, 9-10.

73. Tasker, *Working Girls*, 133.

74. Claudia Springer, *Electronic Eros: Bodies and Desire in the Postindustrial Age* (Austin: University of Texas Press, 1996), 10, 104.

75. Tasker, *Working Girls*, 131.

76. Davies and Smith, *Gender, Ethnicity and Sexuality*, 39-40.

77. Similar anxieties are also evident in French films of the period, such as *L'Emploi du Temps* (*Time Out*) (2001) and *Le Couperet* (*The Ax*) (2005), which also chart the effect of unemployment on white male characters.

78. Segal, *Slow Motion*, ix.

79. The racially motivated murder of Stephen Lawrence in 1993 highlighted this problem. Lawrence's parents claimed that the police had failed to fully investigate the case because the victim was a black youth. Their tireless campaigning led to a national inquiry, which resulted in the MacPherson Report (1999), which criticized the British police force for its institutionalized racism.

80. Moya Luckett, "Image and Nation in 1990s British Cinema," in *British Cinema of the 90s*, ed. Robert Murphy (London: BFI, 2002), 95.

81. Kate Domaille, *The Full Monty*, York Notes (London: York, 2000), 32-33.

82. John Hill, "From the New Wave to 'Brit-Grit': Continuity and Difference in Working-Class Realism," in *British Cinema: Past and Present*, ed. Justine Ashby and Andrew Higson (London: Routledge, 2000), 251.

83. Claire Monk, "Underbelly UK: The 1990s Underclass Film, Masculinity and the Ideologies of 'New' Britain," in *British Cinema: Past and Present*, ed. Justine Ashby and Andrew Higson (London: Routledge, 2000), 277.

84. Luckett, "Image and Nation in 1990s British Cinema," 95.

85 Estella Tincknell and Deborah Chambers, "Performing the Crisis: Fathering, Gender and Representation in Two 1990s Film," *Journal of Popular Film and Television* 29 (2002): 149.

86. Luckett, "Image and Nation," 91-94.

87. Monika Baker, "The Missing Monty," *Black Filmmaker* 1, no. 2 (1998): 14; Domaille, *The Full Monty*, 10.

88. Annalee Newitz and Matthew Wray, "What Is 'White Trash'? Stereotypes and Economic Conditions of Poor Whites in the United States," in *Whiteness: A Critical Reader*, ed. Michael Hill (New York: New York University Press, 1997), 174.

89. Clover, "White Noise," 8; Dyer, *White*, 220.

90. Theodore. W. Allen, *The Invention of the White Race*, vol. 1, *Racial Oppression and Social Control* (London: Verso, 1994), 22. See also Noel Ignatiev, *How the Irish Became White* (New York: Routledge, 1996); David Roediger, *The Wages of Whiteness: Race and the Making of the American Working Class* (London: Verso, 1991).

91. At the same time, it must be noted that the homophobic insults that Monty hurls at the black DEA agent who arrests him, combined with his paranoiac fear of being raped in prison, suggests that Monty's acceptance of difference does not extend to homosexuals.

92. Stella Papamichael, "*25th Hour*," interview with Spike Lee, http://www.bbc.co.uk/films/2003/02/25/spike_lee_25th_hour_interview.shtml (accessed August 31, 2007).

93. Eric Lott, "White Like Me: Racial Cross-Dressing and the Construction of American Whiteness," in *Cultures of United States Imperialism*, ed. Amy Kaplan and Donald E. Pease (Durham, NC: Duke University Press, 1993), 476.

94. O'Donnell, *Latent Destinies*, 13.

Chapter Two
Literalizing the Wound:
Paternal Melodramas, Masochism, and
White Heterosexual Masculinity in Popular
U.S. Cinema

Wounded White Men

In a lurid image of male masochism, one which plays into Christian iconography, most obviously the figure of St. Sebastian, Robert Bly elaborates on the problem of the "soft man" who enjoys being tortured and persecuted by a castrating woman: "If his wife or girlfriend, furious, shouts that he is 'chauvinistic,' a 'sexist,' a 'man,' he doesn't fight back, but just takes it. He opens his shirt so that she can see more clearly where to put the lances. He ends with three or four javelins sticking out of his body, and blood running all over the floor. . . . To be attacked by someone you love—what could be more wonderful?"[1] This highly visceral image literalizes the wounds inflicted on the male psyche at the hands of women, though wounds are also inflicted by absent, severe, or emotionally distant fathers in Bly's account.

The wound motif, a version of symbolic castration, is crucial to much '90s mythopoetic men's movement literature, in particular Bly's seminal *Iron John* (1990). Wounds, by their very nature, penetrate bodily boundaries, collapsing the distinction between inner and outer, private and public; in fact, tellingly, the Greek word for wound, τραύμα (trauma), encompasses both a psychic and somatic meaning, as its assimilation into psychoanalytic discourse reveals, and Bly frequently collapses the two. Bly argues that, deprived of initiation rituals, many young men in industrialized nations attempt to take the "grandiose road" and rise above their wounds, losing their humanity in the process, while others take the "depressed road," becoming childlike victims who are in closer contact with their wounds, but are no more humane either; however, rituals in the presence of a "mentor" would offer a third path, allowing young men to acknowledge the scars delivered to the emotional body, most often by remote, harsh, or absent fathers, and regard the wound as a "gift" enabling them to unblock their repressed feelings.[2] Wounds are thus therapeutic and empowering: "where a man's wound is, that is where his genius will be. Wherever the wound appears in our psyches, whether from alcoholic father, shaming mother, shaming father, abusing mother, whether it stems from isolation, disability, or disease, that is precisely the place from which we will give our major gift to the community."[3] In short, just as the threat of castration, which establishes the limits of paternal law within which the male subject must operate, also presupposes potential possession of the phallus, wounds, in Bly's account, allow the articulation of a once unified, primal masculinity.

Vietnam forms a crucial background to Bly's discussion of emotional scarring and paternal betrayal. For instance, he asserts that "being lied to by older men amounts to a broken leg. When the young men arrived in Vietnam and found they had been lied to, they received immeasurably deep wounds."[4] Coinciding with feminism, the civil rights movement, the rise of the U.S. counterculture, and its mistrust of authority and older generations, Vietnam became the key *topos* in which the "white male as victim" drama was played out. The war comprised a national trauma, not only because it was a war that America failed to win, but also because, on the domestic terrain, the myth of American unity was shattered. Intimately tied as they are, the crisis in nation was articulated as a crisis in masculinity, and the veterans, whether they were injured physically or psychologically, allegorized the ailing national body. However, concerns other than male hysteria and national trauma are expressed through the Vietnam narrative. Intrinsic to the *mythos* of Vietnam is the notion that the most difficult wounds to bear were not physical, but those inflicted by the anti-war protesters and feminists (who, myth has it, spat on returning veterans), as well as the lies told by the government and the older generation, particularly fathers. This suggests that discourses of the beleaguered veteran also transcoded concerns about the erosion of traditional white male privilege and paternal authority.

As Lynda Boose has argued, Vietnam installed a traumatic break between fathers and sons: many sons who were conscientious objectors were banished from their fathers' houses, and those who went off to fight felt bitterly betrayed because they never received the hero's welcome they were promised. It is therefore not surprising that in retrospective cinematic representations, Vietnam is often staged as a domestic Oedipal tragedy; indeed, even anti-war films such as Oliver Stone's *Platoon* (1986) and *Born on the Fourth of July* (1989) spare little screen space for the suffering endured by the Vietnamese, preferring to represent the war as signifying the moment when the father was lost and the son betrayed.[5] Often this is acted out through representatives of patriarchal authority rather than biological fathers, such as *Rambo: First Blood Part II* (1985) or *Platoon*, where the protagonist is caught between competing good and bad figures of paternal identification. Moreover, as Boose argues, even when the benevolent father is inserted into the fantasy, such as *Rambo III* (1988) and *Born on the Fourth of July*, his domestication and feminization signal an eroded paternal authority.[6] Importantly for the arguments of this chapter, many retrospective Vietnam films, as Susan Jeffords has influentially argued in *The Remasculinization of America: Gender and the Vietnam War* (1989), screen a trajectory from victimization to the rebirth of a reinvigorated masculinity and, by extension, nation.[7] This sado-masochistic dynamic is visually imprinted on action heroes' bodies, which are subject to endless mutilations but prove their virility in the process.

The fact that many of these retrospective Vietnam films were released in the late '80s, at a time when the achievements of feminism, the civil rights movement, and gay rights activism were becoming apparent, suggests that Vietnam forms a site through which concerns over the status of white heterosexual masculinity as the universal, dominant identity are played out. As Sally Robinson has asked in her insightful book *Marked Men: White Masculinity in Crisis* (2000), "[w]hy is it that when dominant masculinity becomes visible, it becomes visible as *wounded*?" The answer, she suggests, is two-fold:

> On the one hand, the substitution of an individually suffering white male body for a social class or gender and racial identity under attack betrays a desire to materialize, literalize the wounds to white male privilege that come from puncturing the aura of "universality" and "unmarkedness" historically claimed by whiteness and masculinity. On the other hand, individualizing a more properly social wound is a way to evade, forget, deny the very marking that has produced those wounds in the first place. In other words, narratives about wounded white men spring from, but obscure, the marking of white masculinity as a *category*.[8]

For some commentators on the left, such fetishization of wounds is also symptomatic of a political landscape dominated by identity critiques. For example, according to Matthew Wray and Annalee Newitz, while identity politics have been highly beneficial to minorities, "far too often, admission into the multicultural order depends upon one's ability to claim social victimization."[9] White heterosexual men, as the dominant norm, have traditionally been excluded from identity politics, except for their assigned role as oppressor. As we saw in the previous chapter, deploying the common correlation between victimhood and innocence, many straight white men have begun casting themselves as an oppressed group in an attempt to distance themselves from "evil white guy" status. In the process, by claiming marginalized status, they also disavow the privileges that still inhere in the dominant identity.

In the rest of this chapter, I will focus on the tendency of several popular American films of the '90s to literalize the "wounds" borne by straight white men, producing a body of work which Joseph Sartelle has dubbed "disability films," such as *Forrest Gump* (1994), *The Man without a Face* (1993), *Rain*

Man (1998), *Scent of a Woman* (1992), and *Regarding Henry* (1991).[10] I begin by focusing on two such male melodramas, Mike Nichols's *Regarding Henry* and Robert Zemeckis's *Forrest Gump*, both of which represent their protagonist as an everyman figure, despite the fact that one has suffered brain damage and the other has an extremely low IQ. Mirroring the therapeutic discourse of the men's movement, these films shown how the child-like, innocent outlook of the wounded white male puts him back in touch with his feelings, as well as with traditional family values, though the extremity of this solution to straight white men overcoming emotional blockage and "evil white guy" status suggests the difficulties of screening white male innocence. The motif of the wound allows "ordinary" men to inhabit an extra-ordinary, minoritized body, although neither film engages with the problems facing those minorities whose stories are erased in the act of white males claiming the margins for themselves. Importantly, both these child-like protagonists are also fathers, with fatherhood comprising the means by which they are integrated into society and nation. I then turn my attention to a very different and more complex film, *Fight Club* (David Fincher 1999), which rapidly became the decade's archetypal film on white male angst. The hysterical protagonist of this *fin-de-millennium* cult hit takes to the limit the discourse on male wounds from the men's movement, as well as the logic of an empowering victimology that underwrites identity politics, positing masochism as the solution to societal emasculation and the erosion of paternal authority. The film certainly ridicules the melodramatic sentiments of the men's movement and "disability films," as well as the excesses of the "remasculinization through masochistic endurance" motif that predominates in Hollywood representations of the action hero. At the same time, its parodic mode legitimizes its staging of the protagonist's fantasy of resurrecting a lost, primal masculinity, a fantasy that is only partially undercut by the film's autodeconstructive textual strategies.

Regarding Henry: The Damaged White Male and the Child Within

Regarding Henry opens as brutal corporate lawyer Henry Turner (Harrison Ford)—whose name alone suggests a narrative of transformation—triumphs in his case defending a hospital against negligence charges, a case he won by suppressing vital evidence. As with films such as *Wall Street* (1987), *Pretty Woman* (1990), and *The Firm* (1993), *Regarding Henry* deploys an image of a sterile, materialistic, morally bankrupt, but ultimately redeemable middle-class white heterosexual male in order to critique the evils of capitalism. However, these films simultaneously suggest that capitalism need not be overthrown but can simply be done differently by a transformed white man who does not have to give up privilege, but merely rediscover his lost humanity. Henry's wife, Sarah, played by Annette Bening, is largely excluded from this story of transformation, much like Bening's neurotic character in the darker satire *American Beauty* (1999), which lacks R*egarding Henry*'s feel-good, sentimental mode, but charts a similar trajectory of white male redemption. *Regarding Henry* has received much critical attention for its "saccharine indictment of 1980s' hypermasculinity."[11] At the same time, as Fred Pfeil notes, the film's suggestion that "white straight men cannot be changed short of shooting them" is indicative of how closely tied normative masculinity is to the iconic "evil white guy" in popular American representations.[12]

Henry's transformation begins when he inadvertently walks in on a robbery in his local shop. In what must be one of the shortest hold-up scenes in cinematic history, after demanding Henry's wallet, the Latino robber immediately shoots, leaving Henry in a coma. No context is given for the robber's actions (he runs away without taking Henry's wallet), rendering it another example of the senseless, unpredictable violence of poor people of color in popular representations. Henry eventually awakes, but is left severely brain-damaged, suffering from almost total memory loss. While Henry begins the film illustrating Bly's example of men who have taken the "grandiose road," he is cruelly pushed onto the "depressed route," where he is brought closer to his wounds and his emotions, but is barred from adult manhood.

As Fred Pfeil has pointed out, though, help is at hand in the form of "the healing power of Blackness." When Sarah leaves a comatose Henry after one of her visits, a tracking shot picks up the movements of the black female nurse that Sarah greets, following her path to Henry's bed. In a behind-the-shoulder shot, the nurse leans towards Henry, blocking him from view, her white uniform emphasizing the blackness of her neck and hair. As she moves screen right, Henry is again revealed, this time miraculously awakened from his coma.[13] While the blackness of the nurse might seem contingent, the "black healing" motif appears again in the form of Bradley (Bill Nunn), Henry's physiotherapist, one of '90s Hollywood's newest stereotypes of African-Americans—the magical black helper. This representational trend may even make this character an actual angel (*A Life Less Than Ordinary*, *The Family Man*, *Dogma*) or even God himself (*Bedazzled*, *Bruce Almighty*). As Krin Gabbard argues, this places African-Americans outside of white-dominated power structures, thereby rendering those hierarchical structures invisible in the very act of reproducing them. Although these black angels appeal to desires for racial harmony, the only solution to racial conflict deemed possible is fantasy.[14] Not all black helpers are angels, though they are often armed with certain magical powers, reproducing the stereotypical notion that African-Americans are guardians of a lost spirituality that white people can no longer access, powers they use to help white people and not themselves, as we see in *Ghost* (1990), *The Green Mile* (1999), and *The Legend of Bagger Vance* (2000). Even if these black helpers lack spiritual powers, it has become a common motif for African-Americans to tell the white male who he is, as Thomas DiPiero notes, citing *Grand Canyon* (1991) and *White Men Can't Jump* (1992) as examples.[15] In *Regarding Henry*, Bradley fulfils a therapeutic function, as well as helping Henry discover his "true self" (that is, a faithful, sensitive family man). Although Bradley is largely presented in a positive light, the film illustrates that positive images of racial minorities can be "as pernicious as overtly degrading ones," since they assuage white guilt whilst keeping racial hierarchies intact.[16] Bradley's role is solely to heal white male wounds, wounds that allow white heterosexual masculinity to annex the minoritized status historically associated with African-Americans, canceling out white masculinity's racial debt in the process.

From the moment that the ebullient and gregarious Bradley sings and dances his way into Henry's hospital room, Henry's eyes express their first interest in the world around him. As with all buddy movies, though, which are dogged by the demands of screening male intimacy while displacing homosexual anxiety, the film insists on Bradley's heterosexuality with anxious overdetermination: as he performs physiotherapy on Henry, an exercise that requires physical proximity (further enhanced by the use of tight framing), Bradley immediately declares, "this isn't because I like you." Moreover, throughout their meetings, Bradley engages in sexist banter to a yet unresponsive, child-like Henry about nurses in the hospital. Reversing the dynamics of '80s bi-racial buddy movies, such as *Lethal Weapon* (1987) and *Die Hard* (1988), in which the incompetent black cop is remasculinized through his contact with the rampaging white male hero,[17] Henry learns how to become a man again through his contact with a hypersexualized black male, the polar opposite of the feminized, subservient African-American in the binary opposition that structures racial stereotyping.

It is also Bradley who lectures Henry on self-knowledge once Henry finds himself unable to re-enter the vicious world of corporate law. With Henry preferring the company of a black waiter to his former WASP friends, his depression leads Sarah to invite Bradley into their luxury home to dispense valuable, avuncular advice: "Don't listen to nobody trying to tell you who you are." In this moment of intimacy, shot in the kitchen (traditionally the site of the feminine, further highlighting Sarah's marginalization), Bradley relates the story of his own wounds—the knee injury which shattered his hopes of a football career. But, he states, this injury led him to a fulfilling career, allowing him to meet and help people like Henry. In this exchange, fetishized wounds become evidence of identity and self-knowledge, forming the site across which bi-racial male bonding, in the absence of women, becomes possible. Bradley thus fulfils the role of the mentor who helps Henry find Bly's "third way" of acknowledging his wounds and rediscovering his humanity. The fact that this would only seem to be possible through contact with blackness certainly constitutes a critique of the vacuity of whiteness, but also reproduces the stereotypical association of black masculinity with authenticity (see chapter 6). Moreover, the film's focus on Henry as its victim, along with the literalization and concomitant depoliticization of Bradley's wounds, erases the power differential between the two men. In a similar vein, Richard L. Homan considers *Regarding Henry* to be an example of what he terms the "everyman movies" that were released in 1991 (*Switch, The Fisher King, The Doctor, Grand Canyon*), films which follow the thematic concerns and plot trajectory of the medieval morality play *Everyman*: a yuppie protagonist's brush with mortality forces a reconsideration of personal values, while his contact with a character, often African-American, who is lower in social class, brings about his salvation. This enables the protagonist to "rest assured that [these subaltern characters] do not at all begrudge him the privileges from which they are excluded, and he need not feel guilty of those privileges," offering "the appealing prospect of redemption without sacrifice."[18] The film is thus an example of what David Marriot has termed "cinema as therapeutic intervention," since black anger "go[es] missing" in its portrayal of racial reconciliation.[19]

Once Henry is redeemed, however, Fred Pfeil is right to note that the film has difficulty resolving how "the born-again, sensitized White Guy can keep the wisdom of his new-found or reborn childishness without dropping the reins of his power."[20] Henry finds his "inner-child," as the men's movement literature puts it, and in the process has transformed into a "New Man"—*literally*, since his amnesia enables the film to insert a total break with his former self. Yet, at the same time, his sensitivity is inscribed though childlike naivety, awkwardness, and hesitancy, greatly distancing him from traditional configurations of masculinity. The solution to this problem, though, is found in his role as father. Before being shot, Henry had treated his daughter Rachel (Mikki Allen) harshly. After Henry returns home from the rehabilitation centre, however, Rachel takes over the nurturing role from Bradley (further placing Sarah on the periphery) in an overtly coded role reversal, teaching him to read and tie his shoelaces. When Rachel announces that she will be going away to a boarding school, Henry hesitantly states, "I don't want you to go anywhere," adding, "but I am not sure it's up to me." He then yields to Sarah who insists on the decision she and Henry had made earlier; we, like Henry, though, know better, as the film stridently declares that it is "a dangerous, destabilizing idea for a woman to hold that kind of decision-making power."[21] Having been given his pep talk by Bradley on being his own man, Henry rediscovers his patriarchal clout and convinces Sarah that they should become a proper family. The film ends with a long shot of the reconstructed bourgeois nuclear family, with the wife having learned to listen to her child and husband, and Henry and Sarah (both of whom had had affairs before the shooting) having been taught the importance of the monogamous heterosexual bond.

Forrest Gump: Wounded Intellect and White Male Redemption

Forrest Gump, loosely based on Winston Groom's 1986 novel, bagged a total of six Academy Awards and grossed nearly $680 million worldwide. Told almost exclusively through the point of view of a white heterosexual male with an IQ of 75, the film traverses three decades of U.S. history, which act as backdrop to the structuring heterosexual romance. The film was embraced by the U.S. mainstream for its anti-racism and good old-fashioned family values, and was heralded by Republican House Speaker Newt Gringrich for showing that "the counter-culture destroys human beings and conservative values."[22] Numerous critics, however, have lambasted the film for its reconstruction of an innocent white heterosexual masculinity, its rewriting of American history, and its insidious racial and sexual politics.[23] Krin Gabbard, for instance, considers the film to be "surely the most important Angry White Male film ever made."[24] One of the most remarkable feats of the film is that despite Forrest's (Tom Hanks's) goofiness and dull-wittedness, he was immediately seized upon as an everyman figure by the popular media. Obviously this is possible only because he embodied the universal identity, but it is further enhanced by Tom Hanks's star persona as "the extraordinary ordinary man."[25]

The film is structured around a series of flashbacks that unfold as Forrest waits for a bus to take him to his life-long love, Jenny (Robyn Wright Penn), striking up conversations, or rather monologues, with whomever sits beside him. His first interlocutee is a female African-American nurse. As he comments on how comfortable her shoes look, ignoring her bleakly delivered response that her feet hurt, Forrest embarks on a discussion of his own pain, launching the film into its first flashback, which features Forrest's "magic shoes"—the leg braces he had to wear as a child to correct his crooked spine. Before his story of victimhood fully unravels, however, he states that he was named after Nathan Bedford Forrest, "a civil war hero," who led the Ku Klux Klan—described by Forrest as a bunch of men who dressed up in robes and sheets, acting like "ghosts or spooks or something." In one of the film's many digital manipulations of original footage, inserting Tom Hanks into the undeniably racist *The Birth of a Nation* (1915), the horror of white supremacy is rendered comic through Forrest's limited intellectual capacities. The context of this conversation with an African-American woman, therefore, is highly racialized, though Forrest's childlike innocence and instinctive anti-racism, despite growing up in Alabama in the '50s, serves to neutralize America's white supremacist past. Significantly, however, the black nurse is also the only person who fails to be captivated by Forrest's stories. Her presence would thus seem necessary to evoke and then disavow the power of race in the film's reconstruction of U.S. history.

Far from focusing on racial oppression, the film's central discourse on prejudice and social equality is offered by Forrest's mother: "my boy Forrest is going to get the same opportunities as everybody else." Forrest is refused a seat on the bus on his first journey to school by all class mates but Jenny in a scene that borrows scenarios from the south's Jim Crow segregation policy. While black skin is indelible, however, Forrest miraculously overcomes his social disenfranchisement when, chased by bullies, he breaks free from the shackles of his leg braces, becoming such an exceptionally fast runner that he wins a football scholarship to college. Later, Forrest spontaneously begins a three-year coast-to-coast run across America, inadvertently uniting the nation behind him. When asked the political cause for which he was running, Forrest's reply is simply that "I just felt like running," reflecting the film's consistent privileging of the per-

sonal realm. The exchange of leg braces for Nike running shoes not only cele-
brates the individual's identification with the commodity in scenes screening an
invigorated nation, but also completes his triumphant transcendence over his
wounds.[26] The film thus chimes in with his mother's belief that "you have to
make your own destiny," mirroring the American Dream ethos of hard graft and
self-help, with hindrances such as institutionalized discrimination falling by the
wayside to allow for an individualistic narrative of success despite the odds.

So central is the film's need to literalize white male injury and then narrativize its self-healing that it represents it a second time through the figure of Lieutenant Dan (Gary Sinise), who loses both legs in Vietnam. Throughout the Vietnam sequence, the enemy remains off-screen, allowing American soldiers to
function solely as victims, since the suffering caused by their bullets is never
shown. Furious at Forrest for rescuing him and denying him his patrilineal "destiny" of dying in action, Lieutenant Dan soon transmutes into a self-pitying alcoholic amputee, the butt of taunts by emasculating female prostitutes. According to director Robert Zemeckis, Dan is "a metaphor for the crippled part of
America," and his line "this wasn't supposed to happen" was intended to reflect
the feelings of an entire generation; nonetheless, he claims, Dan has to accept the
fate he has been given and "come out the other side" in an important journey of
"spiritual transformation."[27] Forrest, whose damaged intellect renders him too
innocent to require such redemption, thus fulfils the role of Bly's mentor, steer-
ing Dan from the "depressed road" to an acknowledgment of his wounds and his
humanity. With Dan a metaphor for the wounded national body, the fact he turns
up at Forrest's wedding walking with the aid of artificial limbs is suggestive of
national regeneration and reunification. Dan is also accompanied by his Asian
fiancée in an overdetermined gesture of bi-national reconciliation, where America's redemption is allegorized through a heterosexual romance in which America, represented once again by a white male, is cast as reinvigorated and remasculinized, while Vietnam retains its feminine assignation.

Unlike Forrest and Dan, however, Bubba (Mykelti Williamson), Forrest's
African-American buddy, does not overcome his wounds. The film's narrative
of bi-racial bonding begins when Bubba is the only character to allow Forrest to
sit next to him on the army bus, which this time, unlike Forrest's first school
journey, is populated by many African-Americans, who were less likely to escape the draft than white middle-class college students. Bubba is equally as dim-
witted as Forrest. He dies when his function of proving Forrest's anti-racism and
benevolence to the black community has been secured, and he is soon replaced
by Lieutenant Dan, the film's iconic "white male as victim."

The marginalization of African-American oppression is shored up through
the film's representation of U.S. history, filtered through Forrest's uncompre-
hending perspective. As with the treatment of the Ku Klux Klan, George Wallace's famous attempt to prevent the desegregation of Alabama University is
rendered comic when Forrest thinks that the racist reference to "coons" means
"racoons," and when he inadvertently becomes an agent of racial reconciliation

when he picks up a book dropped by an African-American female student in one of the many digitally manipulated sequences that "sidestep and evacuate the very concepts of history and politics alike."[28] Moreover, as Thomas Byers notes, while the film refers to the assassinations of George Wallace, Jack Kennedy, Robert Kennedy, John Lennon, and the botched attempt on Ronald Reagan, the assassinations of black political leaders Martin Luther King and Malcolm X are written out of the film, an act, he suggests, that can only be explained by the film's desire to attribute victim status exclusively to white men.[29]

This marginalization of African-American racial injury is also spatially inscribed in the scene when Forrest is aggressively harangued by a Black Panther on the evils of African-Americans being sent to war by a country that hates them. As the Black Panther launches into his verbal assault, the camera pans around Forrest, pushing his adversary into the extreme periphery of screen right until he is totally masked by a quarter shot of Forrest, leaving most of the screen free to focus on a scene between Jenny and her boyfriend. A cut to Forrest's concerned expression is matched by a reverse shot showing Jenny's boyfriend slapping her across the face. As Forrest rushes to defend her, the Black Panther's diatribe is drowned out by the frenzied soundtrack of "Hey Joe" performed by The Jimi Hendrix Experience (despite its "whitening" of U.S. history, the film is content to include black-authored tracks that were embraced by the white Baby Boomer generation). As well as dispensing with black rage, the film also implies that good blacks (Bubba) are ones who quietly die for America and bad ones (Black Panthers) are those who refuse to do so, an opposition that "is coded as criminality."[30]

Throughout the film, all collective political struggle is negatively portrayed. The Black Panther is hyperaggressive and the anti-war boyfriend abuses Jenny, who requires protection from Forrest, a member of the military. Moreover, for all her dabbling in the counter-culture, Jenny never discovers feminism. Indeed, as Byers notes, the fact that Forrest is *naturally* caring and sensitive reduces patriarchal oppression to a matter of character rather than institutionalized sexism.[31]

Jenny's story is only of interest in so far as it affirms Forrest's goodness and contributes to his pain. Even her disturbingly punitive and perfunctory death from an unnamed virus, presumably AIDS, is screened only as it impacts on Forrest. (The film takes it for granted that Forrest's innocence safeguards him against infection.) As Byers argues, "the attributes of otherness (Blackness, femininity) are assimilated to Forrest himself, while the subject of the real position of such otherness (Bubba, Jenny) must die."[32] Jenny's death immediately after their marriage solves the question of how a mature, intelligent woman could bear to live with an "emotionally and intellectually stunted, asexual idiot,"[33] but not before her narrative function of reuniting the bourgeois nuclear family, however fleetingly, has been achieved.

Lynda Boose argues that the traumatic father-son rift has produced a body of post-Vietnam Oedipal narratives "stamped with the intensity of a generation stuck in its own boyhood and now playing out . . . an unconscious cultural myth that attempts to recover the father."[34] This would certainly seem to be the case with *Forrest Gump*, which, like *Regarding Henry*, uses the trope of fatherhood in order to propel its childlike protagonist into adulthood. Forrest absolves the guilt of the bad fathers of the previous generation—including his own, who abandoned him, and Jenny's, who sexually abused her. As luck would have it, Forrest Gump Junior, one of the brightest children in his class, was conceived on the fourth of July, offering hope not only for a reinvigorated white masculinity, but also nation.

Father Wounds and Paternal Melodramas

Both *Regarding Henry* and *Forrest Gump* can be understood as part of a trend of representing straight white masculinity as paternity—evident in men's movement literature, "New Man" advertising images, and manifesting itself in popular cinema most visibly in comedies (*Three Men and a Baby, Father of the Bride, Mrs. Doutbfire, Liar Liar, Cheaper by the Dozen, Big Daddy*), but also feeding into action movies (*Commando, Terminator 2: Judgment Day, Ransom, Collateral Damage, The Day After*), male melodramas (*Kramer versus Kramer, The Man without a Face, I am Sam, Field of Dreams, Father's Day, Road to Perdition*), and even animations (*Finding Nemo, The Incredibles*).[35] On the surface, these films might seem to respond to feminist calls for greater male participation in child-rearing. However, feminist critics such as Tania Modleski have expressed concern that they demonstrate how it is possible for men to respond to feminist demands "in such a way as to make the women more marginal than ever."[36] While Modleski is rightly concerned by the marginalization of women and the appropriation of the feminine in these films, it is equally important to investigate what anxieties might be screened (in both senses of the word) by Hollywood's current fascination with fatherhood. For instance, the fact that it has now become a cliché of the action genre that the hero is a dedicated father, often forced to rescue his own child, suggests that paternity offers a means of negotiating white heterosexual masculinity at a time when, as Barbara Creed observes, the values of hypermasculinity would seem to be difficult to take seriously.[37] This fixation on fatherhood also suggests the ongoing need to reiterate and shore up the paternal function at a time of heightened anxiety over absent or neglectful fathers and eroded paternal authority. In the last few decades, fears about how absent fathers damage their sons have been endlessly articulated in the U.S. and British media, as well as neo-conservative and neo-liberal political rhetoric, with the supposition being that only a restoration of paternal authority will heal male pain and, by extension, the ailing social body. *Forrest Gump*, for instance, directly addresses the issue of the abusive or absent father, rendering the father the inflictor of wounds, but then also posits the father as the site through which those wounds are healed in the following generation, when the damaged son accedes to a more sensitive paternal function. This trajectory enables white heterosexual men to claim victimhood and entitlement simultaneously, a similar no-lose strategy that Michael S. Kimmel and Michael Kaufman argue is key to the rhetoric of Bly's men's movement: "When men speak as sons, men are angry and wounded by their fathers. When men speak as fathers, men expect veneration and admiration from sons. Men are thus going to have it both ways, particularly whichever way allows them to feel like the innocent victim of other people's disempowering behavior, the victim of what others (fathers or sons) have done to them."[38]

In their obsession with (literally) damaged men, both *Regarding Henry* and *Forrest Gump* can be viewed as examples of male melodramas. As Linda Williams notes, melodrama orchestrates "the moral legibility crucial to the mode" by eliciting sympathy for "the virtues of beset victims," and "if virtue is not obvious, suffering—often depicted as the literal suffering of an agonized body— is."[39] In film studies, melodrama has commonly been associated with the so-called woman's film, despite the host of male melodramas of the '50s and '60s (*Rebel without a Cause, Written on the Wind, Splendor in the Grass*). However, melodrama is a mode which is becoming increasingly popular to tell men's stories "in the service of a beleaguered and victimized masculinity."[40]

The fact that the family melodrama invests heavily in the Symbolic Order but screens "the impossibility of actually living it" suggests that the generic mode is well-suited to exploring the inability of the male subject to live up to the masculine ideal and the demands of paternal law.[41] As Stella Bruzzi notes, male melodramas most often focus on father-son narratives as part of "Hollywood's obsession with defining and redefining masculinity," though "father narratives in Hollywood are frequently son narratives in disguise, the fathers being viewed from the son's perspective," and most often found wanting.[42] In psychoanalytic terms, this lack in the father is explained through the gap between the real father and his symbolic incarnation, elaborated by Freud in his account of the primal horde, which he posits as the origins of patriarchy. Freud relates how, in anger at the primal father's claim over all the women of the tribe, the horde of brothers banded together to kill and then devour the father, an act of identification which caused their repressed affection to emerge "in the form of remorse." However, "[t]he dead father became stronger than the living one had been."[43] The symbolic father is thus "an impossible ideal of masculine authority that none of the sons individually could ever hope to achieve," which underscores the instabilities and incoherencies of both patriarchy and male subjectivity.[44]

While films such as *Regarding Henry* and *Forrest Gump* attempt to bridge the gap between the real and the symbolic father, several '90s films, such as *Affliction* (1997), *American Beauty, Happiness* (1998), and *Magnolia* (1999), "offer an alarming, tortured, fragmentary vision of family and fatherhood in which fathers are violent, neglectful and incestuous, abandoning and destroying their children."[45] Paul Thomas Anderson's *Magnolia* is a particularly poignant representation of the wounds that fathers can inflict on their children. Frank T. J. Mackey (Tom Cruise) runs workshops for all-male audiences entitled "Seduce and Destroy," a satirical screening of the worst versions of the men's movement. In one of Cruise's most mesmerizing performances, he struts up and down on stage in figure-hugging trousers and a leather waistcoat, delivering strategic advice on "the battle of the bush," gyrating his hips to an audience of cheering men, while shouting out slogans such as "Respect the Cock!" or "Tame the Cunt!" However, Frank later crumbles before the African-American female journalist who, in a television interview, probes behind this masculinist façade, grilling him on lies he has told about his family background. As the film's multileveled narrative unfolds, it becomes apparent that Frank's phallic posturing and lies form a self-defensive mechanism designed to veil his pain at his father's abandonment of both him and his dying mother. At his father's deathbed, when his phallic mask finally slips, and he sobs inconsolably, though is still unable to forgive, the scene is pure melodrama. The film's concern with paternal betrayal is also made through two other interconnected narrative threads: an overambitious, pushy father of a child genius, and another dying father who sexually abused his daughter and seeks absolution.

While films like *Magnolia* dramatize the unbridgeable gap between the individual father and his symbolic ideal, Susannah Radstone has argued that any screening of beleaguered masculinity can form "part of a ubiquitous and routine *testing* of masculinity by means of which patriarchal masculinity continues to maintain itself. Such work inevitably entails both the discovery of and the mending of 'cracks' in masculinity. But 'cracks' do not necessarily imply collapse."[46] With that in mind, I now turn my attention to *Fight Club*, which takes the impetus to literalize the wounds inflicted on the white straight male psyche by not only absent fathers, but also women and commodity culture, to its ultimate conclusion in its representation of male hysteria and masochism. While *Fight Club* has no reservations in laying bare the fissures and instabilities of its unapologetically hysterical and masochistic white male protagonist, the film, as Sally Robinson notes more generally of the "(white) masculinity in crisis" discourse, "performs the cultural work of centering attention on dominant masculinity."[47]

Fight Club: Male Hysteria, Male Masochism, and the Politics of Disavowal

David Fincher's neo-gothic *Fight Club*, based on Chuck Palahniuk's eponymous novel, tells the story of yet another everyman figure, as Fincher himself terms him, named Jack in the screenplay but "the narrator" (Edward Norton) in the credits, and his relationship with the anarchic Tyler Durden (Brad Pitt), later revealed to be the narrator's alter ego.[48] "Together" they organize fistfights in order to rid men of the emasculation caused by commodity culture and the erosion of paternal authority, though, importantly, it is enduring rather than inflicting pain that affirms virility. On its release, *Fight Club* was praised in many reviews for exposing the alienation that the (implicitly white) male currently experiences in contemporary America, though an equal number of reviewers expressed fears that the film's screening of remasculinization through violence might have a profoundly disturbing effect on the young men at whom the film was marketed.

In defense of his film, David Fincher reiterated that *Fight Club* is "a fairy tale, a coming-of-age story about choosing a path to maturity."[49] In interviews, he stated his agreement with Tyler's views about "societal emasculation," but he also rejected Tyler's nihilism and the extremity of his methods, insisting that the film should be read as a dark comedy or satire.[50] However, Fincher's comments themselves are illustrative of the textual ambiguity of the film, as well as the difficulties of pinning down its ideological import. *Fight Club* certainly excels at exploring male alienation and alleged male feminization under late capitalism, yet the extent to which we are supposed to take the narrator at face value is less certain. At times, the film seems to invest in the narrator's fantasy of a restored primal masculinity, yet at others, particularly towards the end of the film, when Tyler seems to have spiraled out of control, this fantasy is treated with heavy doses of parody.

Indeed, *Fight Club* is a film that resists easy decoding, since it frequently undercuts its own seriousness: while it critiques the commodification of the male body, the main star, Brad Pitt, spends much of the film bare-chested, showcasing the washboard stomach that won him fame in *Thelma and Louise* (1991); while its protagonist censures commodity culture, the film itself, featuring two of Hollywood's biggest (and most expensive) male stars, grossed over $100 million worldwide, and has since spawned numerous ancillary products, such as an expensive video game, while Versace, Gucci, and Dolce and Gabbana have even launched *Fight Club* clothing lines; although the film flirts with controversial ideas such as nihilism, anarchy, fascism, homoerotic desire, male masochism, and fantasies of patriarchal restoration, and also delights in pushing the limits of "good taste" and political correctness (not even cancer victims are immune from its caustic humor), it can also deflect criticism by claiming that Tyler is just a figment of the insane narrator's imagination, who is finally expelled when the narrator, albeit in a tongue-in-cheek manner, gains "maturity." *Fight Club* also takes great delight in flouting the codes of realism, evident in its direct addresses to the camera and its groundbreaking, digitally created sequences—most memorably, the IKEA catalogue which emerges in the narrator's living room, complete with prices and descriptors floating in space. These sequences are prime examples of what Laura Mulvey has termed the "technological uncanny," since they create "the sense of uncertainty and disorientation which has always accompanied a new technology that is not yet fully understood."[51] The film also foregrounds its self-reflexivity, such as the penis frame that flickers on the screen in the final scene, a reference to Tyler's penchant for splicing pornographic shots into saccharine family animations while he worked as a projectionist. Most importantly, the film entraps the spectator in the warped consciousness of a perilously unreliable narrator, whose paranoid thoughts and fantasies unfold as instantaneous, rapidly cut images which, as Fincher himself stated, have to be "downloaded."[52] In a manner similar to *The Usual Suspects* (1995), *Fight Club* exploits the conventions of the voiceover, a traditional guarantee of presence, authenticity, and unity, with the psychic split of the hysterical narrator concealed until near narrative closure, necessitating a retrospective re-reading of the film thus far.

Hysteria has long been of interest to feminist critics, who have regarded the hysterical symptoms of the female patients of Jean-Martin Charcot, Joseph Breuer, and Sigmund Freud to have constituted a somatic expression of repressed opposition to patriarchy. More recently, male hysteria has received a great deal of attention from theorists interested in the instabilities of male identifications and the cost that the repression necessary for the assumption of normative male subjectivity necessarily entails for the male subject. In popular cinema, male hysteria takes a variety of forms, be it amnesia, shell shock, neurosis (the verbally incontinent Woody Allen and Hugh Grant being prime examples), gender disturbance in cross-dressing comedies, or the hysterical excess that emerges in the interstices of male heroic texts as a symptom of the repression of homoerotic desire required within patriarchal culture.[53] While male hysteria has a long history in popular cinema, the late '80s onward witnessed a plethora of films in which white heterosexual men flaunt their hysterical symptoms, such as the host of revisionist Second World War films that screen what has now become known as psychosomatic stress disorder (*Thin Red Line, Windtalkers, We Were Soldiers, Saving Private Ryan*); therapy films, such as the melodrama of *The Prince of Tides* (1991) or the high comedy of *Analyze This* (1999), whose male protagonists enlist the help of analysts to unblock their repressed emotions; identity crises in films such as *Face/Off* (1997) and *Being John Malkovitch* (1999); memory loss in films like *Memento* (2000) or *Eternal Sunshine of the Spotless Mind* (2004); and the hysterically split superheroes in the *Superman* (1978) or *Batman* (1989) tradition. However, most interesting for a discussion of *Fight Club* is the current trend for alter ego movies, in which a "soft man" develops a "wild man" double (to use Robert Bly's terms) who vents his repressed rage and anger, primarily at women, evident in *Me, Myself & Irene* (2000), *The Secret Lives of Dentists* (2003), *Secret Window* (2004), and *The Machinist* (2004). The current cultural fascination with male hysteria suggests that it might not provide such a challenge to normative male subjectivity as first appears. Sally Robinson, for instance, regards male hysteria as the perfect vehicle with which to figure the particular dynamics of wounded white masculinity, since it expresses, in personal and bodily terms, the "trauma of the social," enabling a bypassing of the political root causes of that crisis, namely the marking of the universal identity.[54]

Opening inside the recesses of the narrator's brain, *Fight Club* begins at its chronological ending, with Tyler lodging a gun in the narrator's mouth as the two halves of the narrator's psyche battle for supremacy. When, in his numbingly monotone, affectless voiceover, the narrator casually states that suddenly he realizes that all these events have something to do with a girl called Marla Singer (Helena Bonham Carter), we are hurtled back to the chronological beginning of the film, before the appearance of Tyler, as the narrator describes how he had been suffering from chronic insomnia laced with an elaborately scripted death-wish fantasy—death, at least, would rescue him from the inauthenticity and mediocrity of his life. A self-confessed victim of commodity culture and "slave to the IKEA nesting instinct," stuck in a meaningless, unethical job where everything is "a copy of a copy of a copy," the narrator openly expresses the anxiety, prevalent in *Disclosure* (1993) and *The Full Monty* (1997), that the male as passive consumer rather than active producer threatens traditional masculine identifications. He eventually finds relief from his insomnia by visiting self-help groups for people with terminal diseases, since only in the face of death does he feel truly alive, and only when people think you are dying do they really listen to you. In a self-conscious, parodic literalization of the logic of "disability films," the narrator appropriates the suffering of others in order to lay claim to a particularized, extra-ordinary identity that he, as an "ordinary" white middle-class male, lacks. His addiction to self-help groups, with their group hugs and guided meditations, also works to ridicule the New Age therapeutic discourses and "absurd excesses" of the men's movement, even as the film articulates many of the movement's sentiments.[55]

It is no surprise, then, that the narrator's favorite self-help group is "Remaining Men Together" for sufferers of testicular cancer, the group that most clearly establishes the overdetermined relationship between pain, victimhood, and masculinity that the film simultaneously articulates and satirizes. There the narrator finds wholeness and oblivion crying in the arms of Bob (Meat Loaf), an ex-bodybuilder, who has lost his testicles to cancer, caused by his abuse of anabolic steroids. In keeping with the film's caustic humor, Bob, who was once responsible for a chest expansion program on late-night television, has grown what the narrator misogynistically calls "bitch tits" in response to hormone treatment. If the figurative emasculation of men in the film were not sufficiently obvious, in Bob it is cruelly literalized.

Tyler Durden surfaces shortly after the intrusion of a woman, Marla, into this all-male arena. However, four single-frame images of Tyler are spliced into the film before his emergence as a seemingly autonomous character, pointing to the narrator's escalating hysteria, with Tyler waiting in the wings of his psyche, finally materializing as his double. Ever since Otto Rank's *The Double: A Psychoanalytic Study* (1914), the double in literary texts has largely been understood as a psychic projection of mental conflict. The double is the alienated part of the self who acts out the hero's repressed desires, responsibility for which is projected onto another ego, offering an "inner liberation" from the guilt caused by the "distance between the ego-ideal and the attained reality." Inevitably, though, the story ends with the suicidal slaying of the double "through which the hero seeks to protect himself permanently from the pursuits of his self."[56] *Fight Club* had definitely done its homework, flaunting its awareness of both its gothic and psychoanalytic inheritance. The narrator refers to himself and Tyler as Dr. Jekyll and Mr. Hyde, while Tyler, in a line that plays on Brad Pitt's narcissistic, sex-object star persona, explains that he is the narrator's ideal ego, embodying an extra-ordinary masculinity, unfettered by lack: "I look like you wanna look, I fuck like you wanna fuck. I am capable, smart, and most importantly, free in ways you are not."

Through the fact that Tyler emerges soon after Marla's appearance, the film suggests, with postmodern knowingness, that the narrator's creation of an alter ego is the only way he can overcome his fear of the feminine and sleep with Marla (and why, even then, Tyler wears protective rubber gloves!). Indeed, Tyler flippantly refers to the Bobbit case that gripped the U.S. in the early '90s, where the symbolic castration of men at the hands of women was rendered literal: "It could be worse. A woman could cut off your penis while you're sleeping and toss it out the window of a moving car."[57] It is also Tyler who gives voice to the narrator's concern about the alleged large-scale feminization of society when he relates his tale of paternal betrayal, concluding with the key line: "We are a generation of men raised by women, and I'm beginning to wonder whether another woman is really the answer we need."

The blame that Tyler places on mothers for unmanning sons most obviously invites interpretation though Kristeva's theory of the abject, the abject being "what disturbs identity, system, order" and threatens the subject's bodily and psychic boundaries. The maternal body represents ultimate abjection for the male subject because he always fears "his very own identity sinking irretrievably into the mother." Kristeva posits the father as the necessary third term that breaks the mother-child dyad of the Imaginary, saves the child from psychosis, and propels the child into the Symbolic Order.[58] In Kristeva's formulation, as Tania Modleski points out, the more abject the male subject feels, the more he desires paternal law to rescue him.[59] While the narrator's desire for the absent father is rarely overtly articulated in the film, figuring more prominently in Palahniuk's novel, the father haunts the film through his structuring absence. Tyler is established as the group ego-ideal erected in the symbolic father's place, acting like the sadistic, narcissistic primal father who bonds the members of fight club together through their shared transgression of the Law.[60] When it is later revealed that Tyler is in fact a projection of the narrator's unconscious wishes and desires, Tyler's phallic posturing can then be explained as the narrator's psychic defense against paternal abandonment, much the same as Frank's masculine histrionics in *Magnolia*.

The fact that Tyler appears once Marla has destroyed the pleasure the narrator takes in crying "pressed against Bob's tits" also implies that the narrator creates Tyler in order express the homoerotic desire that is forcibly repressed within patriarchal culture, a repression that results in hysterical symptoms. The film is therefore unusual in pointing to the fragility of (male) heterosexual identifications and foregrounding the homoerotic desire that is most often subsumed or rerouted in Hollywood texts. Whereas Otto Rank notes that the double tends to be "the rival of [the hero's] prototype in anything and everything, but primarily in the love for a woman," in *Fight Club*'s erotic triangle, the narrator worries

most about competing for Tyler's, not Marla's, attention.[61] Marla's marginal role
would seem to be that of confirming Tyler's heterosexuality (though not the narrator's) and cementing homoerotic desire, a point explicitly made when the narrator is discovered spying on Tyler and Marla having sex, and Tyler asks, "Do
you want to finish her off?" Having moved in together to the dilapidated gothic
house on Paper Street, the narrator even refers to himself and Tyler as sit-com
characters Ozzie and Harriet: they use the bathroom at the same time, the narrator straightens Tyler's tie before he goes to work, and Tyler wanders around the
house in a pink fluffy bathrobe embroidered with teapots. In a later gruesome
scene, the narrator pulverizes the face of the blond recruit Angel Face (Jared
Leto), who captures Tyler's attention. This is first seen to stem from pathological jealousy intent on disfiguring the object of Tyler's affection, but, retrospectively, when we realize that the narrator and Tyler are one and the same, can be
interpreted as the narrator's anger at Angel Face for arousing his own repressed
homosexuality. As a repository of the narrator's unconscious desires (the unconscious, as Freud taught us, knows no contradictions), Tyler is thus offered up as
an unstable vision of masculinity, at times durably phallic and heterosexual, and
at others more feminine and the object of homoerotic desire. Nonetheless, the
narrator's obsession with Tyler is ultimately displaced onto narcissism when
Tyler and the narrator are revealed as being the same person, so that Tyler functions as defense against homosexuality not only for the narrator, but also, extradiegetically, for the film itself, allowing it to flirt with the screening of homoerotic desire between two of Hollywood's biggest male stars and then disavow
its implications.

Tyler also overtly attributes the narrator's hysterical symptoms to the repression of primordial, male aggression in a society in which the hunter-gatherer
instinct has been squashed by meaningless jobs, rabid consumerism, and an image culture in which a Gucci model represents the masculine ideal. The solution,
Tyler states, is good old-fashioned fistfights, in which the masochistic endurance
of pain proves virility and renders the commodified male body a site of agency
and self-mastery.

Male masochism, much like male hysteria, has received a lot of attention in
recent years from scholars in the field of gender studies. Many theorists working
within a psychoanalytic framework have viewed male masochism to be subversive of phallic masculinity. These theorists take Freud's study of male beating
fantasies in his classic text "A Child Is Being Beaten" as their starting point. The
first stage of the fantasy begins with an inverted Oedipal attitude: "*I am loved by
my father.*" In the second stage, the male subject transforms his transgressive
desire for the father into punishment: "I am being beaten by my father." This
stage is unconscious and reconstructed by Freud. Homosexuality, therefore, is
obviously less culturally sanctioned than masochism, which remains conscious.
In the third stage, the male subject evades his homosexuality by replacing his
father with his mother or another woman, who, nonetheless, is endowed with
masculine attributes.[62] For Freud, this stage is remarkable since "it has for its

content a feminine attitude without a homosexual object-choice," a phrase which, for Kaja Silverman, "wreaks havoc with sexual difference."[63] For Silverman, along with Freud, the male subject "cannot avow feminine masochism without calling into question his identification with the masculine position." The male masochist, consequently, "radiates a negativity inimical to the social order."[64]

However, male masochism has more recently been seen as a specific mode of power that works to bolster phallic male subjectivity, particularly by theorists who do not limit their study to the domain of the Oedipal family or sexual fantasies. For instance, in response to Silverman's analysis, Judith Butler has stated that if masochism is culturally and historically situated, "[phallic] 'divestiture' could be a strategy of phallic self-aggrandizement."[65] Paul Smith has also understood masochism as crucial to the conservation of normative male sexuality within the discourses of popular culture.[66] In a similar vein, David Savran, in his comprehensive study *Taking It Like a Man: White Masculinity, Masochism, and Contemporary American Culture* (1998), argues that psychoanalytic accounts such as Silverman's do not fully examine the material forces that have foregrounded the masochistic male subject. He regards the bifurcation of the male subject not as a radical challenge to hegemonic masculinity, but as a strategy of self-restoration. He explores how current representations of U.S. white heterosexual masculinity are entrenched in a discourse of victimhood, but notes that "cultural texts constructing masochistic masculinities characteristically conclude with an almost magical restitution of phallic power."[67]

Without doubt, the prevalence of the mutilated male body in popular cinema, especially '80s action films such as *First Blood* (1982), *Die Hard*, and *Lethal Weapon* (whose numerous sequels reflect the compulsion for repetition that Freud located in masochism), suggests that masochism can consolidate images of phallic masculinity, since, as Paul Smith puts it, "the place of the exhibitionist/masochist is already accounted for, and already pulled by narrativization into a plot designed to eventually explode the negativity of masochism."[68] The hypermasculine bodies of stars such as Sylvester Stallone, Arnold Schwarzenegger, Jean-Claude Van Damme, and, more recently, Van Diesel, Daniel Craig in *Casino Royale* (2006), as well as Kiefer Sutherland in Fox's hit television series *24*, are often tied up or held down while they are beaten to a bloody pulp. These scenes might even deploy the Christian iconography of crucifixion and eventual resurrection, as we see in *Conan the Barbarian* (1982), *Cyborg* (1982), *Rambo: First Blood Part II*, and *Gladiator* (2000). Such scenarios prove the action hero's virility and ability to "take it like a man," and the audience is well aware that he will soon emerge triumphant to deliver his own violent form of retribution. Moreover, the pulverizing of the male body may also mitigate any homoerotic pleasure gained from the display of the male body, as Steve Neale has argued (see chapter 3), a use to which it is undoubtedly put in *Fight Club*, since, as Tyler instructs, there must only be two men to a fight, one fight at a time, and all participants have to remove their shirts and shoes; in other words, one of the pleasures of fight club, both intra- and extradiegetically, is *watching* bare-chested men wrestling with each other, a pleasure with a potential homoerotic as well as sadomasochistic investment.[69]

Fight Club is well aware of the "regeneration through masochistic endurance" trope that structures representations of masculinity in the Hollywood tradition. In his voiceover, the narrator posits the experience of pain as a means of achieving self-mastery, informing us, "A guy came to fight club for the first time, his ass was a wad of cookie dough. After a few weeks, he was carved out of wood." Here, the soft, amorphous, penetrable, feminized, potentially homosexual body gives way to a hard body with stable boundaries that has been re-phallicized by enduring a little pain.[70] He also informs us that only at fight club did the members feel alive, adding that "afterwards we all felt saved." This very self-consciousness, however, renders *Fight Club* substantially more complex than the conventional action film. For instance, in a later scene, when fight club has spiraled out of control and the narrator brutally pummels Angel Face, leaving him grossly disfigured, the film significantly departs from Hollywood conventions. Not only does the soundtrack cut to silence, bar the gruesome, amplified sound effects of fists pounding flesh, but also the camera oscillates between the narrator's point of view—rendering the spectator complicit in this act of gratuitous violence—and Angel Face's point of view—orchestrating identification with the victim function. Combined with the intercutting reaction shots of the shocked intradiegetic spectators, and the inadequacy of the narrator's justification that he wanted to "destroy something beautiful," the film offers a more critical representation of the libidinal logic undergridding the display of sadomasochistic bodies in many popular films. In several scenes, the film also draws attention to the ludicrousness of its sadomasochistic protagonist, most obviously when he beats himself up in front of his boss (a scene that still suggests the empowering function of masochism, since the boss, panicked that he would be accused of abusing his staff, gives the narrator the paid leave he demanded). Moreover, the visual often conflicts with the discursive; as Edward Norton explains, while Brad Pitt "bulked up" for the role, he, on the other hand, purposefully lost weight and "became Gollum" in order to undermine his character's assertions that mutilation is inherently virility affirming.[71] That said, while Asbjørn Grønstad is right to argue that the film challenges "the narrative paradigm of 'destructibility-and-recuperability' that has traditionally allayed Hollywood's portrayals of masculinity and violence," it is important to note that it does so in the scenes featuring the narrator rather than those featuring Tyler.[72] Indeed, in the early fight scenes, before Tyler's vision of remasculinization reaches ludicrous lengths, the spectator is encouraged to identify with the extraordinary figure of Tyler Durden. For that reason, earlier fistfights deploy the "destructibility-and-recuperability" paradigm more conventionally, with scenes featuring grappling male bodies filmed with an objective camera and intercut with shots of the frenzied, approving spectators, who cheer the fight on, and whose impassioned shouts are accompanied by a musical soundtrack. However, the film can always deflect criticism due to the fact that the inspiration behind these fights, Tyler, is later revealed to be evidence of, rather than solution to, the narrator's failed masculinity.

The revelation of Tyler's true identity also necessitates a retrospective re-reading of many of the scenes featuring sadomasochistic play between him and the narrator. For example, the scene where Tyler sears an imprint of his kiss onto the narrator's hand with lye (the violence barely dislodging the homoerotic implications), informing him that "without pain, without sacrifice we have nothing," depicts a sadistic Tyler leading the narrator to self-realization and remasculinization. However, the reworked flashback of this scene (once Tyler and the narrator are confirmed to be the same person) screens self-abuse or what Freud termed "reflexive masochism," where the subject enjoys pain "*without* an attitude of passivity."[73] It is this refusal of passivity that leads Silverman to argue that reflexive masochism "is ideally suited for negotiating the contradictions inherent in masculinity. The male subject can indulge his appetite for pain without at the same time calling into question either his virility, or his paternal lineage."[74] Historicizing this insight, David Savran regards reflexive masochism to have become "the primary libidinal logic of the white male as victim," allowing him to feel victimized and reempowered simultaneously. In this respect, it functions as an ideal mechanism for white males living in a postfeminist, post-civil rights America: "No longer having others on whom to inflict his power and his pain with impunity, the male subject began to turn against himself and to prove his mettle by gritting his teeth and taking his punishment like a man."[75]

For example, in his analysis of *First Blood*, Savran argues that Rambo's suturing of his own wounds "must be seen as being self-willed, as being the product of his need to prove his masculinity the only way he can, by allowing his sadistic, masculinized half to kick his masochistic, feminized flesh 'to shit.'"[76] If the same logic is applied to the scene where Tyler administers pain to the narrator to help him "hit bottom" and find freedom, what the scene retrospectively reveals is the narrator actively subjugating and punishing the feminine part of his own psyche. However, whereas the *Rambo* series took itself seriously, as do the early, more conventional fight scenes in *Fight Club*, later scenes in the film parody this libidinal logic. For instance, when Tyler orders the narrator's (that is, his own!) castration as punishment for wanting to close fight club, the film stages a lynching fantasy that allows the narrator to inhabit the suffering black male body (much like Nick's racial fantasy in *Falling Down*); but the "space monkeys" (his followers) do not see his desire for castration as feminizing, but as an act of courage and self-sacrifice that demands the greatest respect. But the comic mode in which this scene is filmed, with the protesting narrator pinned down, desperately trying to wriggle free as the castrating space monkeys pull down his trousers, suggests that Tyler's vision of remasculinization through masochistic endurance has reached ludicrous proportions.

While the film might undercut the excesses of Tyler's discourse on male masochism (which it nonetheless also screens), what is more disturbing about the film is the fact that the white male is still firmly represented as a victim figure, with the drama of beleaguered manhood literally inscribed across the battered, mutilated bodies of the overwhelmingly white males that populate fight club. This is not to say that the film does not express some of the genuine suffering of lower- and middle-class (white) men in postindustrial, economically-downsized, consumer-obsessed America. For example, in anti-capitalist rhetoric, Tyler tells fight club members, many of whom are "slaves with white collars," "You are not your job. You are not how much money you have in the bank. Not the car you drive. Not the contents of your wallet." Furthermore, when a police chief threatens to close down fight clubs, Tyler and his followers follow him into the restroom, hold him down, rip off his pants, menacingly dangle a knife and elastic band in front of him, and threaten him with castration, while Tyler lectures him (in a direct address to the camera): "The people you are after are the people you depend on. We cook your meals. We haul your trash. We connect your calls. We drive your ambulances. We guard you while you sleep." Here, then, Tyler functions as the mouthpiece of class conflict, though the import of his address is undercut by the comic mode in which the threatened castration scene is screened. Yet, as Henry A. Giroux and Imre Szeman assert, despite its ostensible critique of consumerist culture, the film in fact shores up the individualistic ideologies of neo-liberal capitalism by inviting identification with an authoritarian, hyper-individualistic white male, whose exceptionality enables him to overcome the alleged penetration of commodity culture into every aspect of contemporary life. Moreover, "[i]t is never imagined that a whole culture could or should change how it organizes the lives of members."[77] Indeed, the oppression experienced by women, immigrants, people of color, homosexuals and lesbians, and other marginalized groups under a capitalist system is deftly elided. Although the straight white male's others are not overtly scapegoated, the film's inscription of the "angry white male" figure, one who fails to consider sexual and racial inequality as significant dynamics in political struggle, plays into the anti-feminist and anti-affirmative action discourses of neo-conservative rhetoric, even as the film voices nominal opposition to the capitalist imperatives that structure that very rhetoric.

To be more specific, as regards racial differences between men, while *Fight Club* features a few token men of color, all the major characters are white males, and race is never mentioned as a contributing factor to social oppression. Although it could be suggested that the homosociality of fight club is actually figured as a means of securing racial rapprochement, Robyn Wiegman has pointed out that, far from suspending the significance of non-gendered formations of power, narratives of interracial homosocial bonding played out in scenarios devoid of women more often than not facilitate the reinforcement of hierarchical arrangements between men.[78] Indeed, in one of the few bi-racial fights we witness, Tyler defeats his black opponent, while the narrator is beaten to a pulp but smiles and shakes his adversary's hand. Within the sadomasochistic economy of the film, therefore, the narrator can occupy both poles of sadomasochistic desire:

as Tyler, the "angry white male" *in extremis*, he pummels an African-American to the point of collapse, but as himself, he assumes the victim function of being pounded by his black other. It is also significant that Raymond K. Hessel (Joon B. Kim), the trembling, weeping, traumatized man that Tyler holds at gunpoint, threatening to kill him if he does not realize his ambitions to become a vet, is played by an Asian-American in the film, even though the character is white in Palahniuk's novel. This scene cannot escape racial encodings, even if the narrator looks on shocked, the implication being that now Tyler really has gone too far.

However, racial antagonisms are largely displaced onto the more obviously elaborated antagonism between the sexes in *Fight Club*. Women are evacuated from fight club's "wound culture," to use Mark Seltzer's term, wherein the violated body "function[s] as a way of imagining and situating our notions of public, social, and collective identity."[79] As we have seen, women, particularly suffocating mothers, are posited as part of the problem in a film that screens the same lament for the loss of paternal authority, the same fantasy of restoring a lost primal masculinity, and the same implicit blaming of women for the current "crisis in masculinity" and perceived feminization of society that characterized Bly's men's movement and popular media rhetoric of the '90s. Violence is therefore valorized because it is posited as one of the few characteristics to which men can still lay exclusive claim. What is disturbing about the film, then, is that its "cool" status, particularly among young male audiences for whom it soon became cult viewing, in part depends on Tyler's rejection of women and all things feminine.

In *Fight Club*'s final scene, however, the narrator is perfunctorily reconciled with the feminine when he saves Marla from Tyler's clutches. But this scene characteristically foregrounds its own absurdity. By literally shooting himself in the head and expelling Tyler, the narrator gains psychic unity and heterosexuality in one fell swoop, taking the logic of empowering masochism to a ludicrous length. Standing bedraggled in an ill-fitting, baggy overcoat and boxer shorts, his trousers lost to the castrating space monkeys, as bloods spurts out of the hole in the side of his head, the narrator turns to Marla and explains, "You met me at a very strange time in my life." With the two figures hand-in-hand, turning to each other in a deliberately stylized manner, the soundtrack then blares out The Pixies' track "Where Is My Mind?" This patently contrived ending thus makes it difficult to agree with Susan Faludi, who takes the film at face value in arguing that it "ends up as a quasi-feminist tale, seen through masculine eyes," where "the man and the woman clasp hands in what could be a mutual redemption."[80] The tongue-in-cheek nature of this male-female reunification is also underscored when the image of the narrator and Marla holding hands to watch the destruction of eleven skyscrapers housing credit card companies (Tyler's attempt to cancel out debt records and bring about "economic equilibrium") is intercut with two frames of a semi-erect penis—a reference to Tyler's habit of splicing genitalia into family movies—implying the provisional nature of the narrator's psychic healing since, as Fincher notes, "the spirit of Tyler Durden is kinda still out there."[81]

  Fight Club's parodic treatment of wounded white masculinity is suggestive of the difficulties of a youth audience taking seriously the melodramatic excesses of the men's movement's discourse on wounded males and its cinematic incarnation in "disability films," as well as the histrionic posturing of the '80s sadomasochistic action hero (see chapter 3) by the millennium's end. Indeed, even the animation *Finding Nemo* (2003) satirizes the men's movement, when a group of sharks are comically represented in a workshop, trying to get in touch with their sensitive side. However, it is important to note that parody, which, as I argue in later chapters, is an increasingly popular mode through which the contradictions and instabilities of straight white masculinity are articulated, is a double-coded discourse that functions by "inscribing both similarity to and difference from" its target model, constructing "an incongruity that evokes both ironic and pluralistic meanings."[82] *Fight Club* is thus an archetypal example of what Linda Hutcheon terms "the paradox of postmodern complicitous critique," which "manages to install and reinforce as much as undermine and subvert the conventions and presuppositions that it appears to challenge."[83] Tyler's beliefs may well be partially dislodged through the film's autodeconstructive mode, its ludic impulses to literalize the wounds inflicted on the male psyche, and the rereading necessitated when Tyler is revealed to be the symptom of rather than cure for the narrator's hysteria; at the same time, these textual strategies also facilitate a postmodern both/and, legitimizing the screening of Tyler's vision of white male disenfranchisement and eventual restoration, along with the marginalization of the white heterosexual male's others. Whereas *Regarding Henry* and *Forrest Gump*'s ingenuity lay in their reconstruction of normative masculinity through their childlike but innocent protagonists, *Fight Club*'s ingenuity lies in its postmodern treatment of the double, which allows a screening of white heterosexual masculinity that is both lacking and complete, wounded and primal, ordinary and extra-ordinary.

  In the following chapter, I will continue my exploration of how commodity culture has impacted on normative masculinity by focusing both on films that commodify and objectify the extra-ordinary white male body, and on films that posit the commodification of the male body as a source of anxiety to "ordinary" men. As well as exploring the various strategies used to minimize concerns caused by the (white) male body on display in Hollywood texts, I also analyze how many of these films, less overtly than *Fight Club*, screen anxieties about visual and virtual culture, and the alleged loss of the physical values of masculinity. I end by considering the nostalgic return to images of unreconstructed, highly physical, masterful heroes evident in the recent cycle of epic films, films that screen the primal masculinity of Tyler's vision, but without the concomitant need for parody.

Notes

1. Robert Bly, *Iron John: A Book about Men* (Reading, MA: Addison-Wesley, 1990), 63.

2. Bly, *Iron John*, 33-36.

3. Bly, *Iron John*, 42.

4. Bly, *Iron John*, 42.

5. Lynda Boose, "Techno-Muscularity and the 'Boy Eternal': From the Quagmire to the Gulf," in *Cultures of United States Imperialism*, ed. Amy Kaplan and Donald E. Pease (Durham, NC: Duke University Press, 1993), 602.

6. Boose, "Techno-Muscularity and the 'Boy Eternal,'" 605.

7. Susan Jeffords, *The Remasculinization of America: Gender and the Vietnam War* (Bloomington: Indiana University Press, 1989), 134.

8. Sally Robinson, *Marked Men: White Masculinity in Crisis* (New York: Columbia University Press, 2000), 12, 8.

9. Matthew Wray and Annalee Newitz, introduction to *White Trash: Race and Class in America*, ed. Matthew Wray and Annalee Newitz (New York: Routledge, 1997), 5.

10. Joseph Sartelle, "Dreams and Nightmares in the Hollywood Blockbuster," in *The Oxford History of World Cinema*, ed. Geoffrey Nowell-Smith (Oxford: Oxford University Press, 1996), 522.

11. Stella Bruzzi, *Bringing Up Daddy: Fatherhood and Masculinity in Post-War Hollywood* (London: BFI, 2005), xii.

12. Fred Pfeil, *White Guys: Studies in Postmodern Domination and Difference* (London: Verso, 1995), 61.

13. Pfeil, *White Guys*, 40.

14. Krin Gabbard, *Black Magic: White Hollywood and African American Culture* (New Brunswick, NJ: Rutgers University Press, 2004), 144.

15. Thomas DiPiero, "White Men Aren't," *Camera Obscura: A Journal of Feminism and Film Theory* 30 (1992): 126.

16. Robert Stam and Louise Spence, "Colonialism, Racism and Representation," *Screen* 24, no. 2 (1983): 3; K. Anthony Appiah, "'No Bad Nigger': Blacks as the Ethical Principle in the Movies," in *Media Spectacles*, ed. Marjorie Garber, Jann Matlock, and Rebecca L. Walkowitz (New York: Routledge, 1993), 83.

17. Pfeil, *White Guys*, 13.

18. Richard L. Homan, "The Everyman Movie, Circa 1991," *The Journal of Popular Film and Television* 25 (1997): 25.

19. David Marriott, *Haunted Life: Visual Culture and Black Modernity* (New Brunswick, NJ: Rutgers University Press, 2007), 186-87.

20. Pfeil, *White Guys*, 42.

21. Pfeil, *White Guys*, 42.

22. Karen Boyle, "New Man, Old Brutalisms? Reconstructing a Violent History in *Forrest Gump*," *Scope: An Online Journal of Film Studies* (December 2001), http://www.scope.nottingham.ac.uk/article.php?issue=dec2001&id=280&section=article (accessed June 10, 2004).

23. See Boyle, "New Man, Old Brutalisms?"; Thomas B. Byers, "History Re-Membered: *Forrest Gump*, Postfeminist Masculinity, and the Burial of Counterculture," *Modern Fiction Studies* 42 (1996): 419-44; Gabbard, *Black Magic*, 122-23; Pfeil, *White Guys*, 251-61; Robyn Wiegman, "'My Name Is Forrest Gump': Whiteness Studies and the Paradox of Particularity," in *Multiculturalism, Postcoloniality, and Transnational*

Media, ed. Ella Shohat and Robert Stam (New Brunswick, NJ: Rutgers University Press, 2003).

24. Gabbard, *Black Magic*, 122-23.

25. Richard Corliss, "Hollywood's Last Decent Man," *Time*, July 11, 1994, 58.

26. Wiegman, "My Name is Forrest Gump," 238.

27. "Audio Commentary," *Forrest Gump: Special 2 Disc Collector's Edition*, DVD, directed by Robert Zemeckis (Paramount Pictures, 2001).

28. Pfeil, *White Guy*, 252.

29. Byers, "History Re-Membered," 428.

30. Byers, "History Re-Membered," 431.

31. Byers, "History Re-Membered," 431.

32. Byers, "History Re-Membered," 422.

33. Pfeil, *White Guys*, 257.

34. Boose, "Techno-Muscularity and the 'Boy Eternal,'" 602.

35. Masculinity as paternity is also evident in films featuring African-Americans, such as *Boyz N the Hood* (1991), *John Q* (2002), and *Daddy Day Care* (2003).

36. Tania Modleski, *Feminism Without Women: Culture and Criticism in a "Post-feminist" Age* (New York: Routledge, 1991), 88.

37. Barbara Creed, "From Here to Modernity: Feminism and Postmodernism," *Screen* 28, no. 2 (1987): 65.

38. Michael S. Kimmel and Michael Kaufman, "Weekend Warriors: The New Men's Movement," in *Theorizing Masculinities*, ed. Harry Brod and Michael Kaufman (London: Sage, 1994), 282.

39. Linda Williams, *Playing the Race Card: Melodramas of Black and White From Uncle Tom to O.J. Simpson* (Princeton, NJ: Princeton University Press, 2001) 15, 29.

40. Kathleen Rowe, "Melodrama and Men in Post-Classical Romantic Comedy," in *Me Jane: Masculinity, Movies and Women*, ed. Pat Kirkham and Janet Thumin (New York: St. Martin's Press, 1995), 185.

41. Christine Gledhill, "The Melodramatic Field: An Investigation," in *Home Is Where the Heart Is: Studies in Melodrama and the Woman's Film*, ed. Christine Gledhill (London: BFI, 1987), 35.

42. Bruzzi, *Bringing Up Daddy*, 35, 139.

43. Sigmund Freud, "Totem and Taboo," in *The Origins of Religion: Totem and Taboo, Moses and Monotheism and Other Works*, trans. James Strachey, ed. Albert Dickson (London: Penguin, 1991), 203-4.

44. Thomas DiPiero, *White Men Aren't* (Durham, NC: Duke University Press, 2002), 212. Kaja Silverman also comments on this instability by referring to Freud's statement in "The Ego and the Id" that the male subject is issued two mutually exclusive imperatives: "You *ought to be* like this (like your father)" and "You *may not be* like this (like your father)—that is, you may not do all that he does; some thing are his prerogative." Sigmund Freud, "The Ego and the Id," in *On Metapsychology: The Theory of Psychoanalysis: Beyond the Pleasure Principle, The Ego and the Id and Other Works*, trans. James Strachey, ed. Angela Richards (London: Penguin, 1991), 374; Kaja Silverman, *Male Subjectivity at the Margins* (New York: Routledge, 1992), 193. The first command, as Silverman notes, comes from the ego-ideal (positive notions of the individual father) and the second from the super-ego formed by "the internalization of the father as Law." Thus, the only way the male child can overcome his libidinal desire for his father is to transform it into identification and become the Symbolic Father, but this is prohibited by the superego (194). As a result, "[t]he prototypical male subject oscillates endlessly be-

tween the mutually exclusive commands of the (male) ego-ideal and the super-ego, wanting both to love the father and to be the father, but prevented from doing either"—a "cruel drama" that the feminine (male) masochist literalizes and plays out on the body (195).

45. Bruzzi, *Bringing Up Daddy*, 180.

46. Susannah Radstone, "'Too Straight a Drive to the Tollbooth': Masculinity, Mortality and Al Pacino," in *Me Jane: Masculinity, Movies and Women*, ed. Pat Kirkham and Janet Thumin (New York: St. Martin's Press, 1995), 155.

47. Robinson, *Marked Men*, 11.

48. Gavin Smith, "Inside Out," *Film Comment*, September/October 1999, 61.

49. Benjamin Svetkey, "Blood, Sweat, and Fears," *Entertainment Weekly*, October 15, 1999, http://www.edward-norton.org/fc/articles/bloodsweat.html (accessed March 30, 2000).

50. See, for example, Smith, "Inside Out"; Svetkey, "Blood, Sweat, and Fears."

51. Laura Mulvey, *Death 24x a Second: Stillness and the Moving Image* (London: Reaktion, 2006), 27.

52. Jonathan Romney, "Boxing Clever," *The New Statesman*, November 15, 1999, http://www.newstatesman.com/199911150043 (accessed May 30, 2000); Smith, "Inside Out," 61.

53. Paul Smith, "Eastwood Bound," in *Constructing Masculinity*, ed. Maurice Berger, Brian Wallis, and Simon Watson (New York: Routledge, 1995), 72.

54. Robinson, *Marked Men*, 174-75.

55. Smith, "Inside Out," 58.

56. Otto Rank, *The Double: A Psychoanalytic Study*, trans. Harry Tucker, Jr. (London: Karnac, 1989), 77, 79.

57. In a televised trial in 1994, Lorena Bobbit was tried for cutting off the penis of her husband, who, she alleged, subjected her to ongoing abuse. She flung his penis out of her car window, though it was later found by police and stitched back on.

58. Julia Kristeva, *Powers of Horror*, trans. Leon Roudiez (New York: Columbia University Press, 1982), 4, 64.

59. Modleski, *Feminism Without Women*, 68.

60. Several Lacanian theorists have argued that symbolic authority is currently being dissolved and that the Oedipal father is now being replaced by the primal father, who is not subordinated by the Law and is only on the look out for his own *jouissance*. For example, see Slavoj Žižek, *The Metastases of Enjoyment: Six Essays on Woman and Causality* (London: Verso, 1994), 206. When it becomes evident that Tyler is the narrator's alter ego, however, the film would seem to screen concerns that the decline in paternal authority is responsible for not only the erection of unacceptable father substitutes, but also a male subject that is psychically split, alarmingly self-punitive, and verging on psychosis. For instance, *Fight Club* almost directly replicates the restless, self-obsessed, feminized, pathologically narcissistic subject that Christopher Lasch profiles in *The Culture of Narcissism: American Life in an Age of Diminishing Expectations* (London: Abacus, 1980).

61. Rank, *The Double*, 75.

62. Sigmund Freud, "A Child Is Being Beaten," in *On Psychopathology: Inhibitions, Symptoms and Anxiety and Other Works*, trans. James Strachey, ed. Angela Richards (London: Penguin, 1993), 170-87.

63. Freud, "A Child Is Being Beaten," 187; Silverman, *Male Subjectivity*, 212.

64. Silverman, *Male Subjectivity*, 190, 206.

65. Liz Kotz, "The Body You Want: Liz Kotz Interviews Judith Butler," *Artforum* 31 (1992): 88.

66. Smith, "Eastwood Bound," 95.

67. David Savran, *Taking It Like a Man: White Masculinity, Masochism, and Contemporary American Culture* (Princeton, NJ: Princeton University Press, 1998), 205-6, 37.

68. Smith, "Eastwood Bound," 90.

69. Steve Neale, "Masculinity as Spectacle," in *The Sexual Subject: A Screen Reader in Sexuality*, ed. Mandy Merck (London: Routledge, 1992), 281, 284.

70. This image is highly suggestive of the male fear of the female body that both Kristeva and Klaus Theweleit, in their accounts of abjection and male fascism respectively, have traced back to the pre-Oedipal mother-child dyad before the construction of a bounded ego. See Kristeva, *Powers of Horror*; Klaus Theweleit, *Male Fantasies*, 2 Vols., trans. Stephen Conway in collaboration with Erica Carter and Chris Turner (Cambridge: Polity, 1987).

71. Robby O'Connor, "Interview with Edward Norton," *The Yale Herald*, October 8, 1999, http://www.edward-norton.org/articles/yaleherald1099.html (accessed February 15, 2002).

72. Asbjørn Grønstad, "One-Dimensional Men: *Fight Club* and the Poetics of the Body," *Film Criticism* 27, no. 1 (2003): 16.

73. Sigmund Freud, "Instincts and their Vicissitudes," in *On Metapsychology: The Theory of Psychoanalysis: Beyond the Pleasure Principle, The Ego and the Id and Other Works*, trans. James Strachey, ed. Angela Richards (London: Penguin, 1991), 125.

74. Silverman, *Male Subjectivity*, 326.

75. Savran, *Taking It Like a Man*, 210, 176

76. Savran, *Taking It Like a Man*, 201.

77. Henry A. Giroux and Imre Szeman, "Ikea Boy Fights Back: *Fight Club*, Consumerism, and the Political Limits of Nineties Cinema," in *The End of Cinema As We Know It: American Film in the Nineties*, ed. Jon Lewis (London: Pluto, 2002), 97.

78. Robyn Wiegman, "Fielder and Sons," in *Race and the Subject of Masculinities*, ed. Harry Stecopoulos and Michael Uebel (Durham, NC: Duke University Press, 1997), 63.

79. Mark Seltzer, *Serial Killers: Death and Life in America's Wound Culture* (New York: Routledge, 1998), 21.

80. Susan Faludi, "It's *Thelma and Louise* for Guys," *Newsweek*, October 25, 1999, 89.

81. Wise, Damon. "Menace II Society," *Empire*, December 1999, 105.

82. Dan Harries, *Film Parody* (London: BFI, 2000), 24.

83. Linda Hutcheon, *The Politics of Postmodernism* (London: Routledge, 1990), 8, 1-2.

Part Two

Coming Apart at the Seams?
White Heterosexual Masculinity
and the Body in Popular Cinema

Chapter Three
Fleshing Out White Heterosexual Masculinity: The Objectified and Commodified White Male Body

Bearing the Burden of Objectification

In a brief but telling scene in *Fight Club* (1999), the narrator's attention is caught by a Gucci underwear advertisement which displays the torso of a white male, cut off at the neck and thighs, offering up the spectacle of a sculptured washboard stomach and amply-filled briefs. The narrator turns to Tyler and indignantly asks, "Is that what a man looks like?" With a grin, Tyler replies, "Self-improvement is masturbation. Now self destruction . . ." His sentence is left unfinished, though in Chuck Palahniuk's novel Tyler actually states, "[m]aybe self-destruction is the answer."[1] Nonetheless, the implication is the same: that masochism and pain offer the modern male a means of reclaiming ownership over the body, and breaking out of the chains of a commodity culture that has reduced masculinity to an image that can be bought or sold. Yet, at the same time, the fact that it is Brad Pitt who stars as the narrator's ideal ego playfully undercuts the narrator's lament—casting that would suggest that in fact, at least as regards the current mediascape of Hollywood film production and advertising, a Gucci model is precisely what a man should look like. As if to make this very point, the next scene features a shirtless Tyler wrestling with an opponent, mediated through the narrator's approving gaze. Tyler eventually wins the fight, stands up triumphantly, allowing the camera to showcase his bare-chested, bronzed body, revealing the developed peps and rippling abdominal and pelvic muscles that launched Pitt's career in *Thelma and Louise* (1991). The film's characteristic conflict of discursive and visual content is highly indicative of the instabilities and contradictions of contemporary white heterosexual masculinity, which is increasingly objectified in the visual culture of late capitalism, despite the obvious anxieties that it causes, especially to the majority of "ordinary" men who fail to measure up to the extra-ordinary, masculine ideal.

Much, then, seems to have changed since Laura Mulvey declared in her seminal article "Visual Pleasure and Narrative Cinema" that "the male figure cannot bear the burden of sexual objectification." Writing in 1975, Mulvey's primary tenet was that "[i]n a world ordered by sexual imbalance, pleasure in looking has been split between active/male and passive/female." In her rigid binary schema, the woman connotes "*to-be-looked-at-ness*" and functions as the passive, eroticized, fetishized object of the controlling male gaze, for the male protagonist as well as for the spectator, who "projects his look on to that of his like, the screen surrogate, so that the power of the male protagonist as he controls events coincides with the active power of the erotic look, both giving a satisfying sense of omnipotence."[2] Mulvey's essay performed an important critical function in inserting gender into apparatus theory, in addressing how unconscious desires and patriarchal ideology are encoded into the grammar of film, and in moving feminist film theory beyond the impasse of stereotypes and "positive images." In designating the cinematic spectator male in a polemical move that emphasized her belief that mainstream cinema engineers spectatorial identifications structured around male pleasure, Mulvey's text not only "gave voice to a radical mistrust of pleasure,"[3] but also unleashed a flurry of publications on the female spectator, to which Mulvey herself contributed when she revised her paradigm in her 1981 essay "Afterthoughts on 'Visual Pleasure and Narrative Cinema' Inspired by King Vidor's *Duel in the Sun* (1946)."[4] Her rigid formulation has been criticized for ignoring other identity categories that inform cinematic spectatorship, for not taking into account psychoanalytic insights about the fluid nature of gendered identifications, not to mention her failure to theorize the potential masochistic pleasures of spectatorship.[5] Her paradigm has also come under considerable pressure from Lacanian theorists who have critiqued apparatus theory's notion of the masterful gaze so important to Mulvey's schema.[6] Nonetheless, Mulvey's article bequeathed feminist film theory a vocabulary and theoretical framework to which it will always be beholden. Indeed, this chapter is indebted to Mulvey's scrupulous attention to sexuality and sexual difference, her gendering of the gaze, her linking of spectatorship and visual pleasure to the cultural and social position of men and women outside of the film text, and her focus on the ways in which the cinematic apparatus attempts to position the spectator via the cinematic apparatus. However, at the same time, I also explore the ways in which contemporary popular films challenge the Mulveyan paradigm in relation to representations of the straight white male body. I also employ a less rigid concept of spectatorial identification. What's more, as well as considering how the male body now has to "bear the burden of objectification," I also consider representations of the male body in terms of differences other than gender, namely race, class, sexuality, and nation.

Of course, written over three decades ago, "Visual Pleasure" now seems rather dated, particularly with the development of the action heroine, contemporary Hollywood's willingness to screen images of more vulnerable, emotional, or ambiguous masculinities,[7] and, most importantly for the concerns of this chapter, the heightened visibility of the commodified male body. However, this is not to say that the male body was previously kept under wraps: the careers of Rudolph Valentino, Kirk Douglas, Marlon Brando, and James Dean soon put this idea to rest. Indeed, in her recent book *Death 24x a Second: Stillness and the Moving Image* (2006) Mulvey accepts that Miriam Hansen's study of Valentino and his "to-be-looked-at-ness" "upsets [her] 1975 assumptions about the gendering of visual pleasure."[8] In fact, male bodies have always been on display, but the cinematic codes through which they are conveyed are historically contingent. For instance, as William Luhr argues, action stars of earlier generations often displayed their torsos (John Wayne, James Cagney, Clark Gable, for instance), but they did not have to possess the sculptured, pumped-up look of contemporary Hollywood stars, and while "[t]he representation of masculinity has always been inextricably tied up with issues of power, . . . that power has not always been represented in bodily terms."[9] It is also the case that new viewing technologies affect cinematic representations of masculinity, as Mulvey herself demonstrates in *Death 24x a Second*. Reflecting on how the spectator's "newly acquired control of the image" might impact on visual pleasure and gendered spectatorship, Mulvey notes that the ability to freeze a frame of the film, for instance, may allow the male body to be objectified and fetishized even if "this form of spectatorship may work perversely against the grain of the film."[10]

However, as early as 1983, Steve Neale, in his influential essay "Masculinity as Spectacle" (1983), contemplated the possibility of the male body being the object of the gaze. His essay, which is one of film theory's first attempts to analyze representations of heterosexual masculinity in cinema, attempted "to open a space within the framework of [Mulvey's] arguments and remarks for a reconsideration of the representation of masculinity."[11] As well as deploying a more fluid notion of identification than Mulvey's "Visual Pleasure," Neale also argued for a more complex, less monolithic notion of masculinity than Mulvey's notion of the male protagonist as unified, omnipotent ideal ego allowed. Building on the work of Paul Willemen, Neale argues that while the male body is frequently on display in films, any gaze at the male body must be motivated in such a way as to disavow homoerotic desire and its potential eroticization. One such way has been through combat scenes, which permit the pleasurable display of the male form, but allay potential homoerotic anxiety by providing the mutilation of the male body as narrative justification for both intra- and extradiegetic gazes.[12] Neale's essay has been essential in aiding understanding of the masochistic tropes in the action movie that I discussed in the previous chapter, and in its recognition that male homosexuality functions as "an undercurrent, as a potentially troubling aspect in many films and genres."[13] However, Neale, like Mulvey, seems to consider cinematic signification to be a sealed, hegemonic system within which homoerotic pleasures are abnegated via disavowal. Indeed, even if the mutilation of male bodies might go some way towards justifying male objec-

tification, that does not mean that those bodies are not consumed as erotic objects, as the huge heterosexual female and gay male following of Hollywood
stars such as Jean-Claude Van Damme and Brad Pitt reveals. Moreover, despite
his problematizing of Muvley's rigid notion of identification, much of Neale's
article retains her binary schema and its attendant problems. For instance, he
slips into the circular logic of assuming that any display of the male body must
necessarily be feminizing.[14] Paul Smith, on the other hand, argues that the male
body is frequently objectified without being feminized, since visual media deploy specific representational strategies for the male body, such as low camera
angles, aggressive gazes, the fetishization of muscles, and the use of phallic
symbols.[15] Neale's agreement with Mulvey that the cinematic apparatus is orchestrated around male pleasure also leads him to emphasize the homoerotic
gaze at the expense of the active, desiring female gaze, which is absent in
Neale's account.

Reading "Visual Pleasure and Narrative Cinema" and "Masculinity as Spectacle" for the first time in 1994, I found the dismissal of overt male sexual objectification at odds with my own experience. Most vividly, I recalled, as a teenager, going to see *Staying Alive* (1983), a film which captured media attention
due to the transformation of John Travolta's body, forged under director Sylvester Stallone's guidance. The popular media fetishized Travolta's newly ex-
panded physique, and obsessively scrutinized how many inches he had added to
his chest, arms, and thighs. Although the musical-dance genre partially (though
never fully) legitimizes the display of the male body, the camera lingered in-
tently over Travolta's oiled pecs and the skimpy loin cloth he donned for one of
the dance performances. Most distinctly, I recall the empowering sense of transgression when, during a scene in which John Travolta takes a shower, I joined in
with the wolf whistles and screams from the teenage girls who made up the majority of the audience. John Travolta, of course, is an interesting case in point,
since he was one of the first male stars to appear on the big screen wearing nothing but his briefs in *Saturday Night Fever* (1977). For Steve Neale, *Saturday
Night Fever* is a "particularly clear and interesting example" of male feminization common to the musical.[16] However, the film is perhaps best understood as
representative of the emergence of new visual codes of representing the male
body at a time when alternative models of masculinity, culturally understood as
more androgynous, were emerging in the post-counter-culture disco age. Travolta also caused a stir when he stripped out of his clothes in *Pulp Fiction*
(1994), revealing a body that was pasty-white and overweight, particularly in
comparison with the slim, toned, black body of co-star Samuel L. Jackson. Reactions to Travolta's weight gain are a sharp reminder that male bodies, just like
female ones, are also caught up in discourses that legitimize certain bodies and
delegitimize others in accordance with the historically dependent ideals perpetuated by visual culture, particularly popular cinema and the advertising industry.

In this respect, the worlds of advertising and popular cinema are inextricably linked. For that reason, I wish briefly to refer to the innovations in represen-

tations of the male body in the arena of advertising, before analyzing the impact that this increased erotic commodification of the white male body has had on popular cinema on both a visual level—how popular cinema screens white male bodies—and a discursive level—how that commodification is offered up as one of the definitive causes of white heterosexual male angst.

Sex, Flies, and Underpants: The White Male Body as Commodity

Advertisements featuring eroticized white male bodies flourished from the mid-'80s onward, both on television, such as Levi's famed "Launderette" (1985) and Diet Coke's "Eleven O'Clock Appointment" (1994), and poster stills, most obviously Calvin Klein's provocative underwear advertisements. A key example of the latter is Bruce Weber's huge, traffic-stopping, Times Square billboard advertisement of pole-vaulter Tom Hinthaus, which inaugurated Calvin Klein's now legendary and hugely successful male underwear campaign in 1983—advertisements that were so popular that poster versions on bus shelters in Manhattan literally disappeared overnight.[17] Hinthaus is every inch the Olympic ideal, shot against a white wall reminiscent of Greek island architecture, showing off his tanned, athletic body to perfection. The advertisement thus plays into the classical imagery of Greek sculptures, and reminds us that despite the Christian and Cartesian discourses of white men transcending their bodies, a point I discuss more fully below, there is a substantial history of white male bodies acting as objects of the gaze. Hinthaus's iconic image is exemplary of the fact that the majority of advertisements used white models. Black models were occasionally used, though often placed in what Susan Bordo terms aggressive "face-off" stances,[18] while for this erotic style of advertisement, Asian male models were rare. One exception is Calvin Klein's promotion of its unisex fragrance, CK One, where stereotypical notions of Asian males as more feminine seemed suited to the fragrance's unisex appeal—a fact that underscores the importance of race in any consideration of the commodified male body. However, even with white models, a bronzed or olive skin tone was preferred, not only to offset the white underwear, but also because of the cultural allusions of exoticism—the lure of what bell hooks terms a "bit of the Other."[19] In other words, while white models are generally preferred, they should not be "too white," a fact that reveals that whiteness is always underwritten by fears of ordinariness.

Hinthaus is also filmed from a low camera angle, which amplifies his towering stature. Although his arm and leg muscles are taut, this image does not readily fall into Richard Dyer's analysis of earlier male pin-ups, where in order to allay anxieties over the violation of visual gender codes, "[e]ven when not actually caught in an act, the male image still promises activity by the way the body is posed."[20] Rather, Hinthaus leans languorously back, with his eyes closed, seemingly unaware of the gaze he is courting, as if lost in a moment of narcissistic self-absorption. As the years progressed, Calvin Klein advertisements, in particular, became even more daring, such as the famed series with white rap-star Marky Mark (now known as Mark Wahlberg), which exploited his gay following caused in part by his penchant for grabbing his crotch on stage. These advertisements do little to undermine the "size matters" supposition. It is fitting, then, that Wahlberg went on to play Dirk Diggler, a porn-star with a thirteen inch penis, in *Boogie Nights* (1997).

For Mark Simpson, these advertisements are subversive of normative white masculinity. He argues that traditional masculinity cannot survive the positioning of men as passive, narcissistic objects, since "it brings masculinity into perilously close contact with that which must always be disavowed: homosexuality."[21] Frank Mort also regards the trend of encouraging men to view themselves and other men as objects of consumer desires to be suggestive of "a space for some new visual codes of masculinity."[22] The same can be said for popular cinema, where some of the codes representing the male body in advertisements have been imported into popular cinematic texts—admittedly, primarily those with an implied female address. While most often the fetishization of the white male body is still accompanied by violence, mutilation, and the kinetic drive of narrative, there are examples of moments when the white male body is offered up as pure sex object in a manner that is in obvious dialogue with the jeans and underwear advertisements of the late '80s onward.

The example that springs most readily to mind is *Thelma and Louise*, Ridley Scott's feminist road movie cum Western, which features Brad Pitt, who, in the same year, found fame for his appearance in the Levi jeans advertisement "Camera." Brad Pitt's character, J.D., is first introduced through Thelma's (Geena Davies's) active desiring gaze, as she asks Louise (Susan Sarandon), "Did you see his butt?" In the celebrated sex scene, in which J.D. gives Thelma what became known as the $6,000 orgasm, the film joins *American Gigolo* (1980) in being one of the few films to posit the function of the male body as being to give pleasure to women.[23] Counter to Mulvey's schema, it is J.D.'s body that initially freezes the narrative: in a three-quarter shot, the camera lingers over his bare chest and unbuttoned jean flies, much like the Levi advertisements to which the film intertextually refers, before slowly panning upward, caressing the undulations of his sculptured physique, which is noticeably slimmer than the pumped-up bodies showcased in the male-addressed action movies of the period. J.D. does not return the gaze of the camera, but stares off-screen at what later turns out to be Thelma lying down before him. As he pulls her towards him, the camera then focuses on Thelma's taut stomach muscles, a parallel shot that draws attention to the similarities rather than differences with which the male and female body are fragmented in this scene. Nonetheless, the camera's gaze at J.D. is objective, preventing Pitt's body from being relayed through Thelma's point of view. In this respect, the film is remarkably similar to its predecessor, *American Gigolo*, which, as Peter Lehman observes, "profoundly equivocates as it offers up Gere's body." The famed nude scene is initially filmed through his female lover's point of view, but cuts to an objective long shot when Richard Gere stands up to look outside the window, which "denies the woman's point of view and de-emphasizes the man's genitals."[24]

The more recent and patently female-addressed *Sex and the City* (2008), however, felt no such compunction concerning its sexually explicit objectification of the male body. The success of the television series—which was renowned for its audacious screening of active female desire, its frank, female-authored dialogues about sex, and its graphic sex scenes filmed from a female point of view—no doubt enabled the film to sustain this reversal of the Mulveyan paradigm, with men featuring as objects of (female) desire and/or scrutiny rather than desiring subjects. The most memorable scene from the film in this respect is when the sexually adventurous Samantha (Kim Cattrall), suffering from the frustrations of her first long-term relationship, follows her dog into the garden of her irresistible next-door neighbor, Dante (Gilles Marini), and happens upon him taking an outdoor shower. In a self-conscious reversal of gender roles, Dante's body is offered up as spectacle through Samantha's active, desiring, voyeuristic gaze, with his body fragmented into fetishized shots of his legs, buttocks, peps, and finally even a brief shot of his penis. At the same time, the humorous voiceover (the conflicted Samantha, we are told, had found her inferno), as well as Samantha's flustered, hyperbolic attempt to restrain herself, mark this scene as knowingly transgressive. In other words, it would still not seem possible to offer up the male body as an object of desire unproblematically, without recourse to humor or postmodern self-reflexivity. This is also the case with the most recent James Bond film, *Casino Royale* (2006), which finds plenty of opportunities, most obviously a protracted, highly sexualized torture scene, to showcase Daniel Craig's body, which is noticeably more pumped-up and objectified than that of James Bonds of the past. Yet, in the one scene when Bond's body is relayed through an admiring female gaze, as he slowly step out the sea in nothing but his swimming trunks, the film overtly references Ursula Andress's famed appearance in *Dr. No* (1962). This knowing, intertextual humor serves to defuse anxieties about gender reversals in a film that is definitely marketed as much to men as women.

These films are certainly illustrative of new visual codes being deployed to screen the male body in popular films, television shows, and advertisements. However, the commodifed male body is not only apparent in popular cinema in terms of visual content, but also emerges as a thematic issue, since, despite cinema's complicity in commodifying the male body, many popular films have recently addressed this tendency as a social problem as part of their ongoing narrativization of "(white) masculinity in crisis."

Anxieties of the Flesh: The Commodified White Male Body as a Social Problem

The anxieties provoked by the objectification of the white male body are inextricable from the fact that it has been the historical right of moneyed white heterosexual masculinity to represent itself as disembodied. Feminist philosophy and Derridean deconstruction have traced the ways in which the mind/body dualism of Western metaphysical thought has been gendered so as to privilege male rationality over female embodiment (a point I develop in the following chapter). While physical strength has been a determining characteristic of modern, capitalist, Western masculinities, especially working-class masculinity, the focus has often been on production and activity, along with a stoical transcendence of pain and bodily needs, which is rooted in the Christian separation of spirit and flesh. Furthermore, as Richard Dyer analyzes, the Christian spirit/flesh distinction has also meant that whiteness has been historically associated with disembodiment, since white bodies were believed to have more spiritual qualities, while black people could be "reduced (in white culture) to their bodies." This is not to suggest that Christianity is essentially a white religion, but to posit it as one of the prime discourses of white superiority deployed by colonialist and imperialist Europe. Christianity has significantly marked Western-European consciousness, and its Manichean dualisms were mapped onto racial difference, reinforcing the doctrines of racial superiority and imperialism.[25] Women and people of color, conversely, have commonly been represented as being at the mercy of their bodies. In the case of African-Americans, this notion of hyperembodiment also has its roots in slavery, where blacks were literal commodities, exploited for their labor (both in the physical and child-bearing sense). Even today, the commonly held assumption is that blacks are more "physical" than whites, not only in terms of their mythical hyperbolic sexuality, but also their alleged "natural" superior athleticism—a belief that conveniently forgets both the hard work that goes into producing such disciplined bodies and the historical reasons that might account for black sporting successes, such as assumptions embedded in the education system about black abilities, black exclusion from more cerebral professions, and sport being the only ticket out of the ghettoes for young blacks.[26]

The very fact that appeals to disembodiment have been a source of historical representational strength for normative white masculinity, allowing it to lay claim to the universal identity, suggests that its "corporealization" would necessarily provoke certain anxieties—not only through the inevitable marking of the universal body as a gendered and raced category, but also because of the fact that it would bring that body perilously close to the side of the mind/body binary historically reserved for its others, unsettling those binary operations, and by extension, white patriarchal hegemonic norms, in the process. Indeed, as Susan Faludi notes in *Stiffed*, "ornamental culture," which propagates the notion "that masculinity is something to drape over the body, . . . that manhood is displayed, not demonstrated," is certainly disruptive of conventional notions of normative masculinity, since it forces men to experience themselves as embodied erotic objects as well as desiring subjects.[27] In '90s popular cinema, these concerns are often expressed through a discourse of white male victimization, while the representational strategies used to screen the male body in such films most often refuse its overt objectification.

A key example is *The Full Monty* (1997), the comic scenarios of which work to both evoke and deny anxieties centered on the white male body. For instance, as the unemployed steel workers exercise in Gerald's gym in order to get fit for their planned strip, Lomper comments, whilst flipping through a pornographic magazine, that a model's "tits are too big," a comment that results in the following amusing dialogue:

> Dave: Well, I just pray they're a bit more understanding about us, that's all.
> Horse: You what?
> Dave: Well, they're gonna be looking at us like that, aren't they, eh? I mean, what if next Friday, 400 women turn around and say, he's too fat, he's too old, and he's a pigeon-chested little tosser? What then?
> Horse: They wouldn't say that, would they?
> Dave: Why not? He said her tits are too big.
> Lomper: That's different. We're blokes.

Of course, it turns out that things are not that different, and the thought of parading their bodies before a female audience causes Gary and his friends to experience self-consciousness about their bodies for the first time, with Dave even wrapping himself up in plastic membrane in the garden shed whilst munching miserably on a chocolate bar in a vain bid to lose weight. The film's narration of "the emergence of the working-class male body as an eroticized object" is largely represented "as a social problem,"[28] and inextricable from the gloomy backdrop of deindustrialization. Whereas these men's bodies had been essential to their identities as working-class men—most of them were skilled manual laborers—they are now called upon to fulfill a purely decorative function, a fact further symbolized by Dave's impotence, which, the film suggests, is rooted in his feelings of emasculation in a social order that denies him the right to work. Moreover, the fact that most of Gary's friends have bodies that are far from the masculine ideal suggests that their masculinity has been compromised by a society characterized by non-production, passive consumption, and domestication.

Stripping, the ultimate form of eroticized display (along with pornography), is designated as emasculating from the outset. When Gary sees a poster advertising the Chippendale male strippers, he immediately classes them as "poofs," ridicules the size of their penises ("There's nowt at the gym that'll help you there, mate"), and later protests, "You call them Chippendales men? Degrading, that's what it were." Here Gary invokes feminist rhetoric, though what the film's humor makes clear is that the male and female body have very different histories of representation.

In fact, despite *The Full Monty*'s discursive suggestion that male bodies are now treated in the same ways as female ones, its representational strategies tell a different story, since the camera does not eroticize the bodies of its male characters. In part, this is attributable to the legacy of British "New Wave" social realism, which cast ordinary-looking actors in its attempt to distinguish itself from Hollywood. Indeed, most humor in the film stems from the fact that Gary's crew are the unlikeliest bunch of strippers imaginable, except for Guy, who later turns out to be gay. Gary and Lomper are scrawny and pasty-white, Gerald and Horse are middle-aged, while Dave is overweight. As a consequence, there is none of the lingering, fetishistic camerawork deployed in *Thelma and Louise*. Rather, during the auditions, when a panel of Gary, Gerald, Dave, and Nathan determine whether those auditioning have good enough bodies or stripping potential, the gazes of the panel are filmed through medium-long and long shots that do not belong to any individual character, thereby defusing a scene with great potential homoerotic anxiety. Similar objective medium-long and long shots are deployed when the men first strip down to their underpants in front of each other. Comedy also mitigates against the possibility of same-sex desire as Dave mutters, "No looking and no laughing, you bastards," Gerald laments, "I used to have a proper job, me," and the men ridicule each other's physique. Only Guy stands up proud, exhibiting his toned, muscular torso. The implied female audience of the strip scene itself, as Kate Domaille notes, does allow more close-ups and bodily fragmentation,[29] though despite the fetishistic police uniforms and leather thongs, this scene, which concludes with a freeze frame revealing a line of naked male buttocks filmed from a long shot, is played for its comic value, as the inter-cutting shots of the laughing audience ensure.

The men's lack of concern about their appearance before they embarked on the strip performance (with the exception of Guy) works to render them authentic in an increasingly inauthentic world. The film is thus infused with melodramatic nostalgia for a time when male bodies were more than pure surface. *Fight Club*'s Tyler Durden, as we have seen, harbors a similar lament, positing violence as a means of reestablishing the body as a site of male agency. The yuppie serial killer narrator of *American Psycho* (2000), Patrick Bateman (Christian Bale), also regards violence, in this case the grizzly dismembering of mainly female victims, as a way in which men can experience the real of the male body and affirm the differences between the sexes in hyperreal culture, a point I further explore in chapter 8. The penetration of consumerism into every facet of '80s yuppie culture is conveyed through the scene in which, as Bateman gets ready for work, his voiceover recites a numbingly boring list of the beauty products he uses. The film would thus seem to concur with Gail Faurschou, who, following Jean Baudrillard, proclaims that "[p]ostmodernity then is no longer an age in which bodies produce commodities, but where commodities produce bodies."[30] The inauthenticity of yuppie culture is also evoked through the fact that, while Bateman and his friends rampantly consume, they are never shown producing; rather their working day consists of an endless round of compliments on appearance, along with attempts to make reservations at exclusive restaurants. As Benjamin Scott King observes in his discussion of the '80s TV series *Miami Vice*, the man as consumer not only violates the traditional gendering of the production/consumption binary, but also brings a crisis in the arena that traditionally distanced men from consumption and helped define their masculinity—their work.[31]

The Real Blonde (Tom DiCillo 1997), a satirical, parodic examination of the American glamour industry, is also concerned with authenticity, or the lack thereof, particularly as regards the male body. The film pivots around the relationship between a struggling actor, Jo (Matthew Modine), an archetypal "angry young man," and Mary (Catherine Keener), a make-up artist, though the "battle of the sexes" narrative screens other concerns about white heterosexual masculinity, which, as with *The Full Monty*, focus relentlessly on the white male body. This angst comes to the fore when the only part Jo is offered is that of an extra in a Madonna video, where even Madonna proves to be a stand-in who, not coincidentally, is not a real blonde. Jo may be one of hundreds of men to appear in the video, but he is the only one to turn up pasty-white in striped boxer shorts: all the other men are tanned, toned, and decked out in tight briefs. Jo, whose body is never eroticized by the camera, is soon sent to the back of the stage because he doesn't have the "right kind of ass." The central role allotted to the "to-be-looked-at-ness" of the male body in this superficial world (where the female model who claims to be "a spiritual person" quotes from Disney's *The Little Mermaid*) is furthered in the photo-shoots that Mary attends. Here, male models elicit more attention than female ones, and the female photographer frequently reminds them that what she wants is "beautiful, tight abs." The artificiality of these bodies is underscored when a make-up artist sprays them with paint to highlight muscle tone. The link between a well-built physique and normative masculinity is further debunked when a camp Italian model farts during a photo-shoot, promptly bursts into tears, and then rushes off into the arms of his gay partner for consolation, mortified that he has passed wind before a lady. Like *The Full Monty*, then, *The Real Blonde* suggests that normative masculinity does not sit comfortably with the commodified male body. However, although both films articulate concerns about male sexuality in a manner which debunks myths about phallic male subjectivity, they do so in narratives that ridicule the objectified male body, in part through designating it homosexual, while offering a comic, feel-good factor through the ultimate triumph of the "ordinary" male protagonists. In the case of *The Real Blonde*, only Jo's masculinity is coded as authentic: he is the film's only "real blonde."

It is not coincidental, therefore, that the actors who end up dancing with Madonna in the video are not only represented as gay, but are also black. Like *The Full Monty*—where Dave asks his wife if she would ever consider going out with a black man because of their great bodies—*The Real Blonde* rehearses anxieties that the white male body is unable to measure up (literally) to its black other, an anxiety that is always undergridded by the mythology of the black male penis. As Kaja Silverman puts it:

> The differentiation of the white man from the black man on the basis of the black man's hyperbolic penis consequently reverberates in disturbing ways within the domain of gender. It places the white man on the side of "less" rather than "more," and so, threatens to erase the distinction between him and the white woman. This is the primary reason, I would argue, why the body of the

black man disrupts the unity of the white male corporeal ego.[32]

In the case of *The Full Monty*, one can only speculate how the film would have been different had the original idea of an all-black cast been adhered to. As it is, the sole black male character, Horse, so-named, the men speculate, because of his "big wanger," buys a penis pump because of his fears of inadequacy. Indeed, while his presumably self-chosen nick-name attests to his own ideological investment in prevalent notions of black hypersexuality,[33] the film in fact demystifies the stereotype, though in a way that might well complicate representations of black masculinity, but also risks emasculating him, thereby allaying white male paranoia.

Once Gary announces they will be going "full monty," the penis and its discontents concern all the male characters except for Guy, who can't sing or dance, but promptly lands the job of stripper when he drops his pants to reveal his wares (off-screen, of course), the size of which can be gauged by the gaping astonishment of the auditioning panel and Gary's quip: "Gentlemen, the lunchbox has landed!" When Gerald first overhears Gary's money-making scheme, he jokes that the audience will have to bring their own microscopes. Later, though, Gerald panics about having an erection on stage, and Lomper worries that women will come armed with scissors. On the one hand, such anxieties disrupt the phantasmatic penis-phallus equation, and reveal how profoundly this equation alienates men from their own bodies.[34] Yet, on the other hand, the fact that the entire narrative thrust of the film builds up to the pseudo-revelation of the male genitals works to reaffirm the import of the penis, allotting it the quintessential role in defining male sexuality. In this sense, *The Full Monty* illustrates Peter Lehman's argument that images of the male body are trapped by the dichotomy of spectacular phallic power or its collapse in the same way that the representation of woman is shaped by the mother/whore dichotomy.[35]

Richard Dyer, following Jacques Lacan, has argued that "the penis isn't a patch on the phallus," since "[t]he limp penis can never match up to the mystique that has kept it hidden from view for the last couple of centuries."[36] Peter Lehman similarly argues that the revelation of the male genitals always risks upsetting the penis-phallus equation upon which patriarchy is founded.[37] It is thus important that despite *The Full Monty*'s willingness to narrate the men's failure to measure up to the phallic fantasy, *visually* the penis is still kept under wraps: in the climactic performance, as the men strip down from their police uniforms (that in the world of the male sex industry have always worked to eroticize state power and institutionalized male authority), police helmets shield the penis from view, and once the helmets are flung aside, we, unlike the intra-diegetic spectators, are only offered a view from behind. In this respect, *The Full Monty* joins countless other films, such as *Basic Instinct* (1992) and *The Piano* (1993), in displaying their stars through rear nudity but shying away from frontal shots. Obviously, a lot of these choices are informed through censorship laws— the display of the male sexual organ normally immediately pushes the film into a

NC-17 ratings category, thereby reducing its ticket sales—a fact that in itself is an indication of the taboo that still surrounds the male genitalia. When Hollywood does occasionally reveal a brief glimpse of male members, they are normally on the large side, and, as Lehman notes, Hollywood now even has a company called Nude Male Casting that specializes in providing men sufficiently endowed and willing to appear in full frontal nudity whilst flaccid.[38] Moreover, unlike art and independent cinema, if Hollywood cinema does expose the male genitals, that revelation is most often designed to shock, and in order to by-pass censorship, the penis is often a prosthetic, as in the case of *Boogie Nights* or *Fight Club*'s final shot, a shot which would seem to reinforce the narrator's postmodern anxiety that everything (even the phallus?) "is a copy of a copy of a copy." As Lee Parpart puts it,

> Hollywood and its semi-independent outskirts may *think* they are ready to embrace new scripts of masculinity by exposing the penis in ways that signal a rejection or distancing from patriarchal concepts of phallic power, but often the organ in question turns out to be a safe, plastic, or barely visible substitute—a fleeting copy of a copy, rather than an image carrying any kind of potentially de-phallicizing, indexical relation to a bodily real.[39]

In the case of *Boogie Nights*, the penis of porn star Dirk Diggler is only revealed in the final minute of the film, though its size is connoted throughout by reaction shots that imply its phallic mystique. However, while the prosthetic itself confirms the "size matters" mantra of the pornography industry, I would like to qualify Parpart's reading; while the exposure scene does not dephallicize the bodily organ, neither does it phallicize it. Indeed, I would join Susan Bordo in noting that "despite its dimensions, Diggler's penis is no masterful tool. It points downwards, weighted with expectation, with shame, looking tired and used."[40] Moreover, earlier the film had screened Dirk's inability to get an erection, caused by anxiety at increased competition from upcoming stars. It therefore joins a host of other contemporary films, such as *The Full Monty*, *Human Traffic* (1999), *How to Kill Your Neighbor's Dog* (2000), *Alfie* (2004), and *The Real Blonde*, that deal with the issue of (white) male impotence, albeit in comic scenarios. As Judith Halberstam puts it, "[i]n the age of viagra and penile enlargements, we might argue, male sexuality and male masculinity in general tends to be a medicated affair in all kinds of situations, and the apparent fragility of erectile function might stand as a symbol for other kinds of masculine vulnerabilities that move far beyond the psychoanalytic formulation of castration anxiety."[41]

All of these body anxiety films engage with the threat posed by the commodification of extra-ordinary white male bodies to "ordinary" white men. However, despite these discursive concerns, the majority of these films do not deploy the fetishistic camerawork that is still used for female stars as a matter of course. Furthermore, most of the films I discussed above, with the exception of the female-addressed *Thelma and Louise* and *Sex and the City*, unfold in nostalgic narratives of white male disenfranchisement. I now wish to turn my attention to action films, the primary feature film genre for showcasing the white male body, albeit through complex and multi-faceted processes of disavowal. These films, of course, have been highly complicit in the circulation of white male bodies as images for visual consumption. By the '90s, however, the parodic strategies deployed in the genre suggest a certain difficulty in taking representations of pumped-up, hypermasculinity seriously, though I argue at the end of this chapter that representations of unified, unreconstructed masculinity seem to have made a comeback at the end of the decade with the return of the epic genre.

White Male Bodies in Action

The '80s was the decade of the action movie, as Hollywood lavished huge budgets on expensive spectacles and notched up box-office successes on an unprecedented scale.[42] The "high concept" action movie was disparaged by many theorists because of its popular appeal, its prioritizing of box-office takings over artistic integrity, and its alleged abandonment of narrative and reliance on special effects—accounts which overlook not only the visual, aural, haptic, and corporeal pleasures of cinematic spectatorship, but also the fact that "[i]n action films, the plot advances *through* spectacle; the spectacular elements are, generally speaking, as 'narrativized' as are the less ostentatious spaces of other genres."[43] In conjunction with explosive special effects, one of the major spectacles, of course, is that of the male body as it moves through time and space, often at vertiginous speeds, in chase scenes or intricately choreographed fight scenes, performing nigh-impossible feats, inflicting or enduring pain, capturing the spectator in a sadomasochistic visual economy. The star body functions as text, narrativizing the discipline and effort that went into its creation, as well as forming sites across and through which discourses of gender, race, class, age, and nation are inscribed.

The overt display of the muscular bodies of key '80s stars, such as Sylvester Stallone, Arnold Schwarzenegger, Jean-Claude Van Damme, and Bruce Willis, must be understood in the context of the increased commodification of the white male body. Not only do these bodies function as the prime attraction of the films, but they are also screened using some similar codes as the advertisements that I have analyzed above, in conjunction with other representational practices that work to disavow their erotic objectification. As Yvonne Tasker notes in her influential *Spectacular Bodies: Gender, Genre and the Action Cinema* (1993), "[a]s with the figure of the showgirl that Laura Mulvey refers to in classic Hollywood films, contemporary American action movies work hard, and often at the expense of narrative development, to contrive situations for the display of the hero's body."[44] The sheer physicality of the genre means that action heroes inevitably glisten with sweat, and soon strip to the waist or a vest T-Shirt, revealing their immaculate and sculptured torsos. The narrative justification for this might be quite flimsy, such as the hyperbolic example from *Lethal Weapon*

(1987) when Riggs (Mel Gibson) rips his shirt off for no apparent reason before grappling with his adversary Joshua (Gary Busey) in wet mud, under a jet of water spurting out from a broken hydrant, in a scene that cannot escape homoerotic implications—hence the homophobic humor of the film, which works to ward off homoerotic anxiety.[45] This example is also interesting in view of the fact that Murtaugh (Danny Glover), Riggs's older, paternalistic African-American partner, merely spectates at a distance. As Tasker puts it, "[t]he scene offers an image of the sexual-power relations of the inter-racial buddie pairing in microcosm. Whilst the white male hero shows off his body, his black buddie stands back, a protective figure who watches from the sidelines."[46] Even though Danny Glover is more powerfully built than Mel Gibson, his body is never eroticized through fragmentary shots or phallic imagery.[47]

As with male advertising models, the action hero's body is marked by its hardness, rendered through the tautening of muscles required for the handling of guns, the punching of fists, or the demonstration of physical prowess that the narratives demand. The camera also tends to fragment male bodies, albeit in a different way to the conventional representation of the female form, lingering over flexed muscles or fetishizing phallic weaponry. (Indeed, if fetishization of the female body wards off castration anxiety in Mulvey's account,[48] fetishization of the male body would seem to disavow the male spectator's knowledge that no one possesses the phallus). These are also bodies in motion, pulled along by frenetic, fast-cut action sequences with thunderous soundtracks, a sensation-overload that works to justify the display of the male body in a genre primarily aimed at a teenage male audience.

Without doubt, the most famous action heroes of the '80s were Sylvester Stallone and Arnold Schwarzenegger, whose iconic bodies must be among the most widely reproduced and consumed images of the last two decades. Ironically, therefore, the very bodies which reaffirm the physical values of white heterosexual masculinity within the films' narratives are also implicated in its commodification and virtualization. As Tasker notes, these pumped-up bodies must be understood in a context in which "bodybuilding as a practice and competitive sport have . . . shifted from freakish marginality to the mainstream of western health culture."[49] Nonetheless, male bodybuilding still straddles contradictory terrain as regards traditional understandings of gendered bodies, since it connotes both masculine activity due to the strenuous (and masochistic) regime that sculpting the body demands, but also passivity and narcissism (culturally aligned with the feminine), since those bodies are constructed primarily to be displayed. This instability is evident in the way that female bodybuilders are often considered masculine, while male bodybuilders are equally as likely to be designated feminine. For instance, Tasker quotes an article from the *Guardian* on *Rambo*, which claims that Stallone's "enormous breasts loom over the screen like Jane Russell in *The Outlaw*."[50] The fact that bodybuilding can be perceived as masculinizing women and feminizing men points to the way in which conceptions of the body are steeped in a binary logic of active/passive, masculine/feminine that has served the patriarchal order, but one which is being increasingly challenged. As Tasker notes, "[w]ith critics caught between breasts and biceps, it is clear that both active and passive, both feminine and masculine terms, inform the imagery of the male body in the action cinema."[51] Moreover, bodybuilding obviously points to the constructedness of the body, carrying the signs of labor required for its formation. For this reason, the bodies of white action stars have aroused, and continue to arouse, sustained, often conflicting critical commentary.

This is most evident in the divergent critical readings that Stallone and Schwarzenegger have provoked. As Tasker points out, the popularity of these stars has been understood both as an assertion of a reactionary, patriarchal, military, nationalistic masculinity, and as a hysterical parody of masculinity.[52] In *Hard Bodies: Hollywood Masculinity in the Reagan Era* (1994), for instance, Susan Jeffords traces the correlation between the "hard bodies" that dominated '80s action cinema and the era that witnessed a resurgence of national and masculine power, both of which were embodied by the president Ronald Reagan, who self-consciously distinguished himself from the "soft" Jimmy Carter.[53] Within this framework, the whiteness of these "hard bodies" is inextricable from the narratives of U.S. imperialism in which they appear. For instance, Stallone's two most famous roles have him triumph over ethnic and/or racial others— Vietnamese and Russian soldiers in *Rambo: First Blood Part II* (1985) and *Rambo III* (1988), and black and Russian opponents in the *Rocky* series. Stallone's tendency to play working-class characters also serves to render him authentic in the face of his "to-be-looked-at-ness." As Tasker notes, along with black bodies, white working-class bodies are always "perceived through an accumulated history of sexual myths and stereotypes," and thus "tell powerful stories of subjection and resistance, so that muscles function both to give the action hero the power to resist, at the same time as they confirm him in a position that defines him almost exclusively through the body."[54] Against the Vietnamese and Russian armies, equipped with the latest technology, Rambo, as lone warrior, relies on his body and the weaponry attached to it, allowing him to triumph in the old-fashioned way—through blood, sweat, and hard graft. As I noted in chapter 2, many critics have suggested that the masochistic battering that his body is subjected to works to displace homoerotic desire, prove his virility through endurance, and allegorize the remasculinization and reinvigoration of the nation.[55] Schwarzenegger has also stood in for the national body in many films, despite his Austrian roots (a fact his appointment as Governor of California only reinforces). For Lynda Boose, "the Schwarzenegger accent, physique, and even the mechanization of the characters he plays are indissociable from the Nazi dream of domination that America's wars in the Third World covertly play out," an association that extra-textual knowledge of Schwarzenenegger's right-wing politics does little to offset.[56] Similarly, bodybuilding inevitably conjures up the Nazi idealization of the white male body, further reinforced by Schwarzenegger's Aryan looks.

Other critics, however, have argued that these hypermasculine bodies are indicative of the contemporary crisis in masculinity in the postmodern era. In "The Signification of the Phallus" Lacan stressed that the male subject only postures at possessing the phallus, an assertion that has been used in cultural and gender studies to extend Joan Riviere's famed theorization of femininity as masquerade to masculinity.[57] Barbara Creed, for instance, argues that Stallone and Schwarzenegger, both of whom resemble "an anthropomorphised phallus," "are simulacra of an exaggerated masculinity, the original completely lost to sight, a causality of the failure of the paternal signifier and the current crisis in master narratives."[58] Queer theorist Mark Simpson also notes that "exaggerated 'masculine' signification" often verges on camp.[59] The apparent paradox—the more prevalent images of phallic masculinity are, the more indicative they are of a crisis—is inextricable from the central contradiction at the heart of masculinity: as Lynn Segal puts it, "the more it asserts itself, the more it calls itself into question."[60]

As Tasker suggests, rather than an "either/or" approach, which chooses between these two seemingly non-commensurate readings, it is more useful to "examine the ways in which [the muscular action hero] represents both [readings], as well as being produced by the ongoing and unsteady relationship between these, and other, images of masculinity."[61] This framework is particularly useful for an analysis of the '90s action hero, not merely because displays of the hyperphallic white male body seemed to require extensive use of self-reflexive jokes or parody, but also because white male bodies were increasingly played off against competing images of masculinity, including action heroes of color and muscular action heroines, who staked a place in the genre in the '90s. *Terminator 2: Judgment Day* (James Cameron 1991) offers a prime example of this shift in representational practices.

Re-Determining White Masculinity: *Terminator 2: Judgment Day*

The opening scene of *Terminator 2* showcases Schwarzenegger's iconic physique by featuring the terminator arriving naked in the fetal position after traveling back to the film's narrative present. The terminator then enters a bikers' bar in order to demand clothes, boots, and a motorcycle from a butch Hell's Angel—costume and props that define his masculinity throughout the remainder of the film. From the moment the terminator enters the bar, his naked body, filmed in a medium shot so that his expansive peps fill the screen, is subjected to relentless scrutiny; while the male bikers look on with aggressive incredulity, the women respond with more appreciative stares, most notably the waitress who looks down to the place the camera never exposes with an approving smile, suggesting that his cybernetically produced body is substantially more generously endowed than the average human one. The bikers in the bar are quick to prove their manhood, though their macho posturing only betrays the phallic lack which fetishistic paraphernalia (guns, knives, leather, bikes, cigars) attempt to belie. Predictably, the bikers come off the worse in the fight scene that ensues, a scene that confirms that Schwarzenegger's muscles perform a more than ornamental function, and that displaces any anxiety of witnessing a naked Schwarzenegger wrestling with leather-clad bikers onto violent spectacle in the manner that Steve Neale has theorized. But immediately following this sequence, the scene swiftly reverts to parody. As the terminator leaves, the extradiegetic soundtrack blares out the blues classic "Bad to the Bones," while the camera lingers first on his motorcycle boots before tilting up his leather-clad body, a pastiche of the camerawork employed in the Western in order to emphasize the hero's stature. When ordered to stop by a huge, bearded biker brandishing a gun, the terminator walks over and, in Eastwoodesque silence, swipes the weapon, and then seizes the biker's sunglasses, donning them with incongruous satisfaction, the suggestion being that this terminator, unlike his predecessor, takes narcissistic pride in his appearance. The Western allusions then continue as Schwarzenegger straddles his motorbike and rides off into the distance.

Richard Dyer has suggested that such tongue-in-cheek humor in action cinema, also evident, for instance, in the *Indiana Jones* or *Die Hard* series, suggests that "the values of masculine physicality are harder to maintain straightfacedly and unproblematically" in an age "of microchips and the large scale growth (in the USA) of women in traditionally male occupations."[62] While I think this to be the case, I would also join Tasker in arguing that self-reflexive jokes perform a double function; they work both to deconstruct the filmic text, but also to pre-empt and thus deflect criticism.[63] Indeed, such facetious or parodic moments tend to last only for a few minutes, allowing film texts to "[cite their] own macho excessiveness, [joke] about it, and then [enact] it with a clearer conscience."[64] Indeed, the dismal box office performance of *The Last Action Hero* (1993), the film that has Schwarzenegger relentlessly parody his own star image, suggests that total parody did not sit well with Schwarzenegger fans. Nonetheless, while *Terminator 2*'s self-reflexive catch-phrases ("I'll be back," "Hasta la vista, baby") or pastiching of the Western might work to legitimize its screening of the semi-naked male body and ritualistic violence, the fact that legitimization is deemed necessary is itself suggestive of the fact that contemporary representations of corporeal, violent masculinity are well aware of the critiques they might provoke.

While Dyer is right to attribute the action movie's recourse to parody to changing definitions of masculinity caused by technological developments and shifts in gender relations, generic revisions, which, of course, are themselves rooted in social change, also need to be taken into account. The '90s witnessed new action formats in which the white hero not only shared the screen with action heroines (*The Terminator, Terminator 2, The Matrix*) and action heroes of color (*Lethal Weapon, Die Hard: With a Vengeance, Training Day*), but, in some cases, was also supplanted by them (the *Alien* series, *The Long Kiss Goodnight, Murder at 1600, Bad Boys, Rush Hour, Avon Flux*). *Terminator 2* offers an interesting example of the action heroine, who, since the phenomenal success of Ripley (Sigourney Weaver) in *Alien* (1979), is now as common as her male counterpart, even if she often still plays second fiddle to the male lead. As with the male hero, the action heroine's body is inscribed in and through both action and display, and may escape the more traditional fetishization that Mulvey located in mainstream cinema's screening of the female body. At the same time, many contemporary films, such as *Charlie's Angels* (2000) and *Lara Croft: Tomb Raider* (2001), cast their heroines as active narrative agents but in parodic scenarios that offer up "eye-candy," insistently eroticizing the heroine through tight, fetishistic, leather outfits, and plunging, cleavage-displaying necklines. The more masculine, muscular action heroine, however, evident in films such as the *Alien* series, *Strange Days* (1995), and *G.I. Jane* (1997), does much to trouble conventional representations of gendered bodies. *Terminator 2*, in particular, seems to me to mark a decisive break, since Sarah Connor's (Linda Hamilton's) body is insistently masculinized in the film, not merely through the display of Sarah's pumped-up muscles, but more insistently through the deployment of visual codes conventionally reserved for male heroes. As I hope to illustrate, the masculinization of the action heroine destabilizes ontological discourses of the body in a way that cannot but impact on the screening of the body of the male hero.

The first glimpse of Sarah Connor is set in the psychiatric hospital to which she has been committed for suffering from paranoid delusions that a nuclear blast, initiated by the machines, will destroy most of humanity in the year 1997. From a long shot of the hospital building, the voyeuristic camera zooms in through Sarah's cell window, closes in on her developed shoulder and arm muscles, and then pulls back to view her in the process of doing chin-ups against her upturned bed frame. A few scenes later, Sarah is shown watching one of her counseling sessions on video as she describes the repeated dream she experiences about the War of Judgment Day. Criminal psychologist Dr. Silberman (Earl Boen) then pauses the video, leaving a frozen image of Sarah's aggressive expression captured while she insisted on how "fucking real" her dream would be for anyone not wearing "two million factor sun block," an image that lingers whilst Dr. Silberman interviews her to decide whether her improved behavior will allow her to be moved into a minimum security wing of the hospital and receive visits from her son John (Edward Furlong). The self-reflexivity of this scene is not confined to us watching Sarah watching herself on video, however, but multi-layered: as the camera pulls back, it becomes evident that Sarah is again filmed by the hospital staff, and some of our access to this scene begins to be mediated through this secondary video screen. When Sarah's request to see her son is refused, she lunges at Dr. Silberman, her face deliberately juxtaposed with the aggressive image left frozen on the video. Her attack causes chaos, which is also filmed intradiegetically, as she wrestles with the staff who rush to save the ineffectual doctor from her grasp. What interests me here is the inability of the intradiegetic cinematic apparatus to subject Sarah to its gaze, an inability which provides a self-reflexive comment on the difficulties caused to traditional codes of cinematic representation when the binaries of active/passive are no longer yoked to a male/female matrix.

Unlike *The Terminator* (1984), in which Sarah first appears as a dizzy, clumsy waitress who unwillingly takes on her role of "mother of the future," by the time of the second film, released seven years later, Sarah has transformed into a muscular, military expert who smokes, swears, orders men around, has no truck with sexual encounters, and is persistently masculinized throughout the film, even referred to as a "son of a bitch" by a female nurse. It is the radical muscularization of Sarah's body that is the most significant development, however, a transformation that gave Linda Hamilton immediate iconic status. Most strikingly, the film deploys the same visual codes normally reserved for the action hero's body. For instance, when Sarah cleans a gun in a sleeveless T-Shirt, the camera lingers over the curves of her rigid, sinewy, veiny arm and shoulder muscles rather than her breasts and legs. Sarah's body is also progressively mutilated in the male hero tradition, proving her ability to "take it like a man." A more humorous and self-conscious example of this process can be found in *The Long Kiss Goodnight* (1996): refusing to give in to the men that torture her for information, Charly (Geena Davies) responds with the insult "suck my dick," also uttered by Demi Moore's female soldier in *G.I. Jane* (1997), a term that, delivered by a male, insults through its homosexual slur, but whose patent misapplication in Charly's case points to her self-styled masculine performance. Indeed, unlike Mulvey's female star, who presents the male viewer with the threat of castration, the action heroine seems to present the threat of female phallicization.

Certain critics have advanced the notion that action heroines like Sarah Connor or Ripley in the *Aliens* series are actually "substitute males," and object to the fact that for a heroine to perform effectively in the action genre she must be masculinized. Certainly, by referring to muscular heroines as "masculinized," we risk reinforcing traditional dualisms. To avoid such binarisms, Yvonne Tasker coins the term "musculinity" to refer to the qualities associated with masculinity that are written over the female body, stating that "'[m]usculinity' indicates the way in which the signifiers of strength are not limited to the male characters."[65] However, as certain queer theorists have pointed out, "female masculinity" (Judith Halberstam's term, which deliberately yokes together a biological and social category in order to destabilize the two) does not make the masculinized woman a man; rather, the dissonance between sex and gender can queer ontological discourses by underscoring the performativity of gender (see chapter 5). However, as Judith Halberstam claims, sexuality determines the subversive potential of these representations. She notes that the buffed Ripley and Sarah Connor offer approved versions of female masculinity that are rendered tame by their heterosexuality, and only in *Alien Resurrection* (1997), in which Ripley flirts with co-star Wynona Ryder, does Ripley's masculinity become threatening or "alien."[66] Nonetheless, the fact that both these action heroines,

Ripley and Sarah Connor, became immediate lesbian icons attests to the opposi-tional readings available in mainstream texts. It is also the case that, once femi-ninity and masculinity are understood as performative categories, the meanings that can be assigned to bodies become unstable and disruptive of the heterosex-ual hegemony, as I illustrate further in chapter 5. For instance, in his queer read-ing of *Terminator 2*, Jonathan Goldberg notes that Schwarzenegger's fetishistic biker gear feeds into images of a butch gay S&M leather man.[67] The film thus unleashed certain images that it was unable to contain.

For this reason, cinematic representations of "female masculinity" have profound ramifications for the representation of the bodies and masculinities of the male characters, revealing that muscularity is not an exclusively male pre-serve. This is made patently clear in a scene in *Aliens* (1986): when Private Vasquez (Jenette Goldstein), a butch, Latina, female soldier with cropped hair, is asked by a male colleague if she has ever been mistaken for a man, she dryly responds, "No, have you?" Moreover, as Jonathan Goldberg argues, pumped-up female bodies not only disrupt patriarchal definitions of femininity, but also point to the fact that "hypermasculinity always transgresses, refuses, and ex-ceeds the phallic measure."[68] This is precisely the case in *Terminator 2*. Sarah's "musculinized" body partly accounts for the film's parodic humor in screening the terminator's excessive masculinity, since she foregrounds the constructed-ness of his hyperphallic body. That said, it is important to join Chris Holmlund in noting that the designation of masculinity as performative does not necessarily rob it of its force, as the adolescent male idolization of Stallone and Schwar-zenegger indicates, and can express nostalgia for a lost "original" identity.[69] In-deed, despite parodic gestures, gender norms are ultimately confirmed by the end of *Terminator 2*: just as Sarah is about to blast the T1000 away, she runs out of bullets and is promptly rescued by the terminator.

The film's discourse on paternity and maternity also goes some way to rein-scribing the conventional gender roles that Sarah's muscularity risks destabiliz-ing. Sarah's desire to protect her son "explains" her militarized "masculinity" and violence; as with *Aliens*, *Strange Days*, and *The Long Kiss Goodnight*, the action heroine is a maternal figure and thus reassuringly still very much "a woman." At the same time, though, Sarah does not represent an image of moth-erhood that sits comfortably with conservative, domestic ideologies. Sarah is also marginalized in her role as mother through the terminator's role as substi-tute father for her son John. This remarkable reversal of the terminator from kil-ler of unborn child in the first movie to idealized father figure in the second is regarded by Susan Jeffords as indicative of a general trend in action movies: whereas masculinity in the '80s was transcribed through the spectacle of physi-cal toughness, the '90s gave way to a more internalized masculine dimension that focused on ethical dilemmas and emotional traumas. For Jeffords, *Termina-tor 2* offers the politically safe solution of "individualism as fathering" as "an alternative to the declining workplace and national structures as sources of mas-culine authority and power."[70] Certainly, the current fusion of the action movie with melodrama common to films such as *Die Hard* (1988), *True Lies* (1994), *Face/Off* (1997), *The Day After* (2004), and *Poseidon* (2006), whose plots revolve around "threats to the family and domesticity,"[71] are suggestive of new representational codes of masculinity in the genre in addition to the spectacle of the pumped-up, hyperphallic body. However, as Stella Bruzzi notes, the integration of the more sensitive male offers "only one aspect of how masculinity and fatherhood has shifted in recent years,"[72] as I hope to show in my discussion of the epic revival at the end of this chapter.

As well as being played off against the vulnerable human bodies of Sarah, the young John Connor, and Dr. Miles Dyson (Joe Morton), the black computer technician who shakes with fear when Sarah threatens to kill him, the terminator is also played off against the only other significant adult white male character: the shape-shifting T1000 terminator (Robert Patrick), whose slimmer, permeable, malleable body forms a stark contrast with the solid, impervious body of Schwarzenegger's T101 model. In *Electronic Eros: Bodies and Desire in the Postindustrial Age* (1996), Claudia Springer has argued that iron-clad cyborgs in films like *The Terminator* series and *Robocop* (1987) "perpetuate and even exaggerate the anachronistic industrial-age metaphor of externally forceful masculine machinery, expressing nostalgia for a time when masculine superiority was taken for granted and an insecure man needed only to look at technology for the power of phallic strength."[73] Springer regards the recycling of phallic imagery from Western society's industrial past as an attempt to cling onto outdated sex roles and disavow the fact that electronic technology is culturally coded as feminine due to its minuteness, passivity, internalization, and fluidity. *Terminator 2* enacts a showdown between industrial/mechanic and electronic/cyber technologies played out over the white male bodies of the terminators and the two different types of masculinity they represent.[74] Schwarzenegger's cyborg is an older model but ultimately defeats the liquid-metal T1000. The T1000 is also played by a much slimmer, mercurial Robert Patrick, whom Cameron reportedly chose because of "his catlike qualities."[75] The T1000's body, which is coded as monstrous precisely because of its formlessness, instability, and leakiness—qualities historically associated with the feminine—airs anxieties about the challenges to traditional white masculinity posed by a technologized and, cyberfeminists would claim, feminized world. On an extra-textual level, the fact that Schwarzenegger's solid, muscular body is known to be flesh and blood (however "constructed" it may be), while the T1000's is a product of the latest special effects technology, further posits Schwarzenegger's cyborg as more authentic. The threat posed by electronic culture is also paralleled with the threat posed by the commodification of the male body in a brief but significant moment when the T1000 looks inquisitively at a metal shop mannequin that bears a resemblance to his own metal figure. The fact that the evil, technologically-superior terminator in *Terminator 3: Rise of the Machines* (2003) is embodied by a woman only lends more credence to this reading, articulating the fear that a future in which muscles are rendered obsolete might also render men themselves unnecessary.

White Male Bodies in the Contemporary Epic Film

In the following chapter I will focus on the shift in the science fiction genre to slimmed-down, flexible white male bodies in virtual reality fantasies, where physical strength is theoretically redundant. Before that, however, I wish to discuss a competing trend: that of the resurgence of the epic genre, in which muscles, physical prowess, and bodily display constitute essential signifiers of white male power, and in which the parody that accompanies the visual or phallic excesses of many '80s and '90s action films is no longer deemed necessary.

Writing in 2000, Steve Neale noted that the term "epic" is essentially used to refer to '50s and '60s films with "historical, especially ancient-world settings" that deployed state of the art technologies and production values in their creation of large-scale stories.[76] However, since the success of key epic films such as *Braveheart* (1995), *Gladiator* (2000), and *The Lord of the Rings* trilogy (2001-02), it would seem that the genre has made a remarkable comeback in recent years (*Rob Roy, Hidalgo, The Last Samurai, King Arthur, Alexander, Troy, 300, Boewulf*).

The resurgence of the epic invites a range of (often conflicting) interpretations. Most obviously, these epic stories offer opportunities to showcase the latest special effects, namely computer-generated imagery. But on a more allegorical level, in a post-Cold-War era, it would be possible to attribute the production and new-found popularity of the epic genre to concerns about Western imperialism, evident, for instance, in *Braveheart*'s anti-English slant. More specifically, in a post-9/11 world, films such as *Troy* (2004) and *Alexander* (2004) could be regarded as mediations of imperialistic narratives, whereby older, historical stories work both to play out, but also defuse their political implications and potentially divisive effects. *Gladiator* could also be seen as offering a comment on the corruption of imperial powers, though it also suggests that the empire can be corrected and remasculinized by an honorable, extra-ordinary white man who represents the idealized imperial/national body (not dissimilar to the sentiments underpinning the *Rambo* series); at the same time, it also invites us to enjoy the extravagant splendor that was Rome, including reveling in the spectacle of gruesomely violent gladiator fights. Moreover, while *The Lord of the Rings* trilogy was in production before the 2001 attacks on the world trade center, its polarized universe, clearly demarcated along the binaries of good and evil, certainly played well into post-9/11 neo-conservative rhetoric, exemplified by George W. Bush's famous declaration that "you're either with us, or against us in the fight against terror." Indeed, Bush scripted the war as a national epic, most often deploying a Western narrative in which he was cast as chief cowboy (the president's body standing in for the national body), and according to which America would be regenerated through violence. It is also tempting to extend Jeffords's allegorical reading and regard these epic warriors as representing a return to the hard bodies of the Reagan era at a time when neo-conservatism returned with a vengeance to the U.S.[77]

At the same time, I would argue that these contemporary epic films also negotiate another set of desires to do with white heterosexual masculinity. Firstly, their historical, ancient, or fantasy settings allow the staging of a nostalgic return to a white masculinity unchallenged by gendered or raced others. These epic narratives are played out almost exclusively among the bodies of white men at a time long before or in a place without the dramas of gender and race that characterize an America long divided by culture wars and identity critiques. In the case of *The Lord of the Rings*, differences of gender, race, and ethnicity are displaced onto differences between humans and other fantastical species. The humans and other benevolent anthropomorphic species, such as the elves or hobbits, are not only overwhelmingly male, but also exclusively white, featuring not a single character of color. The Orcs and Uruk-Hai, on the other hand, and most obviously the monstrous Lurtz, whose "blazing nostrils, deadlock hair and animalistic posturing" directly invoke racist stereotypes of the "all-body negro brute," "demonstrate the film's racial hierarchy and suggested negrophbia."[78] Moreover, while *Gladiator* features one black character, Maximus's (Russell Crowe's) gladiator brother in arms, he is marginal to the main narrative, which is played out between white men, as is the case with its fellow "swords and sandals" movie *Troy*.

The revival of the epic genre also exhibits nostalgia on another level. Its past setting also articulates a desire for a time when the physical values of masculinity were assured, a time when women's role was marginal (unlike the SF genre, which most obviously showcases the female action heroine), a time before the impact of technology that questioned the relevance of physical strength to male identity. Simultaneously, though, these epics also showcase the male body, contributing to its ongoing commodification. These films thus suggest that Jeffords's assertion in 1994 that the warrior-style, rampaging masculinity of the '80s had been superseded by a softer, New Man hero was "both premature and sweeping," as Bruzzi has argued.[79] While the sensitive, more domesticated male Jeffords refers to, even in the action genre, continues to make his presence felt, it is but one of the many, often conflicting representations of white masculinity in current Hollywood production, and must be placed beside the current explosion of more primal, physical masculinities evident in the revived epic and rampage genres. Moreover, as a comparison of *Gladiator* and *Troy* reveals, white male bodies continue to invite multivalent critical responses, even in films sharing the same generic context.

As far as *Gladiator* is concerned, Martin Fradley observes that "Maximus/Crowe's star body was the focus of much critical attention during *Gladiator*'s pre-release marketing campaign," largely due to the transformation it underwent from his role in *The Insider* (1999), for which he gained considerable weight. Fradley notes that in *The Insider* the "flabby body of Crowe's protagonist figured as a visual metaphor for a compromised phallic masculinity and the perceived 'feminisation' of subjugation to a hierarchical corporate structure." Referring to Steven Cohan's assertion that the male body in the epic genre functions as a metaphor for the idealized national body, Fradley argues that Crowe's beefed up body in *Gladiator* encodes "a collective male nostalgia for a more authentic, less performative and/or consumerised and commodified nation."[80] As well as functioning as an allegory for the national body, though, Crowe's body also signals a desire for a return to a primal, physical masculinity equally untainted by commodity culture and consumerism—a similar desire to that articulated in *Fight Club*, though without the doses of parody. Furthermore, as Fradley asserts, the film's "disingenuous contempt for 'the mob' and 'feminine' mass culture, whilst wholly contradictory (though arguably self-mocking) given the hyper-commercial basis of Hollywood entertainment, also help [*sic*] structure Crowe/Maximus's masculinity, whilst simultaneously disavowing the feminizing construction of Crowe/Maximus as object of the gaze and mass-culture's commodified star."[81] Crowe's phallic masculinity and body were rapturously, even hysterically, dissected in reviews of the film.[82] Reviewers reveled in descriptions of his majestic physical presence, magnetism, charisma, commanding voice, roughness, and unreconstructed, outback masculinity.[83]

However, what is interesting about the film is that while Crowe is undeniably a strapping, solid vision of a man in the film, his body does not exhibit the sculptured muscle definition common to contemporary images of the ideal masculine body in advertising images or contemporary Hollywood films, but is rather reminiscent of earlier movie stars such as epic stars Kirk Douglas or Burt Lancaster (the film was compared to *Spartacus* and *Ben-Hur* by numerous critics). For this reason, many reviewers considered Crowe to represent a more authentic masculinity than the pumped-up, contoured body that performs a more ornamental function. Crowe's assured display of male physicality requires no parody or wisecracks; nor is his masculinity articulated as fatherhood—the murder of his wife and son is marginal to the story, though assures us of his heterosexuality and provides the trigger for the revenge plot; nor is his body obviously eroticized by fetishistic camerawork, with Crowe covered in amour throughout most of the film, exposing only his arms and lower legs. Indeed, even in the scene when he is strung up, bare-chested, in a crucifix position, a stance that is often used in action movies to showcase the rippling muscles of the male star in a masochistic spectacle, the shot is cut off at Crowe's shoulders, refusing a view of his bare torso, though the fact that he is stabbed by the evil Commodus (Joaquin Phoenix) in this scene deploys the masculinization through masochistic endurance motif of the action genre.

Brad Pitt's body in *Troy*, however, is decidedly more fetishized. Pitt's body was also the focus of media speculation and interest since Pitt apparently trained for 6 months for the part of Achilles, adding considerable bulk to his already sculptured frame. In reviews of the film, his pumped-up, bulging body was constructed as the film's major spectacle.[84] The very first shot of Brad Pitt marks him as an erotic object and features him naked, lying on his front, displaying the contours of his naked butt, entwined in the arms of two women—a stark contrast to the first glimpses of Maximus in *Gladiator* on the battlefield. Many occasions are found for Pitt's Achilles to remove his amour and reveal his famed, rippling stomach—notably beefier than in *Thelma and Louise* and *Fight Club*—which epitomizes the classical, Greek-sculpture, high-definition look of contemporary bodybuilding. His obviously dyed blonde hair and bronzed tan also recall images of the commodified body of advertising images, as does the fragmentation of his body and Hector's (Eric Bana's) as they don their armor for battle—scenes that recall the fetishization of the female body that Mulvey refers to in "Visual Pleasure and Narrative Cinema."

In the majority of reviews of the film, Brad Pitt was compared unfavorably with Crowe, with many expressing disappointment that he failed to import the primal masculinity that was such a big box-office attraction in *Gladiator*.[85] The adulation of Crowe's Maximus would seem to articulate a desire for an undiluted, corporeal, physical male presence. However, it would seem that an ancient setting is still required in order for this form of extra-ordinary white masculinity to be screened without incredulity or recourse to parodic humor. In the following chapter, though, I will focus on films set in the future that screen white male virtual bodies that might well theoretically be less reliant on physical strength, but still offer the pleasurable spectacle of the white male body on display, even as they simultaneously articulate anxieties about the impact of technology on normative masculinity.

Notes

1. Chuck Palahniuk, *Fight Club* (London: Vintage, 1997), 49.

2. Laura Mulvey, "Visual Pleasure and Narrative Cinema," in *Visual and Other Pleasures* (Houndmills, Basingstoke: Macmillan, 1989), 19-20.

3. Vicky Lebeau, *Psychoanalysis and Cinema: The Play of Shadows* (London: Wallflower, 2001), 95.

4. Laura Mulvey, "Afterthoughts on 'Visual Pleasure and Narrative Cinema' Inspired by King Vidor's *Duel in the Sun* (1946)," in *Visual and Other Pleasures* (Houndmills, Basingstoke: Macmillan, 1989), 29-38. Mulvey considers films that have a female protagonist "torn between the deep blue sea of passive femininity and the devil of regressive masculinity" (30), and addresses the issue of female pleasure that she had previously overlooked by pursuing the ways in which the female spectator can masculinize herself and identify with the male hero. Nonetheless, her binary schema is still retained. For articles on the female spectator, see Janet Bergstrom and Mary Anne Doane, eds., "The Spectatrix," special issue, *Camera Obscura: A Journal of Feminism and Film Theory* 20-21 (1989).

5. Jackie Stacey, for instance, criticizes Mulvey for her heterosexist perspective, noting that "[t]he rigid distinction between *either* desire *or* identification, so characteristic of psychoanalytic film theory, fails to address the construction of desires which involve a specific interplay of both processes." "Desperately Seeking Difference," in *The Sexual Subject: A Screen Reader in Sexuality*, ed. Mandy Merck (London: Routledge, 1992), 256. bell hooks also takes Mulvey to task for ignoring the import of race. *Black Looks: Race and Representation* (Boston: South End Press, 1992), 122-23. Feminist psychoanalytic theorists such as Elizabeth Cowie have also argued for more mobile identifications

in cinematic spectatorship. "Fantasia," in *The Woman in Question: M/F*, ed. Elizabeth Cowie and Parveen Adams (London: Verso, 1990), 149-96. For a discussion of the potential masochistic investment in cinematic spectatorship, see D. N. Rodowick, "The Difficulty of Difference," *Wide Angle* 15 (1982): 4-15; Carol Clover, *Men, Women and Chainsaws: Gender in the Modern Horror Film* (London: BFI, 1992), chap. 6.

6. Lacan makes the distinction between the look (on the side of the subject) and the gaze (on the side of the object), to which no subject has access. Jacques Lacan, "Of the Gaze as *Objet petit a*," in *The Four Fundamental Concepts of Psycho-Analysis*, trans. Alan Sheridan, ed. Jacques-Alain-Miller (London: Penguin, 1991), 65-119. The gaze marks that which is missing from representation, that which prevents the subject from seeing itself from the position from which it is seen. Joan Copjec thus argues that apparatus theory's notion that the cinematic screen functions like the mirror in Lacan's famous mirror stage moment is based on a misconception of Lacan, and "operates in ignorance of, and at the expense of, Lacan's more radical insight whereby the mirror is conceived as screen." In other words, the mirror functions as a screen that protects the subject from the fact that "beyond the visual field, there is, in fact, nothing at all." "The Orthopsychic Subject: Film Theory and the Reception of Lacan," in *Film and Theory: An Anthology*, ed. Robert Stam and Toby Miller (Malden, MA: Blackwell, 2000), 437, 450.

7. Candida Yates, *Masculine Jealousy and Contemporary Cinema* (Houndmills, Basingstoke: Palgrave Macmillan, 2007), 49.

8. Laura Mulvey, *Death 24x a Second: Stillness and the Moving Image* (London: Reaktion, 2006), 169; Miriam Hansen, *Babel and Babylon: Spectatorship in American Silent Film* (Cambridge, MA: Harvard University Press, 1991).

9. William Luhr, "Mutilating Mel: Martyrdom and Masculinity in *Braveheart*," in *Mythologies of Postmodern Violence in Postmodern Media*, ed. Christopher Sharrett (Detroit: Wayne State University Press, 1999), 231.

10. Mulvey, *Death 24x a Second*, 165-67.

11. Steve Neale, "Masculinity as Spectacle," in *The Sexual Subject: A Screen Reader in Sexuality*, ed. Mandy Merck (London: Routledge, 1992), 278.

12. Neale, "Masculinity as Spectacle," 281, 284-86; Paul Willemen, "Anthony Mann: Looking at the Male." *Framework* 15-17 (1981): 16-20.

13. Neale, "Masculinity as Spectacle," 286.

14. Neale, "Masculinity as Spectacle," 286; Tasker, *Spectacular Bodies*, 115; Paul Smith, "Eastwood Bound," in *Constructing Masculinity*, ed. Maurice Berger, Brian Wallis, and Simon Watson (New York: Routledge, 1995), 82.

15. Smith, "Eastwood Bound," 82-83.

16. Neale, "Masculinity as Spectacle," 286.

17. Susan Bordo, *The Male Body: A New Look at Men in Public and Private* (New York: Farrar, Straus, and Giroux, 1999), 181.

18. Bordo, *The Male Body*, 186.

19. hooks, *Black Looks*, 22.

20. Richard Dyer, "Don't Look Now: The Male Pin-Up," in *The Sexual Subject: A Screen Reader in Sexuality*, ed. Mandy Merck (London: Routledge, 1992), 270.

21. Mark Simpson, *Male Impersonators: Men Performing Masculinity* (London: Cassell, 1994), 4.

22. Frank Mort, "Boy's Own? Masculinity, Style and Popular Culture," in *Male Order: Unwrapping Masculinity*, rev. ed., ed. Rowena Chapman and Jonathan Rutherford (London: Lawrence and Wishart, 1996), 198.

23. Teresa de Lauretis, *Alice Doesn't: Feminism, Semiotics, Cinema* (Bloomington: Indiana University Press, 1984), 83.

24. Peter Lehman, *Running Scared: Masculinity and the Representation of the Male Body* (Philadelphia: Temple University Press, 1993), 17.

25. Richard Dyer, *White* (London: Routledge, 1997), 14-17. As Dyer is quick to point out, "Christianity developed initially within Judaism, . . . one of its foundational thinkers was the North African Augustine, and . . . it is now most alive in Africa, South America and the black churches of Europe and North America" (17).

26. Ellis Cashmore, *Making Sense of Sports* (London: Routledge, 1990), 97-116.

27. Susan Faludi, *Stiffed: The Betrayal of Modern Man* (London: Vintage, 2000), 35.

28. Estella Tincknell and Deborah Chambers, "Performing the Crisis: Fathering, Gender and Representation in Two 1990s Films," *Journal of Popular Film and Television* 29 (2002): 152.

29. Kate Domaille, *The Full Monty*, York Notes (London: York, 2000), 28.

30. Gail Faurschou, "Fashion and the Cultural Logic of Postmodernity," in *Body Invaders: Sexuality and the Postmodern Condition*, ed. Arthur Kroker and Marilouise Kroker (Basingstoke: Macmillan, 1988), 82.

31. Scott Benjamin King, "Sonny's Virtues: The Gender Negotiations of *Miami Vice*," *Screen* 31, no. 1 (1990): 286.

32. Kaja Silverman, *The Threshold of the Visible World* (New York: Routledge, 1996), 31.

33. Domaille, *The Full Monty*, 51.

34. Lehman, *Running Scared*, 36.

35. Lehman, *Running Scared*, 31. In a later work, though, Lehman suggests a third category: the melodramatic penis, which is neither phallic spectacle nor its comic collapse. "Crying Over the Melodramatic Penis: Melodrama and Male Nudity in Films of the 90s," in *Masculinity: Bodies, Movies, Culture*, ed. Peter Lehman (New York: Routledge, 2001), 25-41. A key example is Neil Jordan's *The Crying Game* (1992), where the revelation of the penis of the transgendered Dil (Jaye Davidson) is screened in a melodramatic mode (see chapter 5). As Lehman contends, "[p]enises, it seems, must elicit an extremely strong response from us, and if awe and laughter do not define the full range of such responses, melodrama is standing by" (26-27).

36. Dyer, "Don't Look Now," 274-75.

37. Lehman, *Running Scared*, 109.

38. Peter Lehman, "'They Look So Uncomplicated Once They're Dissected': The Act of Seeing the Dead Penis With One's Own Eyes," in *The Trouble with Men: Masculinities in European and Hollywood Cinema*, ed. Phil Powrie, Ann Davies, and Bruce Babington (London: Wallflower Press, 2004), 203.

39. Lee Parpart, "The Nation and the Nude: Colonial Masculinity and the Spectacle of the Male Body in Recent Canadian Cinema(s)," in *The Trouble with Men: Masculinities in European and Hollywood Cinema*, ed. Phil Powrie, Ann Davies, and Bruce Babington (London: Wallflower Press, 2004), 187.

40. Bordo, *The Male Body*, 34.

41. Judith Halberstam, "The Good, the Bad, and the Ugly: Men, Women, and Masculinity," in *Masculinity Studies and Feminist Theory: New Directions*, ed. Judith Kegan Gardiner (New York: Columbia University Press, 2002), 353-54.

42. Tasker, *Spectacular Bodies*, 2.

43. Murray Smith, "Theses on the Philosophy of Hollywood History," in *Contemporary Hollywood Cinema*, ed. Steve Neale and Murray Smith (London: Routledge, 1998), 13.

44. Tasker, *Spectacular Bodies*, 79.

45. For a discussion of homophobic humor in the buddy film, see Fuchs, "The Buddy Politic," in *Screening the Male: Exploring Masculinities in Hollywood Cinema* (London: Routledge, 1993), 202-3.

46. Tasker, *Spectacular Bodies*, 46.

47. It is important to note, however, that black bodies were on display in other action movies, and that black stars in many '90s films, such as Wesley Snipes or Will Smith, have functioned as action heroes in their own right rather than mere sidekicks.

48. Mulvey, "Visual Pleasure," 21.

49. Tasker, *Spectacular Bodies*, 2.

50. Tasker, *Spectacular Bodies*, 80.

51. Tasker, *Spectacular Bodies*, 80.

52. Tasker, *Spectacular Bodies*, 109.

53. Susan Jeffords, *Hard Bodies: Hollywood Masculinity in the Reagan Era* (New Brunswick, NJ: Rutgers University Press, 1994), 21, 13.

54. Tasker, *Spectacular Bodies*, 79.

55. Neale, "Masculinity as Spectacle"; David Savran, *Taking It Like a Man: White Masculinity, Masochism, and Contemporary American Culture* (Princeton, NJ: Princeton University Press, 1998), 197-210; Susan Jeffords, *The Remasculinization of America: Gender and the Vietnam War* (Bloomington: Indiana University Press, 1989).

56. Lynda Boose, "Techno-Muscularity and the 'Boy Eternal': From the Quagmire to the Gulf," in *Cultures of United States Imperialism*, ed. Amy Kaplan and Donald E. Pease (Durham, NC: Duke University Press, 1993), 589.

57. Jacques Lacan, "The Significance of the Phallus," in *Écrits: A Selection*, trans. Alan Sheridan (London: Routledge, 2004), 320-21; Joan Riviere, "Womanliness as Masquerade," in *Formations of Fantasy*, ed. Victor Burgin, James Donald, and Cora Kaplan (London: Methuen, 1986), 35-44.

58. Barbara Creed, "From Here to Modernity: Feminism and Postmodernism," *Screen* 28, no. 2 (1987): 65.

59. Simpson, *Male Impersonators*, 25.

60. Lynn Segal, *Slow Motion: Changing Masculinities, Changing Men*, rev. ed. (London: Virago, 1997), 123.

61. Tasker, *Spectacular Bodies*, 109.

62. Richard Dyer, *Heavenly Bodies: Film Stars and Society* (London: BFI/Macmillan, 1987), 12.

63. Tasker, *Spectacular Bodies*, 91.

64. Linda Mizejewski, "Action Bodies in Futuristic Spaces: Bodybuilders' Stardom as Special Effect," in *Alien Zone II: The Spaces of Science Fiction Cinema*, ed. Annette Kuhn (London: Verso, 1999), 167.

65. Tasker, *Spectacular Bodies*, 149.

66. Judith Halberstam, *Female Masculinity* (Durham, NC: Duke University Press, 1998), 28.

67. Jonathan Goldberg, "Recalling Totalities: The Mirrored Stages of Arnold Schwarzenegger," *Differences: A Journal of Cultural Studies* 4, no. 1 (1992): 190-91.

68. Goldberg, "Recalling Totalities," 179.

69. Chris Holmlund, "Masculinity as Multiple Masquerade: The 'Mature' Stallone and the Stallone Clone," in *Screening the Male: Exploring Masculinities in Hollywood Cinema* (London: Routledge, 1993), 224-25.

70. Jeffords, *Hard Bodies*, 170.

71. Mark Gallagher, "I Married Rambo: Spectacle and Melodrama in the Hollywood Action Film," in *Mythologies of Postmodern Violence in Postmodern Media*, ed. Christopher Sharrett (Detroit: Wayne State University Press, 1999), 203.

72. Stella Bruzzi, *Bringing Up Daddy: Fatherhood and Masculinity in Post-War Hollywood* (London: BFI, 2005), 158.

73. Claudia Springer, *Electronic Eros: Bodies and Desire in the Postindustrial Age* (Austin: University of Texas Press, 1996), 111.

74. Springer, *Electronic Eros*, 10, 111-12.

75. Tasker, *Spectacular Bodies*, 83.

76. Steve Neale, *Genre and Hollywood* (London: Routledge, 2000), 85.

77. However, that said, it is worth noting that there have been trends for black heterosexual males to stand in for the national body in recent years, revealing the gains made by black masculinity (though not so much black femininity, other masculinities of color, or gay masculinities) on the terrain of popular representations. For example, Denzel Washington in *The Siege* (1998) or the remake of *The Manchurian Candidate* (2004). The popular TV series *24* also screens America's first African-American president, David Palmer (Dennis Haysbert). However, the real hero of the series is Jack Bauer (Keifer Sutherland), head of the L.A. Counter-Terrorist Unit. Many scenes in the series return us to the '80s action film tradition, where the battered, mutilated body of the white male represents the national body that may have been attacked (later series are replete with references to 9/11) but which will emerge rejuvenated in the process. The series also reinscribes the dynamics of the interracial buddy movie, since Bauer protects not only the national body, but also the personal, presidential body of his black friend.

78. Sean Redmond, "The Whiteness of the *Rings*," in *The Persistence of Whiteness: Race and Contemporary Hollywood Cinema*, ed. Daniel Bernardi (New York: Routledge, 2008), 96-97.

79. Jeffords, *Hard Bodies*, 176; Bruzzi, *Bringing Up Daddy*, xi.

80. Martin Fradley, "Maximus Melodramaticus: Masculinity, Masochism and White Male Paranoia in Contemporary Hollywood Cinema," in *Action and Adventure Cinema*, ed. Yvonne Tasker (London: Routledge, 2004), 243.

81. Fradley, "Maximus Melodramaticus," 244.

82. Fradley, "Maximus Melodramaticus," 249.

83. See, for example, Jonathan Mahler, "The Making of a Gladiator," *Talk Magazine*, May 2000, http://www.geocities.com/crowesite/talkarticle.htm (accessed January 5, 2007).

84. See, for example, David Edelstein, "War is Hellenic: The Blood and Eroticism of Troy," May 13, 2004, http://www.slate.com/id/2100463/ (accessed January 5, 2007).

85. See, for example, Jackie K. Cooper, "*Troy*," http://www.jackiekcooper.com/MovieReviews/Troy.htm (accessed January 5, 2007).

Chapter Four
Terminal Bodies and Cartesian Trips: White Heterosexual Masculinity in Cyberfantasies

Refiguring the Flesh: From Cyborgs to Virtual Bodies

Due to its fusion of flesh and metal, the organic and the technological, the cyborg has become a key image for both fascinations with and anxieties about the shifting relationship between humans and machines in the high-tech age. Most influentially, in "A Manifesto for Cyborgs" (1985), Donna Haraway posited the cyborg, which blurs traditional metaphysical dualisms such as self/other, mind/body, male/female, and culture/nature, as a model of postmodern, non-essentialist, *postgendered* subjectivity.[1] However, as the previous chapter illustrated, most representations of cyborgs in popular cinematic texts are a far cry from Haraway's postgendered ideal; rather, they bear out Mary Anne Doane's observation that "[w]hen technology intersects with the body in the realm of representation, the question of sexual difference is inevitably involved."[2] As we have seen, Claudia Springer interprets the hyperphallic cyborg as a response to the challenges posed to normative masculinity by electronic technology. Samantha Holland argues along similar lines, suggesting that the hypergendered cyborg works to "counter the threat that cyborgs indicate the loss of human bodies, where such a loss implies the loss of the gendered distinctions that are essential to maintaining the patriarchal order."[3]

If Holland is right, what can be made of the *virtual* bodies that have dominated popular science fiction cinema since the mid-'90s? By the end of the millennium, Schwarzenegger's terminator was dislodged as the iconic figure of the genre by *The Matrix*'s (Andy and Larry Wachowski 1999) Neo (Keanu Reeves), whose slimmer, flexible, virtual body has more in common with *Terminator 2: Judgment Day*'s (James Cameron 1991) shape-shifting, liquid-metal T1000 than

Schwarzenegger's pumped-up, solid, bounded, outdated, yet ultimately triumphant cyborg. As with cyborgs, virtual bodies are hybrid entities, which "[displace] the binary opposition between wired corporeality and organic corporeality."[4] They are also theoretically freed from identities imprinted on the flesh. Indeed, many cybertheorists wax lyrical about the radical potential of cyber- and virtual culture to unshackle us from the confines of the material body. In this respect, virtual culture is considered by many to foreground the performativity of identity, thereby deconstructing ontological discourses that anchor the "truth" of identity in the body, so that, as Scott Bukatman puts it, "[v]irtual reality has become the very embodiment of postmodern *disembodiment*."[5] But in the rather different affair of *cinematic representations* of virtual reality, the bodies featured on screen are always enmeshed in the prevailing scopic regime that inscribes race, gender, age, and ability indelibly on the flesh (however virtual) of characters. These bodies are always caught up in existing hierarchical arrangements— as the positioning of white males as heroic messiahs in both *The Terminator* (John Connor) and *The Matrix* (Neo) trilogies underscores. This policing of gender and racial hierarchies illustrates Anne Balsamo's point that "when seemingly stable boundaries are displaced by technological innovation (human/artificial, nature/culture), other boundaries are more vigilantly guarded."[6]

Many contemporary cinematic cyberfantasies screen the fantasy of leaving "the meat" behind, to use cyberpunk parlance—a fantasy in which the body is little more than "excess baggage for the cyberspace traveller."[7] However, as Allucquère Rosanne Stone notes, "[f]orgetting about the body is an old Cartesian trick, one that has unpleasant consequences for those bodies whose speech is silenced by the act of our forgetting; that is to say, those upon whose labor the act of forgetting the body is founded—usually women and minorities."[8] In this chapter I explore how numerous contemporary cyberfantasies tap into Christian and Cartesian discourses of white male disembodiment. I argue that in most films the fleshless realm of cyberspace is indexed through images of hypernormative masculinity, though not without the concomitant anxiety that the most ordinary of identities is depthless and sterile. Women and people of color, on the other hand, often stand in for the (Baudrillardian) "real." Fusion with the matrix, however, is often coded through monstrous imagery of the female body, which no doubt accounts for the common motif of white male transcendence over technology in narrative closure, but also articulates anxieties about the ramifications of a high-tech age for "ordinary" men.

White Male Disembodiment: The Legacy of Western Metaphysics

As I noted in the previous chapter, white, moneyed masculinity has a history of being represented as disembodied in Western thought, despite the paradox that it is precisely the body that white men possess, culturally coded as unmarked, which affords them that questionable privilege. Plato, for instance, had little but disdain for the body, which, he believed, "takes away from us the power of thinking at all"[9]—though "us" in his account undoubtedly referred to propertied, adult males, since he frequently represented women, along with slaves, free laborers, children, and animals as lacking the capacity for reason.[10] The seventeenth century philosopher René Descartes famously argued that the mind and body are mutually exclusive entities (though he conceded that they interact), declaring that "it is certain that I am really distinct from my body and that I can exist without it."[11] The Cartesian mind/body split was not only indebted to Ancient Greek metaphysics, however, but also the latter's fusion with Christianity during the Middle Ages. Christianity is a notoriously somatophobic religion, despite the paradox that the white male body stretched out on the crucifix is the basis of Western Christian iconography.[12] The hierarchized spirit/flesh dualism of Christian discourse is also enmeshed in sexual and racial ideologies. Women are often associated with the sins of the flesh; menstruation, for instance, has historically been interpreted as Eve's curse. Moreover, as Richard Dyer argues, Christianity, as it was deployed by colonial Western discourse, has also contributed to the association of whiteness with spirituality and therefore something beyond the corporeal.[13] People of color, on the other hand, "can be reduced (in white culture) to their bodies," thereby condemning them to what Robyn Wiegman has termed "the prisonhouse of epidermal inferiority."[14] It is precisely this asymmetrical arrangement that lends political urgency to interrogating Western economies of visibility in order to unveil "the unmarked and invisible, but no less specific, corporeality that hides beneath the abstraction of universality."[15] Indeed, the fact that virtual reality offers the fantasy of the ultimate Cartesian trip at a time when the body is a site of identity critiques may signal a white male "desire to return to the 'neutrality' of the body" at a historical juncture when white heterosexual masculinity's universal status is being challenged.[16] Yet, at the same time, the potential fluidity of gendered, raced, and sexual identities in the virtual realm, a fluidity which deconstructs any recourse to the "natural," has obvious ramifications for normative masculinity, which has secured its traditional privileges through ontological discourses of sexual and racial difference anchored in the body.

A quick glance at some titles of '90s cinematic virtual reality fantasies offers some indication of the way in which cyberspace is often represented as a (white) male terrain: *The Lawnmower Man* (1992), *Digital Man* (1995), and *Hologram Man* (1995). The none-too-subtle *The Lawnmower Man*, loosely based on a Stephen King story, tells the story of the virtual reality experiments of Dr. Lawrence Angelo (Pierce Brosnan), which enabled him to increase the brain capacity of the intellectually-challenged Jobe Smith (Jeff Fahey) by 400%. Jobe convinces his reluctant girlfriend (the town's sex-obsessed widow) to experiment with virtual sex: while their material bodies, kitted out in virtual reality suits and goggles, are plugged into the computer mainframe, a (then) state of the art special effects sequence using computer-generated images evokes the pleasures of cybersexuality. Yet despite the use of fluctuating images to depict the fluidity of subjectivity in the virtual realm, not only is the woman represented by the color pink and Jobe by blue, but also the images representing Jobe eventually morph into a beast who crushes the woman in an embrace that resembles more a virtual rape than consensual sex, leaving the woman brain-dead in "real life." Sexual difference, therefore, is rigorously policed, and, as Anneke Smelik points out, it is the woman who "has to pay the price" for the male desire to transcend the flesh.[17] Eventually, Jobe's ego becomes uncontrollable, and perceiving himself to be the new Jesus Christ, he ultimately succeeds in downloading his consciousness onto cyberspace, fulfilling his desires for omnipotence and immortality. The supposed disembodiment of cyberspace is thus self-consciously articulated through the Christian separation of spirit and flesh. This, combined with Jobe's Aryan looks, maps out virtual reality as a white male space. In terms of the film's sexual and racial politics, then, it is tempting to concur with Angelo's wife, who leaves Angelo (whose name also connotes non-corporeality) because of his obsession with virtuality, scathingly retorting, "It may be the future to you, Larry, but it's just the same old shit to me!"

Many other cinematic cyberfantasies also self-consciously invoke the mind/body split—*The Thirteenth Floor* (1999) even opens with Descartes' founding declaration "I think therefore I am." Other films, however, attempt to resignify Cartesian discourse. Theoretically, as Bukatman points out, in cyberspace "the duality between mind and body is superseded in a new formation that presents the mind as itself *embodied*," "construct[ing] a body at once material and immaterial—a fundamental oxymoron, perhaps, of postmodernity."[18] Likewise, Dani Cavallaro notes that cyberpunk often "dissolves conventional notions of corporeality," requiring the physical body "to reassess the meaning of its concreteness by negotiating with its immaterial counterparts."[19] Certainly, in most cyberfantasies, the jacked-in material body responds *physically* to experiences that befall the virtual body, as we see in *The Matrix*, where after plunging to the ground in the virtual training program, Neo is unplugged to find that his mouth is bleeding. Morpheus (Laurence Fishburne) then informs him that death in the Matrix means death in "real life," since "the body cannot live without the mind." For Peter X. Feng, this aspect of the film provides a "welcome corrective to Baudrillard's celebration of cyberpunk as a means to transcend bodily materiality and deny mortality."[20] However, as I argue below, *The Matrix* still invokes the mind/body dualism in its screening of a white male messiah hero who manages to triumph over both the flesh and the machines. In fact, in most cyberfantasies, it is overwhelmingly white men who seem better able to leave the body behind, while women and people of color are often called upon to represent embodied presence.

In the remainder of this chapter, I will focus on *Strange Days* (Kathryn Bigelow 1995) and *The Matrix, fin-de-millennium* cyberfantasies which screen an apocalyptic vision of cyberculture, articulating anxieties about simulation, hyperreality, and fragmented postmodern subjectivity through the white male protagonist, who is played off against the more grounded subjectivities of his gendered and raced others. Both films screen women and people of color in substantial roles, as the voice of ethics and/or spirituality, while white heterosexual masculinity is posited as a blank, depthless subjectivity—though one waiting to be redeemed. Nevertheless, the representation of simulation technology is articulated through the Cartesian tradition in the case of *Strange Days* and the Christian tradition in the case of *The Matrix*. In both texts, this works to stabilize sexual and racial difference in a virtual realm where, theoretically at least, such differences are rendered obsolete.

Strange Days: Recycling the Cartesian Legacy

The opening shot of *Strange Days*—an extreme close-up of a startled human eye—immediately places the film in self-conscious intertextual relation with two films that begin identically: *Peeping Tom* (1960), a metacinematic interrogation of the voyeuristic pleasures of horror spectatorship, which Bigelow acknowledged as a major influence,[21] and *Blade Runner* (1982), a techno-*noir* exploration of what it means to be human in an age of simulacra, from whose *mise-en-scène* Bigelow borrows significantly in her dystopian portrayal of *fin-de-millennium* Los Angeles.

Set on the eve of the millennium, the film's apocalyptic anxieties are initially articulated through racial tension and the image of "white masculinity in crisis." Los Angeles has degenerated into run-down ghettoes, most evidently when an impervious Lenny (Ralph Fiennes) drives through the city at night in a video-clip sequence: as images of violence and urban decay flash past the car window, a radio discussion about the end of the world blares out the polemical words of a black male speaker who welcomes the coming of the apocalypse, since it marks the demise of white power. Race is thus forcefully inserted into eschatological discourse, making it apparent that one man's apocalypse is another man's emancipation, and suggesting that the apocalyptic mode common to America's religious right wing is intimately connected to the decentering of white heterosexual masculinity.

Concerns about beleaguered white masculinity are also articulated through the film's representation of simulation technology. The in-the-near-future (at least at the time of release) narrative revolves around SQUID (Superconducting Quantum Interference Device) technology, otherwise known as playback. Originally invented by the FBI, SQUID is a wireless device which, when attached to the skull, can download neural impulses in the brain onto disc format, which can then simulate the original wearer's visual, aural, tactile, and psychosensual experiences for another user. While this technology is not strictly speaking virtual, in that a surrogate actually undergoes the original experience, the simulation of the nervous system allows the users to jack-in and embody the phenomenological sensations of the surrogate wearer. SQUID clips are now traded on the black market; in short, in true postmodern style, the last bastion of human individuality—embodied subjectivity—has been commodified. Lenny, an ex-cop and seller of SQUID clips, becomes embroiled in the thriller narrative when he is given a clip by Iris (Brigitte Bako), a prostitute who records on playback the assassination of revolutionary black rap singer Jeriko One (Glenn Plummer) by two cops as punishment for being a black male who has the gall to insult the LAPD. This self-conscious reference to the explosive Rodney King affair underscores that, even in a world immersed in simulation technology, racial identity is still indelibly written on the flesh.

Although playback eventually helps incriminate Jeriko One's killers, and is also shown to have other beneficial functions, such as allowing an amputee to experience running again, *Strange Days* is more interested in the seedier, psychosexual uses to which it is put by the central white male characters. The only women to jack in during the film—Mace (Angela Bassett) and Iris—do so not for pleasure, but at male bequest, and to enable the techno-*noir* plot to unfold. All Lenny's clients are men and, except for one stereotypical Japanese businessman (whose state of the art hardware articulates anxieties about Asian technological superiority), white. The decentered, fragmented, postmodern subject is thus rendered white and male, while women and people of color, who tend to feature on the other side of the SQUID apparatus, seem less able and willing to escape their enfleshed selves.

Lenny defends his sleazy profession to Mace by arguing that playback facilitates an exploration of our "dark side" (seemingly with no awareness of the racial connotations), protecting the body in a world where even sex can kill you. This association between electronic technology and fantasy is further elaborated when Lenny tells a potential, white, middle-class, male client that he could sleep with the exotic Filipino girl dancing in the corner of the bar, or get tied up and whipped by nuns—all without tarnishing his wedding ring. Eventually the client is seen in a state of rapturous ecstasy as he tests out a clip of a teenage girl having a shower. The film thus points to the potential challenge that virtual culture offers ontological embodied subjectivity, as well as hinting at a male desire to be liberated from the constraints of normative masculinity. At the same time, it is clear that the users of SQUID still retain their own subjectivity, since they respond to the clips as "themselves," so that "[a]lthough this technology promises to abduct the spectator, it only does so in relation to his or her prior psychic formation."[22] On the one hand, therefore, playback does not allow white male clients totally to disembody themselves. On the other, as a commercial enterprise, where surrogate wearers are paid like porn stars for their performances, it enables users to colonize the bodies of their others whilst retaining awareness of the power that inheres in that position, and more importantly, all without putting their own material bodies at risk from injury, infection, or social disadvantage.

The film thus suggests that new media devices will be traversed by preexisting networks of power, and the playback scenes, which use seamless point of view camerawork, allow Bigelow to engage in a self-reflexive critique of (white) male voyeurism—though perhaps "voyeurism" is not quite the right term, since playback is not purely visual and is actually "post-cinematic,"[23] offering, as Lenny puts it, "a piece of somebody's life. Pure and uncut. Straight from the cerebral cortex." Bigelow's critique of the (white) male gaze is most obviously played out in the controversial playback clip of the rape and murder of the aptly named Iris. The film's spectator is forced into complicity with the rapist/killer, later revealed to be Lenny's friend Max (Tom Sizemore), through whose point of view the rape is screened as he records his attack onto playback. Even more disturbingly, the killer also jacks Iris into a SQUID device, so that she not only witnesses her own rape and strangulation, but also simultaneously experiences the killer's sadistic titillation, which in turn heightens her fear, which in turn fuels the killer's warped excitement. Thus object/subject, human/technological, male/female oppositions are blurred, though playback is a far cry from the utopian fusion that Donna Haraway envisages in "A Manifesto for Cyborgs."

Bigelow was vehemently criticized for this scene, which she defended by arguing that it was "unflinching" and non-sensationalized, since all camera shots and angles were dictated by the intradiegetic SQUID apparatus, and by stating that she had deconstructed the scene's potentially exploitative nature by putting the film viewer in a position of culpability, as *Peeping Tom* had done over three decades earlier.[24] For instance, the masked face of the killer, whose perspective we share, is reflected in Iris's lifeless eyes (a citing of an equally infamous bathroom scene—the extreme close-up of the murdered Marian's eye in *Psycho*). The killer then stretches out his hands and, like a director searching for the best composition, frames Iris's face, foregrounding the aestheticization of violence common to so many cinematic texts. As Tanya Horeck puts it, the film "calls into question a *benign* view of identification," as well as the notion that looking is passive.[25] Bigelow also critiques this chilling spectacle of rape (that she nonetheless exploits) by intercutting it with the horrified reaction of Lenny when he views the clip and experiences both Iris's terror and the rapist's excitement, eventually vomiting on the pavement—a fully physical response to a simulated experience. While Max literalizes the Mulveyan sadistic male gaze, Lenny's victim-identified response points to the fluidity of gendered identifications and the potentially masochistic dimensions of spectatorship. However, as Christina Lane points out, Lenny's pain is emphasized at the expense of Iris's, allowing Lenny to "[battle] the threat of the female subject-position by territorializing it,"[26] paving the way for his future redemption.

In true *noir* fashion, Lenny is persistently doubled with Max, Iris's killer: both white men are obsessed with playback and the exhibitionist but inauthentic *femme fatale*, ironically called Faith (Juliette Lewis), who sings at the equally overdeterminedly named nightclub "Retinal Fetish." This doubling is made manifest when Lenny jacks into a clip which he thinks shows Faith's rape and murder, but in fact screens her sadomasochistic sex romp with Max. Filmed through a subjective camera, the only means of informing Lenny (and the spectator) as to the identity of the wearer is when "Lenny" turns towards a mirror to be greeted by the image of Max. This uncanny moment thus reverses the dynamics of the Lacanian mirror stage, since it is first an image of misrecognition (the self as other), but then a moment of recognition (the other as self), since Lenny is forced to acknowledge his complicity in Max's gaze.

The film's inscription of an obsessive absorption in simulation technology as a straight white male fixation certainly underscores the power that inheres in the dominant identity as it embodies its others; however, it also articulates a lack of interiority and authenticity in the white male SQUID junkies. The readiness and ease with which these "ordinary" white men colonize the body of the surrogate wearer is suggestive of both the privileges, but also the anxieties, that plague an unmarked body: inhabiting the universal subjectivity, whose very lack of particularity promotes the illusion of disembodiment, has, as a flip-side, the fear that white heterosexual masculinity lacks specific content—hence the need to live vicariously through the other.

This anxiety is emphasized in the manner in which the film self-consciously plays Lenny off against Mace, a black action heroine, who represents embodied presence. Lenny's loser status is partly depicted through his futile obsession with Faith and his parasitical dependence on playback, but is also inscribed through his pasty white, non-muscular, acutely vulnerable body—an example of Bigelow's trademark subversion of gender and genre. The suggestion is that Lenny's passive immersion in cyberculture has resulted in a loss of physicality, which, in the action genre, connotes a loss of masculinity. Lenny repeatedly attempts to worm himself out of physical confrontation with fast-talking and bribes. In one scene, Lenny is punched in the stomach by a pumped-up, white woman, as a male assailant taunts, "We tried to find a smaller girl to beat the shit out of you, but it was short notice." Bigelow even has Lenny faint in the final scene. Lenny's narcissism is also persistently overdetermined. He insists on removing his expensive Armani jacket before being hit, and then begs, "Just don't hurt the eyes." His ties also attract an inordinate amount of comments throughout the film. Consequently, the film suggests that both the commodification of the male body and simulation technology threaten to reduce masculinity to a simulacrum. Thus it would seem that discourses of white male disembodiment only maintain hegemonic norms when they are deployed to safeguard white male transcendence of the body, not the loss of its physical values.

Mace, by contrast, is as tough as her name suggests. Whereas *Terminator 2* partially assimilated the threat that Sarah Connor posed to gender norms through the hyperphallicization of Schwarzenegger's cyborg, Mace is consistently figured as more conventionally masculine than Lenny. While Lenny decks himself out in flamboyant attire, Mace dons trouser suits and leather gear, except for the final scene when she borrows a sexy black number from her sister and receives her first compliment from Lenny; but even then, the gun she pokes in her suspender belt renders this a contradictory image of femininity. As a bodyguard-chauffeur, Mace is well versed in physical combat, and repeatedly rescues Lenny throughout the film.

According to the generic conventions of the action movie, Mace's physicality connotes authenticity, and is therefore inextricable from her vehement opposition to playback, which she considers "porn for wire-heads." Accusing Lenny of being a social parasite (nonetheless one she is in love with), at one point Mace furiously stamps on Lenny's clips of Faith, flings Lenny against a wall, and lectures: "This is your life. Right here, right now. It's real time, you hear me? Real time, time to get real. Not playback. . . . These are used emotions. It's time to trade them in. Memories were meant to fade, Lenny. They're designed that way for a reason." This appeal to the "real" of corporal presence might position Mace as "the moral center of the film," as Bigelow herself intended,[27] but it simultaneously yokes her to historical discourses of black female hyperembodiment. At the same time, as Paul Gormley notes, "it fabricates African-American people and culture as a place where there is a knowledge of a reality underneath the surface simulation of white Symbolic structures."[28] Mace's unwillingness to divest herself of her enfleshed identity is also linked to her investment in the black body as a site of politicized identity. Lenny, on the other hand, cannot appeal to his race or gender as a site of positive political identity, though he is certainly represented as a victimized (and therefore redeemable) white male through his relationship with Faith, a relationship which takes the masochistic impulses of the traditional *noir* hero to extremes. Nor is Lenny concerned by racial and social injustice, and only after a sudden change of heart does he hand over to Mace the clip that indicts Jeriko One's killers.

On his path to redemption, Lenny recognizes his desire for Mace, and, it is suggested, will turn his back on playback. This offers "a progressive theme about the reformation of aggressive masculinity," since Lenny can begin to respond to difference in ways that do not involve mastery and colonization.[29] At the same time, the ending repeats the prevalent motif in fictional cyberpunk texts that present people of color as "more grounded and able to heal white people careening out of control"[30]—a motif that is also common in contemporary Hollywood productions, such as *Johnny Mnemonic* (1995) and *The Matrix*. The final highly romanticized image of a bi-racial kiss deftly displaces attention away from the racial unrest in which the action unfolds and onto the personal realm, more particularly onto a beleaguered white male and his transformation. Talking of the ending of his original screenplay, James Cameron explained (with a neo-Evangelicalism characteristic of recent Hollywood production), "I wanted to do a kind of redemption motif. I always had in mind the fate of this one guy, Lenny Nero, and his ability to find what's right, and what's wrong. If one person can elevate themselves or redeem themselves then, by extrapolation we all can."[31] As a white male, it would seem, Lenny has the privilege of standing for all of humanity. However, his redemption is dependent upon the love of a good black woman, who enables him to re-embody himself, but in a way that risks positing African-Americans and women as exterior to the technological and reinforcing discourses that posit black women as unable to escape the confines of the flesh.

Transcending the Flesh: White Heterosexual Masculinity and Christian Discourse in *The Matrix*

The Matrix (1999), a neo-gothic cyberfantasy famed for its much-imitated special effect and wirework sequences, offers a spectacular trip into the vagaries of the hyperreal, joining other *fin de millennium* films, such as *Pleasantville* (1998), *Dark City* (1998), *The Truman Show* (1998), and *The Thirteenth Floor*, in questioning the status of "reality." *The Matrix* screens the dystopian fantasy of humans having been enslaved by machines that feed off the energy produced by human bodies plugged into fields of womb-like energy extracting devices; in an ironic twist of fate, humans have been reduced to mere batteries. In order to thwart resistance, human consciousness has been wired into the Matrix—an interactive computer program that simulates reality and externalizes the human nervous system, making humans oblivious to their subjugation. Neo, a computer technician and hacker, is emancipated from the Matrix by Morpheus, the leader of the human resistance, who, along with Trinity (Carrie-Anne Moss) and the rest of his crew, frees the few minds capable of accepting the truth—that their lives have been nothing more than a computer-generated illusion. As Morpheus had hoped, Neo turns out to be "the one"—the only human capable of triumphing over the Matrix and saving humankind.

The Matrix borrows extensively from the *Terminator* films in its fusion of science fiction dystopia with Christian discourse, as well as recycling elements from *Vertigo* (1958), *Superman* (1978), *Blade Runner* (1982), *Men in Black* (1997), and John Woo films, to name but a few. Moreover, as Pat Mellencamp points out, "*The Matrix* eclectically blends Asian and American film genres (particularly action adventure, sci-fi, Kung Fu/Hong Kong martial arts), live action and animation (Japanese anime, Warner Brothers Cartoons), and other media (comic books, TV, and computer/video games, in the latter, particularly architectural form and visual style)."[32] As with *Strange Days*, then, for a film that ostensibly screens anxieties about the loss of the real, *The Matrix* is nonetheless a veritable exercise in postmodern citation. In addition to self-conscious allusions to filmic intertexts, it is also peppered with literary references from sources as diverse as the Bible and Lewis Carroll's *Alice in Wonderland*. Neo also hides his illegal discs in a hollowed out copy of Jean Baudrillard's *Simulacra and Simulation* (1981), while Morpheus directly quotes Baudrillard when he shows Neo the devastation that has been wrought upon the world, ironically proclaiming, "welcome to the desert of the real."[33]

For Baudrillard, the order of the real is giving way to the order of the hyperreal, in which the signs of the real are substituted for the real itself; in our media-saturated, image-dominated, cyber-immersed culture, Baudrillard pessimistically declares the impossibility of recovering the real, a vacuum that is being filled by simulacra—copies without originals. He argues that the real has become our true utopia but one "no longer in the realm of the possible, that can only be dreamt of as one would dream of a lost object."[34] *The Matrix* screens the fantasy of reclaiming this "lost object," a fantasy that is packaged up in a postmodern recycling of Christian discourse; it is thus exemplary of popular cinema's penchant for postmodernism at the level of aesthetics, but good old-fashioned humanism and individualism at the level of theme.

The Christian allusions are numerous: indeed, entire web sites have been dedicated to their decoding. Most obviously, the name Neo is also an anagram of "one." Neo is confirmed as "the one" when he is killed in the Matrix and therefore in the material world, but is resurrected by a kiss from Trinity. In *The Matrix Reloaded* (2003), he also brings Trinity back from the dead, while in *The Matrix Revolutions* (2003), he sacrifices himself in a crucifixion-like scene in order to save humanity. Despite the associations of her name, Trinity fills the function of Mary Magdalene in a typically irreverent, postmodern reworking of master narratives. Other Christian allusions include Morpheus's multicultural crew as the Disciples, especially the aptly named Cypher (Joe Pantoliano), who, Judas-like, betrays Neo to the authorities—in this case the agents that patrol the Matrix, seeking out those freed humans that infiltrate the system. Moreover, the name of Morpheus's craft, Nebuchadnezzar, refers to the Biblical King who suffered from bad dreams and eventually became a believer, while the name of the last city of mankind located beneath the Earth's surface is Zion, a reference to the Biblical city of heaven on Earth.

These Christian references are also mixed with references to Ancient Greek mythology, as well as Eastern philosophies. Despite this hybridity, it is striking that in the first film all the main characters with Christian allegorical functions are white (Neo, Trinity, Cypher), while the two central African-American characters bear Ancient Greek names (though the sequels also give Hellenic names to white characters): Morpheus is named after the Greek God of dreams, while Neo's coming has been predicted by the Oracle (Gloria Foster),[35] a homely, cookie-baking, supremely wise black woman, who, like so many African-Americans in popular representations (Morpheus the believer included), acts as the guardian of a lost spirituality and authenticity.[36] Despite the oracle's spiritual dimension and down-to-earth-ness (suggested through her run-down, inner-city abode), which would seem to posit her as the antithesis to simulation and technology, in *The Matrix Reloaded* she turns out to be a computer program. However, importantly, she is one designed to make the Matrix seem more real by offering humans the variable of choice. Her own choice is to help the human resistance and bring about peace by teaching Neo to "know thyself." Along with Morpheus, therefore, she fulfils the role of magical black helper that I discussed in chapter 2, not only in helping Neo to recognize "the secrets" of his identity, but also in bringing the white couple, Neo and Trinity, together.[37]

Despite the trilogy's obvious effort to include a multicultural cast, particularly in the sequels, which feature strong roles for women and people of color,[38] Western racial norms are reinscribed in the association of Christianity with whiteness (though destabilized in the association of Hellenism with blackness), and the assignation of the messiah as a "white" male, blindly followed by Mor-

pheus and worshipped by many of the multicultural inhabitants of Zion. I place
"white" in inverted commas because the complexities of racial identity are particularly apparent in the case of Keanu Reeves. Although in interviews he self-
identifies as white, in actual fact his father is Hawaiian-Chinese (his mother is
white British). For that reason, according to Feng, "Asian American spectators
frequently label Reeves as Asian Pacific passing as white."[39] In most of his
films, he is also invariably positioned as white, his casting as the Victorian Jonathan Harker in *Bram Stoker's Dracula* (1992) being a key case in point. In *The
Matrix*, despite the deployment of his Asian roots in the martial arts sequences,
similar to Bernado Bertolucci's use of Reeves in *Little Buddha* (1993), he is significantly "whitened," given the Anglo Saxon name Thomas A. Anderson—and,
as if to hammer this fact home, he is even told at one point by his friend Choi
(Marc Gray) that he is looking "even whiter than usual." Yet, most importantly,
Reeves is significantly "whitened" by his narrative function of messiah. While
Neo's "whiteness" and maleness are offered up as contingent, within the film's
citation of Christian discourse, they are both essential to his ability to triumph
over the limitations of the flesh.

At the same time, however, within the logic of the virtual reality narrative,
inside the Matrix, differences that are written on the body, notably gender and
race, theoretically become immaterial (in both senses of the word). Unlike
Strange Days, men and women of color frequently disembody themselves in
order to enter the Matrix, though none, of course, are capable of the flesh-
defying feats that Neo performs. *The Matrix* also flirts with gender instability in
its screening of Trinity, the cyberpunk sidekick turned action heroine, whom
Neo had first assumed to be male because of her exceptional hacking skills. In
the realm of virtual reality, of course, muscles and physical strength are rendered
obsolete, which also works to give Trinity's toughness and combative skills narrative justification. Neo and Trinity also look remarkably similar in the Matrix:
both have short black hair, both wear black suits, sunglasses, black leather boots,
and both handle phallic weaponry (however virtual) with ease—a marker of
masculinity in the Hollywood tradition. In other words, the "residual self images" (the mental projection of their digital selves) that Neo and Trinity assume
in the Matrix are both culturally understood as masculine, no doubt functioning
much like the armored body of the cyborg—to ward off the threat of potentially
feminizing electronic technology. The gender dynamics of fairytale conventions
are also reversed when Neo (whose name suggests him to be a "New Man" action hero) is resurrected by a kiss from Trinity, though in the sequel he returns
the favor.

Virtual bodies are also freed from physical limitations, as witnessed in the
breathtaking, fast-cut, gravity-defying action and special effect sequences that
paradoxically offer up cinema at its most visceral. *The Matrix* is a prime example of a film that recognizes that the "specificity of cinema," dependent on an
indexical relationship between the photograph and the real, "[is dissolving]
while other relationships, intertextual and cross-media, begin to emerge."[40] New

special effects, which are showcased in the science fiction genre, not only affect, but also partly determine, the images of masculinity that appear on screen. For instance, Neo's superiority is played out through his speed, malleability, and grace in balletic combat sequences that cite the non-cinematic medium of computer games, as well as the skillfully choreographed fight sequences of martial arts cinema, offering a very different male hero to those that dominated the screen in the Hollywood action film of the '80s and early '90s. While Sarah Connor is played off against the solidity of Schwarzenegger's terminator, Trinity is played off against Neo's greater fluidity; whereas fluidity marked the T1000 a menacingly feminized figure in *Terminator 2*, it marks Neo's triumph over the agents in the Matrix, particularly at the end of the film, when Neo enters the body of Agent Smith (Hugo Weaving), destroying him through implosion.

The fact that these virtual bodies are externalizations of the human nervous system also allows for a reading that underscores the performativity of gender. As Judith Butler has argued, once "gender itself becomes a free-floating artifice" that is no longer anchored in the body, it is freed up from the heterosexual matrix,[41] and Neo's fetishistic leather gear, combined with Keanu Reeves's gay icon status, partly evoked through his willingness to take on homoerotic roles in films like *My Own Private Idaho* (1991) and *Point Break* (1991), certainly lends the film to a queer reading. Thus, as Jenny Wolmark has remarked, "leaving the 'meat' behind does not serve to obliterate all the contradictions inherent in culturally constructed masculinity, nor does it enable a less compromised virtual masculinity to be enacted in cyberspace."[42]

At the same time, *The Matrix* also screens more conventional representations of Hollywood masculinity in its parodic recycling of the generic conventions of the western, such as the shoot-outs, fetishist shots of guns, leather, and hands ready to draw, and newspaper blowing across the ground like tumbleweed—Neo is, after all, in cyberpunk jargon, a "console cowboy." Moreover, certain hegemonic norms are reinscribed not only through the conventions of the action genre (both Morpheus and Trinity are rescued by Neo), but also through recourse to an older, transcendental discourse of disembodiment that marks the "white" male Neo as hero: Christianity. Even though these Christian allusions are articulated in the realm of fantasy, they are no less powerful; as Sharon Willis points out, "[w]hether we are speaking of race, of gender, or of sexuality, fictive constructions and fantasies lend historical and material force to the matter of difference."[43]

Neo's role as white male messiah, however, also performs another ideological function, providing Neo, who is played off against the enigmatic Morpheus and equally intriguing Trinity, with a particularized identity which he otherwise lacks as an "ordinary" white male. As plain Thomas A. Anderson, a computer programmer encased in a white, plastic cubicle in the uniform world of corporate America, Neo looked little different from the agents, who are represented by an overdetermined image of straight white masculinity: they all have the commonest Anglo-Saxon names imaginable—Mr. Smith, Mr. Brown, Mr. Jones—and they all share a blank expression, identical suits, ties, tie-pins, and sunglasses. At one point, Morpheus even tells Agent Smith, in a reversal of racist discourse, "You all look the same to me." This comparison is much aided not only by Reeves's infamous wooden delivery of lines, but also his vacuous star persona, with Reeves often described "as a kind of pure, blank surface, lacking all depth"[44]—all of which render him the apotheosis of the two-dimensional cyber-subject.

J.P. Telotte has observed that images of an "empty human nature" in science fiction cinema are generally masculine.[45] Richard Dyer has also noted an association of whiteness with sterility, meaninglessness, and death in the cinematic representation of cyborgs, citing *Blade Runner* and the *Alien* series as examples.[46] A more recent instance can be found in *I, Robot* (2004): all the robots look identical, all are white, and the leading robot has English Received Pronunciation (much like the 3-CPO robot in *Star Wars*), a marked contrast to the streetwise human hero, Will Smith, and his distinctive African-American cadences. Electronic space in general is coded as white in films such as *THX-1138* (1971) and *The Matrix*, presumably because whiteness connotes absence and non-materiality. The Western city that Neo enters in the training program is also populated solely by whites,[47] all dressed in black suits, except for the blonde woman in red who is designed to distract Neo. Moreover, on a closer inspection, all these city-dwellers are twins, another image that suggests a lack of white self-distinction. A similar representation is evident in *The Matrix Reloaded* with the twin albino assassins, images of hyper-whiteness and a profound lack of individuality. As well as being identical, they both wear white suits, have ghostly white skin and bleached white hair (dreadlocked, however, suggestive of racial appropriation), and lack any outward display of emotion.[48] Ghost-like figures, who pass through objects, they are prime examples of how, as Richard Dyer puts it, whiteness is often represented as an absence of "any *thing*; in other words, material reality."[49] These images all contrast starkly with the highly multicultural city of Zion, particularly in the sequels. Racial difference thus becomes a signifier of humanity, while whiteness is represented as "as much a living tyranny of absence and negation for those who come to embody it, as an empowering and empowered subjectivity."[50]

It is therefore highly significant that it is normative white masculinity that is called upon in *The Matrix* to represent electronic space, which, according to Vivien Sobchack, is depthless and two-dimensional, as well as the excess of surface and the "waning of affect" that Fredric Jameson argues is a characteristic of postmodernism.[51] *The Matrix* is not the first film to make this association, of course. In the influential *Tron* (1982) and more recent *Virtuosity* (1995), computer programs are also represented by white heterosexual men. In the latter film, the chillingly indifferent computer program (Russell Crowe), comprised of the profile of nearly 200 serial killers, is played off against his grounded, passionate, black adversary (Denzel Washington). Such a dynamic, also evident in *Strange Days*, is similarly deployed in *The Matrix Reloaded*: the architect of the

Matrix (Helmut Bakaitis), who informs Neo that he is the sixth version of the messiah, an anomaly of the system, built in to function as a Foucauldian form of control (though Neo eventually proves him wrong, of course), is a white man with a white beard, dressed in white. As Tani Dianca Sanchez points out, the architect is the only character whose racial identity is commented upon in the entire trilogy when a past version of Neo, featured on video screen, angrily shouts, "You can't make me do anything, you old white prick!"—suggesting a rejection of hegemonic forms of whiteness.[52] The architect, who espouses the doctrine of fate and inevitability, is played off against the oracle, who introduces choice into the system. Thus, while the oracle as computer program complicates the association of cyberspace with normative white masculinity, she is also intimately tied to the human resistance, becoming Agent Smith's enemy in *The Matrix Revolutions*. In *The Matrix* Agent Smith is also placed in contradistinction to blackness when he orders agents to beat Morpheus in a scene that evokes the Rodney King affair, a reminder that whiteness does not just connote emptiness, but can also be associated with "the terrible, the terrifying, the terrorizing" in the black imagination.[53] Agent Smith also delivers his speech about hating humanity while Morpheus is bound, gagged, and interrogated—a speech which recalls all the bitterness of white supremacist discourse. Moreover, while the oracle enjoys physical pleasures, such as smoking and eating cookies (albeit within the Matrix), thereby reaffirming common associations of black femininity with embodiment, Agent Smith has nothing but contempt for the flesh, and in *The Matrix Revolutions*, when he enters the material body of a human resistance fighter, he utters with total revulsion, "It's difficult even to think encased in this rotting piece of meat. The stink of it filling every breath, a suffocating cloud you can't escape. Disgusting."

This representation of normative white masculinity as the antithesis of the flesh, an association that is inextricable from its historical claims to noncorporeality, plays out anxieties about white masculinity's potential sterility and lack of self-distinction. In *The Matrix Reloaded* Agent Smith even learns to self-replicate, producing endless images of white masculinity as simulacra. In *The Matrix Revolutions* Smith also tries (unsuccessfully, of course) to make Neo into one of his clones, explaining he has become Neo's "negative." Of course, while Neo ultimately defies the limitations of the flesh, he is largely insulated from these associations of vacuity thanks to his role as messiah, with the flip-side anxieties that his disembodiment provokes displaced onto the agents. Despite this attempt to polarize these antithetical representations of normative white masculinity, as double figures, Neo and Agent Smith persistently slide into each other throughout the film.

Fusing with the Matrix: Pre-Oedipal Imagery and the Monstrous Feminine

The fact that the figure of white heterosexual masculinity is repeatedly called upon to represent not only anxieties about the depthless, postmodern cybersubject, but also human transcendence over the technological, is some indication of the threat that cyber- and virtual culture poses to traditional configurations of male mastery. Indeed, *The Matrix*'s representation of the agents (and therefore the Matrix interface itself) as normative white masculinity works much like the last-ditch attempt to masculinize techno-imagery in the '80s cyborg films. At the same time, the film's use of grotesque womb imagery to represent fusion with the Matrix enacts the violent return of both the repressed body and the repressed feminine that this masculinization and disembodiment involves.

As Claudia Springer and Deborah Lupton have argued, electronic technology shares many characteristics that have historically been associated with the female body—it is miniature, mysterious, dark, leaky, vulnerable to contamination, a site of intense emotional security, but also terrifying engulfment.[54] Many theorists have also pointed out that the etymological root of the word "matrix" is the Latin "mater" meaning both "mother" and "womb." However, as Amanda Fernbach notes, it is important to stress that it is not so much that submersion into the matrix replicates the pre-Oedipal symbiotic relationship between mother and child, but rather (as with the deployment of Cartesian and Christian discourses in these films), due to the absence of narratives with which to describe masculinity in a postmodern, high-tech world, familiar narratives are put into play. Thus pre-Oedipal space is often invoked in cyberpunk fiction in order both to acknowledge and to disavow anxieties that dog contemporary masculinity as it imagines the future.[55]

Pre-Oedipal imagery is used in many films that figure the matrix, like the womb, as an uncanny site of pleasurable plenitude and abject self-annihilation, particularly for the male subject. In her influential *The Monstrous-Feminine: Film, Feminism, Psychoanalysis* (1993), Barbara Creed analyses such imagery in horror cinema through Julia Kristeva's theory of abjection.[56] As we saw in chapter 2, Kristeva argues that all individuals experience abjection when they attempt to break away from the mother, and for the male subject in particular, who within patriarchal culture always fears his own identity "sinking irretrievably into the mother," the maternal body becomes a site of conflicting fears and desires.[57] Notably, many films with active heroines represent cybertechnology through grotesque images of the feminine and/or maternal body, inscribing at the level of *mise-en-scène* the sexual difference binary that tough action heroines and technological advances destabilize. With self-conscious, intertextual allusions to *Alien* (1979), *The Matrix* screens abject images of the maternal body in order to convey fears about male passivity and the annihilation of subjectivity in virtual culture. A bald, naked Neo awakens to find himself in a womb-shaped sac, submerged in viscous fluid, his fetus-like body penetrated by wires resembling umbilical cords, which, far from nurturing him, drain off his energy. Neo's liberation from the Matrix is then figured as a birth; he shoots through a labyrinth of dark, slippery, vaginal passages, landing in a pool of water from which he is rescued by Morpheus's ship. Earlier, in the Matrix, before his liberation, his body had also been infiltrated by a bug that Agent Smith injected into his naval (the place from which children often think babies emerge); Trinity again penetrates his naval to remove the bug in a monstrous image of male pregnancy and labor that cites the famed scene in *Alien* in which Kane (John Hurt) gives birth to the alien gestating inside him. Entering the Matrix from Morpheus's ship also requires penetration through a bioport in the back of the neck, though the film also suggests the pleasures of passively submitting to technology when Neo, lying inert, strapped into his chair, gasps orgasmically when he is jacked in. However, as Cynthia Freeland points out, this is an example of "good penetration" since it is clean and unmessy—a stark contrast to the womb-like human fields. For Freeland, this forms part of the film's fantasy of overcoming the flesh, evident in the black leather, latex costumes of the characters' "residual images," and Neo's eventual ability to dodge bullets and vanquish death.[58]

For this reason, Freeland compares the film unfavorably with another 1999 virtual reality fantasy, David Cronenberg's *eXistenZ*, which "revels in the goo of flesh, gore, and blood."[59] For instance, unlike the phallic-like trode that penetrates Neo's bioport, in *eXistenZ* the characters fuse with the virtual reality game by massaging breast-shaped pods called "umbycords" that are plugged directly into the nervous system. Allegra (Jennifer Jason Leigh), the female game designer, gains great pleasure from caressing these pods, evoking the sexualized "pleasures of the interface," to use Claudia Springer's phrase.[60] The film is also unusual in that Allegra is decidedly more at ease in virtual space than her squeamish male counterpart Ted (Jude Law), who expresses concern about what is happening to his "real" body. Ted is also reluctant to have his bioport fitted: once he has it done, he is left with a vaginal-like hole at the base of his spine which requires stimulation when not in use.

Much like *The Matrix*'s screening of the "monstrous feminine," *eXistenZ* deploys imagery that would seem at least to brook the possibility that, in the words of cyberfeminist Sadie Plant, "[t]here is no escape from the meat, the flesh, and cyberspace is nothing transcendent. . . . Entering the matrix is no assertion of masculinity, but a loss of humanity; to jack into cyberspace is not to penetrate, but to be invaded."[61] For Plant, writing in the playful, parodic, but arguably essentialist mode of Luce Irigaray, cyberspace not only challenges male mastery and self-distinction, but is also a system that is "female and dangerous."[62] However, rather than declaring the future female, it would be more productive to think through the ways in which anxieties about gender relations and male passivity in the high-tech age are articulated through images of feminine flesh mapped across male bodies, as we see in both *The Matrix* and *eXistenZ*. Indeed, in a far cry from Plant's celebratory rhetoric, most contemporary films screen concerns about a so-called feminized future in a backlash mode, as

I analyzed in chapter 1 in my discussion of the virtual reality sequence in *Disclosure* (1994), a film which bears out Springer's observation that feminine images of the technological "are not necessarily feminist."[63]

Disclosure, along with all the films I have discussed in this chapter, bears weight to Anne Balsamo's observation that "[t]here is plenty of evidence to suggest that a reconstructed body does not guarantee a reconstructed cultural identity. Nor does 'freedom from a body' imply that people exercise the 'freedom to be' any kind of body than the one they already enjoy or desire."[64] Rather, these films screen what Braidotti has termed the paradox of the "simultaneous overexposure and disappearance of the body."[65] While they stage the fantasy of virtual disembodiment, the ideologies of gender and race attached to the bodies they depict confirm that bodies are unavoidably saturated with meanings, underscoring the difficulty of escaping what Patrick Fuery, in another context, has termed the "*mise-en-scène* of flesh."[66] Whatever the utopian claims about cyber- and virtual culture liberating us from identities imprinted on the material body, popular cinematic representations of virtual reality still find ways of inscribing difference. Despite the screening of anxieties about male feminization and straight white male emptiness and sterility, the repeated motif of human transcendence over technology and the flesh, figured by the white male protagonist, suggests that white masculinity may well be represented as terminal in both senses of the word (technologized and in crisis) but can still find ways of redeeming itself.

In the following chapter, I discuss the potential liberation from identities inscribed on the body in a rather different context—in cross-dressing comedies and transgender passing narratives. In particular, I analyze the extent to which essentialist notions of gender, namely the notion that the "truth" of gender resides in the body, are dislodged in these films, and explore how the notion of gender as a performative category impacts on "ordinary" men, in terms of both their gender and sexual identity.

Notes

1. Donna Haraway, "A Manifesto for Cyborgs: Science, Technology, and Socialist Feminism in the 1980s," *Socialist Review* 15, no. 2 (1985): 96.

2. Mary Anne Doane, "Technophilia: Technology, Representation, and the Feminine," in *Body/Politics: Women and the Discourses of Science*, ed. Mary Jacobus, Evelyn Fox Keller, and Sally Shuttleworth (New York: Routledge, 1990), 163.

3. Samantha Holland, "Descartes Goes to Hollywood: Mind, Body and Gender in Contemporary Cyborg Cinema," in *Cyberspace/Cyberbodies/Cyberpunk: Cultures of Technological Embodiment*, ed. Mike Featherstone and Roger Burrows (London: Sage, 1995), 159.

4. Dani Cavallaro, *Cyberpunk and Cyberculture* (London: Athlone, 2000), 28-29.

5. Scott Bukatman, *Terminal Identity: The Virtual Subject in Postmodern Science Fiction* (Durham, DC: Duke University Press, 1993), 188. For a discussion of the performativity of identity in cyberspace, see Thomas Foster, "Postmodern Virtualities," in *Cyberspace/Cyberbodies/Cyberpunk: Cultures of Technological Embodiment*, ed. Mike Featherstone and Roger Burrows (London: Sage, 1995), 79-95; Thomas Foster, "Trapped

by the Body? Telepresence and Transgendered Performance in Feminist and Lesbian Rewritings of Cyberpunk Fiction," in *The Cybercultures Reader*, ed. David Bell and Barbara M. Kennedy (London: Routledge, 2000), 439-59; Sadie Plant, "Beyond the Screens: Film, Cyberpunk and Cyberfeminism," *Variant* 14 (1993): 12-17; Harold Rheingold, "A Slice of Life in My Virtual Community," in *High Noon on the Electronic Frontier: Conceptual Issues in Cyberspace*, ed. Peter Ludlow (Cambridge, MA: MIT Press, 1996), 413-36. For a critique of technophilic discourse, see Ziauddin Sardar, "alt.civilisations.faq: Cyberspace as the Darker Side of the West," in *The Cybercultures Reader*, ed. David Bell and Barbara M. Kennedy (London: Routledge, 2000), 732-52; Lisa Nakamura, "Race in/for Cyberspace: Identity Tourism and Racial Passing on the Net," in *The Cybercultures Reader*, ed. David Bell and Barbara M. Kennedy (London: Routledge, 2000), 712-20; Vivian Sobchack, "Beating the Meat/Surviving the Text, or How to Get Out of this Century Alive," in *Cyberspace/Cyberbodies/Cyberpunk: Cultures of Technological Embodiment*, ed. Mike Featherstone and Roger Burrows (London: Sage, 1995), 205-41.

6. Anne Balsamo, "Forms of Technological Embodiment: Reading the Body in Contemporary Culture," in *Cyberspace/Cyberbodies/Cyberpunk: Cultures of Technological Embodiment*, ed. Mike Featherstone and Roger Burrows (London: Sage, 1995), 216-17.

7. Balsamo, "Forms of Technological Embodiment," 229.

8. Allucquère Rosanne Stone, "Will the Real Body Please Stand Up? Boundary Stories about Virtual Cultures," in *The Cybercultures Reader*, ed. David Bell and Barbara M. Kennedy (London: Routledge, 2000), 525.

9. Susan Bordo, *The Flight to Objectivity: Essays on Cartesianism and Culture* (Albany: The State University of New York Press, 1987), 93.

10. Elizabeth V. Spelman, "Woman as Body: Ancient and Contemporary Views," *Feminist Studies* 8, no. 1 (1982): 119.

11. René Descartes, *Meditations and Other Metaphysical Writings* (London: Penguin, 2003), 62.

12. Richard Dyer, *White* (London: Routledge, 1997), 15-16.

13. Dyer, *White*, 14.

14. Dyer, *White*, 14; Robyn Wiegman, *American Anatomies: Theorizing Race and Gender* (Durham, NC: Duke University Press, 1995), 11.

15. Wiegman, *American Anatomies*, 6.

16. Balsamo, "Forms of Technological Embodiment, 229, 233.

17. Anneke Smelik, "The Flight from Flesh: Virtual Reality in Science Fiction Films," http://www.women.it/cyberarchive/files/smelik.htm (accessed September 2, 2002). Permission to quote from this article was kindly given by the author.

18. Bukatman, *Terminal Identity*, 208.

19. Cavallaro, *Cyberpunk and Cyberculture*, xv, 83.

20. Peter X. Feng, "False and Double Consciousness: Race, Virtual Reality and the Assimilation of Hong Kong Action Cinema in *The Matrix*," in *Aliens R Us: The Other in Science Fiction*, ed. Ziauddin Sardar and Sean Cubitt (London: Pluto, 2002), 154.

21. Graham Fuller, "Big Bad Bigelow," *Interview*, November 1995, 44.

22. Brian Carr, "*Strange Days* and the Subject of Mobility," *Camera Obscura: A Journal of Feminism and Film Theory* 50 (2002): 204.

23. Rosi Braidotti, *Metamorphoses: Towards a Materialist Theory of Becoming* (Cambridge, UK: Polity/Blackwell, 2002), 253.

24. Gavin Smith, "Momentum and Design," *Film Comment* September/October, 1995, 49; Fuller, "Big Bad Bigelow," 44.

25. Tanya Horeck, *Public Rape: Representing Violation in Fiction and Film* (London: Routledge, 2004), 109, 106.

26. Christina Lane, *Feminist Hollywood: From* Born in Flames *to* Point Break (Detroit: Wayne State University Press, 2000), 123.

27. Fuller, "Big Bad Bigelow," 44.

28. Paul Gormley, *The New-Brutality Film: Race and Affect in Contemporary Hollywood Cinema* (Bristol: Intellect Books, 2005), 174.

29. Christina Lane, "The Strange Days of Kathryn Bigelow and James Cameron," in *The Cinema of Kathryn Bigelow: Hollywood Transgressor*, ed. Deborah Jermyn and Sean Redmond (London: Wallflower Press, 2003), 186.

30. Claudia Springer, "Psycho-cybernetics in Films of the 1990s," in *Alien Zone II: The Spaces of Science Fiction Cinema*, ed. Annette Kuhn (London: Verso, 1999), 215.

31. "Strange Days Movie Notes," *Ralph Fiennes Interactive Fan Page*, http://ralph fiennes.hypermart.net/strangedays/RalphFiennesStrangeDaysNotes.htm (accessed September 23, 2002).

32. Pat Mellencamp, "The Zen of Masculinity—Rituals of Heroism in *The Matrix*," in *The End of Cinema As We Know It: American Film in the Nineties*, ed. Jon Lewis (London: Pluto, 2002), 84.

33. See Jean Baudrillard, *Simulacra and Simulations*, trans. Sheila Faria Glaser (Michigan: The University of Michigan Press, 1994), 1. Slavoj Žižek also uses this phrase as a title for his lecture on 9/11 (delivered on September 22, 2001), and refers to *The Matrix* when arguing that the attacks introduced U.S. citizens to "the desert of the real," which had been "corrupted by Hollywood." "Welcome to the Desert of the Real," *Re-Constructions: Reflections on Humanity and Media After Tragedy*, http://web.mit.edu/cm s/reconstructions/interpretations/desertreal.html (accessed November 22, 2008).

34. Baudrillard, *Simulacra and Simulations*, 2, 19, 123.

35. After Gloria Foster's death, the oracle was played by Mary Alice in *The Matrix Revolutions*.

36. Tani Dianca Sanchez argues that while the Oracle plays into stereotypes, such as the mammy figure (the Oracle is seen caring for non-black children), she also "disrupts the lingering memory of black female as inferior and also challenges still-current understandings of black females measured by standards of white femininity." "Neo-abolitionists, Colorblind Epistemologies and Black Politics," in *The Persistence of Whiteness: Race and Contemporary Hollywood Cinema*, ed. Daniel Bernardi (London: Routledge, 2008), 108.

37. Thomas DiPiero, "White Men Aren't," *Camera Obscura: A Journal of Feminism and Film Theory* 30 (1992): 126; Krin Gabbard, *Black Magic: White Hollywood and African American Culture* (New Brunswick, NJ: Rutgers University Press, 2004), 68.

38. For a discussion of the trilogy's disruption of patriarchy and whiteness, see Sanchez, "Neo-Abolitionists, Colorblind Epistemologies and Black Politics."

39. Feng, "False and Double Consciousness," 155.

40. Laura Mulvey, *Death 24x a Second: Stillness and the Moving Image* (London: Reaktion, 2006), 18.

41. Judith Butler, *Gender Trouble: Feminism and the Subversion of Identity* (New York: Routledge, 1990), 6.

42. Jenny Wolmark, introduction to *Cybersexualities: A Reader on Feminist Theory, Cyborgs and Cyberspace*, ed. Jenny Wolmark (Edinburgh: Edinburgh University Press, 1999), 8.

43. Sharon Willis, *High Contrast: Race and Gender in Contemporary Hollywood Film* (Durham, NC: Duke University Press, 1997), 2.

44. R. L. Rutsky, "Being Keanu," in *The End of Cinema As We Know It: American Film in the Nineties*, ed. Jon Lewis (London: Pluto, 2002), 187.

45. J. P. Telotte, "The Tremulous Public Body: Robots, Change, and the Science Fiction Film," *Journal of Popular Film and TV* 19 (1991): 16.

46. Dyer, *White*, 212-17.

47. Gabbard, *Black Magic*, 168.

48. Sanchez, "Neo-Abolitionists, Colorblind Epistemologies and Black Politics," 115.

49. Dyer, *White*, 75.

50. Sean Redmond, "The Whiteness of the Rings," in *The Persistence of Whiteness: Race and Contemporary Hollywood Cinema*, ed. Daniel Bernardi (London: Routledge, 2008), 97.

51. Vivian Sobchack, *The Address of the Eye: A Phenomenology of Film Experience* (Princeton, NJ: Princeton University Press, 1992), 302; Fredric Jameson, *Postmodernism, or, The Cultural Logic of Late Capitalism* (London: Verso, 1991), 9-10.

52. Sanchez, "Neo-Abolitionists, Colorblind Epistemologies and Black Politics," 117.

53. bell hooks, *Black Looks: Race and Representation* (Boston: South End Press, 1992), 170.

54. Claudia Springer, *Electronic Eros: Bodies and Desire in the Postindustrial Age* (Austin: University of Texas Press, 1996), 59; Deborah Lupton, "The Embodied Computer/User," in *The Cybercultures Reader*, ed. David Bell and Barbara M. Kennedy (London: Routledge, 2000), 487.

55. Amanda Fernbach, "The Fetishization of Masculinity in Science Fiction: The Cyborg and the Console Cowboy," *Science Fiction Studies* 27, no. 2 (2000): 248.

56. Barbara Creed, *The Monstrous Feminine: Film, Feminism, Psychoanalysis* (London: Routledge, 1993).

57. Julia Kristeva, *Powers of Horror*, trans. Leon Roudiez (New York: Columbia University Press, 1982), 64.

58. Cynthia Freeland, "Penetrating Keanu: New Holes, but the Same Old Shit," in *The Matrix and Philosophy: Welcome to the Desert of the Real*, ed. William Irwin (Chicago: Open Court, 2002), 208, 206, 209.

59. Freeland, "Penetrating Keanu," 206.

60. Springer, *Electronic Eros*, 58

61. Sadie Plant, "The Future Looms: Weaving Women and Cybernetics," in *Cyberspace/Cyberbodies/Cyberpunk: Cultures of Technological Embodiment*, ed. Mike Featherstone and Roger Burrows (London: Sage, 1995), 59.

62. Sadie Plant, "On the Matrix: Cyberfeminist Simulations," in *The Cybercultures Reader*, ed. David Bell and Barbara M. Kennedy (London: Routledge, 2000), 335.

63. Springer, *Electronic Eros*, 104.

64. Balsamo, "Forms of Technological Embodiment," 229.

65. Rosi Braidotti, *Nomadic Subjects: Embodiment and Sexual Difference in Contemporary Feminist Theory* (New York: Columbia University Press, 1994), 60.

66. Patrick Fuery, *New Developments in Film Theory* (Houndmills, Basingstoke: Macmillan, 2000), 71.

Chapter Five
Queering White Heterosexual Masculinity:
Cross-Dressing and Transgender Cinema

Border Crossings

In a discussion of the "representational problem" caused by Michael Jackson's mutable body, Cynthia Fuchs quotes a joke about Michael Jackson's marriage to Lisa Marie Presley which appeared in a "Kudzu" comic strip (August 25, 1994): as one character remarks, "If I heard it once I heard it a thousand times. That skinny white girl doesn't know what she's doing," another replies, "And you should hear what they say about Lisa Marie!"[1] A cheap shot, no doubt, but one characteristic of the ridicule commonly directed at a star "whose image is a spectacle of racial and sexual indeterminacy"[2]—an indeterminacy evoked by Jackson's distinctive appearance (make-up, tousled gelled hair, famed gold-plated codpiece), performance style (high-pitched, breathy vocals, on-stage crotch-grabbing), and surgical/medical alterations (the "whitening" of his facial features and skin tone). The cultural anxiety caused by a body that violates the boundaries between man/woman, black/white, youth/age[3] might also go some way to explaining the relish with which Jackson's disintegrating face has been greeted by the media (even before the charges of pedophilia, which, for many, merely confirmed Jackson's "abnormality"). His somatic indeterminacy also reveals the mutual imbrications of all identity categories. For instance, Jackson's sexual ambiguity is inseparable from his occupation of both poles of the binary opposition of sexual difference that is commonly mapped onto black masculinity—the feminized "coon" and hypermasculinized black male. Reactions to Jackson's "in-betweeness" also point to the hierarchical arrangements of difference. For instance, Madonna's self-styled phallic posturing (even imitating Jackson's famous crotch-grabbing routine with postmodern self-knowingness) was treated with none of the derision of Jackson's high-pitched voice, for instance, primarily because female masculinization functions as a cultural upgrading when acted out

137

in a heterosexual context. Likewise, whereas Jackson's skin lightening is denounced for constituting a rejection of his African-Americaness, a white person who darkens him/herself through tanning loses no prestige, and most likely gains it through demonstrating wealth and a privileged lifestyle.[4] It would seem, therefore, that the erotic lure of consuming what bell hooks terms "a bit of the Other"[5] is inextricably marked by power relations that define the cultural acceptability of border crossing, and retain whiteness, masculinity, and heterosexuality as privileged terms.

In the following two chapters, I analyze what "in-between" figures such as Jackson have to tell us about the constructed nature of gender and race, and their implications for cinematic representations of white heterosexual masculinity. In this chapter, I will focus on the impact that gender border-crossing has on filmic white masculinities, and in the following chapter I will focus on screenings of racial border-crossing, in particular white male appropriations of black culture. By destabilizing ontological notions of the body, border-crossing renders identity a contested site open to potential resignification. At the same time, the hostility that is often leveled at those who disturb our sense of a naturally sexed or raced body reveals not only the hegemonic force of essentialist discourses, but also some of the difficulties of escaping the bodily inscriptions of identity in a sociocultural order in which epistemological primacy is awarded to the visual. In this respect, while border-crossing might reveal identities to be constructions, these are constructions which exert a powerful force. Since border-crossing demonstrates the extent to which identity is always a multifaceted affair, I will also explore how crossing over from one identity category to another affects the other identities that a given body inhabits (however incompletely), and always impacts on normative white masculinity, which discursively positions itself as the universal structuring norm and locus of origins.

This chapter begins with a discussion of queer theorist Judith Butler's theorization of the performativity of gender and the subversive potential of drag, which dominated gender theory in the '90s. Butler's work provides a useful vocabulary and theoretical framework with which to explore the extent to which normative white heterosexual masculinity is "queered" in contemporary cross-dressing and transgender films. I will go on to briefly discuss cross-dressing comedies, which unleash temporary transgression, but tend to reaffirm boys as boys and girls as girls in narrative closure, before dealing with the more interesting '90s development of "new queer cinema."[6] In particular, I will focus on two surprise cross-over box-office successes: *The Crying Game* (Neil Jordan 1992) and *Boys Don't Cry* (Kimberly Peirce 1999), both of which screen transgendered subjectivity in passing narratives. My focus will be whether these films render visible the performative structures of normative white masculinity and destabilize the terms by which its ordinariness has traditionally been secured, or whether they renaturalize ontologically grounded accounts of gender. In my discussion of *The Crying Game* I explore how the presence of a transgendered, mixed race woman underscores the fragility of the white male protagonist's heterosexual identifications, as well as screening a white male desire for pre-feminist gender roles. As regards *Boys Don't Cry*, I analyze the ramifications for "ordinary" white men when they are confronted by the extra-ordinary masculinity of a transgendered male who highlights the imitability and reiterability of their own masculinity.

The Performativity of Gender and the Subversive Potential of Drag

In her now seminal work *Gender Trouble: Feminism and the Subversion of Identity* (1990), Judith Butler famously argued that gender was performative. By this she meant that all gender identifications, including normative heterosexual ones, are simulacra, "*a kind of imitation for which there is no original,*" though it is the kind of imitation that produces the very notion that there is an original gender.[7] Butler argues that the language of presumptive heterosexuality assumes continuity between sex, gender, and desire. However, when this continuity is broken, as it is in drag performances or transgendered identifications, for instance, "gender itself becomes a free-floating artifice, with the consequence that *man* and *masculine* might just as easily signify a female body as a male one, and *woman* and *feminine* a male body as easily as a female one." If gender is no longer tied to sex, it "can potentially proliferate beyond the binary limits imposed by the apparent binary of sex."[8] More contentiously, following Foucault's premise in *The History of Sexuality* (1976), she asserts that "sex," as well as gender, is an effect of regulatory practices and therefore also performative. Refuting the sex/gender dichotomy that has underpinned feminist social constructivist theory, she argues that gender should also refer to the discursive and cultural ways in which the persistent notion of a naturally sexed body is produced.[9] She is not, therefore, claiming that the body is *only* discursive, but that "there is no reference to a pure body which is not at the same time a further formation of that body."[10] As she clarifies in her later and more accessible book *Undoing Gender* (2004):

> "Sex" is made understandable through the signs that indicate how it should be read or understood. These bodily indicators are the cultural means by which the sexed body is read. They are themselves bodily, and they operate as signs, so there is no easy way to distinguish between what is "materially" true, and what is "culturally" true about a sexed body. I don't mean to suggest that purely cultural signs produce a material body, but only that the body does not become sexually readable without those signs, and that those signs are irreducibly cultural and material at once.[11]

Butler's highly influential account restaged the stale debates over essentialism, social constructivism, and sexual difference.[12] The academic interest it generated is also reflective of the more widespread interest in the malleability of the body in the postmodern era (also evident with the popularity of reality TV programs about plastic surgery or *Nip/Tuck*, the FX cable show about two plastic surgeons, which has devoted several episodes to transgendered or transsexual characters). The critical and commercial successes of films such as *The Crying Game* or Jeffrey Eugenides' novel *Middlesex* (2003) are also suggestive of current anxieties about and fascinations with bodies that refuse or fail to line up neatly on one side of the sexual difference binary. Along with Marjorie Garber, Butler argues that it is those who trouble the binary of sexual difference that have most to tell us about that binary and the gender categories it produces.[13]

Famously, Butler argues that drag performances, which foreground the performativity of gender, form a possible arena in which gender can be *re-cited* and resignified in order to reveal the "understated, taken-for-granted quality of heterosexual performativity."[14] In *Gender Trouble* she states:

> The performance of drag plays upon the distinction between the anatomy of the performer and the gender that is being performed. But we are actually in the presence of three contingent dimensions of significant corporeality: anatomical sex, gender identity, and gender performance. If the anatomy of the performer is already distinct from the gender of the performer, and both of those are distinct from the gender of the performance, then the performance suggests a dissonance not only between sex and performance, but sex and gender, and gender and performance. . . . *In imitating gender, drag implicitly reveals the imitative structure of gender itself—as well as its contingency.*[15]

Here, Butler is not denying the existence of anatomy, as she has often been accused of doing; rather, she attempts to separate out anatomy, gender identity, and gender performance. Indeed, for recitation of gender to occur in drag performances, the subversion must be noted, which most often requires awareness of the anatomical corporeality of the performer. Not realizing that a male drag queen has an anatomically male body, for example, would severely qualify the subversive potential of the performance, particularly when male drag queens, as well as male cross-dressers in filmic comedies, often impersonate the most stereotypical aspects of femininity.[16]

In her later *Bodies That Matter: On the Discursive Limits of "Sex"* (1993), Butler concedes that drag can work to reidealize heterosexual and patriarchal norms, and can be "caught in an irresolvable tension" between appropriation and subversion. "At best," she contends, "drag is a site of a certain ambivalence, one which reflects the more general situation of being implicated in the regimes of power by which one is constituted and, hence, of being implicated in the very regimes of power that one opposes."[17] She does, however, suggest that the more heterosexual the context, the less subversive the drag will be when she argues that films such as *Some Like it Hot* (1959) and *Tootsie* (1982), which she dubs "drag as high het entertainment," reveal "that there are domains in which heterosexuality can concede its lack of originality and naturalness" without relinquishing its power.[18] Margaret Thompson Drewal makes a similar point, asking what happens when gay signifying practices "are severed from their gay signifier and put into the service of the very patriarchal and heterosexist ideology of capitalism that camp politics seeks to disrupt and contest?"[19]—an apt framework for discussing representations of white heterosexual masculinity in popular cross-dressing comedies, which may well engage in camp practices, but are also marketed as good clean family fun.

White Masculinity in Cross-Dressing Comedies

As Chris Straayer has noted, the "temporary transvestite film" unleashes provisional transgression while constantly reminding the film's audience of the character's "original" gender, either through extended transformation scenes, gender-coded behavior or gestures, or reminders of the biological body beneath the disguise.[20] Point of view is essential, since the spectator is invariably in the know about the cross-dresser's true biological sex, unlike the diegetic characters, whose cases of mistaken identity form the basis of the films' humor. In short, these films might well screen gender as performance, but they certainly do not screen gender as performative, since the notion of an original gender behind the performance is retained. Moreover, the presence of heterosexual partners throughout "reinforce[s] society's heterosexual hegemony and the absolute alignment of gender, sex, and heterosexual preference."[21] These films thus allow what Butler terms a "ritualistic release for a heterosexual economy that must constantly police its own boundaries against the invasion of queerness."[22] This does not mean that there are not moments of subversion, such as the "paradoxical kiss" between two characters we know to be of the same biological sex, a kiss that can be experienced as heterosexual, homosexual, or bisexual, depending on cinematic point of view, *mise-en-scène*, star personas, or the spectator's own appropriation of the text.[23] Marjorie Garber, for instance, focuses on the subversive potential of these films, arguing that the transvestite occupies a "third term," which is not fixed, but rather "a mode of articulation, a way of describing a space of possibility" which destabilizes the binarity of sexual difference.[24] Using *Tootsie* (1982) as an example, Garber claims that Dorothy's (Dustin Hoffman's) "power inheres in her blurred gender." She also suggests that Michael/Dorothy's roommate "reads the complexity of Michael's interest in cross-dressing better than the critics" when he gingerly enquires, "it's just for the money, isn't it? It's not just so that you can wear these little outfits?"[25] However, invariably, the possibility of queerness or same-sex desire is evoked only to be denied and thus confirm that the male cross-dresser remains steadfastly heterosexual.

One of the pleasures of cross-dressing comedies is that of witnessing the dramatic transformation of the star body in a visual medium. Unlike the novel, for instance, where characters can remain disembodied, such as with the sexually indeterminate narrator of Jeanette Winterson's *Written on the Body* (1993), film, like theatre, depends on the material bodies of actors whose biological sex is visually inscribed. The star bodies that are transformed are overwhelmingly male in the comedies. Watching Dustin Hoffman in *Tootsie* or Robin Williams in *Mrs. Doubtfire* (1993) learning to apply make-up, walk in high heels, negotiate the mysteries of women's underwear, as well as cope with the sexist behavior of men, provide plenty of opportunities for viewing pleasures which can either affirm or unsettle hegemonic norms. For instance, these scenes might confirm that gender is an imitative structure, but may also confirm male viewers' notions of the artifice of the feminine, while providing female spectators with an enjoyable sense of superiority (how difficult can walking in high heels be?) and revenge (now you know what it's like!). Older women tend to be imitated, partly because a young femininity would be hard for many men to approximate, and partly because it provides plenty of opportunities to desexualize and ridicule the older woman's body, as we see with the slapstick, gross-out humor when Mrs. Doubtfire's breasts catch fire. Such films draw attention to male drag's potential for misogyny, since the humorous improbability of a man dressed as a woman can also suggest "the 'improbability' of the female body itself."[26]

Female drag, of course, points to the fact that masculinity has its own performative structures. Most female-to-male cross-dressing films screen a female adoption of a boyish masculinity that is easier for women to act out (*Yentl, Victor/Victoria, The Ballad of Little Jo*), and since (heterosexual) female masculinity is more culturally acceptable than male femininity, it rarely produces the same comic subversion as male drag, unless entire body suits and masks are used, as in the case of *The Associate* (1996) or the sketches of British comediennes Dawn French and Jennifer Saunders in *The French and Saunders Show*, which present maleness in a less than complimentary light.

The reason for cross-dressing also differs between the sexes and has much to say about social hierarchies. In films such as *Yentl* (1983) and *The Associate*, women cross-dress to obtain male privileges, privileges marked by discourses of race and class. For instance, in *The Associate*, Laurel (Whoopi Goldberg), a black female broker, disguises herself as a rich white man to gain recognition in the cut-throat world of Wall Street. While the film makes liberal points about institutionalized sexism and racism, the fact that Whoopi Goldberg is frequently desexualized or masculinized as a black woman in other performances (*Jumpin' Jack Flash, The Player, Fatal Beauty*, and *Ghost*, in which she actually mutates into Patrick Swayze) renders her easy assumption of the masculine less subversive than may first appear, underscoring that sexual norms are always caught up in ideologies of race and class as well. For instance, Tania Modleski, in a critique of Butler, has noted that drag might illustrate Homi Bhabha's observation that a woman of color is often "'not quite' a woman." She illustrates her point with reference to *Jumpin' Jack Flash* (1986), in which Whoopi Goldberg is mistaken for a transvestite by a taxi-driver when she dons a sexy dress and high heels, and walks with the awkwardness usually reserved for the male cross-dresser.[27]

The recent trend of white men cross-dressing to access the alleged "privileges" of (white bourgeois) femininity reveals how many of these comedies feed into narratives of white male victimization: Michael in *Tootsie* can only get a job as a female actor, while Daniel in *Mrs. Doubtfire* dresses up as a nanny in order to spend time with his children, having been granted only limited visiting rights when his wife (Sally Field) files for divorce. However, Michael goes on to become America's most popular "female" soap star, while Daniel, the film suggests, ends up doing a better job of raising his children than his career-orientated ex-wife—a suggestion that must be seen in the context of the host of '80s and '90s films which screen charismatic fathers and marginalized or inadequate mothers (*Three Men and a Baby, Father of the Bride, Terminator 2, Liar Liar, Cheaper by the Dozen, Big Daddy*). In other words, these films might well suggest that men become better people as women, and, in so doing, gesture at popular feminist discourses, but they can also be read through discourses of appropriation. Moreover, the fact that both Michael and Daniel act out conservative, ladylike, prim, older female characters also screens white male nostalgia for pre-feminist versions of femininity.

Even the queer drag movies for mainstream consumption that emerged in the '90s repeat many of the motifs of the heterosexual comedies. For instance, while the Australian *Adventures of Priscilla, Queen of the Desert* (1994) complicates usual characterizations of the drag queen (for example, one drag queen attempts to forge a relationship with his estranged son), one male character considers Bernadette (played by Terence Stamp), a ladylike transgendered woman, to be a better woman than his Filipino wife. As with Terence Stamp's role in *Priscilla*, the film *To Wong Foo, Thanks for Everything, Julie Newman* (1995) also deploys macho star personas to interesting effects—Patrick Swayze and Wesley Snipes both play drag queens—but as with the "temporary transvestite film," dramatic transformation scenes are screened, ensuring that we see the bodies of these known heterosexual stars as recognizably "male" beneath the artifice. *To Wong Foo* also reproduces the racial hierarchies of the buddy movie, with Swayze's maternal Vida playing lead role among multi-racial drag queens.[28] Moreover, the drag queens are positioned as mediating "angels" who help repair the heterosexual bonds between the women of a small, white, U.S. town and their conservative, non-attentive husbands.[29] For Kathryn Kane, therefore, despite the film's ostensibly liberal gestures of inclusion, in fact it solidifies heterosexual and white superiority.[30] The fact that the drag queens teach women of the town to stand up to their husbands also implies that biological men can do feminism better than biological women—a similar suggestion to that seen in *Tootsie* when Dorothy defends herself from lecherous men. Thus *Priscilla, To Wong Foo*, along with *The Birdcage* (1996) may well critique overt homophobia, posit the drag queen as a liberating figure in repressive environments, and suggest that whiteness, heterosexuality, and maleness are more attractive when combined with non-dominant identities;[31] they also, however, reveal how "under the cover of drag's new transgressive status, some very old-fashioned notions about race and gender are being smuggled back into popular culture."[32] Nonetheless, less recoupable into heterosexual norms than their straight cross-dressing counterparts, these films also demonstrate the current marketability of queer themes for mainstream consumption.

More surprise hits were the Oscar-winning films *The Crying Game* and *Boys Don't Cry*, which screen cross-dressing as neither a stage performance nor a temporary disguise, but rather as a psychic need. Both films feature protagonists who are transgender, a term referring to "those persons who cross-identify or who live as another gender, but who may or may not have undergone hormonal treatments or sex reassignment operations."[33] For this reason, the term refuses the fixity of the term transsexual and "embraces more hybrid possibilities for embodiment and identification."[34] *The Crying Game* screens the fictional story of a white heterosexual-identified male, Fergus (Stephen Rea), who falls in love with a mixed race transgendered woman, Dil (Jaye Davidson), while *Boys Don't Cry* is a bio-pic of the real-life Brandon Teena, a transgendered male, who was brutally raped and murdered in 1993. In both films, I am interested in the ramifications for normative white masculinity when a subject refuses his "boying" or her "girling," to use Butler's terms. In my analysis of both films, I also tease out the extent to which the anatomical body is posited as the "truth" of "sex," and whether the binaries of sexual difference and homosexuality/heterosexuality are confirmed or undermined. In so doing, I address how sexual passing affects other identity categories, including class, race, and nation, what these films reveal about the hierarchical arrangements of differences, and how identity categories work through each other to articulate or subvert hegemonic norms.

The Crying Game: Queering White Male Heterosexual Identifications

Despite its controversial political and sexual content, *The Crying Game* was a surprise critical and commercial success. Screened through the point of view of Fergus, an IRA volunteer, the film begins as a political thriller, focusing on Fergus's relationship with Jody (Forest Whitaker), a black British soldier taken hostage. Jody asks Fergus to look up his "special friend," Dil, if anything should happen to him; unable to shoot Jody, who is inadvertently killed by the British troops sent to rescue him, Fergus escapes to England (a literal border crossing, which divides the film's two narrative segments), and makes good on his promise to Jody. Fergus falls in love with Dil, though a Hitchcockian reversal of audience expectations reveals that Dil is a biological man. Not surprisingly, the film was deemed radical in initial reviews, both for its sympathetic portrayal of a member of the IRA and for its sexual content. Nevertheless, Dil's body constitutes the site of some conservative white male fantasies about gender and race, fantasies that the transgressive status of Dil's sexuality works to veil in one of the film's many masquerades.

The Crying Game was originally advertised as a neo-*noir* political thriller. Miramax, the distributor, decided to shift attention away from the political, changing the advertising tag line from "Play it at your own risk. Sex. Murder. Betrayal" to "The movie everyone is talking about but no one is giving away its secrets." Miramax also enlisted the help of reviewers not to disclose the twist: thus its "secret" became instrumental in the film's marketing strategy, facilitating not only a displacement of the IRA plot, but also its queer content—no doubt a fact which enabled it to break beyond the art house circuit.[35]

Point of view is crucial to the film's dramatic disclosure: all events are filtered through Fergus's white male gaze in typical *noir* fashion. For this reason, like the typical *femme fatale* of the *noir* genre, Dil remains two-dimensional and unknowable, at times provocative and confident, at other times tragic and helpless—inconsistencies that underscore that Dil's role is primarily to reflect Fergus's personal and sexual crisis. Crucially, then, the film is yet another story of white heterosexual masculinity thrown into crisis through a confrontation with difference, though one dressed up in art-house chic.[36] Unlike the cross-dressing comedies, the spectator is given no privileged knowledge; there are no comic slips of disguise or transformation scenes, unless we include the scene where Fergus "disguises" Dil as a man to protect her from the IRA, though she still fails to look and act like a convincing man. Thus, much like Hitchcock's *Vertigo* (1958), the epistemological authority usually attributed to the controlling white male gaze in mainstream cinema is evoked only to be found wanting, since in both cases the male protagonist's masochistic submission to a fetish object means that he only sees what he wants to see.

The fact that most film spectators were as shocked as Fergus to discover Dil's biological sex can be attributed to the film's mobilization of cinematic conventions that posit Dil as an eroticized object of heterosexual male desire. The first glimpse of Dil is the photograph that Jody shows Fergus, which immediately frames Dil through Fergus's desiring gaze in an act of bi-racial, homosocial bonding (though the slightly oblique camera angle that films this exchange might well suggest that something else is askew). The next shots of Dil are established through Fergus's voyeuristic gaze and connote Dil's "to-be-looked-at-ness." Dil is first shown when Fergus watches her through the window of the hairdresser's where she works. When Fergus enters the shop, filmed in a long shot from an objective camera, Dil remains partially obscured, positioned at the extreme edge of the frame. Then the scene cuts to a close-up of Dil's hands and painted nails as she runs her hands through Fergus's hair, before she features in her first frontal medium shot. Dil, in other words, is filmed in the traditional manner of a *femme fatale*, though the fetishization of body parts, which in Mulvey's schema is deployed to ward off the threat of castration, is rather ironic in this case, since the threat Dil poses is not lack but presence. The first notable departure from traditional Hollywood codes comes in their first sexual encounter, in which both remain fully clothed. As they kiss and the camera tilts down to show Fergus reaching for her crotch, Dil abruptly pushes Fergus's hand away before unzipping Fergus's flies and lowering her head to perform oral sex. The scene then cuts to Fergus's face as he gasps in orgasmic pleasure, a cut that keeps Fergus's penis off-screen.[37]

Conversely, in the exposure scene, Dil's penis is treated as "some sort of 'special' effect," as Sharon Willis puts it, while Fergus's penis is again obscured, "as if there were nothing to be learned from Fergus's organ and everything to be learned from Dil's."[38] This scene begins conventionally enough. As Fergus and Dil kiss, an objective camera films the scene from behind the red transparent veil that encircles Dil's bed, the symbolism only apparent retrospectively. Dil disappears off to slip into something more comfortable (Dil's femininity is modeled on cliché), before returning in a satin robe. While the dramatic music swirls to its climax, the camera is then aligned with Fergus's white male gaze; when he slips the robe slowly off Dil's shoulders and pulls back, Dil's body is revealed to both Fergus and the film's spectator, as the camera tilts down Dil's body in a continuous shot that reveals a flat-chest and flaccid penis. As Shantanu DuttaAhmed asserts, the fact that Dil's black penis is flaccid, while Fergus's presumably erect, white penis remains, once again, off-screen, allows Fergus's veiled penis to stand in for the phallus, revealing "how issues of race complicate the symbolic investment in the phallus, *despite the imbrication between the two.*"[39]

The Crying Game joins other contemporary films, such as *M. Butterfly* (1992), *The Last Seduction* (1994), and *Trainspotting* (1996), in screening white men being taken in by a transgendered female or transvestite—a trend which can only point to the anxieties that sexual transgression provokes in "ordinary" men, especially anxieties concerning the fragility of heterosexual identifications. Even after the disclosure scene, the joke continues to be on the straight white men in the film, such as when Dil visits Fergus at work and, dressed provocatively in black tights, denim shorts, and high heels, is greeted by wolf whistles from the other builders, who are unaware that the object cementing homosocial desire is biologically male. Likewise, when Fergus's unpleasant boss, Deveroux (Tony Slattery), sarcastically calls Dil a "lady," Fergus replies, "No, she's not that either." Of course, Deveroux uses the term not as a biological marker, but as a signifier of white bourgeois femininity, revealing that while Dil can perform femininity, her performance will always be marked by her non-whiteness and working-class status.

Fergus overcomes his initial homophobic panic, and although he cannot bring himself to have sex with Dil, he carries on treating her as a *woman* in need of his protection. Fergus's chivalrous treatment of Dil is a major reason for the film's most remarkable feat: that Dil continues to be considered a woman by most spectators despite the visual certainty offered by the revelation scene. This is not to ignore the importance awarded the biological body in this scene, but rather to confirm it, since what is disruptive in the film is the fact that, despite Dil's anatomically male body, she remains female in terms of identification and performance. In that sense, Dil causes what Garber terms "a category crisis,"[40] disrupting the notion of sexual difference even as the signifier of that difference, the penis, is awarded epistemological primacy. Indeed, Dil embodies a more excessive femininity than that of the biological women in the film. She performs unreciprocated oral sex on Fergus, brings Fergus his lunch and a cup of tea to work dressed to the nines, faints from nervous blood condition like a swooning nineteenth century lady, and informs Fergus that she will do anything for him as long as he doesn't leave her.[41]

Dil's convincing performance of the damsel in distress allows Fergus to assume the role of chivalric gentleman. While this certainly demonstrates the citationality of Fergus's masculinity, both Fergus and the film seem to be suffering from a yearning for an old-fashioned romance plot, one that represents itself as new, radical even, through the film's queer content. Fergus assumes the role of knight in shining armor from the outset when he protects Dil from her abusive, working-class ex-boyfriend and later from his boss, making Dil exclaim, with camp self-consciousness, "My oh my, Jimmy. How gallant! It made me feel all funny inside!" Irony or no irony, though, Dil allows Fergus to act out an old-fashioned masculinity that he cannot assume around aggressive, independent women like fellow-IRA volunteer Jude (Miranda Richardson). For Slavoj Žižek, who reads the film through the discourse of courtly love, The Crying Game demonstrates that "the sexual relationship is condemned to remain an asymmetrical non-relationship." Therefore, he argues, women like Jude, who oppose patriarchal domination, "simultaneously undermine the fantasy-support of their own 'feminine' identity," and Fergus's relationship with Dil can "realize the notion of heterosexual love far more 'authentically' than a 'normal' relationship with a woman."[42] However, while the film might offer an apt illustration of the Lacanian tenet that there is no sexual relation, Fergus's attraction to this excessive femininity has disquieting gender implications. Indeed, Fergus is another example of the transformed, sensitive white men that populated many '80s and '90s films, the overriding concern of which is how to be a straight white man in a postfeminist age: rather than becoming woman (Tootsie, Mrs. Doubtfire), a father who replaces the mother (Three Men and a Baby, Mrs. Doubtfire, Terminator 2), or a brain-damaged child (Regarding Henry, Forrest Gump), Fergus assumes the role of gentleman to a lady, but can only do so to a biological male who perfectly embodies patriarchal, pre-feminist notions of the feminine.

One of the rather disturbing suggestions that emerges from the film, therefore, is the suggestion that Dil does femininity "better" (in patriarchal terms) than biological women, a trendier take on the premises of Tootsie and Mrs. Doubtfire. Indeed, Jody directly informs Fergus of that fact, even though this interpretation is only available on second viewing: after telling Fergus that "women are trouble," he qualifies his statement to "some kinds of women are," adding, "Dil, she was no trouble, no trouble at all." Mark Simpson, who contends that the film is misogynistic, argues that if contextualized, The Crying Game screens the Good Girl/Bad Girl opposition that dominated Hollywood in the late '80s and '90s—Fatal Attraction (1987) being the prime example.[43] While Simpson underestimates the subversive effect of Dil's ironic and auto-deconstructive citation of femininity, it is certainly the case that the film plays

Dil favorably off against the callous Jude, whose disguise in London is that of phallic career woman, and whose threat is one of aggressive sexuality, much like the neo-*noir femme fatale*, such as Meredith in *Disclosure* (1994) or Bridget in *The Last Seduction* (who is also seen as less "womanly" by the film's victim-hero than the transsexual he unwittingly married).

Dil's femininity and Fergus's response to it must also be examined through the lens of racial dynamics. Garber suggests that the presence of a transvestite in a text often indicates "*a category crisis* elsewhere."[44] In *The Crying Game* that category crisis concerns race, with Dil also functioning as an exotic "in-between" figure as far as her racial identity is concerned. Dil's race is only re-ferred to once in the film, when Jude calls her a "wee black chick," but it is also highlighted through her connection with Jody, "the absent site, perhaps even the *fantasmatic* site, where race is spoken."[45] In one of his first conversations with Fergus, Jody informs him (erroneously) that Northern Ireland is "the only place where they call you nigger to your face." Fergus's flippant reply that Jody shouldn't take it personally underscores the privilege of whiteness to refuse to acknowledge the power that race and racism wield. Likewise, as bell hooks points out, initial reviews of the film either failed to mention race, or if they did, did so only to state that the film's theme was that race and gender do not really matter, and overlooked the fact that it is those with black bodies that are subor-dinated. hooks inserts the racial dynamics that reviewers, along with the film, displaced onto sexual transgression, arguing that Dil "embodies the 'tragic mu-latto' persona that has always been the slot for sexually desirable black female characters of mixed race in Hollywood."[46] Consequently, Fergus's failure to properly "read" Dil might be attributed not only to her convincing performance of patriarchal notions of femininity, but also to a femininity that is racially marked (Dil is both sexually available and a subservient "mammy"), in turn pointing to Fergus's attraction to a paternalistic white male role.

In this respect, *The Crying Game* also parallels Jordan's earlier film *Mona Lisa* (1986), featuring Bob Hoskins as a white male desperately attempting to rescue a black prostitute, Simone (Cathy Tyson), in a similar narrative of white male redemption. Like Dil, Simone harbors a secret that George (Bob Hoskins) is unaware of—she is a lesbian—a secret which similarly renders the white male's investment in the role of the gallant courtly lover pathetically futile. *The Crying Game* is also remarkably similar to *M. Butterfly* (1992), based on David Henry Hwang's play, which Slavoj Žižek jokingly refers to as "*The Crying Game* Goes East."[47] *M. Butterfly* dramatizes the real-life story of a French dip-lomat who fell in love with a Chinese opera singer and ended up spying for China, unaware for years that his lover was a biological man. The film, like the play, suggests that this deception was possible because of Western, patriarchal notions of Asian femininity, since the diplomat Gallimard (Jeremy Irons) attrib-utes the fact that he has never seen his lover, Song Liling (John Lone), naked or the fact that she remains fully clothed during sex to Chinese women's sense of modesty (though the film suggests that he disavows his knowledge of his lover's biological sex). It becomes evident that Gallimard has fallen in love with an idea of exotic, demure Asian womanhood, which bolsters his role as Western patriarch. Thus Song Liling's transgressive body, like Dil's, becomes a repository for regressive white male fantasies about gender, race, and ethnicity.

At the same time, the fact that Fergus is Irish and working-class means that he cannot access all the privileges of white heterosexual masculinity, as his boss's ethnic slurs and superior attitude make clear. The film thus undoes traditional racial configurations of the colonizer/colonized binary, since, in terms of the Irish conflict, the colonized is embodied by a white male, while the colonizer is initially represented by a black male, Jody. However, this binary is further complicated by the fact that Jody, whose chosen military profession serves the British colonial project, is also a colonized subject, since he was born in the former British colony of Antigua. Just as Jody is both colonizer and colonized, so too is Fergus, since, as bell hooks argues, by the film's end he "has not only cannibalized Jody, he appropriates Jody's narrative and uses it to declare possession of Dil." The film thus "offers a romanticized image of the white colonizer moving into black territory, occupying it, possessing it in a way that affirms his identity."[48]

Fergus's obsession with Jody, while partly attributed to his guilty conscience, is also open to a queer as well as a racial/colonial reading. The revelation of Dil's body not only references Jody's queer sexuality, but also, in turn, necessitates a retrospective re-reading of Jody's intimate relationship with Fergus, as well as consideration of how this impacts on Fergus's sexual identity. For instance, the dialogue when Jody tells Fergus that he is "the handsome one" might first be regarded as similar to the homoerotophobic, comic banter common to buddy movies, such as Lethal Weapon (1987) or Tango and Cash (1989), that polices the irruption of homoerotic desire into male relationships. On second viewing, though, this flirtatious exchange acquires homoerotic connotations. Likewise, the male bonding that Jody solicits by showing Fergus Dil's photograph retrospectively foregrounds the homoerotic desire that Eve Sedgwick has located in Western, patriarchal, homosocial ties.[49] The fact that Fergus and Jody bond over Jody's penis is also open to a retrospective queer reading: because Jody's hands are fastened, Fergus has to help him to urinate by unzipping his pants and getting "the fucker" out (Jody's double-edged term). This comic scene, one of the many which posits Jody as child-like, thereby neutralizing the threat of the black male's alleged hypermasculinity, hints at homoerotic desire even on first viewing. Moreover, Fergus's homophobic fear of physical intimacy with Jody suggests that, for Fergus, Jody's penis is not just "a piece of meat," as Jody protests; indeed, as Mark Simpson puts it, it is the "meat" on Dil that causes Fergus to vomit.[50] The laughter that ensues between the men as Jody jokingly states, "I know that wasn't very easy for you," and Fergus replies, "the pleasure was all mine," functions as a release of homoerotic tension. This queer reading of the film is also substantiated when Fergus dresses Dil up in Jody's clothes, ostensibly to protect her from Jude, which Jordan himself views as Fergus's attempt to "reshape [Dil] in the image of the guy he's lost."[51] Heterosexuality in the film is thus marked as precariously unstable. Not only is it always constructed in relation to an abjected other—homosexuality—which always troubles its borders,[52] but also, as Fergus's initial panic at discovering Dil's biological sex underscores, it is also partly dependent on the body and gender identity of the object of desire.

Nonetheless, the sexual transgression unleashed by the film is largely contained by narrative closure, since Fergus is imprisoned, having taken the blame for the murder of Jude that Dil committed in a fit of jealousy. The ending of the film, when Dil visits Fergus in prison, shows them continuing to act out their self-chosen gender roles—Fergus as gallant, protective gentleman, and Dil as the needy damsel in distress—but also avoids exploring the ramifications of this relationship for Fergus's sexual identity, because a glass barrier now divides them. With Fergus having made amends for the death of Jody through his self-sacrifice, the film offers a reworked version of the rather worn narrative of white male redemption, not through the traditional motif of white male redemption through violence, but rather through an extra-ordinary white man's successful negotiation of difference.

Boys Don't Cry: Performing White Masculinity

With *Boys Don't Cry*, director Kimberly Peirce attempted to rescue Teena Brandon's story from sensationalized media coverage.[53] Ironically, though predictably for a Hollywood-financed film about a transgendered male, the film provoked its own media frenzy, not least because of the lawsuits it unleashed, most famously by Lana Tisdel, Brandon's ex-girlfriend—a response symptomatic of the bio-doc genre, in which knowledge that events are based on "real-life" inevitably negotiates interpretation. The popular press also expressed astonishment at Hilary Swank's convincing performance of boyish masculinity, fascinated by the fact that Peirce gave Swank the part on condition that she live as a man for four weeks before shooting. In interviews, Swank explained how she lost touch with her gender identity, calling her husband out to join her after the first few weeks of filming because "[h]e was the only one who could see past my physical appearance and be there for me mentally and emotionally. . . . Without him I don't know if I would have made it through the rest of it." As Chris Straayer asserts, "[i]t was as if Brandon's 'identity crisis' (male identity, female body) had been transferred to Swank (female identity, male performance), which can only imply that the performed body is as powerful as the anatomical body."[54] The press also delighted in commenting on Swank's glamorous appearance at award ceremonies, when "the boyish Brandon transmutes back again into sexy babe as Swank shows up in form-hugging dresses, batting her eyes and thanking her husband."[55] Her appearance thus reassured audiences of an original female identity behind the masquerade, but nonetheless still pointed to "the breadth and ease of gender performativity."[56]

Like *The Crying Game*, *Boys Don't Cry* attracted sustained, critical interest (most notably an ongoing debate in *Screen*), much of which focused on the film's crossover address. Rendering Brandon accessible to straight audiences was precisely Kimberly Peirce's intention. In an article in the lesbian and gay magazine *The Advocate*, Peirce recalls the thrill she experienced as a child watching Howard Hawks's *To Have and Have Not* (1944) and identifying with Humphrey Bogart and his desire for Lauren Bacall, stating that *Boys Don't Cry* enables straight audiences to participate in the transvestism that has been central to queer identity and experience. Peirce suggests that this "erotic leap" was possible because of the fact that "Brandon actually embodied many traits of the traditional Hollywood hero. He had the innocence and tenderness of Montgomery Cliff in *Red River* or a young Henry Fonda, the naïve determination of Jimmy Stewart. He was a rebellious outsider like James Dean, a shy, courtly gentleman around women like Gary Cooper."[57] Fox Searchlight's official website also focuses on the film's portrayal of "the contradictions of American youth and identity," failing to mention transgendered sexuality in its plot synopsis.[58]

Critical reviews, as well as Peirce herself, also universalized the queer subject matter by homing in on the film's *Romeo and Juliet* love story.[59] Unlike the documentary *The Brandon Teena Story* (1998), which paints a reportedly more faithful picture of Brandon seducing a string of young, sexually inexperienced girls, Peirce makes Brandon's relationship with Lana Tisdel (Chloë Sevigny) the narrative focus of her film, mainly because of her self-confessed fascination with Lana's "absolute spiritual love."[60] In this respect, Peirce has been severely criticized for failing to document Brandon's life accurately.[61] However, rather than demanding authenticity in a narrative feature film, a more productive line of enquiry would be to examine what ideological work her deployment of the *Romeo and Juliet* narrative carries out. For instance, the editing out of Brandon's promiscuity certainly renders a film about transgendered subjectivity more palatable to most straight viewers, as does the fated "star-crossed lovers" motif—it is more difficult to imagine mainstream audiences embracing a film that screens a successful relationship involving a well-adjusted transgendered subject, hence Dil's tragic status in *The Crying Game*. Chris Straayer also notes that, while the film succeeds in capturing for Lana the charming masculinity that all of Brandon's girlfriends apparently found irresistible (many of Brandon's ex-girlfriends appeared on talk shows to attest that he was the best boyfriend they had ever had), it "misses the sustaining function that serial seductions likely served his masculinity."[62] Nonetheless, *Boys Don't Cry* does resignify romance conventions outside of heterosexuality. More importantly, as Patricia White points out, the film's romance strategy and marked female address also "makes Lana's desire and way of seeing count."[63]

Lana's way of seeing is not made available until the first sex scene, however; up until that point, events are screened through Brandon's perspective. As with most cross-dressing films, the spectator is made aware at the outset that Brandon is a biological woman. Unlike the comedies, though, or even realist representations of passing, such as Maggie Greenwald's revisionist Western *The Ballad of Little Jo* (1993)—which narrativizes the real life story of Jo Monaghan (Suzy Amis), who dressed as a man to protect herself in the wild West— Brandon does not cross-dress as a means to an end, but as an end in itself.[64] The film opens as Brandon's gay cousin, Lonny (Matt McGrath), finishes cutting Brandon's hair into a boyish crop, though crucially, this transformation scene offers no "pre-passing" image—the only glimpse of a more feminine Brandon throughout the film is a teasingly fleeting shot of his early police records. Instead of offering an original gender identity, the opening scene presents us solely with the performance, as Brandon postures before a mirror, stuffs a sock down his jeans crotch, leading Lonny to joke, "If you was a guy, I might even want to fuck you," to which Brandon grinningly replies, "You mean if *you* was a guy, you might even want to fuck me!" Brandon's reply, of course, underlines not only the performative structures underpinning Lonny's own masculinity, but also the femininity attributed to gay masculinity in heterosexist culture. For Brandon, it becomes clear that possession of the penis is no guarantee of manliness. Lonny, conversely, reinforces the cultural conflation of genitals and gender, and attempts to "reason" with Brandon after he narrowly escapes a beating from a group of men enraged that Brandon had dated one of their sisters:

> Brandon: I don't know what went wrong
> Lonny: You are not a boy. That's what went wrong. That is what went wrong.
> Brandon: Don't get mad. They all say I'm the best boyfriend they've ever had.
> . . .
> Lonny: Why don't you just admit you're a dyke?
> Brandon: Because I'm not a dyke.

For Lonny, Brandon's male identification is part of his general inability to face up to reality, a suggestion that frames the remainder of the film, particularly every time Brandon lies about his past. Nonetheless, Brandon vehemently refuses either lesbian or female identification. Therefore, as Butler notes, "[i]t will not work to say that because Brandon must do himself as a boy that this is a sign that Brandon is a lesbian. For boys surely do themselves as boys, and no anatomy enters gender without being 'done' in some way."[65]

Nonetheless, the film takes pains to stress Brandon's female body beneath his masculine appearance. Not only do other characters remark on his small hands or smooth face, but particular narrative space is devoted to the arrival of Brandon's period. For Jennifer Esposito, these reminders underscore Brandon's failures and the return of the repressed female body, functioning to reaffirm an original gender, much like the slips of disguise that Straayer locates in the "temporary transvestite film." Thus, she argues, Brandon's performance is posited as pure masquerade, while the masculinity of John (Peter Sarsgaard) and Tom (Brendan Sexton III) is reinscribed as natural, since they possess penises, "signifiers in absentia" (Straayer's term).[66] Certainly, these overdetermined reminders of Brandon's female anatomy are open to voyeuristic and sensationalist appeal, and, in accordance with the film's overall tragic structure, point to Brandon's inevitable exposure. Yet, they could also be seen to "*avow* queerness," as Michele Aaron argues, and "extend spectatorial implication within the sexual (and social) workings of the diegesis rather than seal it off."[67] For instance, when we see Brandon leaving the shower, inserting a tampon, binding his breasts, stuffing his pants, and posturing in front of the mirror, Brandon's face suddenly breaks into a smile as he states, "you're an asshole"—a moment of ironizing self-awareness which also points to the imitative structures of all macho masculinity. Moreover, it is precisely the dissonance between biological sex and gender identity that refuses rather than resecures the authentication of masculinity through recourse to the male body. It is also crucial that Brandon's performance fails, not because his "original" gender "betrays" him, but because a court summons arrives, pointing to the discursive formations of a legal system that demands conformity between biology and gender identity. Esposito also underestimates the power of the film's "transgender gaze," as Judith Halberstam terms it, established through Lana's refusal "to privilege the literal over the figurative," even if this gaze is abandoned in the final love scene, a point I will return to.[68]

The first incorporation of Lana's gaze occurs during the film's first sex scene. Lana mutters, "I'm in a trance," a statement that privileges the realm of fantasy, just before Brandon performs oral sex on her (off-screen so that the film could gain a NC-17 rating). The camera lingers on a close-up of Lana's face as she sighs with increasing intensity. The remainder of the scene is then delayed, interrupted by a fleeting shot of Brandon partying in a car with Lana, Candace, and Kate (Alison Folland). Another cut then transports us to the all-female space of Lana's bedroom, as Lana relates a version of her sexual encounter to her friends, an account which diverges considerably from the intercutting flashbacks narrated through Lana's memory. As Lana throws herself back on the bed, covering her eyes and telling her friends that it was "too intense," the camera again lingers on her face in close-up, before cutting to a side-on medium shot of Brandon penetrating her. This is followed by a close-up of Lana's expression as it changes to one of bewilderment, immediately followed by a matching subjective shot which shows a glimpse of Brandon's bound cleavage through his open shirt. A further flashback shows an obviously shaken Lana interrupting their lovemaking, cautiously feeling Brandon's crotch and inspecting his smooth, hairless face, before she mutters "you're so handsome." Back in the film's narrative present, Lana, smiling with self-satisfaction, tells her disbelieving friends that they took off their clothes and went swimming, while a final flashback shows Lana telling Brandon not to be scared, before pushing him gently to the ground and kissing him. When asked by her friends whether they did it, Lana replies, "What do you think?"—positioning the film's spectator as one of the girls,[69] and leaving the rest of the sexual encounter unscreened.

The film, then, suggests that Lana disavows her knowledge of Brandon's biological sex. Indeed, the above scene is paradigmatic of how cinematic signification—with its lingering close-ups and subjective shots, and use of parallel editing, which allows the viewer to move in time and space, in this case revealing Lana's reconstructed account of what she had earlier seen—can construct a fetishistic gaze. At the same time, it reverses the Freudian paradigm in which fetishism is solely a male preserve. Rather than the Freudian scenario of fetishism in which the boy postulates a maternal penis where in fact there is none in order to "triumph over the threat of castration" and "save" the fetishist from homosexuality,[70] this scene constructs a *female* fetishistic gaze that posits a penis where there is none—a gaze that might well attempt to maintain heterosexual identifications, but one which actually queers Lana's heterosexuality in the process. Lana thus installs a temporal distance between the moment of vision and retrospective interpretation, which, as Mary Anne Doane notes, for Freud was solely a male prerogative.[71] Lana's disavowal of Brandon's biological sex continues throughout the film. When Lana finds Brandon in the female section of the prison, and Brandon informs her that he is a hermaphrodite who is more "she" than "he," Lana tenderly tells him, "I don't care if you're half monkey or half ape, I'm getting you out of here." Lana also informs Brandon that she doesn't need to see him naked: "Think about it. I know you're a guy."

It is precisely Lana's refusal to accept Brandon's femaleness that so infuriates John and Tom, who attempt to reinscribe a system of gender and genital equivalence when they strip Brandon naked and expose his vagina. As Halberstam notes, their brutal action "is clearly identified as a violent mode of looking, and the film identifies the male gaze with that form of knowledge which resides in the literal."[72] "All I need's the truth, little buddy," John states, before restraining a struggling Brandon while Tom forces down his pants, opens his legs, and declares, "It don't look like no sexual identity crisis to me!" However, unlike *The Crying Game*, this scene has nothing to tell the spectators that they don't already know, and consequently, attention is not focused on the exposure of Brandon's body so much as Lana's reaction. As John drags Lana into the bathroom and pushes her face towards Brandon's crotch, Lana keeps her eyes closed, screaming out "Leave him alone!" Lana's use of the male pronoun would seem to give Brandon back his male identity: as the soundtrack cuts to silence, a shot of Brandon from Lana's point of view is quickly followed by an eye-line match showing the figure of Brandon, fully-dressed in masculine garb, standing with Lana's mother and friends, singled out by a bright light in the now darkened hallway. This lingering shot is then returned, as for a few seconds Brandon sees a frozen image of his naked self strung up by Tom and John, before this brief respite returns us to the visual and audio frenzy of the attack. This shot/reverse shot, divided between Brandon as subject and object of his own gaze, underscores Brandon's horror at being publicly exposed (a stark contrast to Dil's erotic disclosure), as well as revealing the importance of what Lacan terms "the look of the Other" to his male subjectivity; but it also constitutes a refusal of Tom and John's literal gaze, since Brandon's self-representation remains male identified. In other words, as Halberstam puts it, the shot/reverse shot "serves both to destabilize the spectator's sense of gender stability and also to confirm

Brandon's manhood at the very moment that he has been exposed as female/castrated."[73]

Nonetheless, after the rape scene, Lana's way of seeing changes, and along with it the film's representation of Brandon's maleness. Many critics have expressed their irritation with the fact that the final love scene is assimilated into the terms of lesbianism, as if Brandon being raped forced both Brandon and Lana to accept Brandon's "original" gender identity.[74] As Lana holds Brandon maternally in a tightly framed pietà-like shot, she now tells Brandon that he's "pretty" rather than "handsome." She also asks Brandon whether "before all this" he was like her—"a girl-girl"—to which Brandon replies, "yes, a long time ago," before adding he was then "just like a boy-girl, and then I was just like a jerk." This is also the moment that Brandon confesses to lying about his past, framing this sex scene with an arrival at self-knowledge. Despite their previous sexual encounter, Lana also tells Brandon, "I don't know if I'm going to know how to do it," before a shot of her removing Brandon's top dissolves into tender, post-sex pillow talk. The actual sex remains off-screen, presumably because it has little to tell us, unlike the first encounter involving a dildo, and with Brandon's breast binds cut away by the hospital nurse, the scene taps into the cliché of "idealistic lesbian reciprocity."[75]

When asked about the lesbianization of Brandon in this scene, Peirce defended her choice in humanist terms, arguing that after being raped, "Brandon could be *neither* Brandon Teena *nor* Teena Brandon, and thus truly becomes 'himself' and 'receives love' for the first time as a human being."[76] What is disturbing about this assertion is that it attributes to rape the transformative power that John and Tom intended for it, as well as suggesting that transgendered subjectivity constitutes a tragic state of in-betweeness and non-belonging. Nevertheless, Peirce, like Lana, continues to attribute the pronoun "he" to Brandon, a stark contrast to John, Tom, and Lana's mother's use of "it"—a designation that underscores Butler's point that to qualify as human, bodies must correspond to the norms of sexual difference.[77] Several journalists, however, writing both of Brandon Teena and *Boys Don't Cry*, insisted on Brandon's femaleness and reclaimed Brandon as a confused butch lesbian, provoking anger and activism from the transgendered community.[78] The various claims made on the real-life and filmic Brandon as a woman, man, lesbian, transvestite, transgendered subject, and transsexual thus point not only to the "category crisis" that Brandon presents, but also the leakiness of all identity categories. In a generous reading, then, even if the final sex scene does inscribe Brandon with the more socially legible identity of lesbian, this might also drive a wedge between gender identity and sexual practices, as well as gender identity and biological sex, creating a queer space in which sexuality is fluid enough to "escape being an either-or proposition."[79]

Brandon's convincing performance of masculinity succeeds in foregrounding the performative structures of John and Tom's normative masculinity, underscoring Lacan's insight that, in the words of Butler, "[t]he masculine only *ap-*

pears to originate meanings."[80] Femininity has more commonly been associated
with artifice and masquerade, while masculinity has been culturally associated
with authenticity. But as Hilary Neroni asserts, "masculinity is, of course, as
constructed as femininity but part of its construction lies in creating the appearance of not being constructed."[81] In the case of *Boys Don't Cry*, when Lana asks
Brandon why he allowed John and Tom to tie him to the back of a truck and
drag him around like a dog (a virility-testing ritual known as "bumper-skiing"),
Brandon replies, "I just thought that's what guys do around here." Likewise,
Tom challenges Brandon to prove his mettle by mutilating himself with a knife,
a challenge Brandon skillfully deflects by accepting that he's "just a big pussy"
compared to Tom (misogynistic language is part of the turf, it would seem).
Brandon's approximation of white working-class masculinity thus highlights not
only its underlying masochistic investments (the film's original title was *Take It
Like a Man*), but also the constant verification that masculinity requires, even
when acted out by a biological male.

If, then, possession of the penis does not guarantee possession of the phallus, as Lacanian psychoanalysis insists, the phallus, as Butler argues in *Bodies
that Matter*, might be considered transferable property.[82] In her discussion of
"the lesbian phallus," a theoretical *tour de force* which Butler later claimed was
intended as parody,[83] she returns to the well-trodden path of highlighting Lacan's penis-phallus slippage. Butler follows Lacan in arguing that since the phallus symbolizes the penis, it cannot be the penis, but she goes on to conclude that
it could therefore equally stand for any other body part. If the phallus is indeed
"an imaginary effect," part of an imagined morphology, then "its naturalized link
to masculine morphology can be called into question through an aggressive
reterritorialization," and its structural place no longer determined by the heterosexist Lacanian version of sexual difference, where men "have" and women
"are" the phallus (for men). Butler thus argues for the possibility of a "lesbian
phallus," which "offers the occasion (a set of occasions) for the phallus to signify differently, and in so signifying, to resignify, unwittingly, its own masculinist and heterosexist privilege."[84] While Butler might be accused of ignoring the
import of visual difference symbolized by the penis and of collapsing Lacan's
Imaginary and Symbolic Order by conflating Lacan's Imaginary body of the
mirror stage with his notion of the phallus as the privileged signifier of lack in
the Symbolic, she certainly reveals the extent to which the penis and phallus are
"bound to each by an essential relation in which that difference is contained."[85]
Of course, Butler is here referring to a specifically lesbian phallus by inserting
the butch lesbian body into the Lacanian schema.[86] Nonetheless, while Brandon
identifies as male, not lesbian, Butler's arguments about the possible recitation
of the phallus still apply, since Brandon reveals that the phallus is as "plastic," to
use Butler's pun (meaning counterfeit and replicable), as Brandon's prosthesis.
Moreover, the penis is equally transferable in the age of sex-alteration surgery,
and it is surely significant that John's enraged frenzy reaches its peak when he
finds Brandon's leaflet on transsexuality, which contains a section on skin-

grafted penises, presenting the horror of a biologically sexed woman appropriating "the absolute insignia of maleness," to use Robert Stoller's term.[87]

Rape is clearly screened as John and Tom's punishment of Brandon for usurping male privilege, as well as their violent re-imposition of the sexual difference binary. At the same time, this points not only to the insecurities and instabilities of normative masculinity when its exclusive claims to masculinity are challenged, but also the undergridding homoerotic structures that support homosocial identifications. The rape scene itself is shot in flashback while Brandon is being interviewed by a sheriff, who is more interested in Brandon's sexual identity than the crime itself (the film uses the real-life police tapes for this scene[88]). As the off-screen sheriff crudely asks, "When he poked you, where'd he try to pop it in first at?" the camera trains relentlessly on a traumatized Brandon, who hesitates before tearfully muttering "my vagina." While this is obviously the sheriff's attempt to impose femaleness on Brandon, his question leaves the possibility of anal rape hovering as the unsaid, before a further cut back to the rapes themselves. Peirce delimits any potential titillation by avoiding long shots and using oppressively tight framing. John's swift rape in the back seat of the car also deploys a series of dislocating, rapid jump cuts, which Peirce describes as "four frame flashes viscerally knocking into you, like memory knocking on consciousness."[89] Tom's rape is filmed in medium shots that alternate from his contorted facial expressions to side-on shots of Brandon's upper body and face sprawled out on the bonnet of the car, against which his frail body is violently rammed. Brandon is not fully stripped and his breasts are still bound, though I think that Julianne Pidduck is right to note that for most viewers "it is the violation of Swank's lithe, recognizably female body that commands a much more 'universal pathos.'"[90] Like The Accused (1988), this scene focuses on the homoerotic as well as homosocial function rape performs, as John and Tom cheer, whoop, and clutch each other excitedly between turns. The fact that the possibility of anal rape is evoked also suggests that the rape of Brandon might stage homoerotic fantasies projected onto the transgendered body, particularly due to the fact that after the rape, Tom and John continue to refer to Brandon as "little buddy" or "little dude." As with The Crying Game, then, the transgendered subject queers white male heterosexual identifications, and, to paraphrase Butler out of context, resignifies and destabilizes the hegemonic categories by which more internally dissonant, transgressive categories are enabled.[91]

While revealing the imitative structures of normative white masculinity, Brandon embodies a more sensitive, reciprocal mode of masculinity (walking his girlfriends home, putting their sexual pleasure first, listening to their dreams). Consequently, although it is important to note that Brandon does not identify as female, he still presents the possibilities that Halberstam imagines for "female masculinity." "Female masculinity," Halberstam argues, "offers one powerful model of what inauthentic masculinity can look like," in part by uncoupling misogyny from maleness, and masculinity from social power.[92] Whereas in The Crying Game the suggestion that Dil does her gender "better" than biological women rearticulates and valorizes patriarchal notions of femininity, Brandon's performance of masculinity is decidedly non-patriarchal and reworks the power dynamics of the sexual relation by responding to feminist demands for a more nurturing masculinity, a rather different response to a postfeminist context than that offered by Jordan's film.

Brandon's citation of masculinity is also inextricable from discourses of class. The persona that Brandon creates as part of his gender performance is one that is decidedly more upwardly mobile (a sister modeling in Hollywood and a father in the oil business), suggesting that his performance of a chivalric masculinity is imbued with a class transformation fantasy. For instance, in an early scene a girlfriend tells him that he doesn't seem to be from "around here" but from "some place beautiful." Brandon also creates for himself and Lana a fantasmatic "elsewhere" that transcends the limitations of white working-class life, represented in the film not merely through their shared fantasies of escape, but also projected onto the film's recurring shots of the barren Nebraska landscape, traversed by power lines and one-lane roads, a deployment of the conventions of the road movie whereby the road offers a liberating space freed up from the restraints of identity.[93] At the same time, the film is illustrative of the materiality of class, which is posited as less malleable than gender, with little hope of class mobility.

Brandon's sensitive masculinity is also favorably played off against the aggressive masculinity embodied by Tom and John. As Lisa Henderson puts it, Brandon "is a different kind of man—radiant, beautiful, clear-skinned and clean, the promise of masculinity beside Tom and John, who stand instead as its scarred and mottled failures.[94] However, while the film's valorization of Brandon's transgendered masculinity is certainly progressive in terms of gender politics, the representation of Tom and John reiterates commonplace associations of working class men with hyperviolence. This is not to say that *Boys Don't Cry* does not screen John and Tom's masculine rage in a socio-economic context of a dead-end Middle American town, where career prospects run to a canning factory, and social recreation is limited to bumper-skiing, car chases, graffiti, drug taking, and drinking. In particular, John's swaggering, macho bravado is constructed by the film as a defensive strategy, proof of the only power he wields— a reminder that white heterosexual masculinity is not a monolithic category and not a site of automatic privilege. Tom explains that the doctors say that John has "no impulse control," while Tom himself is a self-confessed pyromaniac who mutilates himself in order to feel. Nevertheless, despite these moments of sympathetic portrayal, the film also taps into a '90s representational trend in U.S. popular cinema of linking innately violent pathologies with "white trash" masculinity (see chapter 8). In part, this was obviously dictated by the real-life events on which the film is based. Moreover, it can be interpreted as Peirce's strategy to de-mystify the American heartlands—the mythical signifier of national values— which were idealized in many media representations of Brandon Teena's murder through idyllic images of rolling hills, hardworking, God-fearing, law-abiding citizens, whose American way of life was threatened by a sexually deviant outsider.[95] As Anna Wilson explains, as with the murder of homosexual Matthew Shepherd, the popular media attempted to deal with "the discursive crisis" caused by the "scandal of queers in the heartlands" by producing "a narrative of an unruly but vigorously normal national body, in need of policing but with its vitality reiterated."[96] Peirce certainly counterbalances this representation, with Middle America represented as oppressively conservative, a far cry from *The Crying Game*'s liberal, though still working-class, London. However, along with Lisa Henderson, I am disturbed by the film's class discourse. My intention is not a "liberal recuperation" of John and Tom,[97] nor a demand for documentary style authenticity, nor an insistence on positive images, which, as Robert Stam and Louise Spence note (writing of race), often "[provide] a bourgeois façade for paternalism."[98] Rather, my concern is that the film's cross-over success might in part be explained through its negative representation of "white trash" masculinity "for an audience of cultural consumers perhaps too primed for such a judgment and too attracted by [the film's] gritty and exotic brand of realism."[99]

Peirce has also been criticized for her exclusion of Philip DeVine, a black disabled male murdered by John and Tom along with Brandon Teena and Lisa Lambert (called Candace in the film for legal purposes)—criticism that underscores the inevitable mediation of "real life" events in interpreting bio-pics. In interviews, Peirce explained this decision by referring to Aristotle's notion of "tragic unity," stating that DeVine was "a subplot" she had no room for—a comment that, predictably, outraged numerous commentators.[100] Jennifer Devere Brody, for instance, comes to the conclusion that "the radical erasure of blackness makes queer stories queerer," adding, "[w]here Peirce has an opportunity, if not an obligation, to record the real confluence of racism, classism, misogyny, transgender discrimination and homophobia, she chose instead to ignore the racist issues at stake in this story."[101] Halberstam makes a similar point, arguing that Peirce missed the opportunity to explore how DeVine, who was dating Lana's sister, represented "a similarly outrageous threat to the supremacy and privilege of white manhood."[102] While it is important to resist the temptation to conflate transphobia, homophobia, misogyny, and racism, reference to DeVine would have allowed an exploration of how "these vectors of power require and deploy each other for the purpose of their own articulation,"[103] how "whiteness" might function as the only property that working-class whites possess, and how Brandon's masculinity interacts with the privilege of exercising "whiteness." DeVine's presence would also have complicated the film's homogenizing image of the American heartlands as "white trash" country, while his blackness and disability would also have demanded a more complex representation of heterosexual male masculinity than that offered by Tom and John.

While *Boys Don't Cry* might well render white masculinity ontologically empty, and thereby problematize its position as originator of meanings, the violent punishment meted out to Brandon by biological males (both on and off screen) illustrates that there are "cruel and fatal social constraints on denaturalization."[104] However subversive of gender norms transgendered subjectivity might be, it is important to remember the tragic status awarded to Brandon and Dil, reinforced by both films' melodramatic titles (Brandon, of course, does cry). As well as suggesting that mainstream audiences are willing to crossover as long as queerness and sexual deviance are dressed up in narratives of fated love and tears, it is also a reminder of the cost all too often paid by those marginal bodies who enact (however unwittingly) the politics of gender trouble. *The Crying Game*, however, the narrative of which is filtered through the point of view of an "ordinary" white male, devotes little screen space to the oppression faced by transgendered subjects; rather, by focusing on Fergus's story of being deceived by Dil's convincing performance, the film feeds into prevalent discourses of white male victimization. The film's structuring point of view works to reinscribe white heterosexual masculinity as the universal identity, and one that, despite being challenged and wounded by confrontations with difference, can always be healed and redeemed. In short, both films reveal, to quote Judith Butler out of context, that white heterosexual masculinity "can concede its lack of originality and naturalness but still hold onto its power"[105]—a point I develop in the framework of race in the following chapter.

Notes

1. Cynthia Fuchs, "Michael Jackson's Penis," in *Cruising the Performative: Interventions into the Representation of Ethnicity, Nationality, and Sexuality*, ed. Sue-Ellen Case, Philip Brett, and Susan Leigh Foster (Bloomington: Indiana University Press, 1995), 15.

2. Kobena Mercer, "Monster Metaphors: Notes on Michael Jackson's *Thriller*," in *Stardom: Industry of Desire*, ed. Christine Gledhill (London: Routledge, 1991), 302.

3. Marjorie Garber, *Vested Interests: Cross-Dressing and Cultural Anxiety* (London: Penguin, 1992), 185.

4. Richard Dyer, *White* (London: Routledge, 1997), 49.

5. bell hooks, *Black Looks: Race and Representation* (Boston: South End Press, 1992), 22.

6. The term "new queer cinema" was coined by B. Ruby Rich to discuss a body of critically-acclaimed films in the '90s that screened queer sexuality in all its complexities. Rich argues that the term is now problematic because queer movies have been commodified. "Queer and Present Danger," *Sight and Sound*, March 2000, 23-24.

7. Judith Butler, "Imitation and Gender Insubordination," in *Inside/Out: Lesbian Theories, Gay Theories*, ed. Diana Fuss (New York: Routledge, 1991), 21.

8. Judith Butler, *Gender Trouble: Feminism and the Subversion of Identity* (New York: Routledge, 1990), ix, 6, 112.

9. Butler, *Gender Trouble*, 7.

10. Judith Butler, *Bodies That Matter: On the Discursive Limits of "Sex"* (New York: Routledge, 1993), 10. For instance, Butler argues that the moment when an infant's sex is declared with the classic phrase "it's a boy/girl!" is also a performative statement (that is, a statement that produces what it purports to describe) since this medical interpellation propels the infant into "the domain of language and kinship": the "it" must shift to a "she" or "he" if the infant is to qualify as human, suggesting that the matrix of sexual

difference is "prior to the emergence of the 'human'" (7).

11. Judith Butler, *Undoing Gender* (New York: Routledge, 2004), 87.

12. Social constructivist accounts of gender have tended to assume the existence of an *a prior* sexual division upon which social processes act; this has the advantage of rendering gender relations mutable and historically specific, but also posits an always already sexed body, and fails to theorize fully the psyche. Psychoanalytic accounts, conversely, concern themselves with sexual difference—"the enigmatic domain which lies in between, no longer biology and not yet the space of socio-symbolic construction." Slavoj Žižek, *The Ticklish Subject: The Absent Centre of Political Ontology* (London: Verso, 1999), 275. Unlike sociological accounts that take as given the internalization of social norms, psychoanalysis recognizes that identification is always a missed encounter. This recognition has been crucial in pointing to perpetual dissonances between the anatomical body and psychic representations of sexual difference. Nevertheless, psychoanalytic discussions of sexual difference have often been accused of essentialism, particularly because of the well-documented penis/phallus slippage. Butler takes a rather different point of departure, however; not only does she take psychoanalysis to task for its heterosexism, but she also attempts to reveal how it is the ideological structure of sexual difference itself that produces sexed bodies rather than constituting their effect. Butler's positing of sexual difference as a performative construct has been challenged by Lacanian theorists, such as Joan Copjec and Slavoj Žižek, who argue that sex is reducible neither to a natural fact, nor discursive construction, but is rather an interaction between the two. For a response to these criticisms, see Butler's own discussion of the sexual difference debate in *Undoing Gender*, chaps. 9 and 10.

13. Garber, *Vested Interests*, 110; Butler, *Gender Trouble*, 137.

14. Butler, *Bodies That Matter*, 237. Here Butler is referring to Jacques Derrida's assertion that the possibility of resignification is intrinsic to all linguistic signs: "Every sign . . . can be *cited*, put between quotation marks; thereby it can break with every given context, and engender infinitely new contexts in an absolutely nonsaturable fashion." Jacques Derrida, "Signature, Event, Context," in *Margins of Philosophy*, (Chicago: University of Chicago Press, 1982), 320. Butler argues that for this reason drag might offer a parodic redeployment of power for lesbian, gay, and queer political struggle, a position that has been criticized by some theorists, who accuse her of advocating an individualistic and ineffective form of politics.

15. Butler, *Gender Trouble*, 137.

16. For a discussion of the potential misogyny of male drag and a response to Butler, see Carol-Anne Tyler, "Boys Will Be Girls: The Politics of Gay Drag," in *Inside/Out: Lesbian Theories, Gay Theories*, ed. Diana Fuss, (New York: Routledge, 1991), 32-70.

17. Butler, *Bodies That Matter*, 128, 125.

18. Butler, *Bodies That Matter*, 126.

19. Margaret Drewall Thompson, "The Camp Face in Corporate America: Liberace and the Rockettes at Radio City Music Hall," in *The Politics and Poetics of Camp*, ed. Moe Meyer (London: Routledge, 1993), 149.

20. Chris Straayer, *Deviant Eyes, Deviant Bodies: Sexual Re-Orientation in Film and Video* (New York: Columbia University Press, 1996), 46-50.

21. Straayer, *Deviant Eyes, Deviant Bodies*, 51.

22. Butler, *Bodies That Matter*, 126.

23. Straayer, *Deviant Eyes, Deviant Bodies*, 54.

24. Garber, *Vested Interests*, 11.

25. Garber, *Vested Interests*, 6, 8.

Chapter Five

26. Mark Simpson, *Male Impersonators: Men Performing Masculinity* (London: Cassell, 1994), 179.

27. Tania Modleski, *Feminism Without Women: Culture and Criticism in a "Post-feminist" Age* (New York: Routledge, 1991), 132. In *Bodies That Matter*, Butler also addresses the issue of race (absent from *Gender Trouble*), and is scrupulous in emphasizing that the Symbolic is also "a racializing set of norms," and that sexual difference is not prior to racial difference (130). She explores how race and class intersect with sex and gender in representations of drag when she analyzes Jennie Livingstone's docu-film *Paris Is Burning* (1991) about multi-racial drag balls in New York City.

28. Yvonne Tasker, *Working Girls: Gender and Sexuality in Popular Cinema* (London: Routledge, 1998), 31.

29. Joyce Hammond, "Drag Queen as Angel: Transformation and Transcendence in *To Wong Foo, Thanks for Everything, Julie Newmar*," *The Journal of Popular Film and Television* 24 (1996): 107.

30. Kathryn Kane, "Passing As Queer and Racing Toward Whiteness: *To Wong Foo, Thanks but No Thanks*," *Genders* 42 (2005), http://www.genders.org/g42/g42_kane.html (accessed June 25, 2006).

31. Annalee Newitz and Matthew Wray, "What Is 'White Trash'? Stereotypes and Economic Conditions of Poor Whites in the United States" in *Whiteness: A Critical Reader*, ed. Michael Hill (New York: New York University Press, 1997), 175.

32. Nicola Evans, "Games of Hide and Seek: Race, Gender and Drag in *The Crying Game* and *The Birdcage*," *Text and Performance Quarterly* 18 (1998): 199.

33. Butler, *Undoing Gender*, 6.

34. Judith Halberstam, "Masculinity Without Men," interview with Annamarie Jagose, *Genders* 29 (1999), http://www.genders.org/g29/g29_halberstam.html (accessed April 14, 2004).

35. Justin Wyatt, "The Formation of the 'Major Independent': Miramax, New Line and the New Hollywood," in *Contemporary Hollywood Cinema*, ed. Steve Neale and Murray Smith (London: Routledge, 1998), 80-81.

36. For an interesting discussion of the similarities and differences between the ways in which *The Crying Game* and *Falling Down* manage difference, see Sharon Willis, *High Contrast: Race and Gender in Contemporary Hollywood Film* (Durham, NC: Duke University Press, 1997), 9-19.

37. Willis, *High Contrast*, 11.

38. Willis, *High Contrast*, 11.

39. Shantanu DuttaAhmed, "'I Thought You Knew! Performing the Penis, the Phallus, and Otherness in Neil Jordan's *The Crying Game*," *Film Criticism* 23, no. 1 (1998): 68. The flaccidity of Dil's penis is no doubt also attributable to film regulations that censor the sight of the erect penis.

40. Garber, *Vested Interests*, 16.

41. Evans, "Games of Hide and Seek," 208.

42. Slavoj Žižek, *The Metastases of Enjoyment: Six Essays on Woman and Causality* (London: Verso, 1994), 108.

43. Simpson, *Male Impersonators*, 165.

44. Garber, *Vested Interests*, 17.

45. Willis, *High Contrast*, 13.

46. bell hooks, *Outlaw Culture: Resisting Representations* (New York: Routledge 1994), 59, 56.

47. Žižek, *The Metastases of Enjoyment*, 105.

48. hooks, *Outlaw Culture*, 59.

49. Eve Kosofsky Sedgwick, *Between Men: English Literature and Male Homosocial Desire* (New York: Columbia University Press, 1985).

50. Simpson, *Male Impersonators*, 171.

51. Neil Jordan, quoted in hooks, *Outlaw Culture*, 59. In the introduction to the screenplay, Jordan explains how he was inspired by two Irish authors, Frank O'Connor and Brendan Behan, both of whom have written of an IRA hostage plot undergridded by "an erotic possibility" between men which "remained subdued." In *The Crying Game*, he continues, "I brought the erotic thread to the surface. Instead of two, there were now three. A hostage, a captor, and an absent lover. The lover became the focus for the erotic subtext, loved by both men in a way they couldn't love each other." Introduction to *The Crying Game: An Original Screenplay* (London: Vintage, 1993), viii.

52. Butler, *Gender Trouble*, 35-65.

53. Danny Leigh, "Boy Wonder: Interview with Kimberly Peirce," *Sight and Sound*, March 2000, 18.

54. Chris Straayer, "Masculinity: Acting and Causality in *Boys Don't Cry*," abstract for VI SAAS Conference, American Mirrors: (Self)Reflections and Self(Distortions), April 9-11, 2003, http://www.vc.ehu.es/castellano/paginas/otros/fiwsaas/program/pa/abst/pa041003cs.htm (accessed June 11, 2004). Permission to quote from the abstract was kindly given by the author.

55. Rich, "Queer and Present Dangers," 25.

56. Michele Aaron, "Pass/Fail," *Screen* 41, no. 1 (2001): 93.

57. Kimberly Peirce, "Brandon goes to Hollywood," *The Advocate*, March 28, 2000, http://www.advocate.com.html.stories/808/808_cvr_peirce.asp (accessed March 14, 20-04).

58. *Boys Don't Cry*, Fox Searchlight Official Site, www.foxsearchlight.com/boys don't cry/index.shtml (accessed April 14, 2004).

59. See, for example, Leigh, "Boy Wonder," 20.

60. Jamie Allen, "*Boys Don't Cry*: Filmmaker Saw Past Violence to Love," *CNN.com*, October 22, 1999, http://www.cnn.com/SHOWBIZ/Movies/9910/22/boys.dont .cry (accessed April 4, 2004).

61. See, for example, Carol Siegel, "Curing ~~Boys~~ Don't Cry: Brandon Teena's Stories," *Genders* 37 (2003), http://www.genders.org/g37/g37_siegel.html (accessed April 14, 2004).

62. Straayer, "Masculinity."

63. Patricia White, "Girls Still Cry," *Screen* 42, no. 2 (2001): 218.

64. Aaron, "Pass/Fail," 94.

65. Butler, *Undoing Gender*, 143.

66. Jennifer Esposito, "Performance of White Masculinity in *Boys Don't Cry*: Identity, Desire, (Mis)Recognition," *Cultural Studies/Critical Methodologies* 3, no. 2 (2003): 239.

67. Aaron, "Pass/Fail," 94.

68. Judith Halberstam, "The Transgender Gaze in *Boys Don't Cry*," *Screen* 42, no. 3 (2001): 295.

69. White, "Girls Still Cry," 220.

70. Sigmund Freud, "On Fetishism," in *On Sexuality: Three Essays on the Theory of Sexuality and Other Works*, trans. James Strachey, ed. Angela Richards (London: Penguin, 1991), 353-54.

71. Mary Ann Doane, *Femmes Fatales: Feminism, Film Theory, Psychoanalysis* (New York: Routledge, 1991), 23.

72. Halberstam, "Transgender Gaze," 295.

73. Halberstam, "Transgender Gaze," 296.

74. See, for example, Butler, *Undoing Gender*, 143; Esposito, "Performance of White Masculinity in *Boys Don't Cry*," 236; Halberstam, "Transgender Gaze," 297; Lisa Henderson, "The Class Character of *Boys Don't Cry*," *Screen* 42, no. 3 (2001): 300; Straayer, "Masculinity."

75. Straayer, "Masculinity."

76. Halberstam, "Transgender Gaze," 297.

77. See note 10.

78. See "Transgendered Picket Village Voice," *NY Transfer News Collective*, May 4, 1994, http://www.qrd.org/qrd/media/print/1994/transgendered.picket.village.voice-05.04. 94 (accessed April 4, 2004).

79. Brenda Cooper, "*Boys Don't Cry* and Female Masculinity: Reclaiming a Life and Dismantling the Politics of Normative Heterosexuality," *Critical Studies in Media Communication* 19, no. 1 (2002): 57.

80. Butler, *Gender Trouble*, 45.

81. Hilary Neroni, *The Violent Woman: Femininity, Narrative, and Violence in Contemporary American Cinema* (Albany: State University of New York Press, 2005), 95.

82. Butler, *Bodies That Matter*, 62.

83. Judith Butler, "Gender as Performance," in *A Critical Sense: Interviews with Intellectuals*, ed. Peter Osborne (London: Routledge, 1996), 121.

84. Butler, *Bodies That Matter*, 84, 86, 88, 90.

85. Butler, *Bodies That Matter*, 90.

86. Judith Halberstam, "The Good, the Bad, and the Ugly: Men, Women, and Masculinity," in *Masculinity Studies and Feminist Theory: New Directions*, ed. Judith Kegan Gardiner (New York: Columbia University Press, 2002), 357.

87. Robert Stoller, *Sex and Gender: On the Development of Masculinity and Femininity*, vol. 1 (London: Hogarth /Institute of Psychoanalysis, 1968), 86.

88. See Susan Muska and Greta Olafsdottir's documentary *The Brandon Teena Story*, which includes taped recordings of Brandon's interrogation by police.

89. Leigh, "Boy Wonder," 20.

90. Julianne Pidduck, "Risk and Spectatorship," *Screen* 42, no. 1 (2001): 101.

91. Butler, *Gender Trouble*, 123.

92. Halberstam, "The Good, the Bad, and the Ugly," 345.

93. For a reading of the film's usage of road movie conventions, see Pidduck, "Risk and Spectatorship."

94. Henderson, "The Class Character of *Boys Don't Cry*," 302.

95. John M. Sloop, "Disciplining the Transgendered: Brandon Teena, Public Representations, and Normativity," *Western Journal of Communication* 64 (2000): 172, quoted in Cooper, "*Boys Don't Cry* and Female Masculinity," 50.

96. Anna Wilson, "National Uses for Bodies," abstract, *The Flesh Made Text: Bodies, Theories, Cultures in the Post-Millennial Era: Book of Abstracts* (Thessaloniki, Greece: Aristotle University of Thessaloniki, 2003), 205. In 1998, Matthew Shepherd, a young gay man, was tied to a fence, beaten, and left for dead in a homophobic attack.

97. Henderson, "The Class Character of *Boys Don't Cry*," 302.

98. Robert Stam and Louise Spence, "Colonialism, Racism and Representation," *Screen* 24, no. 2 (1983): 3.

99. Henderson, "The Class Character of *Boys Don't Cry*," 302.

100. Jennifer Devere Brody, "Boys Do Cry: Screening History's White Lies," *Screen* 43, no. 1 (2001): 94; Henderson, "The Class Character of *Boys Don't Cry*," 301.

101. Brody, "Boys Do Cry," 91, 93.

102. Halberstam, "Transgender Gaze," 298.

103. Butler, *Bodies That Matter*, 18.

104. Butler, *Bodies That Matter*, 133.

105. Butler, *Bodies That Matter*, 126.

Chapter Six
White Skin, Black Masks? Male "Wiggers" in Contemporary Popular Cinema

Racial Crossovers

In a recent Channel Four documentary (2003), *Black Like Beckham*, journalist Paul McKenzie argued that football icon David Beckham is black, citing Beckham's penchant for hip hop fashion, his love of rap music (he has named his dogs Snoop and Puffy), and "bling bling" lifestyle. One black interviewee also suggested that when Beckham was vilified by tabloids as Britain's "most hated man" after being sent off in a match against Argentina in the 1998 World Cup, he "knew what it was like to be a black man." Despite its overall ironic, light-hearted tone, in a more serious mode McKenzie argues that Beckham is Britain's most famous black man, indicative of the massive influence of black urban culture on the British white mainstream. Not surprisingly, though, the program created sustained debate over the meaning of race, with many members of the black community expressing concern about the propagation of narrow conceptions of blackness and black culture largely based on white notions of (male) rap stars' lifestyles, as well as the program's failure to engage with the pernicious effects of racism because of its understanding of race as a purely cultural marker.[1]

In this chapter, I will focus on cinematic representations of male "wiggers"—that is, white emulators of black culture, particularly hip hop—in contemporary popular cinema.[2] In order to ground my discussion theoretically, I begin by offering a brief outline of contemporary understandings of race as a social, performative construct. I then attempt to place wiggers in a history of U.S. white (male) attractions to black culture, which has its roots in the nineteenth-century minstrel show. The minstrel legacy, I argue, enacts a pervasive influence on not only contemporary U.S. popular culture, but also constructions of U.S. white masculinity, which is locked in a mutually defining love-hate relationship with black masculinity. As has been well documented, much U.S. popular culture, particularly music, has been indebted to African-American cultural production, but that debt has not always been acknowledged. However, in the middle of the twentieth century the male-dominated Beat Generation, along with the earlier hipsters, famously dubbed "white negroes" by Norman Mailer, openly expressed their love and envy of both black culture (especially jazz) and black masculinity. As with the Beats, contemporary white male hip hop fans also overtly proclaim their dissatisfaction with the perceived inauthenticity of whiteness; their adoption of black culture is also informed by similar stereotypical images of black masculinity formed in the white imagination. Moreover, as the David Beckham documentary highlights, in a globalized media world, the hip hop phenomenon is making itself felt outside of the U.S. and has a massive fan base in countries as diverse as Canada and Cambodia. It is therefore important to think through the differences within white masculinity played out along the axes of other identity categories, such as nation and ethnicity, as well as class and sexuality, in order to tease out what varying functions approximations of black masculinity might fulfill.

I begin my discussion of white male wiggers in recent popular cinema with representations of male "black wannabes" in the films of Quentin Tarantino, contemporary cinema's wigger *par excellence*, before turning to his most vocal critic, Spike Lee, and his bleak satire on modern minstrelsy, *Bamboozled* (2000). I then look at the parodic *Ali G Indahouse* (Mark Mylod 2002), which maps white male minstrelsy onto a British terrain, in order to explore how discourses of nation impact on representations of male wiggers. I will close by considering the white rapping phenomenon Eminem and his vehicle piece 8 *Mile* (Curtis Hanson 2002) so as to explore the interactions between white masculinity, black masculinity, and class, in particular Eminem's "white trash" roots that authenticate his rap career both intra- and extra-textually. My intention in this chapter is to problematize U.S. white heterosexual masculinity as a coherent, stable category, revealing how it is undergridded by a (often homoerotic) repulsion and attraction to black masculinity, upon which it is dependent for self-definition. I will also explore the underlying anxiety expressed in these films that the fetishization of black masculinity reinforces concerns that white heterosexual masculinity is a sterile and parasitical identity precisely because of its very ordinariness, concerns that are disavowed by the *extra-ordinary* whiteness that male wiggers act out.

Visual Matters: The Performativity of Race

In 1982 Susie Guillory Phillips brought a lawsuit against the state of Louisiana in order to change her racial classification from black to white. Her lawsuit not only failed, but also effected the replacement of the existing state law—which declared anyone with more than one-thirty-second African ancestry black—with the former "one-drop rule," according to which any proportion of African ances-try is sufficient to identify an individual as legally black.[3] By representing "whiteness" as an absence of race, the one-drop rule has perpetuated the myth of white racial purity, along with the notion that African-Americans, to whom the rule exclusively applies, have "most race."[4] Whereas other races have at various historical junctures fallen under the rubric of whiteness, blackness has always formed the polar opposite of whiteness in a rigidly Manichean schema, locking whiteness into a relationship of dependence on blackness for self-definition. The "one-drop rule" thus underscores not only the discursive nature of racial forma-tion, but also the fragilities of whiteness, which can be blackened with alarming ease in a strictly one-way racial economy. Indeed, despite the increasing recog-nition that the U.S. is highly multiracial, with certain geneticists arguing that "95 percent of 'white' Americans have varying degrees of black heritage and 75 per-cent of all 'African' Americans have at least one white ancestor,"[5] the fear of miscegenation continues to haunt the white American imaginary, dramatized explicitly in social problem films such as Spike Lee's *Jungle Fever* (1991) and the Oscar-winning *Monster's Ball* (2001), or in a displaced form in fantasy cin-ema, such as with the racialized clash between vampires and werewolves in the neo-gothic *Underworld* (2003).

Like the phenomenon of passing, the Phillips case also "illustrates the in-adequacy of claims that race is a mere matter of variations in human physiog-nomy, that it is simply a matter of skin color."[6] Rather, critical race theorists currently argue that "race" is a historically contingent social construct, and emerged as a term signifying hierarchical distinctions for socio-economic rea-sons.[7] The instability of racial categories is evident in the contradictions of American race designation: at certain historical moments Asian-Indians and Mexican-Americans have been deemed white by virtue of their non-blackness, while newly arrived Greeks, Italians, Sicilians, Slavs, Irish, and Jews have all been termed non-white at varying moments in U.S. history.[8] Moreover, just as Africans did not think of themselves as black before colonization, so ethno-European immigrants, newly arrived in North America, initially identified not as white, but in accordance with their ethnicity. Whiteness, in other words, was "invented" when, experiencing wage labor and capitalist working conditions for the first time, ethno-European immigrants joined an imaginary white community in order to define themselves against black slaves.[9] Changes to the U.S. census in 2000 that attempted to unify racial classifications also underscore that race is a site of constant contestation (for both racist and anti-racist meanings). Before 2000, someone could change "race" merely by traveling from one state to an-other, but in 2000 citizens were asked to self-select their racial identification by ticking all categories that applied, expanding racial categories from five to sixty three, thereby allowing a multi-racial classification.[10] Some theorists also quote scientific research that contests the biological basis of race, since there is often less genetic variation between an average black person and an average white person than the variability within each racial group.[11]

The claim that race is discursively constructed is not an attempt to deny the very real material consequences that the embodiment of a particular racial identity can bring; rather, as Ruth Frankenberg puts it, it is to insist that the social and political reality of these identities is "precisely social and political rather than inherent or static."[12] Indeed, it is essential to resist the idea that race somehow does not exist, since while race might well be a discursive fiction, it always "translates into discernible material effects," and continues to impact hugely on social reality, such as determining who is most likely to get stopped by the police or gain access to quality housing.[13] For example, the fact that those who suffered the worst consequences of Hurricane Katrina in 2005 were primarily African-Americans proved to be a stark reminder of the racial and class inequalities entrenched in U.S. society. These inequalities continue to be ignored by neoconservatives, who effectively declare race to be obsolete in their clamor for color-blind social policies as part of their reactionary attack on affirmative action and multiculturalism.

In the same vein, utopian calls by white anti-racist activists to abolish whiteness (a school of thought known as New Abolitionism[14]) are equally problematic for assuming one can volitionally opt out of one aspect of one's identity. Likewise, the suggestion of Warren Beatty's Senator in the political satire *Bulworth* (1998) that white people, and by extension race, should be abolished by "a voluntary free-spirited, open-ended program of procreative racial deconstruction"—that is, "everybody's just got to keep fucking everybody until we're all the same color"—while illustrative of the racial hierarchies enabled by the ideology of white purity, also suggests that the only possible means to promote racial harmony is a numbing erasure of race itself rather than respect for difference and heterogeneity. Moreover, however well-meaning, the assertion that race is "a state of mind" (for example, by "wiggers" such as Quentin Tarantino or the members of the white rap band who call themselves Young Black Teenagers[15]) ignores the fact that however black a white subject may act, he or she can always revert back to the privileges afforded by possessing white skin.

For this reason, even as we accept that the selection of certain visible markers with the purpose of highlighting group formation "is always and necessarily a social and historical process,"[16] that does little to rob the visual inscription of race of its force in the prevailing scopic regime which posits race as "a constituted 'fact' of the body" that denotes interior as well as exterior attributes.[17] As Henry Louis Gates, Jr. dryly notes, "it's important to remember that 'race' is *only* a sociopolitical category, nothing more. At the same time—in terms of its practical performative force—that doesn't help me when I'm trying to get a taxi on the corner of 125th and Lenox Avenue ('Please sir, it's only a metaphor.')."[18] It is precisely this "epidermalization" of social inferiority that Frantz Fanon poignantly explores in his groundbreaking *Black Skin, White Masks* (1952), a study that brings to the fore, but also racializes, the aggression inherent in Lacan's mirror stage in order to elaborate a theory of the racist imaginary.[19] In his famed "Look, a Negro!" passage, where a traumatized white child convulses in terror at the sight of a black male, Fanon explores the "racial epidermal schema" that not only posits the black male as a phobic object of European and Anglo-American cultures, but which also causes "the dereliction of [the black male's] *own* self-representation through that culture."[20] Expanding upon Fanon's "recitation of the racist interpellation" in her discussion of the Rodney King affair, Judith Butler argues that LAPD cops were acquitted despite the video footage showing them viciously beating and kicking a defenseless black male precisely because a "racially saturated field of visibility" produced black masculinity as a site of brutal, primitive, meaningless violence. This serves to remind us that "[t]he visual field is not neutral to the question of race; it is itself a racial formation, an episteme, hegemonic and forceful."[21]

Cinema, as a visual medium, is particularly pertinent to these discussions, since the performing body is always unavoidably racially marked. It is this fact that renders Scott McGehee and David Siegel's experimental art-house thriller *Suture* (1993) such a disturbing viewing experience. The film rehearses a typical *noir* plot of lost memory and mistaken identity: the rich Vincent Towers (Michael Harris) attempts to murder and frame his working-class half-brother, Clay Arlington (Dennis Haysbert), with whom he is said to share a disarming physical similarity. Clay survives but suffers from amnesia, and, along with everyone else around him, believes that he is Vincent. Nonetheless, Vincent is white while Clay is black, a fact that no one seems to notice. The conflict between the visual and discursive is perhaps most effectively deployed when the ironically named Renée Descartes (Mel Harris), Clay's plastic surgeon and eventual lover, analyzes Clay's physiognomy, filmed in close-up, offering a description that bears no resemblance whatsoever to Clay/Haysbert's features: "your fine straight hair, almost always a sign of good mental temperament, not to mention digestion. And your mouth: thin, smooth lips, slightly open lips that are a sign of an affectionate, kind-hearted, and generous person." Renée's description is obviously racially inflected, since features aligned with whiteness (straight hair, thin lips) invoke positive ethical attributes, pointing to the processes whereby people of color have been condemned to "the prisonhouse of epidermal inferiority."[22] However, such racist discourses are also subverted, since the physical profile fits the evil, white Vincent, but the character assessment suits Clay. The very fact that conventions dictate that Clay's blackness rather than Vincent's whiteness should be referenced underscores that, far from being neutral, the cinematic gaze is white by default. As Kalpana Seshadri-Crooks notes, then, *Suture* "literally utilizes the visual medium against the visual regime of race."[23]

Race also inhabits a very different visual economy to gender, as filmic representations of passing illuminate. For instance, while *The Crying Game* queers the notion of an original gender through the *discrepancy* of gender performance and the anatomically sexed body, in films of successful racial passing, such as *The Human Stain* (2003), subversion can occur through the *congruence* between racial performance and the visibly raced body. Both films withhold information about the passer's "original" identity in order to undermine epistemological cer-

tainty in the body as the site of truth, but whereas in *The Crying Game* the biological male passing as female is played by a biologically male actor, in *The
Human Stain*, the light-skinned African-American passing as white is played by
Anthony Hopkins, whose whiteness, reinforced by extra-textual "knowledge" of
Hopkins's "real" racial identity, is essential to the film's project. Since the primary signifier of sex is the genitalia, theoretically, at least, any subject who is
fully clothed could perform (to varying degrees of success) any gender; he or she
could not act out any racial identity, however, since race is signified by a variety
of phenotypes (color of skin, shape of eyes, texture of hair etc.) that are harder to
disguise or perform. While *The Human Stain* makes it clear that race is never
merely a matter of these ideologically laden physical features, since Hopkins's
character is discursively and legally positioned as black despite looking "white,"
it also reasserts the hegemony of the visual regime of race, since a dark-skinned
African-American would simply be unable to pass.

From Minstrels to Wiggers

As *The Human Stain* reveals, passing for African-Americans has been a means
of escaping the horrors of systematic racism. It was even a matter of life or death
in times of slavery. Moreover, black integration into white culture, while often
disparaged by both black and white communities, has often been a question of
enforced assimilation rather than volitional mimicry. Nonetheless, blacks who
have passed have been accused of complicity in structures of racial domination,
while white passing is often deemed liberating, even ennobling, since it entails a
loss (normally temporary) of social power.[24] A key example is white journalist
John Howard Griffin, who blackened his skin through medication and ultraviolent light so as to pass as African-American in the American south, in order
to write his best-seller *Black Like Me* (1960)—later made into a film—a controversial attempt to document racism at first hand from the authoritative white
perspective.

Eric Lott has suggested that the white desire to inhabit a black body as a
form of interracial bonding occurs "when the lines of 'race' appear both intrac-
table and obstructive, when there emerges a collective desire (conscious or not)
to bridge a gulf that is, however, perceived to separate the race absolutely."[25] Yet
he still places Griffin's passing in *Black Like Me* in the tradition of minstrelsy.[26]
This is indicative of the uneven power dynamics that will always haunt racial
crossovers, since whites can "get a bit of the other" secure in the knowledge that
the privileges of whiteness, however unevenly allotted across the axes of class,
gender, sexuality, and ethnicity, are still theirs for the taking. It is for this reason
that white performances of blackness, particularly in the blackface tradition, can
be accused of theft and racism, an impossible accusation to level at blacks performing whiteness, such as Eddie Murphy's famous *Saturday Night Live* skit
"White Like Me" (1984), a spoof on Griffin's novel, since they lack the institutionalized force that the *practice* of racism and appropriation requires.[27]

White approximations of blackness have largely been a male affair, attributable both to the fact that whiteness is buttressed by patriarchy (women embody
the risk of miscegenation) and the fact that black masculinity presents white
masculinity with the threat of a disturbing sameness as well as otherness, a threat
which can be neutralized through fetishistic appropriation, which both installs
and disavows difference. These dynamics are most apparent in nineteenth-
century minstrel shows, the performers of which were mainly white males, particularly Irish-Americans, performing for principally white male audiences.
These shows offered up white-authored, racist conceptions of black people as a
spectacle for white consumption. Donning blackface, performers appropriated
black songs and dances whilst caricaturing black people as child-like buffoons.
With their commodification of black bodies for white enjoyment, their exclusion
of black Americans from their own representations, their deployment of crude,
injurious, stereotyped characters (such as Sambo, a dim-witted, lazy, infantile
slave, and Uncle Tom, a downtrodden, spineless black male), and their use of the
grotesque blackface mask, minstrel shows certainly epitomized the racist and
supremacist attitudes of the time. However, recent readings of minstrelsy have
begun to problematize a monolithic interpretation of minstrelsy, as we see with
studies of black artists who later performed in minstrel shows, not only revitaliz-
ing the form but also complicating their relationship to minstrelsy, or with research that explores the function that minstrelsy served white audiences, particularly in helping to forge a common white identity among ethno-Europeans.[28] For
the purposes of this chapter, I will focus on Eric Lott's controversial but groundbreaking study *Love and Theft: Blackface, Minstrelsy and the American Working
Class* (1993), which explores the mutually reinforcing dialectic of envy and repulsion of African-Americans that underwrites not merely minstrelsy, but also
the structures of U.S. white heterosexual masculinity.

Lott begins by rehearsing conventional views that read minstrelsy through
the lens of white supremacy and the material relations of slavery. But Lott then
complicates this view by delving into "the social unconscious of blackface"
through a psychoanalytically informed historical analysis that argues that blackface was "less a sign of absolute white power and control than of panic, anxiety,
terror, and pleasure," "based on small but significant crimes against settled ideas
of racial demarcation," and "a nearly insupportable fascination" with the culture
whites were plundering.[29]

Lott traces how minstrelsy appealed to working-class men precisely because
it helped forge a shared notion of whiteness (and, by extension, Americaness)
"capacious enough to allow entry to almost any non-black worker." Minstrelsy
was also "resilient enough to mask class tensions that were worked out in the
modality of race."[30] Along with fellow labor historian David Roediger, Lott argues that minstrelsy also gave white workers access to preindustrial permissive-
ness and physical pleasures lost in the stultifying effects of capitalism and industrial morality, though any envy of black bodies was disavowed through racism
and ridicule.[31]

Lott develops his argument through reference to Žižek's Lacanian discussion of the theft of enjoyment by the racial other. Žižek analyses how subjects often fantasize that the racial other "wants to steal our enjoyment (by ruining our 'way of life') and/or . . . has access to some secret, perverse enjoyment" (exotic food, songs and dances, insatiable sexual appetite)—fantasies that support contradictory ideologies, such as accusations that the racial other is both "a workaholic stealing our jobs" and "an idler living on our labor."[32] Lott is particularly interested in the fantasy that the racial other has access to a forbidden *jouissance*, a fantasy that allows subjects to experience that *jouissance* vicariously. However, "because the Other personifies their inner divisions, hatred of their own excess of enjoyment necessitates hatred of the Other."[33] Lott thereby complicates the notion that minstrel characters were simply the projection of white racist fantasies onto black bodies that could be enjoyed at a safe distance; rather, they represented the "other within"—repressed aspects of white consciousness.[34]

Minstrel representations of black masculinity thus allowed white men to adopt certain forms of masculinity that were repressed under capitalism: "To wear or even enjoy blackface was literally, for a time, to become black, to inherit the cool, virility, humility, abandon, or *gaité de coeur* that were the prime components of white ideologies of black manhood."[35] While the fetishization of black male bodies undoubtedly forged homosocial bonds among white males, it also overlapped with appropriations of a highly sexualized masculinity, suggesting that minstrelsy fulfilled a homoerotic function as well. Lott's work thus provides an illuminating framework with which to analyze contemporary white male attractions to blackness, which might no longer require burnt cork, but unfold through similar dynamics. Indeed, as Lott argues, "the special achievement of minstrel performers was to have initiated and formalized the white male fascination with the turn to black," which he regards as "so much a part of most American white men's equipment for living that they remain entirely unaware of their participation in it."[36]

Leslie Fielder, as Lott points out, has famously described this dynamic as follows: "Born theoretically white, we are permitted to pass our childhood as imaginary Indians, our adolescence as imaginary Negroes, and only then are expected to settle down to being what we really are: white once more."[37] Despite Fielder's insistence on the ontology of whiteness in the last instance ("what we really are"), adult white masculinity is only arrived at after a cannibalization of non-white (male) identities (women's whiteness would seem to be a less complex, hybrid affair). Fielder is unusual in reflecting on the constitutive role played by Native Americans in the formation of white masculinity (still apparent in the cowboyism of George W. Bush and his threats to "smoke out" terrorists in the wake of 9/11). However, it is important to note that in Fielder's account, it is blackness that is associated with "the onset of pubescent sexuality,"[38] thereby consolidating the myth of black male hypersexuality, while white masculinity is associated with adulthood, "settling down," and all the restrictions and responsibilities that implies.

It was precisely this dissatisfaction with what they perceived to be the inauthenticity and sterility of white, bourgeois values that fuelled the Beat love affair with black culture in the 1950s. Most famously, in an oft-quoted and much discussed passage in Jack Kerouac's Beat classic *On the Road* (1955), the narrator, Sal Paradise, informs us:

> At lilac evening, I walked with every muscle aching among the lights of 27th and Welton in the Denver colored section, wishing I were a Negro, feeling that the best the white world had offered was not enough ecstasy for me, not enough life, joy, kicks, darkness, music, not enough night, . . . I wished I were a Denver Mexican, or even a poor overworked Jap, anything but what I was so drearily, a 'white man' disillusioned . . . wishing I could exchange words with the happy, true-hearted, ecstatic Negroes of America.[39]

Whereas nineteenth-century minstrel audiences were interlocuting with blackness as a means of securing their whiteness, by the middle of the twentieth century Kerouac was openly wishing himself a Negro and rejecting the "dreariness" of white manhood. Like other Beats, Kerouac is reacting against hegemonic, conformist images of '50s masculinity, in particular the "family man" or the "organization man," and repudiating the consumer-driven, bourgeois, suburban values that buttress those ideologies. While Sal suggests that the adoption of any racial otherness would rescue him from the oppressive tedium and ordinariness of white masculinity, his initial desire falls on black Americans, who are twice associated with joy and ecstasy in this naively idyllic and romanticized portrayal of African-American life.

A similar white male romanticization of blackness, specifically black masculinity, appears in the now infamous essay by Norman Mailer, "The White Negro," a text which, as Lott argues, mythologizes as much as analyzes "the twentieth-century reinvention of [the] homosocial and homosexual fascinations" of minstrelsy.[40] Mailer claims that the white hipster was born from a "*ménage-à-trois*" between the bohemian, the juvenile delinquent, and the Negro, a "wedding" to which the Negro brought "the cultural dowry," namely jazz.[41] With this sexual metaphor, Mailer makes little attempt to disguise the homoeroticism of this homosocial scenario from which women are decidedly absent. Much like blackface performers, he attributes to the Negro bodily pleasures unavailable to white males, stating that the horrors of racial subjugation caused the Negro to "[relinquish] the pleasures of the mind for the more obligatory pleasures of the body, and in his music he gave voice to the character and quality of his existence, to his rage and the infinite variations of joy, lust, languor, growl, cramp, pinch, scream and despair of his orgasm."[42] As David Roediger scathingly puts it, Mailer "squarely premised an admiration for black culture based on that culture's capacity to produce orgasms in white males."[43]

Mailer's reinscription of blackness as hyperembodiment and his mythologization of black sexual potency have received severe criticism. James Baldwin, for instance, in what he himself refers to as a "love letter" to Norman Mailer,

registers his "fury" that Mailer maligns "the sorely menaced sexuality of Negroes . . . in order to justify the white man's own sexual panic." Noting that "to
be an American Negro is also to be a kind of walking phallic symbol," he concludes that "[t]he relationship, therefore, of a black boy to a white boy is a very
complex thing."[44] Eldridge Cleaver, on the other hand, virulently condemned
Baldwin's "flippant, schoolmarmish dismissal" of "The White Negro," which he
deemed part of Baldwin's "despicable underground guerilla war, waged on paper, against black masculinity," and which he indirectly attributed to Baldwin's
homosexuality. For him, Mailer's "incisive essay" showed "the depths of fer-
ment, on a personal level, in the white world. People are feverishly, and at great
psychic and social expense, seeking *fundamental and irrevocable liberation*—
and, what is more important, *are succeeding in escaping*—from the big white
lies that compose the monolithic myth of White Supremacy/Black Inferiority."[45]
In other words, for Cleaver, white male admiration and imitation of black culture
has potential political value, since it offers up possible lines of racial cross-
identification.

On this point, Andrew Ross notes that by the end of the '50s, when the civil
rights movement was in full swing, white minority interest in R&B (unlike the
more mainstream teen embrace of R&R) did register white expressions of racial
solidarity.[46] However, as David Roediger notes, Ralph Ellison had understood
over three decades ago that a love of black culture need not rule out racist attitudes: "What, by the way, is one to make of a white youngster who, with a tran-
sistor radio, screaming a Stevie Wonder tune, glued to his ear, shouts racial epithets at black youngsters trying to swim at a public beach?"[47] Moreover, many
cultural forms that have absorbed black culture fail to acknowledge their indebt-
edness, thus provoking accusations of theft and appropriation.[48] For instance,
Fred Pfeil has shown how the white male-dominated world of rock defines itself
"in diacritical distinction from Blackness." Rock "comes with access to the mu-
sical-libidinal resources of Blackness, but unlike Mailer's fantasized hipster-
ideal, with no additional risk or requirement to become a 'white Negro' one-
self."[49] In any case, as Ross argues, after the civil rights movement and the
emergence of black separatist pride, "the category of the 'white negro' was no
longer so easily available." He adds, "there was no such thing as a 'white
Black.'"[50]

But as the David Beckham documentary I discussed in the opening of this
chapter illustrates, for better or worse, now there is such a thing as "white
Black." Most commonly, however, white devotees of black culture, particularly
hip hop, the '70s cultural movement out of which rap emerged, are now dubbed
"wiggers." By fusing white and "nigger," this term is indicative of an attempt by
many African-Americans, particularly within the hip hop scene, to reappropriate
and resignify what has historically been deemed the most debasing of racial epithets, a fact I develop in my discussion of the films of Quentin Tarantino.

Given that rap was originally a form of "black cultural expression that pri-
oritizes black voices from the margins of urban America," it is perhaps surpris-

ing that the biggest *official* buyers of rap are white teenage males from the American suburbs.[51] Rap is a form which initially resisted easy co-option since it generally refuses "to practice the subterfuge usually necessary to sidestep sanctions when bringing lower class vernacular into the public domain"[52] Partly, this has to do with the material and political conditions, namely extreme economic deprivation, social alienation, and deeply entrenched institutionalized racism, that produced rap. Rap was therefore originally a highly politicized form of music making that actively articulated its opposition to the white mainstream, not only through its thematic content, but also through its use of distinctly African-American speech patterns and slang, as well as language considered profane by Middle America. However, recent years have witnessed a proliferation of white-owned hip hop record companies, MTV's careful selection of rap that is palatable to the white mainstream, and the commercial successes of white rap stars such as Eminem, whose rise to stardom via a black cultural form has prompted comparisons with Elvis.

Recalling Lott's assertion that minstrelsy allowed class anxieties to be worked through in the modality of race, no doubt it is rap's railings against social alienation and poverty that appeal to white working-class hip hop fans, who are excluded from many of the so-called privileges of whiteness. But how can the embracing of rap by white, suburban, middle-class, teenage males be explained? In part, I would argue, rap mediates concerns about their economic future in a downsized economy, the adverse knock-on effects of which are being keenly felt by the middle-classes. Identification with black (male) rage can facilitate a shared sense of disenfranchisement, one that enables a disavowal of the advantages that still inhere in whiteness. The fact these suburban male wiggers are increasingly proclaiming not only their affinities with black culture, but also their dissatisfaction with whiteness at a time when African-Americans, males in particular, are deemed by many to be an endangered species, is also some measure of the successes of the civil rights movement's critique of whiteness and its positive investment in blackness as a badge of identity. The illumination of the sterile and parasitical nature of American whiteness by the political and cultural struggle of activists of color has also inevitably affected straight white males the most, since they have no claims to gender or sexual particularity either. The embracing of black culture by white males, then, can also constitute a strategy of particularizing normative masculinity in response to contemporary identity critiques, marking male wiggers as *exceptionally* white and thus insulated against the charges of being an evil and/or a boring white male.

This male rejection of whiteness is often played for comedy in popular films. In *Bulworth*, for instance, a middle-aged senator's adoption of black street cool frees him from a stultifying life of corrupt politics, while his romance with a mixed race woman, played by Hale Berry, offers the prospect of racial rapprochement. Similarly, in *Bringing Down the House* (2003), Steve Martin learns to overcome his fastidious middle-class whiteness through his contact with female rap artist Queen Latifah. Both films implicitly suggest that inside every boring white male is a spontaneous, uninhibited black man struggling to get out. By commodifying white men in blackface for mainstream audiences, these films certainly risk rehearsing the power dynamics of minstrelsy, but they also have the more subversive potential of highlighting that "ordinary" white men are haunted by fears of their inauthenticity and vacuity. As Tania Modleski notes in her psychoanalytic reading of blackface, a reading informed by Homi Bhabha's notion of racial mimicry, fetishization might well "restore the wholeness and unity threatened by the sight of difference, yet because it enters into the game of mimicry it is condemned to keep alive the possibility that there may be 'no presence or identity behind the mask.'"[53] The price that wiggers pay for the fetishization of black masculinity, then, is a reinforcement of anxieties that white heterosexual masculinity is an empty identity, even if it is that very emptiness that has historically allowed white heterosexual masculinity to act as the default identity.

As with minstrels before them, male wiggers, both on and off screen, also act out stereotypes of black masculinity formed in the white imagination. As David Roediger argues, wiggers tend to essentialize black culture as "male, hard, sexual, and violent" in a more extreme form than R&B and soul.[54] Lott's Žižekian reading of minstrelsy is also pertinent here, since it is my sense that undergridding contemporary white male attractions to rap, especially "gangsta rap"—which, despite its damning critiques of institutionalized racism, also perpetuates stereotypes of black masculinity as ultra-virile, violent, sexist, and homophobic—is not only homoerotic fascination with black male posturing, but also the assumption that black males have license to flout the demands of political correctness because of their minoritized status. This assumption, of course, ignores objections to violent, sexist, and anti-gay lyrics that emanate from within the black community itself. That said, most black theorists are careful to contextualize rap in order to avoid re-circulating thinly veiled racist discourses that scapegoat rap, and, by extension, black urban males, for all number of social ills. Many commentators have regarded black male posturing and misogynistic, homophobic lyrics to form a self-defensive strategy against the emasculation caused by economic disenfranchisement. bell hooks also argues that misogyny and homophobia in rap should be understood as "a reflection of the prevailing values in our society, values created and sustained by white supremacist, capitalist patriarchy" for the purposes of its own maintenance.[55] Indeed, misogyny and male posturing are as much a staple of rock music as they are of rap. Moreover, the verbal and sexual violence of rap not only responds to the institutional demands of the music industry, but also sells well to its official biggest buyers—white adolescent males.[56]

As David Roediger argues, while hip hop also provides disaffected white youths with "an explicit, often harsh, critique of whiteness" from a black perspective, it is important to note that not "every white hip hop fan is finding a way out of whiteness, let alone racism."[57] Moreover, because these cross-identifications tend to be mapped onto commodities rather than political struggle, race is conceptualized in purely cultural terms, divorcing the category of race from issues relating to racism, property, and political power, and sidelining the pressing need to translate individual acts of racial solidarity into structural and institutional change. In short, wiggers can adopt otherness without giving up privilege. Consequently, as with permeating the boundaries of sexual difference, racial crossovers can work to evacuate racial categories of their essentialist force, but can simultaneously work to resecure the categories and stereotypes upon which any transgression depends—as I attempt to show in my discussion of filmic wiggers below.

Quentin Tarantino: White Cool, Black Masks

In the '90s Quentin Tarantino emerged as popular cinema's wigger *in extremis*, waxing lyrical about his close affinity with black culture in interviews: "I kind of grew up surrounded by black culture. . . . It is the culture I identify with. . . . Don't let this pigmentation fool you; it's a state of mind."[58] Tarantino borrows heavily from various black cultural forms in his filmmaking, such as the burnt-out urban scenes of rap videos evident in *Reservoir Dogs*, his violent, often profane, but expressive dialogues that self-consciously mimic rap lyrics, his use of black soundtracks, and overt references to Blaxploitation films, along with what Manthia Diawara has termed "the new Black realism"—though *Kill Bill Vol. I* (2003) and *Vol. 2* (2004) showed him borrowing from other cultures too, such as Hong Kong Kung Fu films and Japanese anime.[59] The quintessential example is *Jackie Brown* (1997), designated as "a black film" by Tarantino,[60] which puts a Blaxploitation spin on Elmore Leonard's heist novel *Rum Punch* (1992), changing the white heroine into a black woman played by the iconic Blaxploitation star Pam Grier, complete with a R&B and soul soundtrack. Like Blaxploitaiton films, which were predominately white-controlled, Tarantino's films also exploit racial stereotypes of black women as sexy but castrating, and black manhood as violent, criminalized, hypersexualized, but always incredibly cool. Indeed, in an interview with Lisa Kennedy, Tarantino proudly states, "[s]omeone said to me at Sundance when *Reservoir Dogs* was there, 'You know what you've done, you've given white boys the kind of movies black kids get.' . . . Blacks have always had those movies . . . Being bad, looking cool being bad, with a fuck-you attitude."[61]

Numerous commentators have been angered by Tarantino's use of black culture to create his hip cinema of "white cool," partly because of suspicions that he merely wishes to demonstrate his familiarity with black culture in order to reference his extraordinary whiteness, and partly because he promotes images of blackness that have been formed in the white popular imagination. In the homosocial world of Tarantino's gangster chic, black masculinity is the ultimate in cool; white masculinity, by contrast, becomes a blank screen onto which blackness can be projected. This lays bare the nexus of anxieties surrounding the emptiness and ordinariness of white masculinity, even as it reveals how whiteness can colonize blackness without relinquishing hold of its privileges, neutralizing the threat of difference into a safe (white male) fantasy.

The coolness attributed to black masculinity is made abundantly clear in *Reservoir Dogs* (1992) when the various codenames are distributed to the all-white gangsters, and Mr. Pink and Mr. Brown express dissatisfaction with their allotted color.[62] Mr. Pink (Steve Buscemi) worries that his name is the equivalent of Mr. Pussy, and Mr. Brown (Quentin Tarantino) that his is too close to shit. When they ask whether they could choose their own names, their boss replies, "It doesn't work out. Put four guys in a room and let them pick their own colors, everybody wants to be Mr. Black." Even though one of the men is assigned the name Mr. White (Harvey Keitel), which is also an ethnic maker, it has none of the lexical coolness of its binary opposite.

But it is *True Romance* (1993), based on a Tarantino screenplay, which screens a white male desire to embody black masculinity with Tarantinoesque self-consciousness. As director Tony Scott explained to actor Gary Oldman, his character Drexl is "a white guy who thinks he's black," and with his dread-locked hair, gold-capped teeth, ostentatious display of jewelry, and his half-Rasta, half-Queens accent, Oldman might as well have been in blackface.[63] Despite his white skin, Drexl discursively constructs himself as black through his constant highlighting of the protagonist's (Christian Slater's) whiteness, securing a fantasmatic identification with blackness as his prerogative. His assumption that race is a volitional identity perpetuates the superficial notion that blackness can "be put on and taken off at will."[64] Thus, as Sharon Willis argues, "Drexl's posturing ventriloquizes his fantasy—a white male fantasy—of black masculinity, where racial difference is reduced to a cultural icon for the dominant culture."[65] Drexl is undoubtedly ridiculed by the film for his posturing (opening up the possibility that he forms a self-reflexive comment on Tarantino's self-confessed wannabe-ism), but this also works to safeguard the film from criticism, even as it screens white authored stereotypes of black masculinity that it does little to dislodge or deconstruct. Indeed, the swaggering masculinity that Drexl approximates is violent, misogynistic, and criminalized: not only is Drexl a pimp who beats his "girls," but he is also introduced in mid-conversation with a group of black friends discussing whether "niggers" "eat pussy"—sexist dialogue that would seem to be competing with gangsta rap, as if the mediation of blackness somehow legitimized transgression. While this discussion would primarily seem to fulfill a bi-racial bonding function, as Eve Sedgwick has taught us, homosociality is always undergridded by repressed homoerotic desire.[66]

Indeed, it is worth noting here that a fantasy of bi-racial anal sex between men violently erupts in the all-male universe of both of Tarantino's gangster films. In *Reservoir Dogs*, this fantasy emerges when the borders of whiteness are transgressed by white men acting black: Nice Guy Eddie (Chris Penn) takes Mr. Blonde's (Michael Madsen's) use of black slang on his release from prison to mean that "all that black semen been poke up your ass backed up so far in your brain it's comin' out your mouth." In *Pulp Fiction*, white red-neck racists choose Marsellus (Ving Rhames), the black mafia boss, as their first rape victim, a choice that suggests the ease with which aversion and attraction can slide into each other. Both these examples point to Tarantino's self-conscious screening of what would normally remain repressed in other film texts—in this case, the fact that white male attractions to black masculinity are always enmeshed in a circuit of homoerotic desire, which is often rerouted, but not cancelled out, by the blatantly homophobic hate speech of his characters—a point I develop further in the following chapter.

Nowhere is Tarantino's appropriation of blackness more controversial than in the compulsive repetition of the word "nigger" in his screenplays. With his finger ever on the cultural pulse, Tarantino was well aware of the huge political force the word wielded in the '90s, with some African-Americans attempting resignification and others arguing that it was impossible to unyoke such an abusive term from prior usages.[67] Tarantino himself claims that he attempts to strip "the most taboo word in the English language" of its power.[68] In this respect, his self-proclaimed project falls in with Judith Butler's arguments about hate speech set out in *Excitable Speech: A Politics of the Performative* (1997). Butler accepts that all injurious names have acquired a "sedimentation" of usages, and inflict their blows by invoking that historicity and accompanying trauma. However, for Butler, "[k]eeping such terms unsaid and unsayable can also work to lock them in place, preserving their power to injure." Instead, because signs are unstable and always exceed the purposes for which they were intended, Butler proposes a Derridean strategy of resignification which "*uses* that word, but also *displays* it, points to it, outlines it as the arbitrary material instance of language that is exploited to produce certain kinds of effects."[69] However, Butler offers no clear strategy as to how interpellatives might be redeployed or recontextualized, and prefers to illustrate her point with words such as "lesbian" and "queer" which have been reappropriated with more success than "nigger"; nor does she engage with the crucial issue of "semantic consensus," since while a single speaker might unmoor a term from its prior meaning, it is less certain that the resignification will be recognized as such.[70]

Similar problems are raised by Tarantino's alleged attempts to point to the semantic arbitrariness of "nigger" and rid it of its injurious residue. Importantly, it is Tarantino's African-American characters who use the epithet most extensively, such as *Pulp Fiction*'s Marsellus's affectionate addresses to Vincent (John Travolta) as "my nigger," which arguably frees the word from its racial and racist referent. However, when "nigger" is used as a descriptor by a non-black character, or worse as hate speech, far from sanitizing the word, these usages consolidate its power to wound. While it would be a simplification to regard these speeches as instances of Tarantino's racism, rather than racist dialogue from racist characters, these examples merely confirm that efforts to "highlight the instability of 'race' as a category . . . cannot escape capture in a circuit of cultural meanings that strive to stabilize race."[71] Moreover, even if Tarantino does attempt to empty out the term, he seems rather more interested in the residue that remains, a residue that translates into either discomfort or pleasure, in scenes designed to offer transgressive pleasure precisely because of the meanings that racist usages have historically accrued.

Tarantino's whiteness also inevitably influences the reception of these scenes, and many critics have harbored the suspicion that the obsessive repetition of "nigger" in his screenplays allows him to maintain a certain "hipness quotient," proving that he is "conversant in the nuances of black culture in the most sophisticated way."[72] The most obvious example is Tarantino's own cameo role as Jimmy in *Pulp Fiction*, a role that is impossible to divorce from Tarantino's persona as *white* auteur. Incredulous that Jules (Samuel L. Jackson) and Vincent brought Marvin's (Phil LaMarr's) body to his suburban house, Jimmy rants, mirroring the prosodic features of African-American speech patterns, "When you came pulling in here did you notice a sign on the front of my house saying 'dead nigger storage'? . . . No, because storin' dead niggers ain't my fuckin' business." While Jimmy's overdetermined, infantile repetition of "nigger" could arguably function as a defamiliarization strategy, the very fact that the scene is designed to shock renders Tarantino's self-stated aim of eliminating its power to injure dubious, especially when the stylization of this overtly-coded performance piece seems to function as an inbuilt defensive strategy that allows audiences to take pleasure in Jimmy's sheer outrageousness. As Willis argues, Tarantino's dialogue depends "on imagining that some of us—individually or collectively—must be working to censor such speech. It imagines, in other words, something like a cultural id that functions on an analogy with individual unconscious processes." Jimmy's tirade is also sanctioned by the fact that the African-American Jules is unruffled, and Bonnie, Jimmy's wife, is also posited as black. Thus, as Willis observes, "[e]verything proceeds as if, by figuring Jimmy's wife as African American, the film could insulate the director's own image from the racist edge of his discourse. Bonnie functions, then, as his alibi; she is supposed to exempt him from cultural rules, from ordinary whiteness."[73]

Spike Lee's *Bamboozled*: Male Minstrelsy in the 21st Century

For black filmmaker Spike Lee, famously angered by Ordell's (Samuel L. Jackson's) use of "nigger" 38 times in *Jackie Brown*, Tarantino is *not* exempt from "ordinary whiteness": "I want Quentin to know that all African-Americans do not think that word is trendy or slick. . . . Quentin is infatuated with that word. What does he want to be made—an honorary black man?"[74] Spike Lee's own screening of a stunning series of monologues in *Do The Right Thing* (1989), each one featuring a male member of a different ethnic group delivering a stream of racial abuse about an ethnic/racial other, discourages identification through direct address, oblique camera angles, and the absence of any narrative function. The historical weight of these abusive racial epithets is thus foregrounded, though the fact that all monologues are delivered by men perpetuates the film's overall premise that "racism, as well as the struggle against it, is something that happens exclusively between men."[75]

In the same film, Lee also explores how a white (male) love of black culture does not rule out racist attitudes in an exchange between Mookie (played by Lee himself) and Pino (John Turturro), a racist Italian-American. Mookie asks Pino who his favorite basketball player, film star, and rock star are, to which Pino unhesitantly replies Magic Johnson, Eddie Murphy, and Prince respectively, quickly changing his last answer to Bruce Springsteen (a white working-class male icon) once he cottons on to Mookie's game. In defense, Pino argues that "Magic, Eddie, Prince, they're not niggers. I mean, they're not black"—an argument that underscores how absorption into the cultural mainstream "whitens" stars of color, ridding them of their threatening otherness. In response, Mookie replies, "Deep down inside I think you wish you were black. Laugh if you want to. You know, your hair is kinkier than mine. What does that mean? Now, you know what they say about dark Italians." Mookie thus deconstructs race by pointing to the discursive nature by which certain phenotypes are selected and interpreted as part of the social construction of race, as well as pointing to Italian-American fears about the fragility of their ethnically-inflected whiteness— indeed, racist slurs in the film such as "wop" and "guinea" show that historically Italians have not always been considered "white enough." Lee thus understands race to be a cultural and social construction, but one that unfolds against a backdrop of white supremacy, a historical fact that will never render race the level playing field that Tarantino suggests it to be.

Spike Lee's biting satire *Bamboozled* (2000) self-consciously refers to his public spat with Tarantino, upon whom the film's male wigger *par excellence*, Dunwitty (Michael Rapaport), is rumored to be based.[76] Dunwitty, a white TV producer, brazenly informs the only African-American writer in the network, the embittered, Harvard-educated "buppy," Pierre Delacroix (Damon Wayans), "You know I grew up around black people all my whole life. I mean, if the truth be told, I probably know niggers better than you. And don't go getting offended by my use of the quote unquote N-word. I've a black wife with two bi-racial kids so I feel I have a right. And I don't give a goddamn what that prick Spike Lee says. Tarantino was right. Nigger is just a word." Dunwitty then repeats "nigger" with childish relish, much like *Pulp Fiction*'s Jimmy, behavior that is branded offensive through an intercut fantasy scenario of Delacroix repeatedly pounding him. Dunwitty continues to flaunt his wigger credentials, demonstrating his knowledge about the black sport icons that adorn his office (all-male, suggestive of an undergridding homoerotic dialogue with black masculinity), and asserting, "I'm blacker than you. I'm keeping it real. I 'bout it 'bout. I got the roll. You're just frontin' trying to be white." For Dunwitty, blackness is a matter of style and cultural knowledge, unrelated to issues of power or racism. He also evacuates blackness of its diversity by accusing Delacroix of acting white because Delacroix does not fit the model of black masculinity that Dunwitty himself approximates, though the film also takes pains to stress that Delacroix is uncomfortable in his black skin, most obviously through the pretentious middle-class accent he adopts.

Intent on showing that white-controlled TV is only interested in black people on screen if they are "coons" or "buffoons," Delacroix pitches a new show to
Dunwitty entitled "Mantan: The New Millennium Minstrel Show," which recy-
cles old stereotypes of two "lazy, ignorant, uneducated, and unlucky" "coons"
called Mantan (Savion Glover) and Sleep 'n' Eat (Tommy Davidson), both
based on real-life black male minstrel stars. Delacroix's experiment takes an
unexpected turn, though, when the show becomes a runaway success, since it
"[offered] whites a chance to alleviate white anxiety and guilt concerning America's racist history under a new black sanctioning."[77] Despite their initial unease,
members of the multi-racial audience eventually black up for the show, gleefully
declaring themselves "niggers." As one white male puts it,

> I'm a Sicilian nigger, which means I'm more nigger than any nigger here. Be-
> cause you know what they say about Sicilians. We're darker than most niggers.
> We're bigger than most niggers. And we rap better than most niggers. [he raps]
> I'm white, not black / but not all the time / I'm in blackface / and I'm feelin'
> fine / No matter what color / no matter what race / You know you cool chillin' /
> when you're in blackface.

Throughout the movie, Lee critiques the fetishism involved in this white
(and implicitly male) desire to be black. As Delacroix's stand-up comedian father makes clear, whites want to pick and choose what aspects of blackness they
will adopt: "I hope they start hanging niggers again. I'm going to find out who's
black." A similar point about the indelibility of black skin is made when the police shoot at The Mau Maus, an Afrocentric rap group, killing all the rappers but
1/16th Blak (M.C. Serch), who, as his name suggests, has one-sixteenth African
ancestry, but was recognized as white by the police. With the exception of 1/16th
Blak, whose adoption of blackness is politically motivated, the film's underlying
suggestion is that white men act black not as a form of anti-racist struggle, but
because they have fallen victim to corporate capitalism's redeployment of identity politics as a niche marketing strategy which circulates black masculinity as a
commodity fetish—commodification which has its roots in slavery. This is apparent in Lee's superb parody of a Tommy Hilfiger advertisement. Tommy Hilfiger, a white designer of urban fashion, is transformed into Timmi Hillnigger, a
middle-aged white male, surrounded by women gyrating orgasmically around
him in a parody of rap videos (which, Lee implies, have become assimilated into
advertising culture in another form of minstrelsy) and iconic black males, who
verify the street-cool of his high-street products. Peddling his over-hyped, over-
priced designer wear through the use of black slang and a commodification of
the black urban experience, Hillnigger addresses the camera: "If you want to
keep it real, never get out of the gheeto [mispronounced], stay broke, and continue to add to my multi-billion dollar corporation, keep buying my gear. The
Timmi Hillnigger corporation. We keep it so real, we give you the bullet hole."
    Lee's project throughout *Bamboozled* is to show that minstrelsy never dis-
appeared, a point he underscores in the final scene's disturbing extra-narrative

montage that charts the progress of cinema and television versions of blackface once its stage incarnations disappeared, from Al Johnson to racist cartoons. While it may no longer require blackface, Lee suggests it still exists, not only embodied by wiggers like Dunwitty, but also in black sitcoms and gangsta rap (Lee's most contentious point), in which blacks imitate white conceptions of blacks. To make his point, Lee restages minstrelsy in order to recontextualize it, even running the risk of making his new millennium minstrels amusing at times. Esther Godfey notes that "[c]ontemporary reviews of *Bamboozled* often note that theatre audiences usually stopped laughing about halfway through the film. At some point, minstrelsy's power to recreate the very binary logic it has the power to deconstruct overwhelms and reverses the 'race trouble' it has attempted to make."[78] Whereas the intra-diegetic show was a huge success, *Bamboozled* itself did not fare well at the box office, an indication of the success of Lee's resignification of minstrelsy, but also sadly proving Delacroix's point. *Ali G Indahouse*, on the other hand, a joint British-American production, deploys minstrel codes in a less obviously political context, with critics caught between whether it satirizes the posturings of British male wiggers or, as comedian Felix Dennis suspects, "allows the liberal middle-class to laugh at black street culture in a context where they can retain their political correctness."[79]

Ali G Indahouse: British Male Wiggers, American Minstrelsy?

In 1999 British comedian Sacha Baron Cohen gave birth to his comic creation, Ali G, during a five-minute slot of the satirical Channel Four series *The 11 O'clock Show*, amassing a large enough cult following to be given his own program, *Da Ali G Show*. Part of the fascination with Ali G was his racial indeterminacy, with audiences unsure of how to respond, aware that by laughing they might well be crossing the lines of political correctness, a line that Cohen knows how to tread. Dressed in garish yellow shell suits, yellow-tinted sunglasses, a Tommy Hilfiger skullcap, sporting copious bling, and a thin goatee, with constant allusions to the ghetto and his homies, Ali G dressed, acted, and referenced himself as black. But comments about his uncle Jamal, who owns a local curry house, along with his Asian-sounding first name also made him a possible Asian, or at least an Asian wannabe black. His accent was equally ambivalent, an artful mixture of Asian and black slang, delivered in a West Indian cum Asian cum Estuary English accent. Yet, his physical features are neither Afro-Caribbean nor Asian, though his hair and complexion are dark enough to render his ostensible whiteness questionable. Indeed, when Ali G was still a little-known cult figure, the white authority figures he ridiculed, through asking wonderfully inane questions that they often took at face value, were always thrown by Cohen's catchphrase: "is it cos I is black?" With Cohen remaining silent on the intentions behind his creation, Ali G was inscrutable, leading to communities as diverse as Greeks, Sikhs, Jews, Indians, Scots and the Welsh claiming him as one of their own.[80] Once Cohen's white middle-class Jewish background was confirmed, this extra-textual knowledge paradoxically rendered Ali G more un-stable, with discussions ranging from whether Ali G was a white wannabe black, a white acting like an Asian wannabe black, a Jew acting like an Asian wannabe black, or a Jew acting like a white wannabe black—the latter question not only raising the question of the precarious nature of Jewish whiteness, but also re-hearsing similar dynamics to *The Jazz Singer* (1927), which screens the Jewish Al Johnson gaining full access to whiteness, and therefore Americaness, by put-ting on blackface.[81]

According to Paul Gilroy, part of the attraction of youth audiences to Ali G was their ability to understand the postmodern ironies and verbal codes of which the straight white authority figures that Ali G interviewed were so painfully un-aware, with Ali G even tricking Labour Minister Roy Hattersley into inadver-tently calling Tony Blair a "dong," slang for penis.[82] Thus, as Tony Blair's gov-ernment was rearticulating out-dated, right-wing notions of Britishness in an era marked by what Gilroy terms "post-colonial melancholia," Ali G was moving across cultural and linguistic codes, inviting the viewer "to become literate, if not exactly fluent, in an updated British Culture."[83]

However, with Ali G's Hollywood vehicle *Ali G Indahouse* (2003), Cohen was less able to sustain his racially indeterminate persona and wily exposure of the values of the British white establishment that his mock talk-show format allowed, despite a plot which dramatizes Ali G's culture clash with uptight (white) British MPs when he is elected to Parliament. Rather, the feature film format lapsed into the scatological humor of the British *Carry On* tradition.[84] While Cohen's transgression of the boundaries of both race and "good taste" might have been popular with cult youth British audiences, his entry into the mainstream led to a scrutinizing of his political intentions (about which he still maintained a resolute silence). The film's gala opening was picketed by protest-ers angered at the pimping of black culture for white profit, while *The Daily Mail*, one of Britain's most right-wing tabloids, accused Cohen of being the new Al Johnson. That this anti-immigration tabloid should suddenly see fit to be the vanguard of anti-racism would seem to suggest that Gilroy is right to suspect that some of these responses have more to do with anxieties about "a larger process of dilution and mongrelization in which the protective purity of largely racial cultures is being lost, leaving them vulnerable to unprotected encounters with difference that can only involve risk, fear and jeopardy."[85]

In the light of the country's minstrel past, it is not surprising that the film only gained a limited theatrical release in the U.S due to concerns about its non-bankability. Indeed, many reviewers in the U.S. who saw the film were outraged by the perceived denigration of black culture.[86] Interestingly, many of these re-sponses focused on Cohen's extra-textual Jewishness, rhetorically asking how Cohen would like it if a black male imitated a Jew in order to mock Jewish cul-ture, a response which oversimplified the multi-layered nature of Cohen's per-formance, but also points to the asymmetries of racial impersonation, since there is no history of "Jewish-face" or of Jewishness being circulated as commodity.

Cohen was also seen to be repeating a history of Jewish blackface performers who used blackface as a vehicle to express Jewish sorrow, but nonetheless could always "pass" as the normative ethnicity.[87] However, despite the decision not to give *Ali G Indahouse* a general U.S. release, in 2003 Cohen took his TV show to the U.S. under the auspices of the much-respected network HBO. He soon gained a cult audience, as well as generating controversy, though Ali's Britishness (as well as sheer ridiculousness and stupidity) no doubt worked to insulate Cohen from charges of minstrelsy and racism to some extent.

National context thus plays a crucial role in both the production and reception of representations of white male wiggers. As regards reactions to Ali G, it must be noted that the black community in Britain has a very different history from that of African-Americans. In the 1950s, the majority of Afro-Caribbean and Asian blacks in Britain had *voluntarily* immigrated after the break-up of the British Empire in response to the British government's calls for (menial, poorly paid) labor, though many whites soon panicked about the potential loss of British homogeneity, with Enoch Powell famously leading the call for repatriation. This wave of immigration "produc[ed] a specific set of urgencies that are not translatable to the violent origin in slavery of many African-Americans, nor to the patterns of ethnic immigration in the U.S."[88] Blacks in Britain have faced poverty, social exclusion, alienation, and racism, but unlike the U.S., Britain does not have 400 years of slavery or segregation on its own soil in its racial past. For this reason, whereas racial boundaries in the U.S. often seem to be impenetrable, in Britain they are seen by many to be more fluid or "up for grabs,"[89] with notions of "cultural ownership and experiential copyright" having less of the force they wield in the U.S.[90] Moreover, the signifier "black" in Britain has at times been adopted by both Afro-Carribeans and black Asians, functioning much like the American umbrella term "people of color." As Kobena Mercer notes, this was an achievement "specific and unique to British conditions,"[91] though it is a tendency that is now in decline,[92] particularly with the reterritorialization of identities along ethnic and religious lines in the wake of post-9/11 Islamophobia. As I argued in the first chapter, none of this is to make light of the painful and bloody history of British racism and colonialism, or the colonial-inspired inbuilt sense of superiority that infuses British forms of whiteness. Nor is it to overlook the history of British fascism, which is on the increase with the immigration panic currently sweeping Britain. However, it is certainly the case that white British masculinity is not in dialogue with black masculinity in the same way as its American counterpart; rather British whiteness is always informed by imperialist discourses of nation that are further traversed by entrenched discourses of class. Nevertheless, Ali G reveals how, in a globalized media world, American popular culture, in this case hip hop, impacts significantly on British culture, with hip hop adopted by British blacks and whites alike.

Analyzing the function that racial mimicry serves British white masculinity in *Ali G Indahouse* will always be dogged by the unanswerable question of whose white masculinity we are referring to—Ali G's or Cohen's?—and whether Cohen is believed to be satirizing British white male desires to approximate a gangsta rap persona that does not translate into a British reality or hip hop itself. Indeed, the film's parodic mode does not allow a simple answer to that question. In a similar way to characters' behavior in Tarantino's cinema, Ali's antics are always heavily coded as performance, thereby deflecting criticism through constant reminders of the film's artificiality and lack of serious intent.

This strategy of self-legitimizing autodeconstruction is apparent from the first scene, which opens with a montage sequence of South Central Los Angeles, accompanied by the prototypical track of gangsta rap "Straight Outta Compton" by N.W.A. (Niggaz With Attitude), known for its incendiary lyrics about violence against cops. Ali arrives on the scene in his garish yellow wigger attire, representing a white adolescent male's fantasy of black manhood, able to deflect bullets with his gold ring and endowed with a penis that reaches his knees. Nonetheless, Ali's attempts to emulate 'hood masculinity are pathetically eroded, particularly through codes of infantilization, such as when he runs out of bullets and childishly imitates the sound of a machine gun. This scene undergoes a further level of undercutting when it is revealed that this sequence was just a dream, marking white stereotypes of black masculinity as just that—stereotypes—but screening them nonetheless. The unbridgeable gap between Ali G the homeboy and the less generously endowed Alistair Leslie Graham (an obligatory penis exposure scene makes it clear he fails to measure up), who lives in suburban Staines with his white grandmother (a confirmation of Ali's whiteness that the TV series never granted), is a constant source of the film's humor. As Ali jumps into his Renault 5, carefully obeying the speed limit, his 'hood—screened in slowly cut crane shots that contrast starkly with the rapidly-cut montage of South Central—turns out to be a leafy, spacious suburb made up of identical semi-detached houses, with the turf of his gang, Westside Massive, marked out by mini-roundabouts and nurseries. Ali's adoption of African-American gang codes also comes in for derision, such as when one of his "homies" turns up in green rather than the gang yellow because his mother had washed his top with his brother's football socks, leading Ali to observe that "in the ghetto, washing non-color-fast synthetics at 60° could cost your life." Ali G thus functions as a typical buffoon, with the wigger device allowing a new take on the Benny Hill/*Carry On* style of British humor, with jokes revolving around men who refuse to grow up. But whereas minstrelsy can be accused of featuring infantile characters because of racist impulses to ridicule black masculinity, Cohen's "hyper-minstrelsy" has the dubious inbuilt defense that he is not ridiculing gangsta posturing, but British, suburban, white male wannabes.

The same is true of the film's parodies of R&B and rap videos. Parody, as we have seen in chapter 2, deploys the codes of the object it parodies in order to communicate a second level of meaning.[93] While reception can never be controlled, it can be influenced through specific modes of address. Spike Lee's parody in *Bamboozled* of an advertisement for a soft-drink, "Da Boom," is a case in point. Encircled by half-naked, black women, dancing provocatively to a groovy soundtrack, the show's host, Honeycutt (Thomas Jefferson Byrd), directly addresses the camera to sell the product through niche marketing: "Clinical testing has shown that Viagra doesn't work on black Johnsons. That's why our scientist has developed Da Bomb for you. It makes you feel like a man, yo! And it makes them bitches feel like natural women, I mean hos!" Here, Lee restages the codes of gangsta rap videos in order to lambaste their sexism and pandering to corporate capitalism. The sequence is inserted as an extra-narrative segment, thus averting easy identification. It is also framed by a critique of minstrelsy—indeed the film opens with a dictionary definition of satire and Stevie Wonder's track "Never Be a Misrepresented People." Thus Lee, whose racial politics are well-known, addresses a spectator "capable of resisting ideological systems built on the damaging discourse of stereotypes."[94] *Ali G Indahouse*, on the other hand, parodies hip hop videos in order to ridicule Ali's sexual desires for unobtainable women. Interrupting the narrative and coded as pure fantasy, these videos feature Ali surrounded by variously raced women, clad in skimpy bikinis, gyrating for his pleasure, one scene screening the white boy fantasy of being dominated by a phallic Naomi Campbell (playing herself). Followed immediately by shots of the diegetic Ali clumsily playing with his nipples or uncouthly grinding his pelvis, these segments obviously deflate his painful attempts to approximate a mythical, hypersexualized black masculinity. But, at the same time, Cohen's whiteness cannot be divorced from these parodic scenes, which, devoid of any obvious political import, can also work to render ridiculous the phallic posturing of many black rap artists, as well as allowing the film to circumvent charges of sexism by deflecting it onto black cultural forms. Whereas Lee addresses a non-racist spectator able to unpack the political message, *Ali G Indahouse* constructs an adolescent (white) male spectator who will enjoy Ali's sexist gags and objectification of women, along with Cohen's self-legitimizing parody—with neither pleasure necessarily canceling the other out. Recalling Žižek's arguments about the theft of enjoyment by the racial other, it would seem that Ali attributes to black males the pleasures of sexism that are denied to white men under the "tyranny" of political correctness.

In a generous reading, Gilroy argues that the underlying joke of Ali G is expressive of an "antipathy towards the stultifying US styles and habits that have all but crushed local forms of the black vernacular in the UK and replaced them with the standardised and uniform global products of hip hop consumer culture."[95] However, Gilroy does not comment as to whether Cohen should be leading this defense of British blackness, despite the fact that his reading suggests a problematic white paternalism. For many other theorists, who stress the political roots of hip hop, "white English boys taking the mickey out of black American culture seems at best gratuitous and at worst offensive."[96] With Ali G's cutting edge status dependent precisely on his instability, it is no surprise that Cohen is keeping quiet about his intentions.

8 Mile: Eminem, "White Trash" Masculinity, and Rap Authenticity

Unlike the white suburban Ali G, Eminem has largely been insulated against accusations that he is a mere black wannabe, gaining authentic status through his working-class Detroit roots, his backing from Dr. Dre of N.W.A (Niggaz with Attitude) fame, and his decision to "'address' his whiteness in relation to appropriated culture, rather than just presuming it."[97] For instance, in "Without Me," Eminem raps, "Though I'm not the first king of controversy / I am the worst thing since Elvis Presley / To do black music so selfishly / And use it to get myself wealthy."[98] Moreover, while Eminem refers to his whiteness as an initial disability in lines that rehearse white male victimology—"Some people only see I'm white, ignorin' skill"—other lyrics acknowledge that his white skin soon became his greatest asset: "Look at my sales / Let's do the math. If I was black, I would've sold half." [99] At the same time, whereas rap has been attacked on an unprecedented scale as "part of a long-standing sociologically-based discourse that considers black influences a cultural threat to American society,"[100] Eminem's incendiary lyrics in conjunction with his "baby blue eyes" and "dimples," as Eminem himself puts it in his track "White America," disrupt the racially saturated discourses that pathologize black urban masculinity.

Eminem's violent, sexist, and homophobic lyrics have resulted in some rather unholy alliances between the likes of the neo-conservative Lynne Cheyney and GLAAD (Gay and Lesbian Alliance Against Defamation), with GLAAD making an unprecedented appeal for censorship. Eminem defends himself by ridiculing his detractors for failing to understand the distinction between violence and its representation. However, it is instructive that despite his litanies of abuse directed at women and homosexuals, he has never uttered a racist lyric, no doubt aware that it would damage his standing in the hip hop community. If contextualized, his tracks are symptomatic of prevalent levels of anti-female and anti-gay feelings that exist in the mainstream where they sell so well, as well as rap's generic conventions that demand that MCs "battle" each other by robbing their opponents of their manhood. It is also the case that the same fears of emasculation haunt poor urban white males as their black counterparts, while Eminem's homophobic lyrics might also fulfill the function of deflecting homoerotic tension caused by his emulation of black masculinity.

While his use of an originally black (though increasingly hybridized) cultural form enables him to express his own experiences of social alienation, poverty, and job insecurity, revealing a lack of existing white working-class models at his disposal, Eminem's rap differs from black-authored rap in several respects. Firstly, whereas black gangsta rap is renowned for its visceral revenge fantasies of cop-killing that unfold against a backdrop of police racism and brutality, revenge fantasies in Eminem's tracks are staged primarily in the domestic sphere, as he spits out first-person, present tense tales of white-on-white violence against his (or his rap persona's?) mother and wife, most famously with the tracks "97

Bonnie and Clyde" and "Kim," both of which dramatize the murder of his now ex-wife.[101] At the same time, Eminem raps lyrical about his daughter, her purity played off against adult womanhood, with his self-styled presentation as a devoted father working to soften his rap persona; paternity, as in so many Hollywood films, provides the trope to manage white masculinity in a postindustrial, postfeminist, multicultural age. Secondly, he references his whiteness by foregrounding his "white trash" roots, which have been crucial to his authentic status, unlike middle-class white rappers before him, such as Vanilla Ice, whose career plummeted when it transpired that stories of his ghetto roots and gangsta past were mere marketing strategies. Eminem's feuds with his wife and mother, publicized in his own lyrics, have also been treated in the media like a "white trash" soap opera, with black rap artist Ice-T describing him as the "Jerry Springer of rap."[102] Along with generic self-aggrandizements, Eminem's lyrics also wallow in a self-debasement that is rarely found in black rap, which tends to promote black pride. Noting a similar strategy of self-deprecation in the work of white artists, such as Beck's "I'm a Loser Baby" or Radiohead's "Creep," Annalee Newitz suggests that the contemporary critique of whiteness (which rap has amplified), along with the failure that is built into the very structure of whiteness, can result in expressions of self-loathing and nihilism, which nonetheless render "the speaker both hip and impervious to criticism" through a strategy of pre-emption.[103] Indeed, Eminem's lyrics often slide into masochism, with *The Slim Shady LP* littered with references to self-immolation: "You see this bullet hole in my neck? It's self-inflicted . . . Cause my split personality is having an identity crisis / I'm Dr. Hyde and Mr. Jekyll."[104]

Similar to when *Fight Club*'s narrator refers to himself as Jekyll and Hyde, alluding to a repressed, embittered, aggressive, repressed "other within," Eminem joins the ranks of the "angry white males" (one of his world tours was aptly entitled "Anger Management Tour") who rail against their perceived disenfranchisement (though women and homosexuals are his scapegoats of choice, not affirmative action), and defend themselves against criticism through self-denigration and appeals to victim status. In this light, Eminem has much in common with the paranoid "angry white male" protagonist of *Falling Down*, sharing not only D-FENS's masochistic subjectivity, but also his appropriation of black discourses, as I discussed in chapter 1. Indeed, Paul Gormley has cited *Falling Down* as an example of white "brutality films" that appropriate the rage of new black realist cinema by simply transferring it to a white character, decontextualizing and primitivizing that rage by eliding the material conditions that produced that raw anger in the first place.[105] In this respect, as David Wellman argues, in their self-representation as America's latest victims and their borrowing of the discourse of identity politics, it is certainly possible to regard "angry white males" (both on and off-screen) as the latest development in a long history of minstrelsy.[106]

In that the "angry white man" has proved a popular figure in contemporary U.S. cinema, it is interesting to explore how *8 Mile* (2002), a fictionalized account of Eminem's early career, translates his persona to the big screen. Most notably, the "angry white male" of Slim Shady fame is massively toned down, diluted by that other great '90s Hollywood icon, the "sensitive white male," with an American dream narrative thrown into the mix for good measure. The Oscar-winning signature anthem "Lose Yourself" became Eminem's first number one hit, with the wife-beating, mother-raping, gay-bashing lyrics replaced by an individualistic, Anglo-Saxon, capitalist work ethic: "You can do anything you put your mind to, man."[107] Not surprisingly, in reviews, the film prompted numerous comparisons with *Rocky* (1976). Despite its evident commercialism, however, *8 Mile* is the first Hollywood film to depict the underground hip hop scene, though white mainstream interest in the most heavily policed musical form to date would seem to require the mediating figure of a hard-grafting white boy succeeding in a black man's world.

The slight differences between the lives of Eminem and his character, Jimmy, enable a recuperation of Eminem for the mainstream by having him play the part of a vulnerable, damaged white male. All the women in Jimmy's life disappoint him (his ex-girlfriend fakes pregnancy, his new lover cheats on him, his irresponsible mother refuses to work and drinks herself into oblivion, leaving her daughter to fend for herself), with the exception of his baby sister, who enables the film to cash in on Eminem's devoted father persona. He even becomes a defender of a gay colleague, dissing a homophobic rapper to the tune that he "may be gay, but you're a faggot," a distinction that Eminem himself made in an interview with MTV's Kurt Loder: "The lowest degrading thing that you can say to a man when you're battling him is to call him a faggot and try to take away his manhood. Call him a sissy, call him a punk. 'Faggot' to me doesn't necessarily mean gay people."[108] While here Eminem participates in the devaluation of the feminine that is common to much male rap, *8 Mile* provides a class context for this discourse. As Jimmy puts it, "we're still as broke as fuck and live with our moms." Jimmy's Oedipal dramas with his mother—such as when she wants to discuss her sex life, causing him to slam the door in her face in horror—also imply that male rap's misogyny might be explained through a male fear of the suffocating maternal and feminine, which economic disenfranchisement and absent fathers exacerbate.

Poverty unites all male characters, regardless of racial identity. As with Lott's assertion that minstrelsy allowed the working through of class anxieties, it is suggested that it is hip hop's rage at social exclusion, alienation, and poverty that speaks to these white male characters, whose whiteness is sullied by their class status, while it also offers what Roediger terms "the spontaneity, experimentation, humor, danger, sexuality, physical movement and rebellion absent from what passes as white culture."[109] The characters' desperation is reflected in Rodrigo Prieto's social realist cinematography, which, at another level of minstrelsy, borrows heavily from new black realist films and their attention to the local 'hood, as the camera lingers on abandoned, decaying buildings, boarded-up businesses, and desolate neighborhoods filmed in grainy film stock and desaturated color. The film's title is taken from the symbolic road that divides the overwhelmingly white suburbs from the city of Detroit, which is 76% African-American, according to the 2000 census.[110] With Jimmy being a minority white, and exposed to critiques of whiteness from within the hip hop community, it is suggested that he lives his whiteness differently than middle-class whites from the suburbs.

While *8 Mile*'s mediating black subject matter has ironically led to it being one of the few sympathetic representations of the white urban poor in a Hollywood feature film, it also risks overlooking the advantages of possessing white skin, whatever one's class status. Jimmy's black friend, the politicized DJ Iz (De'Angelo Wilson), does state of white rappers, "it's always easier for a white man to make it in a black man's medium. Right B?"—but his question remains unanswered, since conveniently, at this exact same moment, Jimmy spots his adversary Papa Doc (Anthony Mackie) and rushes off to attack him. The film, though, would suggest the exact opposite and taps uncomfortably into the prevalent "angry white male" accusations of reverse racism in post-affirmative action America. Most of the invectives hurled at Jimmy in the battles insult his whiteness, accusing him of being a tourist, Elvis, Vanilla Ice, a hillbilly, Hitler, and trailer trash. However, his mentor, Future (Mekhi Phifer), never stops believing in him, reversing conventional racial dynamics by stating, "Once they hear you, it won't matter what color you are." In this respect, *8 Mile* follows *White Men Can't Jump* (1992) (which also screens a white male in a black environment in which the odds are uncharacteristically stacked against him) in positing a black male "as possessing a profound and intimate knowledge of the white men's fears and desires."[111]

The final battle scene suggests that hip hop authenticity resides not in skin color but "power, class, and privilege."[112] Jimmy wins over the hostile crowd by exposing that self-styled gangsta Papa Doc went to a private school and lives at home with his happily married parents. Jimmy also pre-empts all of Papa Doc's insults, aware that they would merely rehash stereotypes about white rappers: "I'm a piece of white trash, I say it proudly / . . . / Here, tell these people something they don't know about me." His silencing of Pap Doc underscores just how effective a strategy (white male) masochistic self-loathing is in deflecting criticism, though adopting "white trash" as a badge of pride could be read as another act of minstrelsy, aping the African-American resignification of "nigger."

On the one hand, then, *8 Mile* is interesting for insisting that economic class is the overwhelming divider of society (though, unlike the British *The Full Monty*, requires racial discourse to do so), and that a working-class cultural form like hip hop might constitute a means of bridging racial demarcations. In the process, it also problematizes white masculinity as a monolithic category. On the other hand, issues such as institutionalized racism are sidelined and displaced onto the black racisms of the hip hop community. It is thus fitting that the film ends with Jimmy going back to finish his factory shift, which ostensibly mitigates against a Hollywood ending (though our extra-textual knowledge of

Eminem assures us Jimmy will ultimately make the big time), but also means that the advantages that Eminem's whiteness brought him once he had broken into the hip hop world remain unexplored.

Of course, Jimmy is not Hollywood's first white male to adopt another culture and then do it better. Nor need this culture necessarily be African-American, as demonstrated in films such as *Dances with Wolves* (1990) and *The Last Samourai* (2003), both of which screen the white male protagonist's embrace of an exotic other on the path to white male (and American) redemption. The current trend for the "Asianization" of the action movie also points to new borrowings, as seen in *The Matrix* and *Kill Bill*, for instance, which reveal the potential of other cultures to act as signifiers of the new, the hip, and the authentic in white postmodern culture.[113] However, despite the variety of manifestations of white masculinity granting its racial others "the simultaneous privilege and responsibility . . . of defining what it is,"[114] the indelible history of slavery and minstrelsy has meant that the "dominant codes of masculinity in the U.S. [are still] partly negotiated through an imaginary black interlocutor."[115] Any white male annexations of black masculinity, though, will always be haunted by anxieties that white heterosexual masculinity is an inauthentic, barren identity, forced to borrow if it wishes to fill the gaping void.

While one way of coping with the lack-in-being of white heterosexual masculinity (as, indeed, with all identities) is the fetishistic appropriation of otherness, another way is the vehement rejection of that otherness, expressed through virulent hate speech or even physical violence. However, as Kobena Mercer argues, "negrophilia" inhabits same fantasy space as "negrophobia," merely "invert[ing] and revers[ing] the binary axis of the repressed fears and anxieties that are projected onto the Other."[116] In the next chapter, I explore this dynamic by building on my discussion of Quentin Tarantino. In particular, I focus on how white male violence erupts in his gangster films when white heterosexual masculinity is threatened by otherness, with violence providing a means of reconsolidating the always precarious borders of identity.

Notes

1. Tony Snow, "Black Like Beckham," *Channel Four, Black and Asian History Map*, http://www.channel4.com/history/microsites/B/blackhistorymap/articles_02.html (accessed October 1, 2004).

2. David Roediger cites research exploring early usages of the term "wigger" in Detroit, where it functioned as a derogative term for whites that were "overly" influenced by black culture, a meaning it has accrued elsewhere in the U.S. The term has also been deployed as a classist slur from white suburban kids to white working-class Detroiters. Yet "wigger," Roediger notes, has also become a term of affection from blacks towards whites who seriously embrace black culture rather than being mere wannabes. "Guineas, Wiggers, and the Drama of Racialized Culture," *American Literary History* 7, no. 4 (1995): 659-60.

3. Adrian Piper, "Passing for White, Passing for Black," in *Critical White Studies: Looking Behind the Mirror*, ed. Richard Delgado and Jean Stefancic (Philadelphia: Temple, 1997), 427.

4. Gayle Wald, *Crossing the Line: Racial Passing in Twentieth-Century U.S. Literature and Culture* (Durham, NC: Duke University Press, 2000), 13-14.

5. Susan Gubar, *Racechanges: White Skin, Black Face in American Culture* (New York: Oxford University Press, 1997), 32.

6. Michael Omi and Howard Winant, *Racial Formation in the United States: From the 1960s to the 1990s*, 2nd ed. (New York: Routledge, 1994), 54.

7. Theresa Meléndez, "Race Dialogues for the New Millennium," in *Race in 21st Century America*, ed. Curtis Stokes, Theresa Meléndez, and Genice Rhodes-Reed (East Lansing: Michigan State University Press, 2001), xxvi.

8. David Roediger, *Towards the Abolition of Whiteness* (London: Verso, 1994), 181-87.

9. See Theodore W. Allen, *The Invention of the White Race*, vol. 1, *Racial Oppression and Social Control* (London: Verso, 1994); Noel Ignatiev, *How the Irish Became White* (New York: Routledge, 1996); David Roediger, *The Wages of Whiteness: Race and the Making of the American Working Class* (London: Verso, 1991); Ella Shohat and Robert Stam, *Unthinking Eurocentrism: Multiculturalism and the Media* (London: Routledge, 1994), 19.

10. While this change was welcomed for accepting that many individuals do not fit neatly into given racial categories, ironically, it also re-enforced the one-drop rule, since those who selected white in addition to a minority classification were registered as a minority. This effectively threatens to dismantle civil rights legislation to the point where "all differences count equally, while none do." Michael Hill, *After Whiteness: Unmaking an American Majority* (New York: New York University Press, 2004), 39. This change also suggests that race is a volitional identity, which precludes discussion of how institutions regulate racial identifications and the practice of racism.

11. Michael J. Bamshad and Steve E. Olson, "Does Race Exist?" *Scientific American.Com*, November 10, 2003, http://www.sciam.com/article.cfm?id=does-race-exist (accessed July 2, 2004); Richard Delgado and Jean Stefancic, introduction to *Critical White Studies: Looking Behind the Mirror*, ed. Richard Delgado and Jean Stefancic (Philadelphia: Temple, 1997), xvii.

12. Ruth Frankenberg, *White Women, Race Matters: The Social Construction of Whiteness* (Minneapolis: University of Minnesota Press, 1993), 11.

13. Henry A. Giroux, *Impure Acts: The Practical Politics of Cultural Studies* (New York: Routledge, 2000), 102.

14. For an example of New Abolitionism, see Noel Ignatiev and John Garvey, "Abolish the White Race by Any Means Necessary," in *Race Traitor*, ed. Noel Ignatiev and John Garvey (New York: Routledge, 1996), 9-14.

15. Paul A. Woods, *King Pulp: The Wild World of Quentin Tarantino* (London: Plexus, 1998), 201-2; Shohat and Stam, *Unthinking Eurocentrism*, 238.

16. Omi and Winant, *Racial Formation*, 55.

17. Robyn Wiegman, *American Anatomies: Theorizing Race and Gender* (Durham, NC: Duke University Press, 1995), 23.

18. Henry Louis Gates, Jr., "The Master's Pieces: On Canon-Formation and the African-American Tradition," in *Loose Canons: Notes on the Culture Wars*, ed. Henry Louis Gates, Jr. (Oxford: Oxford University Press, 1992), 37-38.

19. Frantz Fanon, *Black Skin, White Masks,* trans. Charles Lam Markmann (New York: Grove, 1967), 11. For a discussion of Fanon's use of Lacan's mirror stage in his formulation of a racist imaginary, see Vicky Lebeau, *Psychoanalysis and Cinema: The Play of Shadows* (London: Wallflower, 2001), 115-16; David Marriott, *Haunted Life: Visual Culture and Black Modernity* (New Brunswick, NJ: Rutgers University Press, 2007), 219-24.

20. Fanon, *Black Skin, White Masks,* 111-14; Vicky Lebeau, "Psychopolitics: Frantz Fanon's *Black Skin, White Masks,*" in *Psycho-Politics and Cultural Desires,* ed. Jan Campbell and Janet Harbord (London: Taylor and Francis, 1998), 115.

21. Judith Butler, "Endangered/Endangering: Schematic Racism and White Paranoia," in *Reading Rodney King, Reading Urban Uprising,* ed. Robert Gooding (New York: Routledge, 1993), 18, 15, 17.

22. Wiegman, *American Anatomies,* 11.

23. Kalpana Seshadri-Crooks, *Desiring Whiteness: A Lacanian Analysis of Race* (London: Routledge, 2000), 131.

24. Wald, *Crossing the Line,* 16.

25. Eric Lott, "White Like Me: Racial Cross-Dressing and the Construction of American Whiteness," in *Cultures of United States Imperialism,* ed. Amy Kaplan and Donald E. Pease (Durham, NC: Duke University Press, 1993), 475.

26. Eric Lott, *Love and Theft: Blackface Minstrelsy and the American Working Class* (New York: Oxford University Press, 1993), 5.

27. Susan Gubar, for instance, draws a comparison between Ted Danson's infamous appearance in blackface at a Friars Club roast (1993) and Eddie Murphy's *Saturday Night Live* skit "White Like Me," in which Murphy reverses the codes of minstrelsy and dons whiteface. Danson's appearance attracted widespread condemnation, while Murphy's performance "signals a kind of antic clownishness." Gubar attributes this asymmetry to Fanon's observation that "not only must the black man be black, he must be black in relation to the white man." The reverse, Fanon states, can never be true, since "[t]he black man has no ontological resistance in the eyes of the white man." Gubar, *Racechanges,* 38; Fanon, *Black Skin, White Masks,* 110.

28. See, for example, Louis Chude-Sokei, *The Last "Darky": Bert Williams, Black-on-Black Minstrelsy, and the African Diaspora* (Durham, NC: Duke University Press, 2006); Michael Rogin, "Blackface, White Noise: The Jewish Jazz Singer Finds His Voice," *Critical Inquiry* 18, no. 3 (1992): 417-53; Roediger, *The Wages of Whiteness,* 127; George Lipsitz, *The Possessive Investment in Whiteness: How White People Profit from Identity Politics* (Philadelphia: Temple University Press, 1998), 99; Lott, *Love and Theft,* 156.

29. Lott, *Love and Theft,* 3, 6, 4, 6, 8.

30. Lott, *Love and Theft,* 156.

31. Lott, *Love and Theft,* 143, 149; Roediger, *The Wages of Whiteness,* 107.

32. Slavoj Žižek, *Looking Awry: An Introduction to Jacques Lacan through Popular Culture* (Cambridge, MA: MIT Press, 1991), 165.

33. Lott, *Love and Theft,* 148.

34. Lott, *Love and Theft,* 149. Lott's study has been criticized for this reason. Michael Rogin, for instance, argues that "postmodern" accounts like Lott's are so eager "to find points of identification across racial lines that, protests notwithstanding, they dwell insufficiently both on the exclusion of actual African Americans from their own representations and on the grotesque, demeaning, animalistic blackface mask." *Blackface, White*

Noise: Jewish Immigrants in the Hollywood Melting Pot (Berkley: University of California Press, 1996), 37.

35. Lott, *Love and Theft*, 52.

36. Lott, *Love and Theft*, 53.

37. Leslie Fielder, *Waiting for the End* (New York: Stein and Day, 1972), 134; Lott, *Love and Theft*, 53.

38. Lott, *Love and Theft*, 53.

39. Jack Kerouac, *On the Road* (London: Penguin, 1972), 169-70.

40. Lott, *Love and Theft*, 54.

41. Norman Mailer, "The White Negro," in *Advertisements for Myself* (London: Flamingo, 1994), 293.

42. Mailer, "The White Negro," 294.

43. Roediger, "Guineas, Wiggers, and the Drama of Racialized Culture," 662.

44. James Baldwin, *Nobody Knows My Name: More Notes of a Native Son* (London: Corgi, 1973), 180-81, 172.

45. Eldridge Cleaver, *Soul on Ice* (New York: Dell, 1968), 159, 102, 98.

46. Andrew Ross, *No Respect: Intellectuals and Popular Culture* (New York: Routledge, 1989), 98.

47. Ralph Ellison, "Little Man and Chehaw Station," in *Going to the Territories* (New York: Random, 1986), 21, quoted in Roediger, "Guineas, Wiggers, and the Drama of Racialized Culture," 658.

48. "The everyday, plagiaristic commerce between white and black musics . . . has been generic and not exceptional. But it is important to remember that this *overexchanged* and *overbartered* record of miscegenated cultural production everywhere bespeaks a racist history of exploitation exclusively weighted to dominant white interests. Given such a history, it is no wonder that terms like 'imitation' are often read as 'theft' and 'appropriation' and that white definitions of 'authenticity' are mismatched with black essentialisms like 'roots' and 'soul.'" Ross, *No Respect*, 68.

49. Fred Pfeil, *White Guys: Studies in Postmodern Domination and Difference* (London: Verso, 1995), 79, 75.

50. Ross, *No Respect*, 97.

51. Tricia Rose, *Black Noise: Rap Music and Black Culture in Contemporary America* (Hanover: Wesleyan University Press, 1994), 2. Rose notes that the percentage of white consumers of rap might be overrepresented because of the absence of chain music stores and prevalence of bootleg products in poor communities, as well as the "higher pass-along rate" of products among poor consumers of color (7).

52. Tom Jennings, "Br(other) Rabbit's Tale," *Variant*, Spring 2003, www.variant.randomstate.org/17texts/17tom_jennings.html (accessed August 15, 2004).

53. Tania Modleski, *Feminism Without Women: Culture and Criticism in a "Postfeminist" Age* (New York: Routledge, 1991), 119; Homi Bhabha, "Of Mimicry and Man: The Ambivalence of Colonial Discourse," *October* 28 (1984): 128.

54. Roediger, "Guineas, Wiggers, and the Drama of Racialized Culture," 663.

55. bell hooks, *Outlaw Culture: Resisting Representations* (New York: Routledge 1994), 116.

56. Robin D. G. Kelley, "Straight from the Underground," *The Nation*, June 8 1992, 793-96, quoted in Roediger, "Guineas, Wiggers, and the Drama of Racialized Culture," 661.

57. Roediger, *Towards the Abolition of Whiteness*, 16.

58. Paul A. Woods, *King Pulp: The Wild World of Quentin Tarantino* (London: Plexus, 1998), 201-2.

59. For Manthia Diawara, "the new black realism" includes such films as *Boyz N the Hood* (John Singleton 1991), *New Jack City* (Mario Van Peebles 1991), and *Menace II Society* (Allen and Albert Hughes 1993). Diawara suggests that the characters in these films "look *real* because they dress in the style of hip hop, talk the lingo of hip hop, practice its world view toward the police and women, and are played by rap stars such as Ice Cube." "Black American Cinema: The New Realism," in *Black American Cinema*, ed. Manthia Diawara (New York: AFI/Routledge, 1993), 22.

60. Woods, *King Pulp*, 205.

61. Lisa Kennedy, "Natural Born Filmmaker," *Village Voice*, October 25, 1994, 32.

62. Sharon Willis, *High Contrast: Race and Gender in Contemporary Hollywood Film* (Durham, NC: Duke University Press, 1997), 210.

63. Jeff Dawson, *Quentin Tarantino: The Cinema of Cool* (New York: Applause, 1995), 114.

64. Roediger, "Guineas, Wiggers, and the Drama of Racialized Culture," 662.

65. Willis, *High Contrast*, 210.

66. Eve Kosofsky Sedgwick, *Between Men: English Literature and Male Homosocial Desire* (New York: Columbia University Press, 1985).

67. See Randall Kennedy, *Nigger: The Strange Career of a Troublesome Word* (New York: Vintage, 2002).

68. Dawson, *Quentin Tarantino*, 116.

69. Judith Butler, *Excitable Speech: A Politics of the Performative* (New York: Routledge, 1997), 36, 38, 99.

70. Sara Salih, *Judith Butler*, Routledge Critical Thinkers (New York: Routledge, 2002), 114-16.

71. Willis, *High Contrast*, 213.

72. Todd Boyd, "Tarantino's Mantra?" *Chicago Tribune*, November 6, 1994, 2.

73. Willis, *High Contrast*, 205, 207.

74. Woods, *King Pulp*, 200.

75. Susan Fraiman, *Cool Men and the Second Sex* (New York: Columbia University Press, 2003), 27.

76. The title is taken from a speech by Malcolm X: "You've been hoodwinked. You've been had. You've been took. You've been led astray. You've been bamboozled." The speech is directly invoked through a clip of Lee's film *Malcolm X* (1992) when Denzel Washington utters these very words.

77. Esther Godfrey, "'To Be Real': Drag, Minstrelsy and Identity in the New Millennium," *Genders* 41 (2005), http://www.genders.org/g41/g41_godfrey.html (accessed June 25, 2006).

78. Godfrey, "'To Be Real."

79. Pat Kane, "Ali G: Da New White and Black Minstrel," *Sunday Herald*, March 10, 2002, www.sundayherald.com/22797 (accessed July 11, 2004).

80. Dan Friedman, "Genuine Authentic Gangsta Flava," *Zeek*, April 2003, http://www.zeek.net/film_0304.shtml (accessed July 11, 2004).

81. Sander L. Gilman, *The Jew's Body* (New York: Routledge, 1991), 238; Rogin, "Blackface, White Noise," 95.

82. Paul Gilroy, "Ali G and the Oscars," *OpenDemocracy.net*, April 4, 2002, http://www.opendemocracy.net/arts-Film/article_459.jsp (accessed July 11, 2004).

83. Paul Gilroy, *Joined-Up Politics and Post-Colonial Melancholia* (London: Institute of Contemporary Arts, 1999), 15; Gilroy, "Ali G and the Oscars."

84. The *Carry On* film cycle began with *Carry on, Sergeant* (1958). Famed for their double-entendre toilet humor, each film more risqué than the last, the films are now cult viewing.

85. Gilroy, "Ali G and the Oscars."

86. *The Cultural Learnings of America to Make Benefit Glorious Nation of Kazakhstan* (Larry Charles 2006), on the other hand, which stars Cohen as a spoof Kazakh journalist Borat Sagdiev, became a surprise box-office hit. The film, which revels in political incorrectness, has generated equal levels of controversy as *Ali G Indahouse* because of the sexism, homophobia, and racism of Borat (wrapped in the multi-layered, self-legitimizing veneer of parody and excess), with the Kazakhstan government censoring the film, angered at Cohen's negative and racist depiction of the country and its inhabitants. Middle Americans, who, in conversations with Borat, unwittingly exposed their prejudices and ignorance, have also threatened to sue. Nevertheless, the fact that the film, unlike *Ali G Indahouse*, did receive a general U.S. release and went on to become a box office hit reveals that a white male impersonating a (possibly Muslim) Kazakh is deemed less politically incendiary and unpalatable than Ali G's impersonation of black masculinity.

87. Shohat and Stam, *Unthinking Eurocentrism*, 229-30.

88. Matthew Tinkcom and Amy Villarejo, introduction to *Keyframes: Popular Cinema and Cultural Studies*, ed. Matthew Tinkcom and Amy Villarejo (London: Routledge, 2001), 24.

89. Friedman, "Genuine Authentic Gangsta Flava."

90. Gilroy, "Ali G and the Oscars."

91. Kobena Mercer, *Welcome to the Jungle: New Positions in Black Cultural Studies* (London: Routledge, 1994), 28.

92. Paul Gilroy, *There Ain't No Black in the Union Jack: The Cultural Politics of Race and Nation*, rev. ed. (London: Routledge, 2002), xiv.

93. Linda Hutcheon, *The Politics of Postmodernism* (London: Routledge, 1990), 101.

94. Michael H. Epp, "Raising Minstrelsy: Humor, Satire and the Stereotype in *The Birth of a Nation* and *Bamboozled*," *Canadian Review of American Studies* 33, no. 1 (2003): 20.

95. Gilroy, "Ali G and the Oscars."

96. Kane, "Ali G: Da New White and Black Minstrel."

97. Cynthia Fuchs, "With or Without You," *Pop.Politics.Com*, June 17, 2002, http://www.poppolitics.com/articles/2002-06-17-eminem.shtml (accessed August 20, 2004).

98. Eminem, "Without Me," *The Eminem Show*, Interscope Records, 2002.

99. Eminem, "Role Model," *The Slim Shady LP*, Interscope Records, 1999; Eminem, "White America," *The Eminem Show*, Interscope Records, 2002.

100. Rose, *Black Noise*, 130.

101. Eminem, "97 Bonnie and Clyde," *The Slim Shady LP*, Interscope Records, 1999; Eminem, "Kim," *The Marshall Mathers LP*, Interscope Records, 2000.

102. Jennings, "Br(other) Rabbit's Tale."

103. Annalee Newitz, "White Savagery and Humiliation, or a New Racial Consciousness in the Media," in *White Trash: Race and Class in America*, ed. Matthew Wray and Annalee Newitz (New York: Routledge, 1997), 146.

104. Eminem, "Low, Down, Dirty," *The Slim Shady LP*, Interscope Records, 1999.

105. Paul Gormley, *The New-Brutality Film: Race and Affect in Contemporary Hollywood Cinema* (Bristol: Intellect Books, 2005), 58-59. To support his arguments, Gormley quotes director Joel Schumacher's comments in an interview that "there have been several movies in the U.S. about anger in the streets but they had all been by African-Americans. Well they're not the only angry people in the United States" (58).

106. David Wellman, "Minstrel Shows, Affirmative Action Talk, and Angry White Men: Marking Racial Otherness in the 1990s," in *Displacing Whiteness: Essays in Social and Cultural Criticism*, ed. Ruth Frankenberg (Durham, NC: Duke University Press, 1997), 324.

107. Eminem, "Lose Yourself," *8 Mile*, Interscope Records, 2002.

108. Richard Kim, "Eminem—Bad Rap?" *The Nation*, March 5, 2001, http://www.thenation.com/doc.mhtml?i=20010305&s=kim (accessed August 20, 2004).

109. Roediger, *Towards the Abolition of Whiteness*, 15-16.

110. Anthony Bozza, *Whatever You Say I Am: The Life and Times of Eminem* (London: Corgi, 2003), 254.

111. Thomas DiPiero, "White Men Aren't," *Camera Obscura: A Journal of Feminism and Film Theory* 30 (1992): 126.

112. Dan Friedman, "'Ringleader of a Circus of Worthless Pawns': Eminem and Class Rage," *Zeek*, December 2002, http://www.zeek.net/film _9212.htm (accessed 15 August, 2004).

113. Gormley, *The New-Brutality Film*, 191.

114. DiPiero, "White Men Aren't," 133.

115. Lott, *Love and Theft*, 53.

116. Kobena Mercer, "Looking for Trouble," *Transition* 51 (1991): 187.

Part Three

Marking White Male Violence:
The Gangster and the Serial Killer

Chapter Seven
White Male Violence in Quentin Tarantino's Gangster Films

Quentin Tarantino and His Cinema of Postmodern Cool

By 1994, the adjective "tarantino-esque" had been firmly established in film critical vocabulary, despite the fact that at that point, Tarantino had only written and directed *Reservoir Dogs* (1992), a surprise critical and commercial success which provoked a media storm, and *Pulp Fiction* (1994), which cost $8 million to make but took $213 million at the box office—though Tarantino had also written the original screenplays for *True Romance* (Tony Scott 1993) and *Natural Born Killers* (Oliver Stone 1994). *Reservoir Dogs* and *Pulp Fiction*, in particular, spawned numerous imitations, such as the laddish "Cool Britannia" films of Guy Ritchie, *Lock, Stock and Two-Smoking Barrels* (1998) and *Snatch* (2000), which translated Tarantino's gangster chic onto a British terrain, and films like *Things to Do in Denver When You're Dead* (1995), *Two Days in the Valley* (1996), and *Gross Pointe Blank* (1997), which employed Tarantino's iconography and penchant for small-time crooks and hit men, but failed to pull off his distinctive hip dialogue and unnerving mix of violence and humor.

Tarantino is generally considered the postmodernist filmmaker *par excellence* due to his penchant for intertextual allusions, ranging from Blaxploitation films to Hong Kong Kung Fu cinema. Yet it is French New Wave cinema that his two gangster films, *Reservoir Dogs* and *Pulp Fiction*, cite stylistically, in particular Francois Truffaut's *Tirez sur le Pianiste* (1960) and Jean-Pierre Melville's *Le Samouraï* (1967), which, in turn, paid homage to American gangster movies of the '30s and '40s. Like French New Wave directors, Tarantino employs non-linear narratives, which take unexpected twist and turns, and often seem designed to seduce the spectator with their cleverness. As with French New Wave, Tarantino's camera is often static and meditative, and his preference for long takes refuses the MTV-style rapid cutting that dominates contemporary

Hollywood production, though at other times, his camera roves disembodied in a Hitchcockian manner, unhinged from any character's point of view, a technique that precludes easy identification. Tarantino also follows the avant-garde tradition with his use of oblique, disorientating camera angles, his novelistic style of storytelling complete with chapter title cards, and his metacinematic foregrounding of his films' fictional status.

In terms of content, however, Tarantino's films are quintessentially American, populated by two-dimensional characters plucked straight from the pages of 1950s crime pulp fiction, and flung into a contemporary context, along with constant allusions to the popular culture of the 1970s he grew up in. Tarantino also takes delight in resurrecting the flagging careers of '70s American stars, capitalizing on their star personas, often for comic effect: John Travolta's famous boogie in *Pulp Fiction* cannot fail to provoke memories of his dance-floor reign in *Saturday Night Fever* (1977), while Tarantino's use of the iconic Pam Grier imports Blaxploitation cool into *Jackie Brown* (1997). His characters also talk of all things American, from TV programs to McDonald's.

Despite this wealth of allusions, Tarantino was heralded for producing something new: the ultimate '90s aesthetic—a ludic, postmodern fascination with surface, intertextuality, and parody, with no ostensible message or political point, much like the pulp fiction his stories were based on, which, as Tarantino himself has stated, were designed to be read compulsively and then given or thrown away.[1] He was immediately loved or hated for the same reasons. His fans loved his cinema of guilt-free spectacle, hip dialogue, and generic hybridity, along with the viewing pleasure afforded simply by getting the reference; with references ranging from popular culture to avant-garde cinema, his films could be consumed as cult culture or as an academic treatise on postmodernism. His detractors regarded him as a product of the vacuous, amoral, cynical postmodern age, and accused his films of exhibiting a loss of affect, history, and social reference. Others claimed that his films hide real political issues about gender, race, and sexuality that the "seductive veneer of spectacle" masks.[2] Paul Gormley, for instance, argues that Tarantino's films "are extraordinarily political in the way they evoke and crystallize the sensations and affects around questions of 'race' that were embedded in 'the white cultural imagination' in the US of the 1990s."[3] As far as representations of white heterosexual masculinity are concerned, his films are particularly interesting due to the way they self-consciously deconstruct the gangster, foreground the performative structures of masculinity, and highlight the importance of black masculinity to white heterosexual male identifications. What is also distinctive about Tarantino's gangster films is their thematic concern with *white male* violence, and their recognition of the increased difficulty of normative white masculinity occupying a universal, unmarked position in contemporary U.S. society. This is most apparent in the racist, misogynistic, and homophobic dialogue of his white male gangsters, often legitimized through their utterance in a highly stylized mode. Tellingly, white male hate speech erupts in the form of white male paranoia when the borders of white heterosexual masculinity are posited as unstable or violated.

"Are you going to bark all day, little doggie, . . . or are you going to bite?" Deconstructing the Gangster Ideal

In the light of Tarantino's love of both French New Wave and American popular culture, it is little wonder that it was the gangster genre that Tarantino first chose to reinvent. The gangster, along with the cowboy, is the most iconic image of violent white masculinity in American film history. Hollywood gangsters from the 1930s until the 1970s were almost exclusively white ethnic characters, normally Italian- or Irish-American, in pursuit of "individual enterprise and immigrant acculturation."[4] Later, the Italian-American gangster was mythologized in the nostalgic cinema of Francis Ford Coppola, Martin Scorsese, Brian de Palma, and Sergio Leone. Coppola's *The Godfather* (1972) opens with the lines "I believe in America," and in so doing, "rekindled the notion of the gangster as the definitive American, one whose life was based on a violence at once rational and irrational, public and private, and native to the national character."[5] In other words, violence is posited as a means by which working-class, urban, white, but ethnically-inflected males can have their stab at the American dream.

The contemporary gangster film, however, is often populated by all number of ethnicities. In particular, the '90s witnessed the commercial successes of black gangsta cinema with films such as *New Jack City* (1991), *Boyz N the Hood* (1991), and *Menace II Society* (1993), which cited '70s Blaxploitation and black gangster films, but placed African-American gangs in a '90s social and cultural postindustrial urban landscape.[6] They also explored how "race mediates issues of crime, violence, and justice in the black ghetto and positions its underclass inhabitants outside normative notions of what constitutes citizenship."[7] As I noted in the previous chapter, Tarantino has been accused of appropriating these films by some theorists who draw attention to his run-down, claustrophobic, ghetto-like setting in *Reservoir Dogs*, his use of black-authored soundtracks, his rap-influenced dialogue, and his representation of black masculinity as irredeemably violent, but always the epitome of cool. Tarantino self-consciously racializes the power struggle between aggressive rival masculinities, though his gangsters in *Reservoir Dogs*, *Pulp Fiction*, and *Jackie Brown* are either African-American or white, offering up a rather Manichean vision of American race relations. Unlike black gangsta films, however, violence is given no obvious rationale or social context; indeed, as Fran Mason asserts, Tarantino seems more concerned with "articulating the semiotic codes of the gangster genre to map identity and lifestyle as a form of cultural expression as opposed to using them to explore the psychology of the gangster and the social reality he inhabits."[8] Moreover, unlike *The Godfather* trilogy, Tarantino's gangsters are coded as members of an urban underclass—he is more interested in hit men or small-time crooks than mafia bosses. And in a far cry from Coppola's tragic mode, Tarantino follows the French New Wave impulse to deconstruct the gangster ideal, starting a trend of parodying the white gangster that would be prevalent throughout the '90s, most obviously in the films of Guy Ritchie, but also in comedies such as *Analyze This* (1999), a film which deploys Robert de Niro's star persona to comic effect when he plays a Mafioso who hires therapist Billy Crystal to help him to overcome panic attacks and a sudden aversion to killing. Similarly, the hit TV series *The Sopranos* has the mafia-head Tony Soprano (James Gandolfini) go into therapy to deal with his mother complex. *The Sopranos* is also indebted to Tarantino's postmodern self-consciousness, with characters often comparing themselves to the screen gangsters that they fail to live up to, or complaining about the stereotyping of Italian-Americans. Tarantino's gangsters are not deconstructed through existential angst, however (they have little interiority), but through generic subversion, with Tarantino finding humor in taking genre characters and putting them in non-generic situations.

In part, his ironic destabilization of the gangster is inscribed through costume. As Stella Bruzzi has argued in *Cinema: Clothing and Identity in the Movies* (1997), the gangster has always been a contradictory figure of masculinity: "The trait that distinguishes the screen gangster from the majority of other masculine archetypes is his overt narcissism, manifested by a preoccupation with the appearance of others and a self-conscious regard for his own." Screen gangsters "have both cultivated an aggressively masculine image and are immensely vain," but their "sartorial flamboyance, far from intimating femininity or effeminacy, is the most important sign of their masculine social and material success." For Bruzzi, the screen gangster's obsessive concern with his appearance (evident in the number of scenes of gangsters having suits fitted) foregrounds his need to define and redefine himself against a gangster ideal that he is invariably unable to approximate.[9]

In both *Reservoir Dogs* and *Pulp Fiction*, this failure is deployed for comic effect. Gangsters begin both films decked out in chic black suits that allude to 1950s *film noir*, French New Wave gangster movies, rat pack movies such as *Ocean's Eleven* (1960), as well as John Woo's Hong Kong "bullet fests."[10] Indeed, Tarantino himself recognizes that clothes maketh the gangster, stating in an interview, "You can't put a guy in a black suit without him looking a little cooler than he already looks." This coolness soon collapses, though, as Tarantino delights in smearing these black and white suits with dirt, sweat, and blood, thus exposing the fragility of the body that the sharp, conventionalized, masculine suits mask.[11] In particular, in *Pulp Fiction*'s "The Bonnie Situation" segment, Jules (Samuel L. Jackson) and Vincent's (John Travolta's) macho assurance is established only to be pathetically eroded when Mr. Wolf (Harvey Keitel) orders the humiliated pair to strip out of their blood-stained suits before hosing them down and dressing them in the geek T-shirts and Bermuda shorts belonging to Jimmy (played by Tarantino himself), who relishes in telling them "you look like dorks." The film's closing image of Jules and Vincent simultaneously tucking their guns into the waistband of their Bermuda shorts before strutting away is wonderfully incongruous; as Tarantino (always the biggest fan of his own films) states, "[w]hat's interesting is how they get reconstructed . . . their suits get more and more fucked up until they're stripped off and the two are dressed in the exact antithesis." Bruzzi thus concludes, "[t]he immaculate attire spied only briefly at the beginning of Tarantino films fulfils a similar function to Lacan's elusive phallus, persuading the characters to go in search of an ideal that they think they once embodied, but which was never theirs for the taking."[12]

Tarantino's gangsters do not just mess up their suits; they spectacularly mess up in all number of ways. *Reservoir Dogs* is structured around a failed heist, and those not killed by cops are killed by each other in the closing Mexican standoff, when three gangsters point guns at each other in a stylized triangular formation, and, refusing to stand down and risk compromising their masculinity, shoot simultaneously—a homage to Kubrick's *The Killing* (1956). In *Pulp Fiction*, most humor is derived from Vincent's un-gangster-like behavior: he boogies unforgettably on the dance floor, and then spends the rest of the evening coping (badly) with Mia's (Uma Thurman's) heroin overdose, he accidentally kills Marvin (Phil LaMarr), an informant, and is then killed himself when he takes an ill-timed visit to the bathroom, leaving his machine gun on the side ready for Butch (Bruce Willis) to use.

The distance between the gangster ideal and Tarantino's non-generic gangsters is also inscribed in the banal conversation that his characters engage in during the lengthy interstices that punctuate action—the kind of idle, narrative-delaying banter that most films steer well clear of, but that Tarantino makes the epicenter of his films. At odds with the laconic model of virile masculinity epitomized by Jeff (Alain Delon) in *Le Samouraï*, and more akin to the talkative gangsters of Trauffaut's parodic *Tirez sur le Pianiste*, Tarantino's gangsters are positively garrulous, with humor derived from the incongruous topics that clutter their dialogues, from the ethics of tipping waitresses (*Reservoir Dogs*) to Jules and Vincent's famous dialogue (immortalized in *Pulp Fiction*'s top-selling soundtrack) about the differences between European and American McDonald's. Another particularly memorable example is the opening scene of *Reservoir Dogs*, which screens the gangsters in mid-conversation (French New Wave style), but rather than discussing the upcoming heist, they are deconstructing the lyrics of Madonna's "Like a Virgin," debating whether the song is about a girl whose "pussy should be Bubble Yum by now" experiencing "a big dick" for the first time, or whether it is about a vulnerable girl who eventually meets the sensitive guy of her dreams. Obviously, political correctness is not Tarantino's intention, and as spectators we are directed toward wholesale delight in Tarantino's verbal wizardry, misogyny and all. Whether offended or amused, the spectator is offered no stable viewing position, since the camera slowly circles behind the men seated around a table, their backs often obscuring the face of the current speaker, a distancing device that makes identification difficult. In a similar mode, in *Pulp Fiction*, on their way to perform a hit, Jules and Vincent argue over whether, in terms of marital infidelity, a foot massage is on a par with cunnilingus, which Jules terms "stickin' your tongue in her holiest of holies." While the preceding dialogue is screened in a backward tracking shot, Jules, Vincent, and the camera stop still for this discussion in a static, symmetrical medium shot, rendering the matter incongruously important, as well as foregrounding the scene's artificiality and precluding easy identification with these two-dimensional characters.

In a generous reading, the verbal incontinence of Tarantino's gangsters can be interpreted as his recognition that phallic posturing screens the lack that traverses masculine subjectivity. In *Pulp Fiction* the unflappable Mr. Wolf, who embodies the gangster cool that Vincent's affectations fall pathetically short of, orders Vincent to keep his "spurs from jingling and dangling." Similarly, in *Reservoir Dogs*, the menacing Mr. Blonde (Michael Madsen) responds to Mr. White's (Harvey Keitel's) blustering tirade by asking, "are you going to bark all day, little doggie, . . . or are you going to bite?"—a quote which acts as title card after the film's opening credit sequence, and which alludes to the film's deliberately esoteric title (a possible homage to Peckinpah's ultraviolent *Straw Dogs* [1971]). Tarantino himself has characterized *Reservoir Dogs* as "a total talk fest, a bunch of guys yakking at each other."[13] Indeed, the ingenuity of the film is the fact that it takes place after the failed heist that is never actually screened, though events leading up to and immediately proceeding it are shown in a complex pattern of flashbacks that accompany each gangster's narrative of events; in other words, the heist only exists as a series of rhetorical performances, which often end up being testosterone-charged, hysterical rants.

The film's narrative is structured around whether undercover cop Mr. Orange's (Tim Roth's) performance of gangster masculinity will be sufficiently convincing. A series of flashbacks screen Mr. Orange's rehearsals of an imaginary narrative that his black police chief, Holdaway (Randy Brooks), has deemed necessary for a persuasive performance. In other words, a black male, placed in a position of authority, is given the job of assessing whether Mr. Orange's rendition of gangster masculinity is sufficiently authentic. As Sharon Willis notes, this is exemplary of "the [racial] address of the masculine posturings that emerge as the central subject of Tarantino's films."[14] Mr. Orange's final rendition in front of Joe Cabot (Lawrence Tierney), Nice-Guy Eddie (Chris Penn), and Mr. White then unfolds on screen, made "real" by his convincing theatrical skills. His anecdote tells the story of him walking into the men's room, carrying large quantities of marijuana, encountering a group of cops, one of whom is telling his own macho story about a recent arrest. As Mr. Orange stands still in the imaginary bathroom, encircled by a roving, objective camera, he then begins to narrate the self-same story he is telling, this time to the audience of cops, a Brechtian distancing device that reminds us that his story is pure fabrication.

Theatricality is not limited to this particular verbal performance, though, but characterizes the film's *mise-en-scène* and mode of enunciation. The narrative present unfolds in one setting, the abandoned warehouse in which the gang meet after the heist. Most warehouse scenes use long shots with a fairly static camera, while rapid cutting and shot-reverse shots are eschewed for long takes, and the sound is almost exclusively diegetic, rendering the viewing experience akin to watching a play unfold on stage. Performativity is also highlighted in *Pulp Fiction* when Mr. Wolf terms those involved in "The Bonnie Situation" "the principals," whom he then proceeds to direct, or when after the "foot massage" dialogue, Jules tells Vincent to "get into character" just before they appropriate their hit-men personas, which Jules acts out with particular thespian aplomb, ominously spouting a passage from the book of Ezekiel that he considered "a cold-blooded thing to say to a motherfucker before you popped a cap in his ass."

The extent to which Tarantino's deconstruction of the gangster is subversive of phallic masculinity is much contended. For Bruzzi, "the image of masculinity is destroyed in the most spectacular way."[15] On the other hand, Jude Davies and Carol R. Smith assert that while Tarantino's macho mode is only achieved "by virtue of ironies and self-reflexivity at the level of form," this works to "[renaturalize] white masculinity rather than drawing attention to its performance."[16] But perhaps rather than an either/or, what Tarantino's films achieve is the postmodern both/and. Parody, as we saw in chapters 2 and 3, is a double-coded discourse, a doubleness that must be noticed for the text to be read specifically as parody. Parody functions precisely by "inscribing both similarity to and difference from its target texts and [constructing] an incongruity that evokes both ironic and pluralistic meanings."[17] For Linda Hutcheon, this double address means that parody both legitimizes and subverts what it parodies, making it an ideal vehicle for the political contradictions of postmodernism at large.[18] This is precisely the reason that Tarantino's films elicit such conflicting responses, often in the same spectator. Certainly, Tarantino's fragmentation of the gangster ideal has none of the poignancy of Melville's *Le Samouraï*, for instance, which gradually strips Jeff of his cool suit to expose a fragile wounded body, not for comic effect, but in order to screen Jeff as an existential hero of his times, whose alienation and inability to live up to the phallic ideal are given tragic dimensions. However, Tarantino's films do underscore the imitative structures and fragility of masculine subjectivity. Tarantino's self-referential cinema also draws attention to past cinematic representations of gangster masculinity, since it is only by recognizing how his gangsters depart from this model that parody is generated, thereby "signal[ing] how present representations come from past ones and what ideological consequences derive from both continuity and difference."[19] Parody thus facilitates both the deconstruction of macho masculinity and the simultaneous reassertion of the phallic model (and the concomitant sexism, racism, and homophobia, a point I will return to), even if it is a model to which Tarantino's incompetent gangsters can only hope to aspire.

White Heterosexual Masculinity in Tarantino's Cinema of Hyperreal Violence

In accordance with generic conventions, Tarantino's gangster films present men, however raced, to be capable of sudden, unpredictable acts of violence. However, Tarantino's ultraviolent aesthetic self-consciously distinguishes itself from the ritualized violence of Hollywood action formats or the glamorized violence of the traditional gangster movie. Indeed, his films have been heralded as examples *par excellence* of "new brutalism," a media catchphrase that designated a body of Hollywood and independent films whose graphic violence unleashed controversy on release, including *Reservoir Dogs* (1992) and the Tarantino-authored *Natural Born Killers*, but also films such as *Man Bites Dog* (Rémy Belvaux 1991) and *Bad Lieutenant* (Abel Ferrara 1992). As Julia Hallam and Margaret Marchment observe, these films all shared a preoccupation with violence perpetuated by individuals against individuals. In terms of style, their graphic representations of violence were considered more "realistic" than their Hollywood counterparts, often due to a *cinema verité* style and loose narrative structures which refused to offer satisfactory motivations, social or psychological, for the violent acts committed. They therefore attracted "audiences bored with Hollywood's predictable action movies, their larger-than-life hero figures and crude moral pieties."[20] Many of these films engage with the debates centered on identity that raged in the '90s, albeit an engagement which is often articulated through white male characters who are overtly racist, misogynistic, and homophobic, whose violence erupts in response to perceived threats to their hegemony. The question that has concerned theorists, then, is whether these films endorse racism, misogyny, homophobia, and classism, whether they cite and perform them, or whether, in fact, there is a difference.

While Tarantino's films have been accused of screening hyperreal, cartoonish violence, he himself defends his films by recourse to appeals to "real life," stating that they reflect the way that gangsters behave. He also claims that the duration of his screen violence—either uncomfortably protracted or else shockingly brief—"[stops] movie time and [plays] the violence out in real time. Letting nothing get in the way of it and letting it happen the way real violence does."[21] As Manohla Dargis notes of *Reservoir Dogs*, "[w]hat makes the violence hurt isn't some outrageous, literally deadening body count but the way Tarantino decelerates pain, squeezing it out drop by anguished drop."[22] Indeed, *Reservoir Dogs* seems to be structured around the time it takes a writhing Mr. Orange to bleed to death from a gun-shot wound to the stomach,[23] his contorted face becoming whiter and whiter as his shirt gets redder and redder from the volumes of blood that soak his once chic suit. This is not the virility-affirming masochism that I outlined in my discussion of Hollywood action films in chapter 2; quite the opposite, since Mr. Orange does not transcend physical pain or re-emerge triumphant.

In interviews, Tarantino refuses any causal link between real and reel violence. For instance, he has asserted that violence in movies "is a totally aesthetic subject," one devoid of morality or politics.[24] Not surprisingly, such comments have angered many theorists who rightly refute the notion that screen violence can unfold in a social vacuum and somehow free itself from associations that accrue around identity categories in social reality.[25] Their concern is not only that Tarantino fails to examine the external political, social, and economic conditions that foster violence in the first place, but also that he perpetuates existing stereotypes that, in turn, produce concrete, material effects (such as supporting harsh discriminatory crime policies or fuelling a racist imagination). While each negative image of underrepresented people acquires what Michael Rogin refers to as a "surplus symbolic value,"[26] whereby the violent behavior of a minority identity is able to indict an entire social group, white heterosexual male violence, on the other hand, can be seen to stem from individual pathology or even heroism in the cases of the iconic screen gangster, cowboy, or soldier. Class is also key to this debate: although the urban poor tend to be signified by people of color in the American popular imagination, poor whites, along with urban and rural poor of all colors, are also insistently criminalized in many mainstream films (a point I explore further in chapter 8), as well as docudrama/reality TV, such as the long-running show *Cops*.

The racial asymmetries of representations of violence are apparent in the fact that the overwhelmingly white male cast and white-on-white violence of *Reservoir Dogs* has meant that it has received substantially less critical commentary in terms of racialized violence than *Pulp Fiction, Jackie Brown, Kill Bill Vol. 1* (2003), or *Kill Bill Vol. 2* (2004). Nevertheless, it would be a simplification to argue that white heterosexual masculinity is unmarked in this film, since, as I will argue below, it is represented as raced, gendered, classed, and always constituted in relation to its others. Indeed, as Amy Taubin notes of the film's masochistic mode of violence, "[i]t's the privilege of white male culture to destroy itself, rather than to be destroyed by the other. Violence is the only privilege these underclass men have. It's what allows them to believe that they're the oppressor and not the oppressed (not female, not black, not homosexual)."[27]

The most controversial scene involves the inexplicably psychotic Mr. Blonde torturing a white cop. Mr. Blonde's whiteness (emphasized by his name) prevents his twisted lust for violence being attributed to any racialized pathology, unlike *Jackie Brown*'s equally malicious Ordell (Samuel L. Jackson), whose brutality could well fuel pernicious racist stereotypes. Paul Gormley, however, one of the few theorists to analyze *Reservoir Dogs'* torture scene in terms of race, suggests that Mr. Blonde is in fact a mimesis of African-American gangsta masculinity, and asserts that this scene "both plays on and disrupts the construction of blackness as the source of an affective violence by placing a white body and white genre as the centre and cause of violence." For Gormley, this miming of black masculinity functions as a "reminder of the violence that lies at the heart of white American national identity and the cultural imagination associated with this," particularly in traditional gangster films that new black realism mined and reworked.[28] However, Gormley fails to address the visual import of race that I explored in the previous chapter. It also overlooks the fact that Mr. Blonde's delight in torture could also be read as confirming classist stereotypes of white, male, working-class hyperbrutality, and risks reinscribing the notion that senseless, meaningless violence must somehow be black-authored.

Mr. Blonde's delight in torturing the cop is given no psychological motivation; indeed, the flashback entitled "Mr. Blonde" is rather a red herring that teases with the promise of explanation that it refuses to deliver. Informing the cop that he will torture him not so much to get information but simply because he enjoys it, Mr. Blonde switches on the radio and breaks into a spontaneous dance to the '70s hit "Stuck in the Middle With You"—a self-conscious performance designed to chill both the cop and the film's spectator precisely because of its ominous incongruity. With cold-blooded poise, Mr. Blonde then proceeds to mutilate the cop, though the camera slowly averts its eye, refusing the tie-in shot of the mutilation itself, panning to the top corner of the warehouse, focusing on a painted warning that reads "watch your head"—knowingness that implicates the spectator in his/her voyeurism, as well as encouraging identification with the victim function. We are thus left to guess what fate has befallen the screaming cop until we are shown Mr. Blonde toying with and talking into a bloody, severed ear. Mr. Blonde then jokes with mock concern, inserting homoerotic aggression into the scenario: "Was that as good for you as it was for me?" The inappropriate, up-beat, diegetic music plays throughout this ordeal until Mr. Blonde walks outside into an eerie silence, his steps tracked by an objective camera. As he fetches petrol from the boot of his car, and walks inside, the song again blares out, with Mr. Blonde shuffling a few dance steps before dousing the cop in petrol. Only then are we finally given the sight of the cop's disfigured face. Surprisingly little gore is shown in the scene, its affective power residing in its departure from cinematic conventions. Like Hitchcock, Tarantino recognizes the power of that which remains off-screen, as well as the masochistic dimensions of spectatorship. Tarantino has further suggested that the scene unsettles not because of the violence *per se*, but because it makes the viewer a co-conspirator and leaves him/her unsure of how to react.[29] As Sharon Willis writes of Tarantino's films,

> [t]weaking our internal social censorship mechanisms as they do by the mismatches that they effect between the funny and the horrifying, the abject, or the frightening, these films leave us to manage that affective excess, which we may do by turning shock into embarrassment, or by taking satisfaction in the alibi they provide, so we can feel that we are getting away with laughing when we should not.[30]

This "affective excess" has rather different connotations when the violence is no longer carried out exclusively among white men, however, and can therefore no longer appeal to gendered or raced neutrality. For instance, in *Jackie Brown* comic pleasure in seeing the incompetent Louis (Robert de Niro) being mercilessly taunted by Melanie (Bridget Fonda) for forgetting where he had parked the getaway car is unexpectedly ruptured when Louis shoots at her off-screen. The shock-factor of this scene often translates into embarrassed laughter that stems from viewing discomfort and Tarantino's break with the worn-out, formulaic conventions of mainstream Hollywood violence. What is perhaps most disturbing about this scene is its refusal to offer a tie-in shot of Melanie's body or any identification with the victim function (her death is lent none of the tragic dimensions of Mr. Orange's in *Reservoir Dogs*, for instance). This punitive murder at the hands of a man who offers our only point of identification cannot escape gender implications. On the one hand, it feeds into regressive male fantasies of silencing emasculating women. At the same time, it underscores the fragility of Louis's male ego, allowing the film to have its proverbial cake and eat it too: the shock factor and self-legitimizing critique. The scene would also have had very different ideological implications if Ordell, a black male, had killed Melanie. Yet while Louis's aggression escapes racial stereotyping, though is enmeshed in discourses of class, it is worth noting that the affectless, bland, laconic Louis is the apotheosis of the vacuous, depthless white male, who is deliberately played off against Samuel Jackson's dynamic and animated Ordell. Recalling that Melanie, with whom Louis had been having an affair, is Ordell's "blond-haired surfer girl," whose whiteness, Ordell believes, affords him status as a black male (that is, access to some of the privileges of whiteness), it becomes difficult to separate Louis's uncontrollable anger from insecurities about the erosion of the authority and privileges that are supposed to inhere in both his gender and race. Indeed, as Susan Fraiman notes of Tarantino's films, coolness, to which most white male characters aspire, "involves a distinctly masculine desire for mastery, in which domination of the feminine is tied up with white male anxiety about, among other things, black masculinity."[31]

White male violence against black men is more overtly racialized in *Pulp Fiction*. A key example is when Vincent accidentally shoots Marvin. This scene, played for its shock value, courts uncomfortable laughter, sanctioned by Jules and Vincent's lack of concern about Marvin, but panic over the car that has been splattered with blood and fragments of flesh, brains, and bone. While Marvin's racial identity might have been read as coincidental up until this point, when they drive to Jimmy's (Quentin Tarantino's) house to embark on the clean-up campaign, Jimmy foregrounds Marvin's blackness in controversy-courting dialogue, objecting to his house being used for "dead nigger storage." I have already discussed Tarantino's use of the word "nigger" in the previous chapter. Here, I am concerned with the accentuation of Marvin's blackness by a white character, and one played by Tarantino himself, no less. What is, of course, outrageous in this scene is that its transgression is dependent on the suggestion that the death of a black male is insignificant (Jules overtly states that Marvin won't be missed). Nonetheless, it might also cause an uncomfortable affective overload at the ease with which Marvin's death at the hands of a white man had provoked apprehensive laughter a few scenes earlier, inserting the possibility that Marvin's blackness is *not* in fact beside the point. Unlike the Hollywood action tradition, race in Tarantino's films is never swiftly displaced onto other differences and/or officially ignored (such as in the *Lethal Weapon* series); indeed, Tarantino's films screen an America in which masculinity, like femininity, is always raced— as we see when Mr. Wolf jots down Vincent and Jules's names, adding the descriptors white and black respectively in parenthesis. However, this recognition often comes at a heavy price, since race tends to be referenced in moments of physical and verbal aggression, most often in abusive hate speech, a point I will return to.

Similar strategies of foregrounding race are at work in the scene where Butch and the ultra cool mafia boss, Marsellus Wallace, whom he has attempted to swindle, are captured by the two white racist hillbilly rapists (a stereotype of "white trash" masculinity if ever there was one). This scene of white male violence is racially encoded from the outset, when the rednecks, one of whom is a cop, deliberately choose Marsellus as their first victim through a fixed rendition of "eeny meeny miney moe, catch a nigger by the toe." As Butch manages to struggle free, Marsellus's agonizing cries coming through the door of an adjacent room prompt Butch to rescue the man that he had previously attempted to run down with his car. Humor is then derived from Butch's slow but deliberate choice of weapon, and his final selection of the least appropriate, a samurai sword,[32] all of which is accompanied by an up-beat rockabilly soundtrack. This pleasure is then rudely interrupted when Butch opens the door, with suspenseful slowness, revealing the sight of Marsellus being raped. In the words of Sharon Willis, "[w]e get caught laughing at an anal rape—caught, figuratively, with our pants down—and at the very moment when Marsellus is literally caught with his pants down."[33] While Bruce Willis, who imports his tough wise guy persona from *Die Hard* films, gets to ride off into the sunset on one of the rednecks' motorbike (the ultimate horror of anal rape being enough to heal the rift between Butch and Marsellus), it is the black stud stereotype (whose castration had been hinted at on his first appearance by a shot of a Band-Aid stuck on the back of his shaved head) that is ritually humiliated by a white cop—the representative of white supremacist state power. For bell hooks, whose views sum up the feeling of a significant number of black critics, "in case viewers haven't figured out that Marsellus ain't got what it takes, the film turns him into a welfare case—another needy victim who must ultimately rely on the kindness of strangers (i.e., Butch, the neoprimitive white colonizer, another modern day Tarzan) to rescue him from the rape-in-progress that is his symbolic castration, his return to the jungle, to a lower rung on the food chain."[34] Tarantino does not steer clear of these racial implications, however. In revenge Marcellus shoots his rapist in the crotch to the tune of "I'll get a couple of hard pipe fitting niggers to go to work on Mr. Rapist here with a blowtorch and pliers." As Willis notes, "[i]f the film had any ambition to sanitize the anal rape of its racial overcodings," Marsellus's threat "certainly reinstates the racialized edge of this homoerotic attack."[35] Indeed, with quintessential postmodern self-consciousness, Tarantino's films knowingly deconstruct themselves and pre-empt critical readings, foregrounding potential interpretations that in a Hollywood text might require substantial mining.

Dana Polan is right to note that the scene does not endorse Marsellus's humiliation and "is not handled with the jokey and gleeful relish that other acts of violence receive in the film," and that rather than regard the scene as easy racism, it is perhaps more appropriate to view it through the lens of classism and homophobia.[36] Certainly, we are positioned to identify with Butch, the white heterosexual rescuing hero, who slices the stomach of the sexually aroused, lip-licking redneck watching the rape, a scene that smacks of gay-bashing. Indeed, the film's hillbillies confirm that white masculinity is always also marked by discourses of class and sexuality, not just gender and race. Arguments over whether the scene itself is an enactment or performance of racism and/or homophobia and/or classism revolve around whether Tarantino's formal strategies of distance and irony are sufficient to insulate the scene from such charges. Certainly, the laughter that accompanied the close-up of Marsellus's gagged face as he was being violently assaulted in the screening I attended (and subsequent screenings with students, the majority of whom are white males), while partly caused by sheer embarrassment, is difficult to divorce from the racial and sexual dynamics of a black male being ritually humiliated by a white male; in other words, there is more than a sneaking suspicion that Tarantino's cult appeal is in part due to his packaging up of racism and homophobia as "marketable concepts" for a "hip" audience.[37] Nonetheless, as Polan points out, Marsellus is soon reinstated as "a figure of cool control and resolve," illustrating Tarantino's unequivocal admiration for all things black.[38]

White Male Hate Speech in Tarantino's Gangster Films

Pulp Fiction's rape scene screens the homoerotophobic racial violence which runs throughout Tarantino's films, but which most often remains at the level of dialogue. In chapter 6, I discussed this in relation to Tarantino's tendency to screen what lies repressed in Hollywood films texts—that the white male emulation of black masculinity is often caught up in a circuit of homoerotic desire, which is often rerouted as racism and/or homophobia. In the case of Marsellus's rape, though, it is important that the rapists are also racists who would seemingly have most to lose from any "contamination" of whiteness. In chapter 1, I noted similar structures in *Falling Down* (1993), where Nick the neo-fascist imagines himself to be a black inmate raping D-FENS. *American History X* (1998) also screens white neo-fascists punishing Derek (Edward Norton) for race treason by raping him in the shower in order to make him into a "nigger." What these screenings of (real or imagined) bi-racial anal rape by white racists suggest is how intimately connected we are to those we hate, even if it is by virtue of their function of constituting what we are not; as Jonathan Dollimore puts it, "[t]o be against (opposed to) is also to be against (close-up, in proximity to) or, in other words, up against."[39]

In this section, I would like to explore how paranoia and verbal violence erupt in Tarantino's gangster films when the borders of white heterosexual male identity are rendered unstable because of its polluting proximity to its others. As we saw in chapter 1, paranoia "has more to do the more susceptible those boundaries [between self and other] are to transgression and erasure."[40] The positing of a white male body whose boundaries are permeable and susceptible to contamination is most evident in the homophobic hate speech, often with racist overcodings, which surfaces in Tarantino's straight white male characters' simultaneous fascination with and aversion to homosexuality, a point I explore below. To date, Tarantino's only substantial homosexual characters are the rapists of *Pulp Fiction*, both of whom are violently dispatched (gay men would seem to have none of the "cool" of black masculinity to import into his films). But homosexuality figures obsessively in dialogue. As with the racist or misogynistic charges, whether the films themselves are homophobic or performances of homophobia, is a hotly debated issue, though I would argue that Tarantino's "hip" dialogue offered up as sheer performance, the lack of space inscribed for critical intervention, as well as the fact that his only homosexual characters in the homosocial gangster world are rapists, certainly means that his films risk being consumed homophobically, whatever Tarantino's authorial intentions might be (Tarantino is uncharacteristically reticent on the subject).

As might be expected, homophobic hate speech works to strengthen homosocial desire, "at once the most compulsory and the most prohibited of social bonds."[41] In *Pulp Fiction*, the horror of anal penetration by a man is sufficient to secure bi-racial male bonding between two sworn enemies, Butch and Marsellus. Thus it would seem that the more homosocial the ties, the more homophobia is required to police them, demonstrating Eve Kosofsky Sedgwick's insight that homosociality and homosexuality are mutually imbricated, often "assum[ing] interlocking or mirroring shapes."[42] Sedgwick's comment can help illuminate how the homosocial world of Tarantino's gangster films is also replete with an obsession with (bi-racial) male-on-male anal sex. For example, in *Pulp Fiction*, Jules asks one of the white students who has attempted to swindle Marsellus out of drug money, "Does Marsellus look like a bitch? . . . Then why you tryin' to fuck him like a bitch?" The irony, of course, is that it is indeed Marsellus who ends up being "fucked like a bitch," while white male anxieties about homosexuality remain at the level of homoerotophobic fantasy.

Reservoir Dogs includes an equally telling example of a white-authored, biracial, homosexual fantasy. When Vic Vega/Mr. Blonde, newly released from prison, meets up with Nice-Guy-Eddie, the two men's verbal posturing in front of Nice-Guy-Eddie's father, Joe Cabot, soon transforms into a physical tussle, the aggression of which is knowingly coded with frenzied homoerotic desire:

> Eddie: Daddy, he tried to fuck me. . . . You've been fuckin' punks up the ass, I'd think you'd appreciate a nice prime rib when you see it. . . .
> Vic: If I was a butt cowboy, I wouldn't even throw you to my posse. I might break you in, but I'd make you my dog's bitch.
> Eddie: All that black semen been poke up your ass backed up so far in your brain it's comin' out your mouth. It's a sad sight, Daddy, a man walkin'

into prison white and comin' out talking like a fuckin' nigger.

In this dialogue, homoerotic desire is abnegated by being transformed into homophobic and racist abuse. But what again is articulated in this exchange is
anxiety over the fragile borders of white heterosexual masculinity. The abject
image of semen underscores that whiteness, like all categories, is leaky; indeed,
this exchange suggests that it can be contaminated by its mere proximity to
blackness. This inevitably recalls Frantz Fanon's famed account of a child expressing fear upon seeing a Negro before him, a fear with its roots in the notion
that "the virgin sanctity of whiteness will be endangered by that proximity."[43] In
discussing Fanon's insertion of race into Lacan's mirror stage, and Fanon's
speculation that white male aggression directed at the black male other stems
from the white subject's internal aggressivity, David Marriot states that "Fanon
suggests that the imago of the black other is an instinctual component of the
white psyche, linked inextricably to the psychic process in which aggressive
drives associated with phobic anxiety and fear become psychically effective in
and through a racial substitute object or delegate." Noting Fanon's deployment
of "metaphors of breaching, staining, and contamination," Marriott adds that for
Fanon, "the ego experiences racial difference as a violent rupture of bodily
ego."[44] The above dialogue from *Reservoir Dogs* expresses fears of "somatic
contagion" and the "dangerous violation of white bodily integrity" in homophobic as well as racist terms,[45] with being anally penetrated by a black male posited
as the equivalent of being blackened. However, this is strictly a one-way process; as with the "one-drop rule," whiteness can be blackened with alarming ease,
while blackness can never be fully whitened. Indeed, the precariousness of the
myth of white racial purity is precisely why Mr. Blonde's alleged crime of
"speaking black" is so threatening. Bearing in mind that, in Lacanian terms, as
Fanon was so aware, aggressivity directed towards the other is always rooted in
aggressivity against the self,[46] it is certainly possible to read this homophobic
and racist diatribe to be expressive of insecurities pivoting around the instabilities of heterosexual and racial identifications. At the same time, this diatribe
serves a recuperative function, since the undesirable, permeable, and amorphous
body is designated as black, feminine, and homosexual, which works to shore up
a solid, impenetrable white heterosexual male body in opposition.[47]

Reservoir Dogs is a particularly interesting filmic example of white heterosexual masculinity's dependence on its abjected others for self-definition. As
Amy Taubin notes, it is an insularly white male film: women get no more than
thirty seconds of screen time, and the only person of color is Mr. Orange's police chief; nonetheless, not a minute goes by without references to either "niggers," "jungle bunnies," male rape, and castrating women.[48] Presumably a conscious strategy, this screens Tarantino's understanding of white heterosexual
masculinity as always marked by the categories of gender, race, and sexuality,
though this recognition is largely achieved through abusive hate speech, making
it, in bell hooks's words, "multiculturalism with a chic neofascist twist."[49] Mr.

Pink, for example, defines his notion of professionalism (coded white) against an image of black male posturing; angered by Mr. Blonde and Mr. White's bickering, he states, "You guys act like a bunch of fuckin' niggers. You ever work a job with a bunch of niggers? They're just like you two, always fightin', always sayin' they're gonna kill one another." At the same time, this outburst suggests that an underlying fear is that, as members of an urban underclass, these "dogs" also suffer from the anxiety that they are not quite white enough.

In *True Romance*, similar verbal aggression erupts over fears concerning the ease with which white masculinity can be contaminated when Worley (Dennis Hopper) embarks on a controversy-courting, suicidal rant that aims at insulting mafioso Don Vincenzo's (Christopher Walken's) Sicilian ethnicity. Remarking to the unnervingly unruffled Don Vincenzio that "Sicilians were spawned by niggers," Worley continues,

> You see, way back then, Sicilians were like the wops from Northern Italy. They all had blonde hair and blue eyes. But then the Moors moved in there, they changed the whole country. They did so much fuckin' with Sicilian women that they changed the whole bloodline forever. That's why blond hair and blue eyes became black hair and dark skin. You know it's absolutely amazing to me to think that, to this day, hundreds of years later, Sicilians still carry that nigger gene. I'm quotin' history. It's a fact. It's written. Your ancestors are niggers. Your great, great, great grandmother fucked a nigger and she had a half nigger kid. Now, if that's a fact, tell me, am I lyin'? 'Cause you, you are part eggplant.

Like Jimmy's tirade about "dead nigger storage" in *Pulp Fiction*, this rant is offered up as sheer performance, which gestures at sanctioning any pleasure that its very transgressiveness unleashes. Whereas Jules seemed to use "nigger" as pure descriptor, though, Worley uses it as racist abuse, qualifying the efficacy of any such potential distancing devices. Indeed, Worley's rant bears an uncomfortable resemblance to white supremacist discourses, the major locus of anxiety of which is miscegenation, anxiety that revolves around control over the white woman's body. This ethnic/racial slur thus plays on white male anxieties that the regulation of whiteness is in the hands of women, not men; as Richard Dyer has noted, heterosexuality is the site in which whiteness is reproduced, but also the site where it can be contaminated.[50] This insult to Sicilian ethnicity functions precisely through the suggestion that as dark-skinned Europeans, Sicilians do not have access to fully-fledged whiteness, a point that the film later seems to confirm when the Sicilians are dubbed "wops" or "guineas" by WASP cops. At the same time, Worley is coded as "white trash" and is therefore also exempt from the economic and social advantages that whiteness is supposed to bring. As David Roediger points out, whiteness and property are yoked together in the popular cultural imagination, which might help explain why many poor whites hang onto whiteness as the only property they own.[51]

White Male Infantilism and Aggression in Tarantino's Gangster Chic

Much like homosexuals and people of color, women circulate only at the level of dialogue in *Reservoir Dogs*, and their function is primarily to cement white homosocial ties in what is often misogynistic and racist discourse. For instance, when the all-white gangsters discuss the differences between white and black women, Mr. Pink authoritatively states, "What a white bitch'll put up with a black bitch wouldn't put up with for a minute. They've got a line and if you cross it they fuck you up." The image of the sexualized, castrating black woman continues when Nice-Guy Eddie tells an anecdote about a black "man-eater-upper" cocktail waitress named Elois, who stuck a man's penis to his stomach with crazy glue. That no man can resist Elois, though, articulates a white male masochistic fantasy of being dominated by an authoritative black woman.

The black phallic woman reappears in *Pulp Fiction*'s "The Bonnie Situation," in which Jules and Vincent desperately attempt to clean up the bloody mess made by the remains of Marvin's body before Bonnie gets home from work. Humor stems from the fear instilled in these ruthless gangsters at the idea of incurring a black woman's wrath, with Jules ringing up Marcellus to the tune of "you've got to understand how explosive a factor this Bonnie situation is." Marsellus agrees and sends in an expert, the anal Mr. Wolf (possibly a reference to Freud's Wolfman case[52]), to supervise the clean-up job. As Tarantino himself explains (in an unfortunate, but no doubt knowing analogy between a dead black male and shit), Jules and Vincent are like boys who have messed up the house and are afraid of their mother's impending fury: "You spilled shit on the carpet—clean up the mess you made from screwing around before your mom gets home."[53] For Sharon Willis, this "central address to absent feminine authority might explain some of the pleasures of Tarantino's films for the young white males who largely constitute his fan audience," since it both addresses but also wards off the pre-Oedipal figure of the phallic mother.[54]

In her psychoanalytic reading, Willis argues that Tarantino's films obsessively rehearse Oedipal structures, in particular through appeals to paternal authority (Joe Cabot, Mr. Orange's boss, Elvis, Mr. Wolf, Marsellus), but these structures are often interrupted by ferocious pre-Oedipal desires. For instance, Willis observes that both Tarantino's films and characters take pleasure in the abject, with defiling and cleaning acting as "central organizing processes for these films—at the literal and the figurative levels." Examples include the pristine white shirts of Mr. Orange, Jules, and Vincent being smeared with garish blood, the abject bodily fluids of Mia's overdose, or the sheer number of bathroom scenes, the bathroom being a site where blood and violence are connected to anal eroticism and smearing.[55] Regressive anal and oral desires are particularly evident in *Pulp Fiction*. Anal eroticism is played out not only through the homoerotophobic obsession with male anal sex, but also in "The Gold Watch" sequence, where a young Butch is visited by Captain Koons (Christopher Walken). Koons gives Butch his paternal legacy of a gold watch to the accompaniment of his Vietnam narrative, which begins in all earnestness and then veers off unexpectedly as he elaborates on how long, as a prisoner of war, he "hid this uncomfortable hunk of metal up [his] ass." Polan and Willis also note that bathrooms function as structuring devices in Tarantino's films; for example, in *Pulp Fiction*, every time that Vincent emerges from the toilet, he finds the scene he left radically changed.[56] As regards oral desires, Tarantino's films are littered with fetishizing discussions of food, such as Jules waxing lyrical about hamburgers or Vincent's unreserved admiration for a five-dollar milkshake.[57]

The infantilism of Tarantino's male characters provides a useful framework for analyzing the unpredictable eruptions of verbal and physical violence in his films. While his *Pulp Fiction* characters often wander around with a "wide-eyed innocence" (for instance, Butch's witnessing of a primal scene with Marsellus's rape), or engage in babyish, romantic banter (most notably, Butch and Fabienne [Maria de Medeiros], and Pumpkin [Tim Roth] and Honey Bunny [Amanda Plumber]), the flipside of this is often a sadistic cruelty.[58] Tarantino himself has stated that his macho gangsters are "a cross between criminals and actors and children playing roles . . . little boys with real guns": "If you ever saw kids playing—three little kids playing Starsky and Hutch interrogating a prisoner—you'll probably see more *real*, honest moments happening than you would ever see on that show, because those kids would be so into it."[59] Tarantino foregrounds this infantilism in *Reservoir Dogs* when a condescending Mr. Blonde interrupts the testosterone-charged tussle between Mr. Pink and Mr. White by stating, "You kids shouldn't play so rough." Likewise, Joe Cabot informs the dogs that they are like "a bunch of broads in a schoolyard," an insult that also works through designating them female. Outpourings of obscenities can also be understood through the lens of infantilism, with Tarantino's characters like kids taking relish in "defying the rules of propriety" and uttering what parents wouldn't want to hear.[60]

Willis suggests that the infantilism of Tarantino's male characters might well account for the appeal of his films to female spectators:

> If the absence of women . . . does not put off female spectators, it may be because Tarantino's films offer a masculinity whose worst enemy is itself. Or, it may be because the film interpellates women spectators into the reassuring posture of judge, adjudicator, or evaluator. In this case, self-deconstructing adolescent white masculinity is on parade before the discerning, and perhaps satisfied feminine gaze, a gaze that can take its distance from a transgressive eruption designed precisely to provoke her.[61]

The fact that white masculinity is associated with infantilism, while black masculinity is figured as the epitome of cool, and black femininity aligned with phallic womanhood (Elois, Christy Love, Pam Grier, Jackie Brown, Bonnie), might also help explain Tarantino's appeal to certain black audiences. Yet, at the same time, this infantilism undoubtedly undergrids the pleasures of Tarantino's films for his largely young white male fan base. I am not only referring to Willis's argument that Tarantino's films both address and ward off the phallic mother. I would add that despite gesturing at a fragmented, fragile masculinity, paradoxically infantilism can also function to create a vision of transgressive (white) masculine "cool," which, as Susan Fraiman points out, is epitomized by the male teenager's histrionic defiance of maternal authority as part of his attempt to reach "a state of cool imperviousness."[62] In other words, the infantile antics of Tarantino's (white) male characters form a means of rejecting the feminine and articulating a fantasy of macho transcendence, a fantasy that is legitimized through parody and autodeconstructive textual strategies.

I would also locate this representation of infantile white heterosexual masculinity elsewhere. Tarantino's self-conscious strategy of flouting political correctness, often in the mouths of white male members of the urban working-class, no doubt accounts for his popularity with certain young white males (among others), who are thrilled at being allowed to get away with laughing at or enjoying things that are normally prohibited. One potential viewing position constructed by Tarantino, therefore, is that of child or adolescent, a position that allows guilt-free pleasures in physical and verbal violence and potentially offensive humor. Tarantino's films disregard such restrictions and actively attempt, through stylistic innovation, to elicit the uneasy residue and excess that prohibition usually leaves behind. This recalls Freud's theorizing of jokes as a means of voicing aggression that is inhibited by social interdiction. Using racism and sexism as dominant paradigms, Freud states that "the joke will evade restrictions and open sources of pleasure that have become inaccessible."[63] In view of the infantilism of Tarantino's white male characters, it is also interesting to note that Freud regarded jokes as a means of accessing pleasures from "the mood of our childhood . . . when we had no need of humour to make us feel happy in our life"[64]—that is, a time before social prohibition, and, in the case of Tarantino, a time before the demands of political correctness, which acts as the dominant discourse regulating the "sayable" and "unsayable."

A similar trend can be found in the whiter-than-white '90s gross-out film cycle, such as There's Something about Mary (1998) or American Pie (1998). Gwendolyn Foster notes that white bodies are often a source of humor because of their abject leakiness and instability.[65] I would add that these bodies tend to be figured as white adolescent male bodies. For example, American Pie is replete with examples of male characters masturbating, ejaculating (often prematurely), vomiting, or accidentally drinking semen. The scene that gives the film its title has its virgin hero masturbate into a fresh-out-of-the-oven apple pie because he has been told that it is like "third base," only to be interrupted by his father, causing them both to panic about mom returning home to find her pie looking rather the worse for wear—a similar fear of maternal authority to that screened in Pulp Fiction's "The Bonnie Situation."[66] These gross-out films lack the sophistication of Tarantino's cinema, but function similarly by encouraging us to laugh at the white male characters' sexism and homophobia, with their immaturity acting as a self-legitimizing defence. What this trend of violating the codes of political correctedness and good taste would seem to bear out, therefore, is Butler's observation that prohibition is what "fantasy loves most," and that restrictions often displace and reroute the violence they attempt to control.[67]

Sharon Willis rightly states that "Tarantino's films are nothing if not symptomatic."[68] He has white phallic masculinity autodeconstruct before our eyes, though parody and intertextuality prevent this fragility or infantilism being treated too seriously. He problematizes traditional modes of consumption, but his films are also prime examples of a cynical postmodern *ennui*; as bell hooks puts it, Tarantino "would have everyone see racism, sexism, homophobia but behave as if none of that shit really matters."[69] What makes Tarantino interesting is his recognition that "ordinary" white guys are always also extra-ordinary—that is, inextricably enmeshed in discourses of gender, race, sexuality, and class. However, that recognition is most often referenced through verbal and/or physical aggression, with violence being the only means his white heterosexual male characters have of policing and regulating the always precarious borders of their identity.

In the following chapter, I further explore representations of white male violence, this time through the equally iconic figure of the serial killer. Whereas Tarantino's films present white masculinity as an always raced and gendered category, serial killer films tend to figure the violence of the white male serial killer as an individual psychopathology (with a few notable exceptions, such as *The Silence of the Lambs*, which explores serial killing in the context of patriarchal violence). In my attempt to foreground the whiteness, along with the maleness, of white male serial violence in these films, I again explore how aggression works to shore up white male identity as in Tarantino's films, despite the serial killer film's very different aesthetic strategies. Moreover, while the two-dimensionality of Tarantino's gangsters offers a ludic, postmodern play with surface and a parodic exploration of the performativity of masculinity, in many serial killer films, this two-dimensionality indexes concerns about virtual, mass-mediated, postmodern culture, as well as anxieties about the inauthenticity and sterility of "ordinary" white men.

Notes

1. Dana Polan, *Pulp Fiction*, BFI Modern Classics (London: BFI, 2003), 24.
2. Polan, *Pulp Fiction*, 7.
3. Paul Gormley, *The New-Brutality Film: Race and Affect in Contemporary Hollywood Cinema* (Bristol: Intellect Books, 2005), 25.
4. Liam Kennedy, *Race and Urban Contemporary American Culture* (Edinburgh: Edinburgh University Press, 2000), 129.
5. Manohla Dargis, "Dark Side of the Dream," *Sight and Sound*, August 1996, 16.
6. Fran Mason, *American Gangster Cinema: From* Little Caesar *to* Pulp Fiction (Basingstoke: Palgrave Macmillan, 2002), 141.
7. Kennedy, *Race and Urban Contemporary American Culture*, 130-31.

8. Mason, *American Gangster Cinema*, 161.

9. Stella Bruzzi, *Undressing Cinema: Clothing and Identity in the Movies* (London: Routledge, 1997), 67, 70.

10. Jeff Dawson, *Quentin Tarantino: The Cinema of Cool* (New York: Applause, 1995), 78.

11. Bruzzi, *Undressing Cinema*, 89.

12. Bruzzi, *Undressing Cinema*, 91.

13. Paul A. Woods, *King Pulp: The Wild World of Quentin Tarantino* (London: Plexus, 1998), 46.

14. Sharon Willis, *High Contrast: Race and Gender in Contemporary Hollywood Film* (Durham, NC: Duke University Press, 1997), 203.

15. Bruzzi, *Undressing Cinema*, 90.

16. Jude Davies and Carol R. Smith, *Gender, Ethnicity and Sexuality in Contemporary American Film* (Edinburgh: Keele University Press, 1997), 19.

17. Dan Harries, *Film Parody* (London: BFI, 2000), 24.

18. Linda Hutcheon, *The Politics of Postmodernism* (London: Routledge, 1990), 101.

19. Hutcheon, *The Politics of Postmodernism*, 93.

20. Julie Hallam and Margaret Marshment, *Realism and Popular Cinema* (Manchester: Manchester University Press, 2000), 224-25.

21. Henry A. Giroux, "*Pulp Fiction* and the Culture of Violence," *Harvard Educational Review* 65, no. 2 (1995): 308.

22. Manohla Dargis, "Who's Afraid of Red, Yellow and Blonde?" *Artforum* 31, no. 3 (1992): 11.

23. Willis, *High Contrast*, 191.

24. Graham Fuller, "Answer First. Questions Later," in *Quentin Tarantino Inteviews*, ed. Gerald Peary (Jackson: University Press of Mississippi, 1998), 60.

25. See, for instance, Giroux's "*Pulp Fiction* and the Culture of Violence."

26. Michael Rogin, "Blackface, White Noise: The Jewish Jazz Singer Finds His Voice," *Critical Inquiry* 18, no. 3 (1992): 417.

27. Amy Taubin, "The Men's Room," *Sight and Sound*, December 1992, 5.

28. Gormley, *The New-Brutality Film*, 29, 93.

29. Woods, *King Pulp*, 47.

30. Willis, *High Contrast*, 190.

31. Susan Fraiman, *Cool Men and the Second Sex* (New York: Columbia University Press, 2003), 3.

32. Willis, *High Contrast*, 200.

33. Willis, *High Contrast*, 200.

34. bell hooks, *Reel to Real: Race, Sex, and Class at the Movies* (New York: Routledge, 1996), 48-49.

35. Willis, *High Contrast*, 200.

36. Polan, *Pulp Fiction*, 62.

37. Gwendolyn Audrey Foster, *Performing Whiteness: Postmodern Re/Constructions in the Cinema* (Albany: State University of New York Press, 2003), 64.

38. Polan, *Pulp Fiction*, 62-63.

39. Jonathan Dollimore, *Sexual Dissidence: Augustine to Wilde, Freud to Foucault* (Oxford: Clarendon, 1991), 229.

40. Patrick O'Donnell, *Latent Destinies: Cultural Paranoia and Contemporary U.S. Narrative* (Durham, NC: Duke University Press, 2000), 18-19.

41. Eve Kosofsky Sedgwick, *Epistemology of the Closet* (Berkeley: University of California Press, 1990), 187.

42. Eve Kosofsky Sedgwick, *Between Men: English Literature and Male Homosocial Desire* (New York: Columbia University Press, 1985), 20.

43. Frantz Fanon, *Black Skin, White Masks*, trans. Charles Lam Markmann (New York: Grove, 1967), 111-12; Judith Butler, "Endangered/Endangering: Schematic Racism and White Paranoia," in *Reading Rodney King, Reading Urban Uprising*, ed. Robert Gooding (New York: Routledge, 1993), 18.

44. David Marriott, *Haunted Life: Visual Culture and Black Modernity* (New Brunswick, NJ: Rutgers University Press, 2007), 220-21.

45. Marriott, *Haunted Life*, 207, 221.

46. In his discussion of narcissistic identification in his seminal text "The Mirror Stage" (1949), Jacques Lacan explores how the infant's recognition of its image in the mirror is always a misrecognition because the unified *gestalt* conflicts with the infant's own experiences of bodily fragmentation. "The Mirror Stage," in *Écrits: A Selection*, trans. Alan Sheridan (London: Routledge, 2004), 3. For Lacan, this moment is also underpinned by aggression, since "the human individual fixes upon himself an image that alienates him from himself." Aggressivity directed at the subject's others, therefore, also stems from the subject's internal aggressivity, which always accompanies "the coming-into-being (*devenir*) of the subject." "Aggressivity in Psychoanalysis," in *Écrits: A Selection*, trans. Alan Sheridan (London: Routledge, 2004), 21, 24.

47. This inevitably recalls Klaus Theweleit's arguments in *Male Fantasies* that the fascist male desire for a hard body is grounded in the male subject's fears of being overrun by otherness, fears which often translate into violence against those others that threaten the ego's sense of a masterful, unified self. *Male Fantasies*, 2 Vols., trans. Stephen Conway in collaboration with Erica Carter and Chris Turner (Cambridge: Polity, 1987).

48. Taubin, "The Men's Room," 4.

49. hooks, *Reel to Real*, 49.

50. Richard Dyer, *White* (London: Routledge, 1997), 20.

51. David Roediger, *Colored White: Transcending the Racial Past* (Berkeley: University of California Press, 2002), 24, 240.

52. Devin Anthony Orgeron, "Scatological Film Practice: *Pulp Fiction* and a Cinema in Movements," *Postscript* 19, no. 3 (2000): 38.

53. Gavin Smith, "You Know You're in Good Hands," in *Quentin Tarantino Interviews*, ed. Gerald Peary (Jackson: University Press of Mississippi, 1998), 101.

54. Willis, *High Contrast*, 207.

55. Willis, *High Contrast*, 202, 192, 189-92.

56. Polan, *Pulp Fiction*, 30; Willis, *High Contrast*, 192.

57. Polan, *Pulp Fiction*, 49.

58. Polan, *Pulp Fiction*, 47-51.

59. Smith, "You Know You're in Good Hands," 101.

60. Polan, *Pulp Fiction*, 57.

61. Willis, *High Contrast*, 207.

62. Fraiman, *Cool Men and the Second Sex*, 3.

63. Sigmund Freud, *Jokes and their Relation to the Unconscious*, trans. James Strachey, ed. Angela Richards (London: Penguin, 1991), 147.

64. Freud, *Jokes and their Relation to the Unconscious*, 302.

65. Foster, *Performing Whiteness*, 22.

66. I am indebted to Mandy Merck for alerting me to this point. Mandy Merck, "Mom's Apple Pie" (paper presented at the international conference "Bodies, Theories, Cultures in the Post-Millennium Era," Aristotle University of Thessaloniki, Thessaloniki, Greece, May 16, 2003).

67. Judith Butler, "The Force of Fantasy: Feminism, Maplethorpe, and Discursive Excess," *Differences: A Journal of Feminist Cultural Studies* 2, no. 2 (1990): 111, 119.

68. Willis, *High Contrast*, 207.

69. hooks, *Reel to Real*, 47.

Chapter Eight
Everyman and No Man: White Masculinity in Contemporary Serial Killer Movies

Gendering and Racing the Serial Killer

Jon Amiel's *Copycat* (1995) opens with renowned criminal psychologist Dr. Helen Hudson (Sigourney Weaver) giving her stock lecture on serial killers in which she explains that serial killers murder for recognition and power, usually over women, who constitute the majority of victims; with each killing leaving them unfulfilled, they kill again driven by the hope that next time might be perfect. To highlight the group that poses most risk, Helen asks all male members of the audience to stand, and then invites those under 20 or over 35, and those of Asian and African-American descent, to sit down, an exercise designed to highlight that 90% of serial killers are young adult white males. Adding that most women in the audience would probably date the men still standing, she notes that the majority of serial killers appear to be totally "normal" on the surface. What interests me about this scene is not only the unusual highlighting of the whiteness and maleness of serial killing, but also the suggestion that there is something about white masculinity that makes it fertile terrain for the spawning of such horrendous crimes. Helen implicitly links the apparent "normality" of the serial killer with the invisibility afforded by white masculinity. At the same time, she suggests that this very anonymity is intrinsic to the pathology, since serial killers kill precisely to gain recognition. In other words, undergridding her lecture is the suggestion that white masculinity is a rather empty, depleted identity, which, in the serial killer, produces a chain of violent acts intent on attaining a form of subjectivity that remains ever elusive.

Copycat is one of the many serial killer films released in the '90s in the wake of the Oscar-winning success of *The Silence of the Lambs* (Jonathan Demme 1991), which gave a genre with its roots in the slasher cycle a newfound respectability. The popularity of the genre was immediately seized upon by the

U.S. popular media and packaged up in *fin-de-millennium* anxieties about the state of the nation, while neo-conservatives used the opportunity to scapegoat reel for real violence. These sensationalized accounts not only eclipsed any discussion of the violence of American domestic and foreign policies during the same period,[1] but also sidelined the gendered and raced nature of serial killing. As Richard Dyer notes, Helen's assertion that "nine out of ten" serial killers are white males follows official statistics, and those who dispute this figure "only manage to demonstrate small increases in percentages of women and non-white serial killers."[2] Because, as we have seen, white masculinity has the privilege of functioning as the universal, neutral term—a positioning dependent on the burden of excess signification carried by those bodies that are marked—the maleness and whiteness of serial killing, both on and off screen, can remain obscured in discourses of individual pathology or more generalized discussions about the violence endemic to U.S. society.

In this chapter, I would like to foreground the whiteness as well as the maleness of serial killing in my analysis of the contemporary serial killer movie in order to explore the anxieties that the genre articulates about contemporary U.S. white heterosexual masculinity. On the surface, screen serial killers have little to tell us about normative white masculinity, since they occupy a position of monstrous otherness, often achieved through pathologizing discourses of sexual deviance and/or class inferiority. However, I begin by tracing how cinematic representations of non-phallic or "white trash" serial killers point to what must be excluded for the constitution of "ordinary" white heterosexual masculinity. Considering that uncanny doublings between detective and killer have become a staple of the genre, I then explore the effect of the detective being embodied by a white male, whose identity is always troubled by his proximity to the serial killer. I further tease out the very different implications of this doubling in generic revisions where the detective is a woman or person of color, who is better able to insulate him/herself from the violence of the serial killer. This stems not only from his/her visually inscribed gendered and/or racial otherness, but also his/her ability to access the positive investment in minoritized identity. As I have argued throughout this book, identity politics and the attendant celebration of difference have resulted in anxieties that, by virtue of its very ordinariness, white heterosexual masculinity lacks specific content, apart from its assigned role as oppressor. With this in mind, I end by turning my attention to a body of films which, far from othering the serial killer, represent him as "abnormally normal," to use Mark Seltzer's term.[3] These filmic representations of the white male serial killer as unnervingly two-dimensional and vacuous allow an interrogation of contemporary concerns about commodity-driven, mass-mediated, hyperreal, postmodern culture, but in the process, they reinforce associations of white heterosexual masculinity with sterility and emptiness in the manner that Helen's lecture in *Copycat* implicitly suggests.

The Sexually Deviant Serial Killer

The common trend of marking the screen serial killer monstrous through representations of non-phallic sexuality has its roots in *Peeping Tom* (Michael Powell 1960) and *Psycho* (Alfred Hitchcock 1960), whose legacies are evident in the slasher film and its upmarket relation, the '90s serial killer movie. In *Peeping Tom*, Mark (Carl Boehm) kills his female victims using a blade that he has fixed to his camera, attempting to capture the image of perfect fear on film; he also attaches a distorting mirror to his camera, not only forcing his female victims to watch their own murder, but also to regard themselves as monstrous. Sadistic though his actions are, they also reveal his need to bolster his failed sense of masculinist control, with his pathology attributed to the systematic abuse his scientist father inflicted on him as part of his investigation into the effects of fear on the nervous system. *Psycho*'s Norman Bates (Anthony Perkins) kills women that sexually arouse him because he has psychically introjected the persona of the castrating mother he killed, installing the motif of transvestitism and transsexuality that would be repeated in numerous films, most obviously Brian De Palma's blatant imitation *Dressed to Kill* (1980). Ever since, psychosexual killers have invariably been posited as products of a sick family, ensnared in Oedipal dramas that prevent them from achieving phallic subjectivity. As Carol Clover has argued in *Men, Women and Chainsaws: Gender in the Modern Horror Film* (1992), in slasher films the masculinity of the serial killer is "severely qualified," and however phallically encoded their stabbing and slashing of female victims might be, it always belies the fact that phallic subjectivity eludes them.[4]

Clover's observations can equally be applied to those contemporary serial killer movies that recycle slasher narratives. For instance, in *Copycat*, in front of his domineering, bed-ridden wife/girlfriend, Peter Foley (Michael McNamara), the film's copycat killer, is as awkward and childlike as *Psycho*'s Norman Bates. Helen also momentarily disarms him by taunting him with accusations of impotence, while, in the final chase sequence, her weapon is her hysterical but mocking laughter, which unnerves him long enough for Detective Monahan (Holly Hunter) to shoot. In *The Cell* (Tarsem Singh 2002), the need that Carl (Vincent D'Onofrio) has to transform his victims into dolls reveals his insecurities about his masculine identity, which are again rooted in the abuse he suffered as a child. In *The Silence of the Lambs*, which reworks *Psycho*'s transvestite serial killer narrative, Buffalo Bill (Ted Levine) kills size 14 women in order to make himself a bodysuit out of female skin. The most renowned scene features a series of extreme close-ups of Buffalo Bill erotically twisting his nipple ring, putting on jewelry, and applying lipstick whilst asking his mirror reflection, "Will you fuck me? . . . I'd fuck me." Then, dancing before his own video camera, he fumbles below screen, and, as he dances backwards, reveals that he has tucked his penis between his legs; raising his colorful shawl like outstretched wings, he then completes his fantasmatic identification both with femininity and his symbol of transformation—the signature death-head moth that he leaves in his victims' mouths. As Judith Halberstam notes, this particular scene would seem more designed to scare men than women, screening the image of "a fragmented and fragile masculinity, a male body disowning the penis."[5]

The fact that these films feature not only killers who are marked by phallic lack, but also often tough female heroines with whom we are encouraged to identify (a point I will return to) considerably complicates the rigid schema put forward by Laura Mulvey whereby the cinematic apparatus engineers identification with the sadistic, masterful male gaze.[6] At the same time, the referencing of phallic lack in these films would also seem to necessitate the demonization of non-phallic sexuality and/or sexual deviance. By othering the serial killer in this way, the values of normative, heterosexual masculinity are shored up, and "ordinary" white men are insulated from serial violence.

The Silence of the Lambs reveals the slippery process of othering at work in its representation of Buffalo Bill and Hannibal Lecter (Anthony Hopkins), the film's second serial killer. In many ways they are doubled: both violate the self/other distinction by incorporating their victims, though Lecter chooses to cannibalize his prey rather than dress in their skin. Lecter also "tears a leaf out of Buffalo Bill's casebook" when he escapes from captivity by "wearing" the face of a security guard he has skinned.[7] Moreover, while Buffalo Bill wants to get into women's skin, Lecter wants to penetrate the psyche of the heroine, Clarice (Jodie Foster), and gain access to her deepest, most intimate traumas. This is represented visually through one of their many skilfully filmed exchanges when the ghostly reflection of Lecter's face is projected onto the protective glass barrier as we gaze at Clarice from his perspective, a scene in which he seems to have got inside her head, both literally and figuratively. However, while Lecter, as a vicious serial killer, could by no means be termed a positive representation of white masculinity, he nonetheless functions as a fascinating, charismatic figure, gaining iconic status as popular cinema's first serial killer hero (vampires aside). Indeed, as many reviewers of the film noted, *The Silence of the Lambs* knowingly plays its two serial killers off against each other, positioning spectators to enjoy Hannibal Lecter's escape from the authorities, but also to root for Clarice as she blows Buffalo Bill away.[8] While *The Silence of the Lambs* was embraced by many feminist critics for its strong female protagonist, it was picketed by lesbian and gay activists, angered at the film's representation of Buffalo Bill, and the concomitant suggestive analogies between non-normative sexuality and serial killers at a time of rampant paranoia over the AIDS epidemic.[9] Indeed, Buffalo Bill's gruesome murders of women are directly attributed to his gender confusion and his psychic need for female identity, which the film represents through a variety of images of sexual transgression: polymorphous perversity, male effeminacy, homosexuality, transvestitism, and would-be transsexuality.

Lecter, on the other hand, is only seen killing male victims (the photograph of a nurse whose face he mutilated and cannibalized remains safely off-screen), and unlike Buffalo Bill, is implicitly coded as heterosexual through his erotic interest in Clarice, despite the camp overtones in the delivery of his wittiest lines.[10] Lecter's iconic status owes much to Hopkins's compelling performance, in particular his emphatic, rasped delivery, his unnervingly stiff and restrained body postures punctuated by sudden bursts of shocking violence, and his mesmerizing, piercing, blue eyes, which blink with reptilian deliberation. More importantly, unlike Buffalo Bill, Lecter is posited as a charismatic, if demonic, figure of identification, engineered through the use of controlled, tightly framed close-ups during his tense exchanges with Clarice.[11] One meeting, which opens with Lecter ironically informing Clarice that "people will say we are in love," is particularly erotically charged: on handing her a file to help her with the case, a close-up cut-away shot focuses on Lecter caressing Clarice's fingers. Lecter is also capable of perverse acts of heterosexual gallantry, such as when he talks fellow inmate Miggs (Stuart Rudin) into killing himself as punishment for verbally abusing Clarice and throwing semen into her face. Thus Lecter "occupies the place of the charming but mysterious and potentially violent gothic male" to Clarice's gothic heroine,[12] while Buffalo Bill occupies the place of "the ultimate monster,"[13] positionings inextricable from the film's discourse on sexuality.

Nevertheless, Lecter's desire for Clarice always also renders him a potential threat—indeed, his insistence on learning about her deepest trauma in return for help capturing Buffalo Bill is posited as akin to a psychological rape. The fact that most other white heterosexual men in positions of patriarchal authority in the film show similar erotic interest in Clarice or subject her to varying degrees of sexist behavior and/or violence also links them with the threat that both Buffalo Bill and Lecter pose, a point I explore further below. Lecter thus functions as "the other within" the category of middle-class white heterosexual masculinity, implicating it in his violence. However, as Elizabeth Young notes, any "feminist critique of male violence against women" is severely mitigated by the film's demonized representation of Buffalo Bill, since it "displaces that violence—which in social practice is overwhelmingly committed by heterosexual men—onto the fictive scapegoat of male homosexuality."[14]

Lecter is not only played off against Buffalo Bill in terms of sexuality, though; he is also differentiated in terms of his eloquence, wit, intellectual genius, and refined, middle-class tastes—he even performs the gruesome murder of his prison guards in style to the accompaniment of Bach. In other words, the otherness of Buffalo Bill is also inscribed through his portrayal as "white trash," signified through his run-down abode, clothes, accent, and inarticulateness, a characterization in which other '90s serial killer films follow suit.

"White Trash" Serial Killers

The derogatory descriptor "white trash" has recently received academic attention, most notably from Annalee Newitz and Matthew Wray, who argue that "[y]oking a classist epithet to a racist one, as white trash does, reminds us how often racism is in fact directly related to economic differences." "White trash," they argue, is a non-dominant form of whiteness that undermines notions that white identity is necessarily "the primary locus of social privilege and power."[15] Nevertheless, this function would seem to come at a high cost in '90s films such as *Copycat, Kalifornia* (Dominic Sena 1993), and *Natural Born Killers* (Oliver Stone 1994), where the serial killer is demonized through the deployment of crude stereotypes of white, working-class, rural masculinity, and played off against the middle-class whites whose lives he threatens. As with the abusive, redneck sadists in John Boorman's influential *Deliverance* (1972), simply being "white trash" would seem to give sufficient narrative justification for these killers' murderous impulses.

Copycat's first serial killer, Daryll Lee Cullum (Henry Connick, Jr.), whose threat to the white, bourgeois Helen is explicitly sexual, is an unshaven, swaggering, redneck lout, with bad teeth and a crude vocabulary, who screams out in glee after shooting a cop and spitting on his body. *Kalifornia* makes no bones about the class of its serial killer: as Brian (David Duchovny) and his girlfriend Carrie (Michelle Forbes) meet Early Grayce (Brad Pitt) (whose name alone renders him an atavistic throw-back) and Adele (Juliette Lewis), Brian's voiceover informs us: "If you looked in the dictionary under 'poor white trash,' a picture of Early and Adele would have been there." Early has unkempt, greasy hair, scruffy clothes, and spits, swears, burps, grunts, and drinks beer for breakfast. Indeed, Carrie's original suspicions about Early are alerted solely because he offends her middle-class sensibilities, as a scene at a diner makes clear when a close-up of Early playing with his sweaty socks at the dinner table is intercut with her disapproving gaze. Brian, on the other hand, is initially attracted to Early, and enjoys the homosocial rituals of getting drunk and learning to fire a gun with him in the face of Carrie's disapproval, the suggestion being that Brian's masculinity has been jeopardized by his bourgeois, consumer-led lifestyle and his relationship with a dynamic, career-driven woman. When it becomes obvious that Early poses a sexual threat to Carrie, however (his long-term abuse and murder of Adele are dealt with more perfunctorily), the film rehearses the common trope of remasculinization through violence. While Brian had earlier argued against the death penalty with his middle-class friends, refusing the existence of innate evil, he soon jettisons his liberal beliefs, shooting Early at close range, guiltlessly dispensing a punishment that not only reaffirms existing class hierarchies, but also differentiates him from his "white trash" other in the very act of proving that his own primal masculinity is still very much intact.

Oliver Stone's experimental, though ideologically incoherent *Natural Born Killers*, on the other hand, offers a more complex representation of the "white trash" serial killer. In the tradition of the outlaw couple inaugurated by *Bonnie and Clyde* (1967), gender norms are violated by the fact that Mallory (Juliette Lewis) relishes in the killing spree as much as Mickey (Woody Harrelson), though her violence is contextualized against the sexual abuse she suffered at the hands of her father (Rodney Dangerfield), as well as other male authority figures. Similarly, in the bio-doc *Monster* (2003), based on the life of one of the few known female serial killers, Aileen Wuornos, female aggression is posited as a response not only to class injustice, but also patriarchal violence. While *Natural Born Killer*'s Mickey is also given an abusive family background, unlike Mallory he is endowed with satanic dimensions, even morphing into the figure of a bald, blood-drenched, devilish figure surrounded by engulfing flames in several intercutting shots throughout the film. Indeed, the stereotypically wise Native American that Mickey kills—thus forging a link between the white violence on which modern America was founded and the whiteness of serial killing—sees "demon" projected across Mickey's chest, but believes Mallory to be suffering from "sad sickness." Mickey, who, unlike most "white trash" serial killers, is compellingly eloquent, justifies his violence as an attempt to rise above the banality of a defiling image culture (implicitly coded as feminizing), proudly declaring himself a "natural born killer" in a scene that encapsulates the film's pivotal discursive contradiction: blaming violence both on the contaminations of the media and an innate, primal aggression that is indexed through representations that are unavoidably classist.

The '90s trend for "white trash" serial killers can partly be attributed to their white-on-white, straight-on-straight, gender-indiscriminate violence (though women are subjected to sexual abuse, with Early and Mickey both raping female captives), which largely escapes the identity critiques that revolve around the categories of gender, race, and sexuality. In her discussion of rednecks in the horror genre, for instance, Clover argues that "the displacement of ethnic otherness onto a class of whites" is "the most significant 'ethnic' development" in recent popular culture.[16] However, it would be reductive to read these "white trash" killers solely as symbolic stand-ins for racial minorities, a reading that would overlook entrenched histories of prejudice against rural and urban, white, working-class people, who are often held responsible for their poverty. Indeed, Clover's reading is itself also symptomatic of the ways in which class—particularly in the U.S.—is often subsumed into racial discourse. Newitz, on the other hand, has argued that films in which middle-class whites are abused by "white trash" villains free privileged whites from the guilt of exercising white power whilst allowing them to prove their superiority and innocence.[17] This works to confirm classist assumptions about the abusive hypermasculinity of white working-class males and legitimize a violent resurgence of punitive power that attempts to purify middle-class whiteness, particularly middle-class white heterosexual masculinity, of any contamination.

However, as Newitz and Wray note, "white trash," being inside and outside the category of whiteness, always constitutes "both an internal and external threat."[18] This threat is evident in Stone's more critical *Natural Born Killers*, which, less subtly than *The Silence of the Lambs*, parallels the serial killer's violence with the violence enacted by all white male authority figures—Mallory's father, Scagnetti the killer cop (Tom Sizemore), Tommy Lee Jones's hysterical prison warden, and the unctuous reality TV presenter, Wayne Gale (Robert Downey, Jr.), who ends up participating in the killing spree. The film thus destabilizes the opposition between institutionalized white patriarchal violence and the violence of the serial killer, even as it deploys the image of the "white trash" serial killer to represent primal, unadulterated, "natural born" aggression. In the following section I further explore films that self-consciously double white male representatives of the law with the serial killer, interrogating what anxieties about white heterosexual masculinity are screened in the process.

"You caught me because we are very much alike": Uncanny Doublings between the Detective and Serial Killer

The common trend of highlighting uncanny resemblances between the detective and killer has its roots in the doubling of the hero/ine and monster that attends the gothic tradition, where the monster represents "the other within"—that is, those fears and desires that the hero/ine has had to repress in civilized, bourgeois society. The monster figure might well function as an othered figure, therefore, but also troubles the hero/ine's identity. In the police procedural style serial killer movie, the serial killer often delights in highlighting uncanny similarities between himself and the detective, suggesting that they merely operate on different sides of the law. When the detective is embodied by a white male, any doubling between investigator and killer inevitably calls into question the detective's sense of innocence. Of course, in most films, the detective is redeemed in narrative closure, most often through his violent dispatch of the killer, which resecures the boundaries of his identity and repeats the common motif of "regeneration through violence" that Richard Slotkin has located in frontier literature and mythology, and which is endlessly repeated in popular American cinema.[19] At the same time, the difficulty the white male detective initially faces in establishing an identity distinct from the white male serial killer not only raises questions of white heterosexual masculinity's complicity in patriarchal violence, but also represents concerns about the difficulty of white male self-distinction in "a culture that appears to organize itself around the visibility of differences and the symbolic currency of identity politics."[20]

   Red Dragon (Brett Ratner 2002), the prequel to *The Silence of the Lambs* and remake of the earlier *Manhunter* (Michael Mann 1986), knowingly highlights similarities between the white male profiler and serial killer. One of the opening scenes reveals FBI profiler Will Graham (Edward Norton) enlisting the help of famed forensic psychoanalyst Hannibal Lecter (Anthony Hopkins), whose bourgeois and professional status initially safeguards him from suspicion. As a profiler, Will's very job is to identify with the killer's psychic processes. When Will states, "I'm starting to be able to think like this one," Lecter cannily replies, "You're able to assume the emotional point of view of other people, even those that might scare or sicken you. It's a troubling gift, I should think. How I'd love to get you on my couch." When it dawns on Will that Lecter is in fact the killer he pursues, in the violent struggle that follows the two men are visually paralleled. Both are dressed in dark suit trousers and white shirts (symbols of moneyed, patriarchal authority), and both stab each other's left side, marking their pristine white shirts with almost identical, bloody stains. After his arrest, Lecter informs Will, "you caught me because we are very much alike." In addition, when Will's use of an irritating journalist as bait leads to the latter's gruesome murder at the hands of the film's second serial killer, Francis Dolarhyde (Ralph Fiennes), Lecter asks Will whether he enjoyed orchestrating the journalist's death. Then, manipulating Will's guilt at putting his own family at risk, he taunts him by claiming, "no one will ever be safe around you." Lecter thus deploys his skills as a brilliant psychoanalyst in order to play on Will's darkest fears of his own complicity. While Will asserts that there is a major difference between him and Lecter—*he* is not insane—the suggestion of shared characteristics is nonetheless voiced. Indeed, the final shot of Will reunited with his wife and son in the privatized space of the bourgeois family suggests that he has turned his back on the profession that rendered his own identity and sense of innocence a fragile affair.

The Watcher (Joe Charbanic 2000) and *Blood Work* (Clint Eastwood 2002), which rehearse homoerotic narratives of a highly personal game of cat and mouse between serial killer and detective, also screen the difficulties the white male detective faces in distancing himself from the killer. *The Watcher*'s serial killer, David Griffin, is played by Keanu Reeves, whose vacuous star persona renders him the apotheosis of not only the cybersubject (as I argued in chapter 4), but also the two-dimensional, affectless serial killer profile. Indeed, Griffin's only passion is his relationship with the film's profiler, Joel Campbell (James Spader). In the film's narrative past, Griffin had kidnapped Campbell's girl-friend in order to keep Campbell and him "together forever," describing this event as "our finest moment." While Campbell manages to track Griffin down before his girlfriend is killed, his decision to leave her tied to a chair while he went in pursuit of Griffin proves disastrous when the house catches fire and she is subjected to an agonizing death. Racked by guilt, Campbell is reduced to an insomniac, tranquilizer-dependent wreck who retires from the force and moves to Chicago in order to be near his girlfriend's grave. Griffin, however, soon locates him, shadowing his every move, and forces him out of retirement by sending him pictures of future victims. When Campbell's female therapist suggests that Griffin reinstated their relationship because he missed him, her question "did *you* miss him?" angers Campbell but nonetheless remains unanswered. Griffin, though, much like Lecter with Will in *Red Dragon*, delights in drawing attention to their mutually informing relationship: "We need each other. We define each other. We're yin and yang."

Blood Work rehearses a similar narrative. The serial killer leaves profiler Terry McCaleb (Clint Eastwood) "love letters," that is a numerical code as clue, after every killing in order to entice him into the chase. When McCaleb suffers a massive coronary on the job, the serial killer, who turns out to be McCaleb's irritating neighbor, James Noone (Jeff Daniels), murders organ donors who share McCaleb's unusual blood type in order to supply McCaleb with the new heart he needs, and thus keep their relationship alive. Noone tells McCaleb that their relationship is "meant to be," while Mc Caleb had earlier confided that his pursuit of the killer makes him feel more "connected" with the world around him.

The detective and killer in *The Watcher* and *Blood Work*, therefore, become locked in a relationship of mutual dependence, one which screens the precarious nature of white male self-definition, with the investigator "in danger of losing his identity" because of his "obsessive pursuit" of the killer.[21] Moreover, the detective is also made an unwilling accomplice in the serial killer's crimes, although he achieves redemption and transcendence in narrative closure when he violently kills his adversary. At the same time, both films also knowingly screen the homoerotic desire that threatens to erupt in all scenarios of homosocial bonding, airing anxieties about the instabilities of (male) heterosexual identifications. Indeed, Noone's self-chosen nickname "Buddy" is no coincidence in a film that reworks the homoerotic dimensions of the buddy movie.

The fact that "a lack of distance between hunter and hunted" foregrounds "questions of desire and sexuality"[22] becomes more evident in those few films with female serial killers and white male investigators in the hybrid genre of the erotic thriller. The prime example, of course, is *Basic Instinct* (1992), which reverses the conventions of the profiler movie, since the evil serial killer, Catherine Tramell (Sharon Stone), seems to have intimate knowledge of the detective, Nick Curran (Michael Douglas), which, as Yvonne Tasker notes, "serves to reinforce the suggestion of similarity between them."[23] This similarity is highlighted throughout the film: both have killed (Nick killed some tourists while high on cocaine), both have passed a polygraph test that acquitted them, and, as Catherine herself delights in pointing out, both revel in taking risks, professionally and sexually. As his professional identity slowly slips away from him due to his erotic involvement with Catherine—a collapsing of the private/public distinction which is common to the genre—Nick is eventually questioned by Internal Affairs in a scene that self-consciously deploys almost identical *mise-en-scène*, camerawork, and dialogue to Catherine's earlier interrogation. Indeed, on being asked to extinguish his cigarette, Nick echoes Catherine's exact same line: "What are you going to do? Charge me with smoking?" Thus the film not only posits him as an equally monstrous figure as the killer he pursues, but also articulates traditional *noir* instability over male identity caused by the aggressive sexuality of the *femme fatale*. While the film certainly plays into backlash fantasies by screening the monstrous threat posed by sexually active and professionally successful women in a narrative of white male victimhood, it also screens concerns that Nick lacks an identity, forced to borrow words and phrases from the woman who manipulates him at will.

As well as expressing anxieties about normative masculinity's lack of a specific, positive identity, the difficulties these white male profilers have in distancing themselves from the serial killer articulates concerns about white heterosexual masculinity's relation to power and violence. This becomes all the more apparent when the above films are compared to those in which the detective is embodied by a woman (normally white) or person of color (normally African-American male)—generic shifts which themselves testify to some of the successes of identity politics in the realm of representation (at least as far as white women and African-American males are concerned), with Hollywood ever keen to co-opt the discourses of politicized identity in order to capture wider audiences for its product.[24] These non-white male investigators are able to lay claim to specific, minoritized identities which are unavailable to white male detectives, thereby installing a distance between themselves and the white male serial killers they pursue.

The female detective, as Carol Clover has noted, has her roots in the slasher genre, in which increasingly the male rescuer/survivor function has been rendered "marginal or dispensed with altogether," resulting in a female victim-hero figure that Clover dubs "the final girl." Complicating Laura Mulvey's binary schema, Clover argues that horror films tend to install a *sadomasochistic* visual economy, engineered through point of view shots that oscillate between the killer (sadistic identification) and victim (masochistic identification). According to Clover, the "final girl"—who is invariably boyish, "not fully masculine," "not fully feminine," and "sexually reluctant" to boot—acts as a stand-in with which the predominately young male audience can identify in order to experience but then disavow the pleasures of masochism. With "abject terror" still "gendered feminine," therefore, Clover does not applaud the prevalence of the "final girl" as a feminist development, but rather regards her as "an agreed-upon fiction" that the male viewer can use "as a vehicle for his own sadomasochistic fantasies in an act of perhaps timeless dishonesty."[25]

Personally, I would credit the "final girl" with more subversive potential than Clover, particularly as regards female viewing pleasure, which remains rather secondary in Clover's account. But it is also important to remember that Clover's primary focus is the slasher film, out of which the contemporary, sleek serial killer movie emerged, and in which the boyish, desexualized "final girl" (typified by Jamie Lee Curtis in John Carpenter's *Halloween* [1978]) has transmuted into an attractive, professional woman, often obliged to field sexual advances that threaten her professional identity. While it is important to stress that the white female heroines of these films are not necessarily masculinized, an argument that would result in a rather circular logic (they are "figurative males" because of their narrative positioning and function), it is still the case that they are placed in positions of traditional patriarchal authority, as we see in such films as *The Silence of the Lambs, Copycat, Hannibal* (2001), *Blue Steel* (1990), *The Bone Collector* (1999), and *Taking Lives* (2004). While the problematic positioning of female heroines as representatives of the law limits these films' ability to engage in any comprehensive critique of patriarchy and its institutions, they are nonetheless able to tap into popular feminist discourses, rendering their female detectives less troubled by their proximity to the violence of the serial killer or by the anxieties of self-(non)distinction that plague their white male counterparts.

The Silence of the Lambs offers a particularly interesting example of the female detective. As Yvonne Tasker has noted, in accordance with generic conventions, Clarice is doubled with Buffalo Bill, since Clarice is also seeking self-transformation, though in terms of class (she wishes to transcend her working-class roots) rather than gender.[26] In her role as profiler, she also has to enter the psychic processes of the serial killer in order to comprehend his pathology, much as Will does in *Red Dragon*. However, as the generally positive feminist response to the film indicates, Clarice's very femaleness also allows her to access the positive identity of a feminist heroine protecting fellow women from the insanity of male violence. At the same time, as I noted above, white heterosexual male authority figures in the film are coded as at best ineffectual and at worst abusive, largely through the process of doubling. The repellent Dr. Chilton (Anthony Heald) and FBI chief Agent Crawford (Scott Glenn) are both likened to Lecter due to their obvious erotic interest in Clarice, which threatens her professional identity. Moreover, Chilton betrays Clarice for spurning his unsolicited advances, which Elizabeth Young regards as an implicit "literalization" of Miggs's "disgusting act" of throwing semen in Clarice's face, differing "in degree but not in kind."[27] Crawford, despite functioning as a substitute paternal figure, also uses Clarice as bait to capture Buffalo Bill, rendering her the sacrificial lamb of the title. Thus, the film "dramatiz[es] the violent asymmetry of gender relations."[28] Although Clarice finally kills Buffalo Bill to protect both herself and his latest female victim, women are represented as the *victims* of gender violence, not its agents.

Similar strategies are at work in *Copycat*, where Helen, who publishes and lectures on the topic of serial killing, is at one point accused of being complicit in glorifying serial violence. As with profilers, she also has the uncanny ability to comprehend the killer's motives and *modus operandi*. However, Helen is attacked by both of the film's killers in erotically charged scenes which deploy slasher style camerawork, orchestrating masochistic identification with the victim function in the manner that Clover suggests. In other words, the victim and aggressor roles are distinctly gendered in the film. Helen also joins forces with Monahan (whose white male partner is killed off remarkably perfunctorily in an unrelated case), forging a female alliance against (white) male violence.

African American male detectives also occupy positions of symbolic and moral authority in serial killer films such as *The Bone Collector*, which screens an alliance between African-American forensic expert Lincoln Rhyme (Denzel Washington) and a white female cop Amelia Donaghy (Angelina Jolie), and *Se7en* (David Fincher 1995). *Se7en* is a particularly interesting film in terms of its reworking of the dynamics of the bi-racial buddy movie typified by the *Lethal Weapon* series, in which Danny Glover embodied the protective, safe, aging family man played off against Mel Gibson's explosive, mentally unstable, rule-breaking, violent, but heroic cop. Despite *Se7en*'s African-American protagonist and its apocalyptic screening of the bleak, corrupt, decaying, postmodern city, race receives no mention throughout the film. Rather, as with *Lethal Weapon*, *Se7en* displaces racial difference onto the other differences that characterize its two detectives—William Somerset (Morgan Freeman), a jaded, resigned, intellectual African-American detective who is about to retire, and David Mills (Brad Pitt), a younger, impulsive, physical rather than cerebral white cop. Unlike Glover's character in *Lethal Weapon*, however, Somerset is by no means a secondary character, but rather leads the investigation, with the less experienced and impatient Mills left lagging behind. Both detectives, though, are doubled with the film's serial killer, John Doe (Kevin Spacey), but in differing ways that have implications for the film's representation of white masculinity. Somerset shares the disgust that Doe, a neo-conservative religious zealot, feels at the immoral and degenerate city that surrounds him. He also shares Doe's literary knowledge and erudition, which enables him to comprehend Doe's *modus operandi*, according to which each murder punishes a representative of one of the seven deadly sins, and each sin forms the means of the murder.[29] Mills, on the other hand, has to resort to Cliff's Notes. Somerset is also methodical and patient, unlike the impetuous Mills, who expressly states that he hates all the waiting around the job entails. But Somerset is markedly different from both John Doe and most detectives in the action and serial killer genre, since he refuses to regard violence, however punitive, as a means of transcendence or redemption. In fact, in his long career he has never pulled the trigger and he begs Mills not to kill Doe in the film's final scene. Whereas a reluctance to use his gun feminizes Bruce Willis's black buddy in *Die Hard* (1986) (until his remasculinization when, after contact with the rampaging white hero, he blows one of the bad guys away), in the case of Somerset it signifies restraint and prudence, and ensures that, unlike most detectives in the genre, he is never posited as being complicit in the brutality of the serial killer or the sanctioned, patriarchal violence of the police force.

The doubling between Mills and John Doe, on other hand, suggests that a common psychopathology underlies the sadomasochistic tendencies of both the serial killer and the rampaging white action hero. John Doe and Mills share a vision of a Manichean universe made up of good and evil, and both believe that punitive violence offers a path to regeneration. Indeed, as conventions dictate, Doe draws attention to their similarity by stating that Mills would like nothing better than to beat him senseless behind a locked door, and would act on this desire if there were no consequences. He is proved right when the film's climax has Mills shoot Doe in cold-blood in revenge for the murder of his wife and unborn child. Mills thus unwittingly fulfils Doe's spectacular plans to stage the final deadly sin of "wrath." Whereas in most action films the rampaging white hero emerges triumphant after killing or incarcerating the villain, the final scene of *Se7en* has Mills carted away by police, now occupying the wrong side of the law, guilty of the white male violence he was supposed to prevent.

The "Extra-Ordinarily Ordinary" Serial Killer

The anxieties about the lack of white heterosexual male distinction that I have outlined above are also played out in the figure of what Mark Seltzer, in his insightful study of real-life and fictional serial killers, *Serial Killers: Death and Life in America's Wound Culture* (1998), has dubbed "the abnormally normal serial killer," who, alongside the sexually deviant and "white trash" killer, populated cinematic screens in the '90s. Seltzer argues that the profile of the serial killer emerges as the very icon of *"the mass in person"*— "the species of person proper to a mass-mediated public culture." For example, he notes that it is commonplace for coverage of real-life serial killers to comment on their dead average looks (read white male), such as the court psychiatrists of Jeffrey Dahmer, who commented: "Dress him in a suit and he looks like ten other men."[30]

Seltzer's comments also apply to many serial killer films where the killer is "the man next door," literally in the case of *Blood Work*, since Noone resides in the boat next to Clint Eastwood's FBI profiler. Moreover, his very name—"no one"—self-consciously highlights the anonymity of the serial killer profile. In *Stepfather* (1987), the serial killer is even closer to home; he is a stepfather who moves from family to family, killing his new wife and stepchildren when they disappoint him. *Blue Steel*'s female cop, Megan Turner (Jamie Lee Curtis), unwittingly dates the film's psychokiller, while in *Resurrection* (1999), the killer masquerades as a profiler in whom Detective Prudhomme (Christopher Lambert) confides intimate details of the case. In *The Bone Collector*, the serial killer is a seemingly inconsequential medical technician, just one of the many faces that come and go in Rhyme's apartment. In all these cases, the killer's unremarkable appearance is afforded through the universal, anonymous status allotted to white middle-class masculinity. Indeed, one of the few films that screens an African-American serial killer, *Switchback* (Jeb Stuart 1997), reveals just how ingrained the profile of the extra-ordinarily ordinary white male serial killer is in cultural representations. Bob Goodall (Danny Glover) seems an unlikely suspect even in a genre that delights in unexpected twists and reversals, precisely because he does not fit the profile. Moreover, Danny Glover's star persona as a paternal, supportive African-American, cultivated primarily by his role as Mel Gibson's buddy in the *Lethal Weapon* series, also works against easy audience acceptance of his villainous status, with the title itself alerting us to the switching of generic roles.

For Seltzer, serial killing must be understood within the context of a "machine culture," characterized by mass-mediated societies, economic modes of mass production, serial consumption, and an intimate "identification with technology that seems to empty out the very category of the subject." Seltzer contends that in such a culture, attempts at self-origination, of which serial killing is a part, will always be marked by failure since self-invention has now been routinized and the self-made man has been absorbed into the indiscriminate mass. Even the "abnormal normality" of the killer is dependent on "primary imitation"—looking and acting like everyone else—which is "premised on the self as an empty category and as an effect of imitation and not its cause." Seltzer addresses the issue of the maleness of serial killing by suggesting that the serial killer channels "the withering of self-distinction . . . in the direction of a distinctively gendered violence," which "produces the torn and leaking and opened body—the un-male body—as its 'proof.'"[31] Implicit in his argument is also the fact that new modes of work, the demands of consumerism, and technologies of simulation impinge particularly on the male subject, since the association of masculinity with productivity and self-definition is violated. However, he does not address the issue of the race of the serial killer profile, with whiteness assuming its privileged position of representing the dominant norm. What interests me, though, is how concerns about "machine culture" and the failures of identity are indexed in contemporary cinema through images of the serial killer, whose emptiness and lack of self-distinction are inextricable from his white male status.

One noteworthy example is the virtual reality fantasy, *Virtuosity* (Brett Leonard 1995), which features a computer program made up of an identikit of the personalities of nearly 200 serial killers, which is not surprisingly (virtually) embodied by a white male (Russell Crowe). His two-dimensionality is played off against the "surplus symbolic value"[32] awarded to his passionate, grounded, African-American adversary (Denzel Washington), a victim of racist abuse in the prison in which he has been incarcerated. *Virtuosity* thus conflates the serial killer with the cybersubject, who, I argued in chapter 4, is most often represented by images of hypernormative white men, in order to explore anxieties about the disembodiment and depthlessness of virtual culture, as well as the implied sterility of "ordinary" masculinity.

American Psycho (Mary Harron 2000), based on Bret Easton Ellis's bitingly satirical novel, also puts the figure of the vacuous serial killer to transactional use, deploying it to explore (and exploit) the horrors of patriarchal, capitalist culture, and the loss of the (Baudrillardian) real. Set in '80s America, and comprising an acerbic critique of commodity culture, the film, like the book, trades on analogies between serial consumerism and serial killing through its serial killer protagonist, Patrick Bateman (Christian Bale), a monstrous incarnation of a yuppie, the diametrical opposite of "white trash."[33] Bateman's choice of predominately female victims also suggests complicity between patriarchy and capitalism, with his wealth allowing him to buy victims, such as the prostitute he lures into his home, and to evade capture because of the invisibility his moneyed white heterosexual male status affords him.[34]

As with the novel, Bateman is the film's narrator, following a trend of making the serial killer uncannily familiar that films such as *Henry: Portrait of a Serial Killer* (1986), *Natural Born Killers*, and *Man Bites Dog* (1991) have also deployed, though his dully delivered voiceover works more to portray his inner-emptiness and chilling postmodern *ennui* than render him psychologically complex. For instance, when Bateman is getting ready for work, his voiceover lists his beauty routine, including a monotonous inventory of brand products. As he

applies a facemask that, combined with hard lighting and Christian Bale's unnervingly affectless performance, renders his face uncannily mannequin-like, he
informs us in a voiceover: "There is an idea of Patrick Bateman. Some kind of
abstraction. But there is no real me. Only an identity. Something illusory. . . . I
am simply not there." While this lack of affect could be explained in psychoanalytic discourse as a self-protective gesture that enables him to avoid feeling at all
in order to ward off trauma, in the terms of the film itself, this emptiness is represented as inextricable from the hyperreal culture he inhabits. Bateman is pure
simulacrum, a clichéd recycling of previous screen serial killers, his very name
(a play on Norman Bates) rendering him nothing but a copy of a copy. His monstrous need to penetrate and dissect the bodies of his victims seems to function
as a means of puncturing the tyranny of the image, and in the case of female
victims, serves to reaffirm sexual difference and secure male self-distinction in
the manner Seltzer suggests.

That Bateman is immersed in hyperreality is represented through Harron's
postmodern stylistics, such as obvious pastiches of the slasher film, complete
with chainsaw, dramatic music, and masochistic identification with the female
victim function. The murder of his rival Paul Allen (Jared Leto) (for having a
better business card!) is also screened in an ultra-stylized mode that prevents
easy identification and highlights its status as pure performance. As Allen sits on
the sofa, Bateman dons a plastic raincoat and dances around the room to the '80s
pop hit "It's Hip to Be Square" by Huey Lewis and the News, whose banal lyrics
Bateman deconstructs as an insightful comment on the pleasures of conformity.
With this upbeat pop song as soundtrack, the film deploys a Tarantino-
influenced, unnerving mixing of humor and violence, though the actual murder
is performed off-screen, shifting attention to Bateman's sterility and the culture
that produced him. Nonetheless, the film was still critiqued for glorifying the
violence of the serial killer by critics who felt that Harron's parodic strategies
functioned as an act of self-legitimization, allowing audiences to enjoy consuming celluloid violence in a guilt-free mode. At the same time, though, these
strategies simultaneously communicate the "waning of affect" and depthlessness
that Fredric Jameson has argued is intrinsic to postmodern culture, and that the
film posits as constitutive of moneyed white heterosexual masculinity.[35]

In keeping with this hyperreal mode, the film ends with the suggestion that
Bateman's murders are merely a figment of his warped imagination. As with
Fight Club, it is implied that we have been anchored into the perverse fantasy
life of an unreliable narrator who views violence as the only means available for
men to break the chains of an oppressive, feminizing commodity culture in
which masculinity circulates as an image. Whether the murders that unfold as
real on screen actually happened or not, then, is a moot point, as the film questions our ability to separate not only people from commodities, but also violence
from its representation.

Another such example of the "abnormally normal" serial killer can be found
in David Fincher's apocalyptic *Se7en*. Doe's appearance is overdeterminedly

average, and, and, as Richard Dyer notes, until he gives himself up, skillful camera-work, lighting, and editing render him faceless, "a silhouette of a pork pie hat and three-quarter length mac."[36] On handing himself in at a train station, he even has to shout several times before detectives Somerset and Mills take notice, and even then his face is lost in the crowd. Kevin Spacey's performance is also the epitome of deadpan, his face expressionless except for the odd ironic smile, and his lines delivered with monotone, colorless precision.[37] Somerset acutely observes that the killer has become "John Doe" by choice. Officially he does not exist: he has no bank records, no social security number, no employment records, and even cuts off the skin on his fingertips to avoid leaving fingerprints. He is both Everyman and no man. Thus, as Dyer argues, on the one hand, Doe does not fit commonplace serial killer profiles (victim of child abuse, mentally disturbed, sexually non-normative) and even mobilizes those discourses to throw police when he leaves behind the fingerprints of his next victim, who perfectly fits the FBI identikit profile. Yet, on the other hand, he represents other aspects of the profile purely by being an anonymous white male.[38] But if it is the privilege of white masculinity to be unremarkable, the casting of Morgan Freeman as Somerset certainly works to make Doe's whiteness, and, by extension, the whiteness of serial killing, more visible, much like Denzel Washington's blackness in *The Bone Collector*.

Of course, John Doe's very ordinariness is the means by which he can escape suspicion on the route to becoming utterly extraordinary, immortalized by his intricately staged murders that have to enter the public realm if his religious crusade is to have its desired results. Killing for Doe is inextricably bound up in the public sphere, even understood as a profession that bestows on him an identity that he lacks but desperately craves: "I am not special. I've never been exceptional. This is though. What I'm doing. . . . My work." In this respect, he mirrors the confessions of several real-life serial killers. Ted Bundy, for instance, referred to his serial rapes and murders as his "professional job," suggesting that his sense of masculinity was profoundly dependent on being a productive worker.[39] Similarly, British serial killer Dennis Nilsen posited his killings as a "career," imagining his arrest at retirement age: "If I had been arrested at sixty-five years of age there might have been thousands of bodies behind me."[40]

Doe's attempts to literalize the seven deadly sins are indicative of the same failure of distance from representation that marks many other '90s serial killers in films that screen what Seltzer terms "the *contagious* relation of the subject to imitation, simulation, or identification, such that identification brings the subject, and the subject's desires, into being, and not the other way round."[41] For instance, whereas Norman Bates killed because he had become m/other, Buffalo Bill kills in order to become other: it is his desperate need for female identity that drives him to kill. Serial killing thus seems to act "in the service of the fantasy" rather than vice versa.[42] In *Taking Lives* the serial killer also kills in order to adopt the identity of his victims, a response to the trauma of being the twin brother his mother loved least, the suggestion being not only that he internalized his mother's antipathy, but also that being a twin rendered self-distinction a difficult affair. In *Red Dragon*, Dolarhyde kills in an act of identification with Blake's empowering image of "The Great Red Dragon," which forms a punishing superego, goading him to kill. Dolarhyde chooses his victims from family movies developed in the photo lab where he works. Thus, as Seltzer notes of Thomas Harris's novel, on which the film is based, Dolarhyde identifies with "mass reproduction generally," "literaliz[ing] the cannibalistic devouring of other people as objects of consumption."[43]

Copycat's Foley also kills solely to gain an identity, copycatting the *modus operandi*, the victims, and crime scenes of famous serial killers that he learnt about through the popular media. In other words, Foley has fully identified with technologies of reproduction, sharing their modes of seriality and simulation, even as the film intimates that it is those very processes that stripped him of identity in the first place. As with *Se7en*, *Copycat* takes pains to empty out its serial killer's identity through his dead average appearance, though in this case, Helen's framing lecture works to make his maleness and whiteness visible in retrospect. Our first glimpses of Foley render him inconsequential: he is one of the men asked to stand up during Helen's lecture, and then he later greets a cop at the police station. In both cases his image is lost in a sea of bodies and his identity is only apparent on second viewing. His first appearance coded as the killer is faceless—just a brief close-up of his glasses that reflect back the image of his computer screen. Moreover, Foley is utterly chameleon-like. Before his dominant, invalid wife/girlfriend, he is an awkward, sexually repressed, boyish figure. Then, when she gives him permission to return to his computer, his expression immediately changes into a smirk as he skips Norman Bates-like down the stairs. As he enters his gothic basement, the mobile camera lingers on the photographs and newspapers clippings of his crimes that he has plastered on the wall. Then, an oddly low-positioned camera trains on Foley donning a doctor's white coat, before panning right to reveal the shocking sight of a woman's legs, and then her body strapped to a bed, with a plastic bag taped to her head, slowly asphyxiating her. As Foley punctures a hole in the bag to enable the woman a few panicked gasps of breath, he assumes the identity of a doctor, and just as he is about to inject her, with an eerily tender bedside manner informs her, "this is going to hurt a little bit, I'm afraid." Like the white male who falsely confesses to the first murder in a desperate bid for recognition, Foley also lacks a coherent sense of self.

This desire for recognition is also evident in the sheer number of screen serial killers who save press clippings or accounts of their crimes (*Copycat, Red Dragon, Se7en, The Silence of the Lambs*), or, more usually, videotape their murders (*Henry: Portrait of a Serial Killer, American Psycho, Copycat, The Cell, Natural Born Killers*), the latter building on the knowing exploration of the pleasures of horror spectatorship first screened in Michael Powell's inaugural, metacinematic *Peeping Tom*, which implicated the spectator in Mark's murderous, white male gaze. Moreover, the genre plays into popular understandings of serial killing as "a symptom of a society in which worth is measured in terms of fame."[44] In other words, it is suggested that it is not enough for these serial killers simply to kill; killing must be performed, witnessed, reproduced, and made spectacle for an imagined external other. Serial killing is thus represented as a response to "the killer's panic about the failure of self-distinction in the mass," as Seltzer puts it[45]—a failure that is posited as predominately a white male predicament.

In this chapter, I have not attempted to engage with the aetiology of real life serial killers, but rather to trace some of the transactional uses to which representations of white masculinity are put in the contemporary serial killer movie. Films with sexually deviant or "white trash" serial killers find ways to demonize those categories *within* white masculinity that threaten it with contamination, though the process of othering is never totalizing and can always yield unexpected instabilities. Those films, on the other hand, that represent the serial killer as hypernormative are more complex, using the figure of the vacuous, affectless white male serial killer to explore contemporary Western anxieties about mass-mediated, hyperreal, consumerist society, as well as airing concerns about the implied emptiness of white heterosexual masculinity. At the same time, it is important to remember that it is precisely because white heterosexual masculinity can stand as the default subjectivity that these killers can represent *general* anxieties; that is, at the very moment that the whiteness and maleness of serial killing are being highlighted, the gendered and raced specificity of serial killing can then be subsumed by broader concerns about postmodern culture and society. This underscores the ongoing ability of contemporary white heterosexual men to represent themselves as both everyman and no man, as both ordinary and extra-ordinary—a violation of binary oppositions that only an identity with the privilege of acting as the universal term can wield.

Notes

1. Christopher Sharrett, introduction to *Mythologies of Violence in Postmodern Media*, ed. Christopher Sharrett (Detroit: Wayne State University Press, 1999), 13.

2. Richard Dyer, *Seven*, BFI Modern Classics (London: BFI, 1999), 38.

3. Mark Seltzer, *Serial Killers: Death and Life in America's Wound Culture* (New York: Routledge, 1998), 9.

4. Carol Clover, *Men, Women and Chainsaws: Gender in the Modern Horror Film* (London: BFI, 1992), 47.

5. Judith Halberstam, *Skin Shows: Gothic Horror and the Technology of Monsters* (Durham, NC: Duke University Press, 1995), 168.

6. Laura Mulvey, "Visual Pleasure and Narrative Cinema," in *Visual and Other Pleasures* (Houndmills, Basingstoke: Macmillan, 1989), 14-26.

7. Halberstam, *Skin Shows*, 175.

8. For a summary of reviewers' discussions of the oppositions installed between Lecter and Buffalo Bill, see Janet Staiger, "Taboos and Totems: Cultural Meanings of

The Silence of the Lambs," in *Film Theory Goes to the Movies,* ed. Ava Preacher Collins, Jim Collins, and Hilary Radner (New York: Routledge, 1993), 142-54.

9. Staiger, "Taboos and Totems," 142.

10. Elizabeth Young, "*The Silence of the Lambs* and the Flaying of Feminist Theory," *Camera Obscura: A Journal of Feminism and Film Theory* 27 (1991): 19.

11. Yvonne Tasker, *The Silence of the Lambs,* BFI Modern Classics (London: BFI, 2000), 10.

12. Tasker, *The Silence of the Lambs,* 69.

13. Staiger, "Taboos and Totems," 150.

14. Young, "*The Silence of the Lambs* and the Flaying of Feminist Theory," 20.

15. Annalee Newitz and Matthew Wray, "What Is 'White Trash'? Stereotypes and Economic Conditions of Poor Whites in the United States," in *Whiteness: A Critical Reader,* ed. Michael Hill (New York: New York University Press, 1997), 169.

16. Clover, *Men, Women and Chainsaws,* 135n21.

17. Annalee Newitz, "White Savagery and Humiliation, or a New Racial Consciousness in the Media," in *White Trash: Race and Class in America,* ed. Matthew Wray and Annalee Newitz (New York: Routledge, 1997), 139-44.

18. Newitz and Wray, "What Is 'White Trash'?" 169.

19. Richard Slotkin, *Regeneration through Violence: The Mythology of the American Frontier, 1600-1860* (New York: HarperPerennial, 1996).

20. Sally Robinson, *Marked Men: White Masculinity in Crisis* (New York: Columbia University Press, 2000), 3.

21. Yvonne Tasker, *Working Girls: Gender and Sexuality in Popular Cinema* (London: Routledge, 1998), 105.

22. Tasker, *Working Girls,* 105.

23. Tasker, *Working Girls,* 105.

24. Jude Davies and Carol R. Smith, *Gender, Ethnicity and Sexuality in Contemporary American Film* (Edinburgh: Keele University Press, 1997), 3.

25. Clover, *Men, Women and Chainsaws,* 60, 40, 18, 60, 53.

26. Tasker, *Working Girls,* 106.

27. Young, "*The Silence of the Lambs* and the Flaying of Feminist Theory," 10-11.

28. Young, "*The Silence of the Lambs* and the Flaying of Feminist Theory," 11.

29. Dyer, *Seven,* 11.

30. Seltzer, *Serial Killers,* 9, 7, 10.

31. Seltzer, *Serial Killers,* 20, 219, 68, 144.

32. Michael Rogin, "Blackface, White Noise: The Jewish Jazz Singer Finds His Voice," *Critical Inquiry* 18, no. 3 (1992): 417.

33. Seltzer, *Serial Killers,* 65.

34. Barry Keith Grant, "American Psycho/sis: The Pure Products of America Go Crazy," in *Mythologies of Violence in Postmodern Media,* ed. Christopher Sharrett (Detroit: Wayne State University Press, 1999), 27.

35. Fredric Jameson, *Postmodernism, or, The Cultural Logic of Late Capitalism* (London: Verso, 1991), 10.

36. Dyer, *Seven,* 41.

37. Dyer, *Seven,* 45.

38. Dyer, *Seven,* 35, 39.

39. Newitz, Annalee, "Serial Killers, True Crime, and Economic Performance Anxiety," in *Mythologies of Violence in Postmodern Media,* ed. Christopher Sharrett (Detroit: Wayne State University Press, 1999), 69.

40. Seltzer, *Serial Killers*, 18-19.
41. Seltzer, *Serial Killers*, 65.
42. Seltzer, *Serial Killers*, 137.
43. Seltzer, *Serial Killers*, 114.
44. Richard Dyer, "Kill and Kill Again," in *Action/Spectacle Cinema: A Sight and Sound Reader*, ed. José Arroyo (London: BFI, 2000), 146.
45. Seltzer, *Serial Killers*, 135.

Afterword

Frank A. Cappello's *He Was a Quiet Man* (2007) opens with the protagonist, Bob Maconel (Christian Slater), informing us in a voiceover: "It was easier in the past. A man knew what it was to be a man. You stood up for the things that were wrong. You had the right to do so. You were expected to do so." Immediately, then, the film self-consciously positions itself in the discourse of the "angry white male," as Bob laments the loss of an imagined, primal masculinity. The blame, Bob states, can be put on the increased bureaucratization (and implied feminization) of society; with lawyers now acting as our shepherds, he states, a man can no longer fight for what is right. Women, not surprisingly, are also deemed responsible for (white) male disenfranchisement: "Woman demanded equality and she got it. Not by getting everything the man had, but by the man being castrated in the form of the woman." Casting himself as an avenging hero, who must sacrifice the herd to cure the disease, as he puts it, and stand up against injustice like a "real man," Bob fantasizes about blowing away his colleagues, and saving the last bullet for himself.

He Was a Quiet Man foregrounds its overt intertextual dialogue with the two definitive '90s films screening white male angst—*Falling Down* (1993) and *Fight Club* (1999). Most obviously, as soon as the opening credits end, the film explicitly borrows the opening shot of *Falling Down*: the screen is filled with an extreme close-up of Bob's bespectacled eyes, and then an equally extreme close-up of his mouth, as his voiceover explains which bullet is designated for which co-worker. As with Michael Douglas in *Falling Down*, Christian Slater, who is also famed for his cocky, arrogant characters, is cast against type, playing an office drone, an invisible cog in a corporate machine. His appearance is equally as nerdy: like D-FENS, Bob wears old-fashioned steel-rimmed glasses, short-sleeved shirts, and is always dressed in a shirt and tie. As well as having thinning hair, a conventional moustache, yellowing, uneven teeth, a slight paunch, and a pasty complexion, many shots of Bob also seem to empty him out of color. Like D-FENS, Bob is also established as a victim figure early on in the film, subject to relentless office bullying by male executives and ungrounded accusations of sexual harassment by the castrating Paula (Sascha Knopf). However, as with D-FENS, we know that Bob's rage will not remain unchecked.

The opening voiceover also obviously begs comparisons with *Fight Club*, not only due to Slater's muted, monotone delivery, but also its content, most notably the blame placed on an allegedly feminized society for the loss of a mythical, original, unified masculinity. *He Was a Quiet Man* also shares *Fight Club*'s dark vision of male alienation in the contemporary workplace, evoked through the isolating work cubicles, the mundane, repetitive, unskilled work that Bob is assigned, as well as some rather surreal camerawork, such as oddly-angled close-ups of Bob's face gliding through the brightly lit, sterile office space—shots which seem to sever Bob totally from his environment. The opening shot of *Fight Club* is also invoked when the camera seems to disappear down Bob's ear hole, taking us deep inside the angst-ridden white male psyche. As with *Fight Club*, *He Was a Quiet Man* also locks the spectator into the insular, insane world of its protagonist, though the latter makes it clear from the beginning that Bob's psychic discontent has reached pathological proportions. Most obviously, when Bob returns to his drab, run-down home, having once again lost the courage to carry out his plans, not only does the camera linger on the laminated versions of suicide notes that Bob has stuck on his fridge, but also Bob enters into dialogue with one of his fish (computer-generated), who taunts him for "chickening out" once again. The film is equally as knowledgeable about male hysteria as *Fight Club*, with the fish reminding Bob that he is merely a psychic projection. As with *Fight Club*, the film also screens events that we later learn only occur in Bob's perverse imagination. For instance, when Bob envisages blowing up his office block with the toy black box, complete with red button, that he brings to work with him inside his packed lunch box, the explosion is initially filmed as if it really happened, before being reframed as pure fantasy.

The film associates profound alienation with the image of a depleted "ordinary" white male a second time when, just as Bob is finally pushed to act by a particularly vicious spate of office bullying, another white male colleague beats him to the job, sparing Bob only because Bob is even "lamer" than he is. When Bob kills the shooter to save the wounded Vanessa (Elisha Cuthbert), whom he has always worshipped from afar, Bob unexpectedly becomes the office hero. No longer invisible or insignificant, he is awarded an executive position, is embraced by his macho colleagues, and also embarks on an at times touching, at times rather disturbing, relationship of co-dependency with Vanessa, who was left a paraplegic by the shooting. Similar to *Fight Club*, however, the film we have watched thus far, filtered through the unreliable perspective of the deranged protagonist, is abruptly undercut when the ending of the film implies that these events unfolded purely in Bob's imagination. The shooting scene is unexpectedly rescreened from a different perspective, this time showing Bob turning the gun on himself in a desperate bid to be noticed, primarily by Vanessa. His suicide note forms the final voiceover: "You may ask why I did what I did. But what choice did you give me? How else could I get your attention? All I wanted was to exist in your world. Just one person that would take time to actually see me and help me find a way out." The films ends as his female neighbor, who thought he had just moved into the neighborhood, even though he had actually lived there for five years, tells a reporter, "He was a quiet man."

Released 15 years after *Falling Down, He Was a Quiet Man* illustrates that the "angry white male" figure remains a compelling media icon, one that still resonates with cultural and social relevance. Indeed, this film raises many of the issues concerning white heterosexual masculinity that I have explored throughout this book. Most importantly, it is yet another contemporary film which suggests that embodying the universal identity can entail as many anxieties as privileges. This is particularly the case for a lower-middle class male like Bob, whose economic status means that he is unable to secure the advantages that his gender and skin color supposedly entail. Moreover, as we have seen throughout this book, when white heterosexual masculinity is made visible as a distinctly raced, gendered, and sexualized identity, as it is in this film through overdetermined representations of white male hypernormativity, it is usually achieved through a narrative of white male victimization. In other words, the marking of white heterosexual masculinity as a category is most often represented as trauma, since it is suggestive of a loss of universality and concomitant power.[1] *He Was a Quiet Man* is also exemplary of the representational trend I have traced of white heterosexual masculinity being represented as a sterile, depleted, vacuous identity, one lacking positive and/or specific content, which I have attributed to the exclusion of straight white men from the positive investment in minoritized identity that is a characteristic of identity politics and the postmodern celebration of difference. As with the uncannily uniform agents in *The Matrix*, or the "extraordinarily ordinary" serial killers I discussed in the previous chapter, *He Was a Quiet Man* also uses the figure of the washed-out, anonymous white male to explore concerns about the loss of productivity and agency in the media-saturated, increasingly virtualized, alienating society of late capitalism. Violence is also seen by Bob, as it is by numerous screen serial killers, as well as Tyler in *Fight Club*, as a means of puncturing the tyranny of the hyperreal, of reestablishing male autonomy, of breaking the shackles of a feminized society, of becoming "real" men again. In these films, similar to Tarantino's gangster films, white male aggression also erupts when white heterosexual masculinity is posited as precariously unstable or vacuous, with violence providing the means by which the white male can shore up the boundaries of his identity and rescue himself from a numbing lack of self-distinction. Unlike the action adventure film, however, Bob's violence does not bring about redemption or regeneration; indeed, Bob's journey from an "ordinary" to "extra-ordinary" male exists purely in his imagination, much like the narrator's fantasy of rephallicization in *Fight Club*.

In *He Was a Quiet Man*, as with most films that screen the "angry white male" figure, it is women that pose the main threat to white male hegemony. Vanessa is only approachable once she is rendered helpless (and equally wounded as the psychically damaged Bob, the film suggests), though Bob's happiness soon subsides when the paranoid fear that she will leave him when she recovers sets in. Paula, on the other hand, a caricature of the office bitch, is a menacing figure throughout. When she accuses Bob of sexual harassment, her assertion that "they have rules to protect women from men like you" also implies that the legal cards are stacked in women's favor, highly reminiscent of Meredith's misuse of feminist-inspired legislation in *Disclosure* (1994). After seducing Bob when he becomes a top executive, Paula later taunts him about his sexual performance and his penis size. In this respect, the film also engages with the body anxieties that I discussed in chapter 3, anxieties that are increasingly foregrounded in popular films. Bob's rather flabby midriff is also suggestive of a non-productive male body, one symbolically feminized, much like the bodies of Gary's stripping crew in *The Full Monty*.

What is noticeably absent in *He Was a Quiet Man* is the perceived threat posed to the "angry white male" by people of color and homosexuals—a threat that *Falling Down*, for instance, makes apparent. In part, this can be explained by the film's desire to posit Bob as an everyman character—racist or homophobic sentiments always risk tarnishing the "angry white male" with the specter of fascism. Accusations that men have lost out to women, on the other hand, would seem to be more culturally sanctioned, and, as we have seen, are openly expressed in films such as *Disclosure*, *Fight Club*, and *The Full Monty*. The absence of people of color in this film also adds to the cultural association of whiteness with sterility, non-existence, and death.[2]

While *He Was a Quiet Man* suggests that there is still much mileage to be made out of the image of "(white) masculinity in crisis" in popular films, it also shows that this rather tired image is subject to perpetual revisions. For instance, *He Was a Quiet Man* not only self-consciously foregrounds its intertextual references to preceding films in this tradition, such as *Taxi Driver* (1976), *Brazil* (1985), and *Falling Down*, but also, like *Fight Club*, deploys a dark, degree-zero mode, which opens up room for critical intervention on the part of the spectator by rendering identification with the white male protagonist problematic. Moreover, as I have attempted to stress throughout this book, popular cinematic representations of white heterosexual masculinity are never monolithic; rather, a diversity of straight white masculinities are offered on the big screen, with the figure of the angsty white male just one of the many manifestations. This diversity, as well as the disproportionate screen space that white men continue to command in popular cinema, has meant that this book has only been able to trace what I consider the most interesting trends in popular cinematic representations of white heterosexual masculinity, in particular those relating to its contested positioning as the "ordinary" identity, and the anxieties, as well as advantages, that this positioning would seem to entail. For this reason, I would like to close by suggesting avenues for future research into this topic.

One such area, which this book has touched on, but which requires substantial development, is the impact of 9/11, along with the subsequent wars in Afghanistan and Iraq, on cinematic representations of white heterosexual men. As we have seen, the white male body often stands in for the national body in popular films, and it would be interesting to examine whether representations of the "war on terror" repeat the trajectory of victimization and remasculinization evident in cultural representations of the Vietnam War.[3] At the same time, it is also imperative to think through the extent to which women and people of color, especially African-American men, are being called upon to represent nation in the light of films such as *Deep Impact* (1998), which stars Morgan Freeman as U.S. President, or the remake of *The Manchurian Candidate* (2004), where the war-damaged veteran is played by Denzel Washington. Concerns about the "war on terror" may also be mediated through other conflicts, be it epic films, which unfold in mythical or past settings, or rampage films, such as *Rambo* (2008), which is set in Burma. Both the epic film and rampage film are also dominated by avenging white men. These films need also be set against more critical treatments of U.S. interventions, often expressed through narratives of "(white) masculinity in crisis," such as *Jarhead* (2005) or *In the Valley of Elah* (2007). The latter film, for instance, directed by Paul Haggis, examines the Iraq War through the lens of a father-son melodrama. Retired military office Hank Deerfield (Tommy Lee Jones) is forced to reassess his long-held traditional beliefs when his son goes missing after a stint in Iraq. Once his son's body is found, Hank requires the help of a white female police officer, played by Charlize Theron, to track down his son's killers, who, it later turns out, are his son's war-traumatized buddies. It also transpires that his son was also mentally unhinged, haunted by the horrendous acts he committed in Iraq. Hank is forced to reevaluate not only his sexisms and racisms (he wrongly accuses a Mexican-American of killing his son), but also his unquestioning patriotism, as conveyed in the rather heavy-handed final scene when he deliberately hangs up the U.S. flag upside-down to signal a nation in distress. Nonetheless, as with the generation of films critical of Vietnam, such as *Platoon* (1986) and *Born on the Fourth of July* (1989), the trauma of the war is largely depicted as a white male tragedy, with little narrative space allotted to the suffering endured by non-U.S. citizens.

Moreover, in the light of the Islamophobia unleashed by 9/11, as well as the influence wielded by Evangelicalism on the political sphere under the George W. Bush administration, another interesting line of inquiry would be an analysis of how religion impacts on cinematic representations of "ordinary" men in a post-9/11 era. One area worthy of attention is the way religion, in particular Christian discourse, is used to secure white male normativity. It is also important to address the ways in which religion cuts across figurations of white heterosexual masculinity, revealing its internal differences and diversities.

Age, a much neglected area in studies of filmic identities, this present book included, is another category that traverses white heterosexual masculinity. For example, contemporary popular cinema has witnessed an array of aging white male stars appearing in narratives of "(white) masculinity in crisis," narratives that often conclude, not unsurprisingly, with white male redemption. Here I am thinking of Clint Eastwood as an aging CIA agent in *In the Line of Fire* (1993) or as a heart transplant patient in *Blood Work* (2002), Jack Nicholson in *The Pledge* (2001), *About Schmidt* (2002), or the comedy in which he learns to give in gracefully to the ageing process, *Something's Gotta Give* (2003), Al Pacino playing older men losing their professional status in *Insomnia* (2002) and *People I Know* (2002), Tommy Lee Jones's disillusioned veteran in *In the Valley of Elah*, and, of course, Sylvester Stallone's decision to resurrect the roles that made him a star with *Rocky Balboa* (2006) and *Rambo* (2008).

The role played by new technologies in cinematic representations of straight white masculinities also warrants substantial research. This book has touched on the innovative camerawork work and digital sequences deployed in stylistically experimental films such as *Fight Club*, as well as suggesting that new viewing technologies will affect our consumption of filmic masculinities, such as the ability to freeze-frame the male body and work against the pull of narrative. But it would also be interesting to explore the impact of computer-generated imagery on representations of gender and race in popular films. This question is particularly pertinent in the light of the resurgence of the epic genre—a genre that obviously showcases the latest special effects. As I suggested in chapter 3, the special effect scenes deployed in the battle scenes of films such as *The Lord of the Rings* (2001) or *Troy* (2004), where battles are carried out almost exclusively between white men, somewhat paradoxically serve to reaffirm the values of white male physicality, screening the nostalgic return to a unified, primal, warrior masculinity. Computer-generated imagery also impacts on representations of white male bodies in films such as Zack Snyder's *300* (2006), which combines live action with computer-generated effects in an attempt to offer a visually faithful filmic rendition of Frank Miller's graphic novel. The film surfeits in a sea of near identical, exaggerated, sculptured, stylized, bronzed torsos that embody the Hellenic ideal, but that no "ordinary" male could approximate.

Of course, writing about such contemporary texts is always accompanied by the anxiety that one is lagging behind the object of inquiry, with every new film released adding to the plethora of representations of white heterosexual masculinities that continually shift in response to social, cultural, economic, and political change. What this anxiety reveals, of course, is that identities are neither static nor monolithic, a fact that points to the need for ongoing work on popular cinematic representations of "ordinary" straight white men, who are, at the same time, always also extra-ordinary as well.

Notes

1. Sally Robinson, *Marked Men: White Masculinity in Crisis* (New York: Columbia University Press, 2000).
2. Richard Dyer, *The Matter of Images: Essays on Representation* (London: Routledge, 1993), 141.
3. Susan Jeffords, *The Remasculinization of America: Gender and the Vietnam War* (Bloomington: Indiana University Press, 1989).

Bibliography

Aaron, Michele. "New Queer Cinema: An Introduction." In *New Queer Cinema: A Critical Reader*, edited by Michele Aaron, 3-14. Edinburgh: Edinburgh University Press, 2004.

——. "New Queer Spectator." In *New Queer Cinema: A Critical Reader*, edited by Michele Aaron, 187-200. Edinburgh: Edinburgh University Press, 2004.

——. "Pass/Fail." *Screen* 41, no. 1 (2001): 92-96.

Allen, Jamie. "*Boys Don't Cry*: Filmmaker Saw Past Violence to Love." *CNN.com*, October 22, 1999. http://www.cnn.com/SHOWBIZ/Movies/9910/22/boys.dont.cry (accessed April 4, 2004).

Allen, Theodore W. *The Invention of the White Race*. Vol. 1, *Racial Oppression and Social Control*. London: Verso, 1994.

Appiah, K. Anthony. "'No Bad Nigger': Blacks as the Ethical Principle in the Movies." In *Media Spectacles*, edited by Marjorie Garber, Jann Matlock, and Rebecca L. Walkowitz, 77-90. New York: Routledge, 1993.

Baker, Monika. "The Missing Monty." *Black Filmmaker* 1, no. 2 (1998): 14.

Baldwin, James. *Nobody Knows My Name: More Notes of a Native Son*. London: Corgi, 1973.

Balsamo, Anne. "Forms of Technological Embodiment: Reading the Body in Contemporary Culture." In *Cyberspace/Cyberbodies/Cyberpunk*, edited by Mike Featherstone and Roger Burrows, 215-37. London: Sage, 1995.

Bamshad, Michael J., and Steve E. Olson. "Does Race Exist?" *Scientific American.Com*, November 10, 2003. http://www.sciam.com/article.cfm?id=does-race-exist (accessed July 2, 2004).

Baudrillard, Jean. *Simulacra and Simulations*. Translated by Sheila Faria Glaser. Michigan: The University of Michigan Press, 1994.

Beavers, Herman. "'The Cool Pose': Intersectionality, Masculinity, and Quiescence in the Comedy and Films of Richard Pryor and Eddie Murphy." In *Race and the Subject of Masculinities*, edited by Harry Stecopoulos and Michael Uebel, 253-85. Durham, NC: Duke University Press, 1997.

Bergstrom, Janet, and Mary Anne Doane, eds. "The Spectatrix." Special issue, *Camera Obscura: A Journal of Feminism and Film Theory* 20-21 (1989).

Bhabha, Homi. "Of Mimicry and Man: The Ambivalence of Colonial Discourse." *October* 28 (1984): 125-33.

Bly, Robert. *Iron John: A Book about Men*. Reading, MA: Addison-Wesley, 1990.

256   Bibliography

Boose, Lynda. "Techno-Muscularity and the 'Boy Eternal': From the Quagmire to the Gulf." In *Cultures of United States Imperialism*, edited by Amy Kaplan and Donald E. Pease, 581-616. Durham, NC: Duke University Press, 1993.

Bordo, Susan. *The Flight to Objectivity: Essays on Cartesianism and Culture*. Albany: The State University of New York Press, 1987.

———. *The Male Body: A New Look at Men in Public and Private*. New York: Farrar, Straus, and Giroux, 1999.

Boyd, Todd. "Tarantino's Mantra?" *Chicago Tribune*, November 6, 1994.

Boyle, Karen. "New Man, Old Brutalisms? Reconstructing a Violent History in *Forrest Gump*." *Scope: An Online Journal of Film Studies* (December 2001). http://www.scope.nottingham.ac.uk/article.php?issue=dec2001&id=280&section=article (accessed June 10, 2004).

Bozza, Anthony. *Whatever You Say I Am: The Life and Times of Eminem*. London: Corgi, 2003.

Braidotti, Rosi. *Metamorphoses: Towards a Materialist Theory of Becoming*. Cambridge, UK: Polity/Blackwell, 2002.

———. *Nomadic Subjects: Embodiment and Sexual Difference in Contemporary Feminist Theory*. New York: Columbia University Press, 1994.

Braidotti, Rosi, with Judith Butler. "Feminism by Any Other Name." *Differences: A Journal of Feminist Cultural Studies* 6, no. 2-3 (1994): 27-61.

Brody, Jennifer Devere. "Boys Do Cry: Screening History's White Lies." *Screen* 43, no. 1 (2001): 91-96.

Bruzzi, Stella. *Bringing Up Daddy: Fatherhood and Masculinity in Post-War Hollywood*. London: BFI, 2005.

———. *Undressing Cinema: Clothing and Identity in the Movies*. London: Routledge, 1997.

Bukatman, Scott. *Terminal Identity: The Virtual Subject in Postmodern Science Fiction*. Durham, NC: Duke University Press, 1993.

Butler, Judith. *Bodies That Matter: On the Discursive Limits of "Sex."* New York: Routledge, 1993.

———. "Endangered/Endangering: Schematic Racism and White Paranoia." In *Reading Rodney King, Reading Urban Uprising*, edited by Robert Gooding-Williams, 15-22. New York: Routledge, 1993.

———. *Excitable Speech: A Politics of the Performative*. New York: Routledge, 1997.

———. "The Force of Fantasy: Feminism, Maplethorpe, and Discursive Excess." *Differences: A Journal of Feminist Cultural Studies* 2, no. 2 (1990): 105-25.

———. "Gender as Performance." In *A Critical Sense: Interviews with Intellectuals*, edited by Peter Osborne, 109-25. London: Routledge, 1996.

———. *Gender Trouble: Feminism and the Subversion of Identity*. New York: Routledge, 1990.

———. "Imitation and Gender Insubordination." In *Inside/Out: Lesbian Theories, Gay Theories*, edited by Diana Fuss, 13-32. New York: Routledge, 1991.

———. *Undoing Gender*. New York: Routledge, 2004.

Byers, Thomas B. "History Re-Membered: *Forrest Gump*, Postfeminist Masculinity, and the Burial of Counterculture." *Modern Fiction Studies* 42 (1996): 419-44.

Carr, Brian. "*Strange Days* and the Subject of Mobility." *Camera Obscura: A Journal of Feminism and Film Theory* 50 (2002): 191-216.

Cashmore, Ellis. *Making Sense of Sports*. London: Routledge, 1990.

Cavallaro, Dani. *Cyberpunk and Cyberculture*. London: Athlone, 2000.

Chude-Sokei, Louis. *The Last "Darky": Bert Williams, Black-on-Black Minstrelsy, and the African Diaspora*. Durham, NC: Duke University Press, 2006.

Clatterbaugh, Kenneth. "Literature of the U.S. Men's Movements." *Signs* 25, no. 3 (2000): 883-94.

Cleaver, Eldridge. *Soul on Ice*. New York: Dell, 1968.

Clover, Carol. *Men, Women and Chainsaws: Gender in the Modern Horror Film*. London: BFI, 1992.

———. "White Noise." *Sight and Sound*, May 1993, 7-9.

Cohan, Steve, and Ina Rae Hark. Introduction to *Screening the Male: Exploring Masculinities in Hollywood Cinema*, edited by Steve Cohan and Ina Rae Hark, 1-8. London: Routledge, 1993.

———, eds. *Screening the Male: Exploring Masculinities in Hollywood Cinema*. London: Routledge, 1993.

Cook, Pam. "Masculinity in Crisis?" *Screen* 23, no. 3-4 (1982): 38-46.

Cooper, Brenda. "*Boys Don't Cry* and Female Masculinity: Reclaiming a Life and Dismantling the Politics of Normative Heterosexuality." *Critical Studies in Media Communication* 19, no. 1 (2002): 44-63.

Copjec, Joan. "The Orthopsychic Subject: Film Theory and the Reception of Lacan." In *Film and Theory: An Anthology*, edited by Robert Stam and Toby Miller, 437-55. Malden, MA: Blackwell, 2000.

———. *Read My Desire: Lacan against the Historicists*. Cambridge, MA: MIT Press, 1995.

Corliss, Richard. "Hollywood's Last Decent Man," *Time*, July 11, 1994.

Cowie, Elizabeth. "Fantasia." In *The Woman in Question: M/F*, edited by Elizabeth Cowie and Parveen Adams, 149-96. London: Verso, 1990.

Creed, Barbara. "From Here to Modernity: Feminism and Postmodernism." *Screen* 28, no. 2 (1987): 47-68.

———. *The Monstrous Feminine: Film, Feminism, Psychoanalysis*. London: Routledge, 1993.

Dargis, Manohla. "Dark Side of the Dream." *Sight and Sound*, August 1996, 16-19.

———. "Who's Afraid of Red, Yellow and Blonde?" *Artforum* 31, no. 3 (1992): 11.

Davies, Jude. "Gender, Ethnicity and Cultural Crisis in *Falling Down* and *Groundhog Day*." *Screen* 36, no. 3 (1995): 214-32.

Davies, Jude, and Carol R. Smith. *Gender, Ethnicity and Sexuality in Contemporary American Film*. Edinburgh: Keele University Press, 1997.

Dawson, Jeff. *Quentin Tarantino: The Cinema of Cool*. New York: Applause, 1995.

De Lauretis, Teresa. *Alice Doesn't: Feminism, Semiotics, Cinema*. Bloomington: Indiana University Press, 1984.

Delgado, Richard, and Jean Stefancic. Introduction to *Critical White Studies: Looking Behind the Mirror*, edited by Richard Delgado and Jean Stefancic, xvii-xviii. Philadelphia: Temple, 1997.

Derrida, Jacques. "Signature, Event, Context." In *Margins of Philosophy*, 309-30. Chicago: University of Chicago Press, 1982.

Descartes, René. *Meditations and Other Metaphysical Writings*. London: Penguin, 2003.

Diawara, Manthia. "Black American Cinema: The New Realism." In *Black American Cinema*, edited by Manthia Diawara, 3-25. New York: AFI/Routledge, 1993.

DiPiero, Thomas. "White Men Aren't." *Camera Obscura: A Journal of Feminism and Film Theory* 30 (1992): 112-37.

———. *White Men Aren't*. Durham, NC: Duke University Press, 2002.

Doane, Mary Ann. *Femmes Fatales: Feminism, Film Theory, Psychoanalysis.* New York: Routledge, 1991.

———. "Technophilia: Technology, Representation, and the Feminine." In *Body/Politics: Women and the Discourses of Science,* edited by Mary Jacobus, Evelyn Fox Keller, and Sally Shuttleworth, 163-91. New York: Routledge, 1990.

Dollimore, Jonathan. *Sexual Dissidence: Augustine to Wilde, Freud to Foucault.* Oxford: Clarendon, 1991.

Domaille, Kate. *The Full Monty.* York Notes. London: York, 2000.

DuttaAhmed, Shantanu. "'I Thought You Knew! Performing the Penis, the Phallus, and Otherness in Neil Jordan's *The Crying Game.*" *Film Criticism* 23, no. 1 (1998): 61-73.

Dyer, Richard. "Charisma." In *Stardom: Industry of Desire,* edited by Christine Gledhill, 57-59. London: Routledge, 1991.

———. "Don't Look Now: The Male Pin-Up." In *The Sexual Subject: A Screen Reader in Sexuality,* edited by Mandy Merck, 265-76. London: Routledge, 1992.

———. *Heavenly Bodies: Film Stars and Society.* London: BFI/Macmillan, 1987.

———. "Kill and Kill Again." In *Action/Spectacle Cinema: A Sight and Sound Reader,* edited by José Arroyo, 145-50. London: BFI, 2000.

———. *The Matter of Images: Essays on Representation.* London: Routledge, 1993.

———. *Seven.* BFI Modern Classics. London: BFI, 1999.

———. *White.* London: Routledge, 1997.

Epp, Michael H. "Raising Minstrelsy: Humor, Satire and the Stereotype in *The Birth of a Nation* and *Bamboozled.*" *Canadian Review of American Studies* 33, no. 1 (2003): 17-35.

Esposito, Jennifer. "Performance of White Masculinity in *Boys Don't Cry:* Identity, Desire, (Mis)Recognition." *Cultural Studies/Critical Methodologies* 3, no. 2 (2003): 229-41.

Evans, Nicola. "Games of Hide and Seek: Race, Gender and Drag in *The Crying Game* and *The Birdcage.*" *Text and Performance Quarterly* 18 (1998): 199-216.

Faludi, Susan. *Backlash: The Undeclared War Against Women.* London: Vintage, 1992.

———. "It's *Thelma and Louise* for Guys." *Newsweek,* October 25, 1999, 89.

———. *Stiffed: The Betrayal of Modern Man.* London: Vintage, 2000.

Fanon, Frantz. *Black Skin, White Masks.* Translated by Charles Lam Markmann. New York: Grove, 1967.

Faurschou, Gail. "Fashion and the Cultural Logic of Postmodernity." In *Body Invaders: Sexuality and the Postmodern Condition,* edited by Arthur Kroker and Marilouise Kroker, 78-93. Basingstoke: Macmillan, 1988.

Feng, Peter X. "False and Double Consciousness: Race, Virtual Reality and the Assimilation of Hong Kong Action Cinema in *The Matrix.*" In *Aliens R Us: The Other in Science Fiction,* edited by Ziauddin Sardar and Sean Cubitt, 149-63. London: Pluto, 2002.

Fernbach, Amanda. "The Fetishization of Masculinity in Science Fiction: The Cyborg and the Console Cowboy." *Science Fiction Studies* 27, no. 2 (2000): 234-55.

Fielder, Leslie. *Waiting for the End.* New York: Stein and Day, 1972.

Foster, Gwendolyn Audrey. *Performing Whiteness: Postmodern Re/Constructions in the Cinema.* Albany: State University of New York Press, 2003.

Foster, Thomas. "Postmodern Virtualities." In *Cyberspace/Cyberbodies/Cyberpunk,* edited by Mike Featherstone and Roger Burrows, 79-95. London: Sage, 1995.

————. "Trapped by the Body? Telepresence and Transgendered Performance in Feminist and Lesbian Rewritings of Cyberpunk Fiction." In *The Cybercultures Reader*, edited by David Bell and Barbara M. Kennedy, 439-59. London: Routledge, 2000.

Fradley, Martin. "Maximus Melodramaticus: Masculinity, Masochism and White Male Paranoia in Contemporary Hollywood Cinema." In *Action and Adventure Cinema*, edited by Yvonne Tasker, 235-51. London: Routledge, 2004.

Fraiman, Susan. *Cool Men and the Second Sex*. New York: Columbia University Press, 2003.

Frankenberg, Ruth. *White Women, Race Matters: The Social Construction of Whiteness*. Minneapolis: University of Minnesota Press, 1993.

Freeland, Cynthia. "Penetrating Keanu: New Holes, but the Same Old Shit." In The Matrix *and Philosophy: Welcome to the Desert of the Real*, edited by William Irwin, 205-15. Chicago: Open Court, 2002.

Freud, Sigmund. "A Child Is Being Beaten." In *On Psychopathology: Inhibitions, Symptoms and Anxiety and Other Works*. Translated by James Strachey. Edited by Angela Richards, 163-93. London: Penguin, 1993.

————. "The Economic Problem of Masochism." In *On Metapsychology: The Theory of Psychoanalysis: Beyond the Pleasure Principle, The Ego and the Id and Other Works*. Translated by James Strachey. Edited by Angela Richards, 413-26. London: Penguin, 1991.

————. "The Ego and the Id." In *On Metapsychology: The Theory of Psychoanalysis: Beyond the Pleasure Principle, The Ego and the Id and Other Works*. Translated by James Strachey. Edited by Angela Richards, 350-407. London: Penguin, 1991.

————. *Jokes and their Relation to the Unconscious*. Translated by James Strachey. Edited by Angela Richards. London: Penguin, 1991.

————. "Instincts and their Vicissitudes." In *On Metapsychology: The Theory of Psychoanalysis: Beyond the Pleasure Principle, The Ego and the Id and Other Works*. Translated by James Strachey. Edited by Angela Richards, 113-38. London: Penguin, 1991.

————. "On Fetishism." In *On Sexuality: Three Essays on the Theory of Sexuality and Other Works*. Translated by James Strachey. Edited by Angela Richards, 351-57. London: Penguin, 1991.

————. "Psychoanalytic Notes on an Autobiographical Account of a Case of Paranoia (Dementia Paranoides) (1911 [1910])." In *Case Histories II: The "Rat Man," Schreber, The "Wolf Man," A Case of Female Homosexuality*. Translated by James Strachey. Edited by Angela Richards, 129-223. London: Penguin, 1990.

————. "Totem and Taboo." In *The Origins of Religion: Totem and Taboo, Moses and Monotheism and Other Works*. Translated by James Strachey. Edited by Albert Dickson, 53-224. London: Penguin, 1991.

Friedman, Dan. "Genuine Authentic Gangsta Flava." *Zeek*, April 2003. http://www.zeek.net/film_0304.shtml (accessed July 11, 2004).

————. "'Ringleader of a Circus of Worthless Pawns': Eminem and Class Rage." *Zeek*, December 2002. http://www.zeek.net/film_9212.htm (accessed August 15, 2004).

Fuchs, Cynthia. "The Buddy Politic." In *Screening the Male: Exploring Masculinities in Hollywood Cinema*, edited by Steve Cohan and Ina Rae Hark, 194-210. London: Routledge, 1993.

———. "Michael Jackson's Penis." In *Cruising the Performative: Interventions into the Representation* of *Ethnicity, Nationality, and Sexuality*, edited by Sue-Ellen Case, Philip Brett, and Susan Leigh Foster, 13-33. Bloomington: Indiana University Press, 1995.

———. "With or Without You." *Pop.Politics.Com*, June 17, 2002. http://www.pop politics.com/articles/2002-06-17-eminem.shtml (accessed August 20, 2004).

Fuery, Patrick. *New Developments in Film Theory*. Houndmills, Basingstoke: Macmillan, 2000.

Fuller, Graham. "Answer First. Questions Later." In *Quentin Tarantino Interviews*, edited by Gerald Peary, 49-65. Jackson: University Press of Mississippi, 1998.

———. "Big Bad Bigelow." *Interview*, November 1995, 42-188.

Gabbard, Krin. *Black Magic: White Hollywood and African American Culture*. New Brunswick, NJ: Rutgers University Press, 2004.

Gallagher, Mark. "I Married Rambo: Spectacle and Melodrama in the Hollywood Action Film." In *Mythologies of Violence in Postmodern Media*, edited by Christopher Sharrett, 199-225. Detroit: Wayne State University Press, 1999.

Garber, Marjorie. *Vested Interests: Cross-Dressing and Cultural Anxiety*. London: Penguin, 1992.

Gardiner, Judith Kegan. Introduction to *Masculinity Studies and Feminist Theory: New Directions*, edited by Judith Kegan Gardiner, 1-29. New York: Columbia University Press, 2002.

Gates, David. "White Male Paranoia: Say It Loud. They're White and They're Cowed. But Are They Victims of Multiculturalism, or Are They Just Bad Sports?" *Newsweek*, March 29, 1993, 48-53.

Gates, Henry Louis, Jr. "The Master's Pieces: On Canon-Formation and the African-American Tradition." In *Loose Canons: Notes on the Culture Wars*, edited by Henry Louis Gates, Jr., 17-42. Oxford: Oxford University Press, 1992.

Gilman, Sander L. *The Jew's Body*. New York: Routledge, 1991.

Gilroy, Paul. "Ali G and the Oscars." *OpenDemocracy.net*, April 4, 2002. http://www. opendemocracy.net/arts-Film/article_459.jsp (accessed July 11, 2004).

———. *Joined-Up Politics and Post-Colonial Melancholia*. London: Institute of Contemporary Arts, 1999.

———. *There Ain't No Black in the Union Jack: The Cultural Politics of Race and Nation*. Revised edition. London: Routledge, 2002.

Giroux, Henry A. *Impure Acts: The Practical Politics of Cultural Studies*. New York: Routledge, 2000.

———. "*Pulp Fiction* and the Culture of Violence." *Harvard Educational Review* 65, no. 2 (1995): 299-314.

Giroux, Henry A., and Imre Szeman. "Ikea Boy Fights Back: *Fight Club*, Consumerism, and the Political Limits of Nineties Cinema." In *The End of Cinema As We Know It: American Film in the Nineties*, edited by Jon Lewis, 95-104. London: Pluto, 2002.

Gledhill, Christine. "The Melodramatic Field: An Investigation." In *Home Is Where the Heart Is: Studies in Melodrama and the Woman's Film*, edited by Christine Gledhill, 5-39. London: BFI, 1987.

Godfrey, Esther. "'To Be Real': Drag, Minstrelsy and Identity in the New Millennium." *Genders* 41 (2005). http://www.genders.org/g41/g41_godfrey.html (accessed June 25, 2006).

Goldberg, Jonathan. "Recalling Totalities: The Mirrored Stages of Arnold Schwarzeneg-ger." *Differences: A Journal of Cultural Studies* 4, no. 1 (1992): 172-204.

Gormley, Paul. *The New-Brutality Film: Race and Affect in Contemporary Hollywood Cinema.* Bristol: Intellect Books, 2005.

Grant, Barry Keith. "American Psycho/sis: The Pure Products of America Go Crazy." In *Mythologies of Violence in Postmodern Media*, edited by Christopher Sharrett, 23-40. Detroit: Wayne State University Press, 1999.

Grønstad, Asbjørn. "One-Dimensional Men: *Fight Club* and the Poetics of the Body." *Film Criticism* 27, no. 1 (2003): 1-23.

Gubar, Susan. *Racechanges: White Skin, Black Face in American Culture.* New York: Oxford University Press, 1997.

Halberstam, Judith. *Female Masculinity.* Durham, NC: Duke University Press, 1998.

———. "The Good, the Bad, and the Ugly: Men, Women, and Masculinity." In *Masculinity Studies and Feminist Theory: New Directions*, edited by Judith Kegan Gardiner, 344-67. New York: Columbia University Press, 2002.

———. "Masculinity Without Men." Interview with Annamarie Jagose. *Genders* 29 (1999). http://www.genders.org/g29/g29_halberstam.html (accessed June 23, 2006).

———. *Skin Shows: Gothic Horror and the Technology of Monsters.* Durham, NC: Duke University Press, 1995.

———. "The Transgender Gaze in *Boys Don't Cry*." *Screen* 42, no. 3 (2001): 294-98.

Hall, Stuart. "Encoding/Decoding." In *The Cultural Studies Reader*, edited by Simon During, 90-103. London: Routledge, 1993.

———. "Introduction: Who Needs Identity?" In *Questions of Cultural Identity*, edited by Stuart Hall and Paul du Gay, 1-17. London: Sage, 1996.

Hallam, Julie, and Margaret Marshment. *Realism and Popular Cinema.* Manchester: Manchester University Press, 2000.

Hammond, Joyce. "Drag Queen as Angel: Transformation and Transcendence in *To Wong Foo, Thanks for Everything, Julie Newmar*." *The Journal of Popular Film and Television* 24 (1996): 106-14.

Hansen, Miriam. *Babel and Babylon: Spectatorship in American Silent Film.* Cambridge, MA: Harvard University Press, 1991.

Haraway, Donna. "A Manifesto for Cyborgs: Science, Technology, and Socialist Femi-nism in the 1980s." *Socialist Review* 15, no. 2 (1985): 65-107.

Harries, Dan. *Film Parody.* London: BFI, 2000.

Harrington, C. Lee, and Denise D. Bielby. "Constructing the Popular: Cultural Production and Consumption." In *Popular Culture: Production and Consumption*, edited by C. Lee Harrington and Denise D. Bielby, 1-15. Malden, MA: Blackwell, 2001.

Henderson, Lisa. "The Class Character of *Boys Don't Cry*." *Screen* 42, no. 3 (2001): 299-303.

Hill, John. "Failure and Utopianism: Representations of the Working Class in British Cinema of the 1990s." In *British Cinema of the 90s*, edited by Robert Murphy, 178-87. London: BFI, 2002.

———. "From the New Wave to 'Brit-Grit': Continuity and Difference in Working-Class Realism." *British Cinema: Past and Present*, edited by Justine Ashby and Andrew Higson, 249-60. London: Routledge, 2000.

Hill, Michael. *After Whiteness: Unmaking an American Majority.* New York: New York University Press, 2004.

———. "Can Whiteness Speak? Institutional Anomies, Ontological Disasters, and Three Hollywood Films." In *White Trash: Race and Class in America*, edited by Matthew Wray and Annalee Newitz, 155-73. New York: Routledge, 1997.

———. "Introduction: Vipers in Shangri-la: Whiteness, Writing, and Other Ordinary Terrors." In *Whiteness: A Critical Reader*, edited by Michael Hill, 1-18. New York: New York University Press, 1997.

Holland, Samantha. "Descartes Goes to Hollywood: Mind, Body and Gender in Contemporary Cyborg Cinema." In *Cyberspace/Cyberbodies/Cyberpunk*, edited by Mike Featherstone and Roger Burrows, 156-74. London: Sage, 1995.

Holmlund, Chris. "Masculinity as Multiple Masquerade: The 'Mature' Stallone and the Stallone Clone." In *Screening the Male: Exploring Masculinities in Hollywood Cinema*, edited by Steve Cohan and Ina Rae Hark, 213-29. London: Routledge, 1993.

Homan, Richard L. "The Everyman Movie, Circa 1991." *The Journal of Popular Film and Television* 25 (1997): 21-30.

hooks, bell. *Black Looks: Race and Representation*. Boston: South End Press, 1992.

———. *Outlaw Culture: Resisting Representations*. New York: Routledge, 1994.

———. *Reel to Real: Race, Sex, and Class at the Movies*. New York: Routledge, 1996.

Horeck, Tanya. *Public Rape: Representing Violation in Fiction and Film*. London: Routledge, 2004.

Hutcheon, Linda. *The Politics of Postmodernism*. London: Routledge, 1990.

Ignatiev, Noel. *How the Irish Became White*. New York: Routledge, 1996.

Ignatiev, Noel, and John Garvey. "Abolish the White Race by Any Means Necessary." In *Race Traitor*, edited by Noel Ignatiev and John Garvey, 9-14. New York: Routledge, 1996.

Jameson, Fredric. *The Geopolitical Aesthetic: Cinema and Space in the World System*. London: BFI, 1992.

———. *Postmodernism, or, The Cultural Logic of Late Capitalism*. London: Verso, 1991.

Jeffords, Susan. *Hard Bodies: Hollywood Masculinity in the Reagan Era*. New Brunswick, NJ: Rutgers University Press, 1994.

———. *The Remasculinization of America: Gender and the Vietnam War*. Bloomington: Indiana University Press, 1989.

Jennings, Tom. "Br(other) Rabbit's Tale." *Variant*, Spring 2003. www.variant.random state.org/17texts/17tom_jennings.html (accessed August 15, 2004).

Jordan, Neil. Introduction to *The Crying Game: An Original Screenplay*, vii-viii. London: Vintage, 1993.

Kane, Kathryn. "Passing As Queer and Racing Toward Whiteness: *To Wong Foo*, Thanks but No Thanks." *Genders* 42 (2005). http://www.genders.org/g42/g42_kane.html (accessed June 25, 2006).

Kane, Pat. "Ali G: Da New White and Black Minstrel." *Sunday Herald*, March 10, 2002. www.sundayherald.com/22797 (accessed July 11, 2004).

Kennedy, Liam. *Race and Urban Space in Contemporary American Culture*. Edinburgh: Edinburgh University Press, 2000.

Kennedy, Lisa. "Natural Born Filmmaker." *Village Voice*, October 25, 1994, 29-32.

Kennedy, Randall. *Nigger: The Strange Career of a Troublesome Word*. New York: Vintage, 2002.

Kerouac, Jack. *On the Road*. London: Penguin, 1972.

Kim, Richard. "Eminem—Bad Rap?" *The Nation*, March 5, 2001. http://www.thenation. com/doc.mhtml?i=20010305&s=kim (accessed August 20, 2004).

Kimmel, Michael S., and Michael Kaufman. "Weekend Warriors: The New Men's Movement." In *Theorizing Masculinities*, edited by Harry Brod and Michael Kaufman, 259-88. London: Sage, 1994.

King, Scott Benjamin. "Sonny's Virtues: The Gender Negotiations of *Miami Vice*." *Screen* 31, no. 1 (1990): 281-95.

Kirkham, Pat, and Janet Thumin, "Me Jane." Introduction to *Me Jane: Masculinity, Movies and Women*, edited by Pat Kirkham and Janet Thumin, 11-35. New York: St. Martin's, 1995.

———, eds. *Me Jane: Masculinity, Movies and Women*. New York: St. Martin's, 1995.

———, eds. *You Tarzan: Masculinity, Movies and Men*. London: Lawrence and Wishart, 1993.

Kotz, Liz. "The Body You Want: Liz Kotz Interviews Judith Butler." *Artforum* 31, no. 3 (1992): 83-89.

Kristeva, Julia. *Powers of Horror*. Translated by Leon Roudiez. New York: Columbia University Press, 1982.

Krutnik, Frank. *In a Lonely Street: Film Noir, Genre, Masculinity*. London: Routledge, 1991.

Lacan, Jacques. "Aggressivity in Psychoanalysis." In *Écrits: A Selection*. Translated by Alan Sheridan, 9-32. London: Routledge, 2004.

———. "Of the Gaze as *Objet petit a*." In *The Four Fundamental Concepts of Psycho-Analysis*. Translated by Alan Sheridan. Edited by Jacques-Alain Miller, 65-119. London: Penguin, 1991.

———. "The Mirror Stage." In *Écrits: A Selection*. Translated by Alan Sheridan, 1-18. London: Routledge, 2004.

———. "The Significance of the Phallus." *Écrits: A Selection*. Translated by Alan Sheridan, 311-22. London: Routledge, 2004.

Lane, Christina. *Feminist Hollywood: From* Born in Flames *to* Point Break. Detroit: Wayne State University Press, 2000.

———. "The Strange Days of Kathryn Bigelow and James Cameron." In *The Cinema of Kathryn Bigelow: Hollywood Transgressor*, edited by Deborah Jermyn and Sean Redmond, 178-97. London: Wallflower Press, 2003.

Lasch, Christopher. *The Culture of Narcissism: American Life in an Age of Diminishing Expectations*. London: Abacus, 1980.

Lebeau, Vicky. *Psychoanalysis and Cinema: The Play of Shadows*. London: Wallflower, 2001.

———. "Psychopolitics: Frantz Fanon's *Black Skin, White Masks*." In *Psycho-Politics and Cultural Desires*, edited by Jan Campbell and Janet Harbord, 113-23. London: Taylor and Francis, 1998.

Lehman, Peter. "Crying Over the Melodramatic Penis: Melodrama and Male Nudity in Films of the 90s." In *Masculinity: Bodies, Movies, Culture*, edited by Peter Lehman, 25-41. New York: Routledge, 2001.

———, ed. *Masculinity: Bodies, Movies, Culture*. New York: Routledge, 2001.

———. *Running Scared: Masculinity and the Representation of the Male Body*. Philadelphia: Temple University Press, 1993.

———. "'They Look So Uncomplicated Once They're Dissected': The Act of Seeing the Dead Penis With One's Own Eyes." In *The Trouble with Men: Masculinities in*

European and Hollywood Cinema, edited by Phil Powrie, Ann Davies, and Bruce Babington, 196-206. London: Wallflower, 2004.

Leigh, Danny. "Boy Wonder: Interview with Kimberly Peirce." *Sight and Sound*, March 2000, 18-20.

Lipsitz, George. *The Possessive Investment in Whiteness: How White People Profit from Identity Politics*. Philadelphia: Temple University Press, 1998.

Lott, Eric. *Love and Theft: Blackface Minstrelsy and the American Working Class*. New York: Oxford University Press, 1993.

————. "White Like Me: Racial Cross-Dressing and the Construction of American Whiteness." In *Cultures of United States Imperialism*, edited by Amy Kaplan and Donald E. Pease, 474-95. Durham, NC: Duke University Press, 1993.

Luckett, Moya. "Image and Nation in 1990s British Cinema." In *British Cinema of the 90s*, edited by Robert Murphy, 88-99. London: BFI, 2002.

Luhr, William. "Mutilating Mel: Martyrdom and Masculinity in *Braveheart*." In *Mythologies of Violence in Postmodern Media*, edited by Christopher Sharrett, 227-46. Detroit: Wayne State University Press, 1999.

Lupton, Deborah. "The Embodied Computer/User." In *The Cybercultures Reader*, edited by David Bell and Barbara M. Kennedy, 476-88. London: Routledge, 2000.

Mahoney, Elisabeth. "'The People in Parenthesis': Space Under Pressure in the Post-Modern City." In *The Cinematic City*, edited by David B. Clarke, 168-85. London: Routledge, 1997.

Mailer, Norman. "The White Negro." In *Advertisements for Myself*, 290-311. London: Flamingo, 1994.

Marriott, David. *Haunted Life: Visual Culture and Black Modernity*. New Brunswick, NJ: Rutgers University Press, 2007.

Mason, Fran. *American Gangster Cinema: From* Little Caesar *to* Pulp Fiction. Basingstoke: Palgrave Macmillan, 2002.

Meléndez, Theresa. "Race Dialogues for the New Millennium." In *Race in 21st Century America*, edited by Curtis Stokes, Theresa Meléndez, and Genice Rhodes-Reed, xxiv-xxxvii. East Lansing: Michigan State University Press, 2001.

Mellencamp, Pat. "The Zen of Masculinity—Rituals of Heroism in *The Matrix*." In *The End of Cinema As We Know It: American Film in the Nineties*, edited by Jon Lewis, 83-94. London: Pluto, 2002.

Mercer, Kobena. "Looking for Trouble." *Transition* 51 (1991): 184-97.

————. "Monster Metaphors: Notes on Michael Jackson's *Thriller*." In *Stardom: Industry of Desire*, edited by Christine Gledhill, 300-16. London: Routledge, 1991.

————. *Welcome to the Jungle: New Positions in Black Cultural Studies*. London: Routledge, 1994.

Merck, Mandy. "Mom's Apple Pie." Paper presented at the international conference "Bodies, Theories, Cultures in the Post-Millennium Era," Aristotle University of Thessaloniki, Thessaloniki, Greece, May 16, 2003.

Mizejewski, Linda. "Action Bodies in Futuristic Spaces: Bodybuilders' Stardom as Special Effect." In *Alien Zone II: The Spaces of Science Fiction Cinema*, edited by Annette Kuhn, 152-72. London: Verso, 1999.

Modleski, Tania. *Feminism Without Women: Culture and Criticism in a "Postfeminist" Age*. New York: Routledge, 1991.

Monk, Claire. "Underbelly UK: The 1990s Underclass Film, Masculinity and the Ideologies of 'New' Britain." In *British Cinema: Past and Present*, edited by Justine Ashby and Andrew Higson, 272-87. London: Routledge, 2000.

Morrison, Toni. *Playing in the Dark: Whiteness and the Literary Imagination*. London: Picador, 1992.

Mort, Frank. "Boy's Own? Masculinity, Style and Popular Culture." In *Male Order: Unwrapping Masculinity*, revised edition, edited by Rowena Chapman and Jonathan Rutherford, 193-224. London: Lawrence and Wishart, 1996.

Mulvey, Laura. "Afterthoughts on 'Visual Pleasure and Narrative Cinema' Inspired by King Vidor's *Duel in the Sun* (1946)." In *Visual and Other Pleasures*, 29-38. Houndmills, Basingstoke: Macmillan, 1989.

———. *Death 24x a Second: Stillness and the Moving Image*. London: Reaktion, 2006.

———. "Visual Pleasure and Narrative Cinema." In *Visual and Other Pleasures*, 14-26. Houndmills, Basingstoke: Macmillan, 1989.

Nakamura, Lisa "Race in/for Cyberspace: Identity Tourism and Racial Passing on the Net." In *The Cybercultures Reader*, edited by David Bell and Barbara M. Kennedy, 712-20. London: Routledge, 2000.

Neale, Steve. *Genre and Hollywood*. London: Routledge, 2000.

———. "Masculinity as Spectacle." In *The Sexual Subject: A Screen Reader in Sexuality*, edited by Mandy Merck, 277-87. London: Routledge, 1992.

Neroni, Hilary. *The Violent Woman: Femininity, Narrative, and Violence in Contemporary American Cinema*. Albany: State University of New York Press, 2005.

Newitz, Annalee. "Serial Killers, True Crime, and Economic Performance Anxiety." In *Mythologies of Violence in Postmodern Media*, edited by Christopher Sharrett, 65-83. Detroit: Wayne State University Press, 1999.

———. "White Savagery and Humiliation, or a New Racial Consciousness in the Media." In *White Trash: Race and Class in America*, edited by Matthew Wray and Annalee Newitz, 131-54. New York: Routledge, 1997.

Newitz, Annalee, and Matthew Wray. "What Is 'White Trash'? Stereotypes and Economic Conditions of Poor Whites in the United States." In *Whiteness: A Critical Reader*, edited by Michael Hill, 168-84. New York: New York University Press, 1997.

O'Connor, Robby. "Interview with Edward Norton." *The Yale Herald*, October 8, 1999. http://www.edward-norton.org/articles/yaleherald1099.html (accessed February 15, 2002).

O'Donnell, Patrick. *Latent Destinies: Cultural Paranoia and Contemporary U.S. Narrative*. Durham, NC: Duke University Press, 2000.

Omi, Michael, and Howard Winant. *Racial Formation in the United States: From the 1960s to the 1990s*. Second edition. New York: Routledge, 1994.

———. "The Los Angeles 'Race Riot' and Contemporary U.S. Politics." In *Reading Rodney King, Reading Urban Uprising*, edited by Robert Gooding-Williams, 97-114. New York: Routledge, 1993.

Orgeron, Devin Anthony. "Scatological Film Practice: *Pulp Fiction* and a Cinema in Movements." *Postscript* 19, no. 3 (2000): 29-40.

Parpart, Lee. "The Nation and the Nude: Colonial Masculinity and the Spectacle of the Male Body in Recent Canadian Cinema(s)." In *Masculinity: Bodies, Movies, Culture*, edited by Peter Lehman, 167-92. New York: Routledge, 2001.

Peirce, Kimberly. "Brandon goes to Hollywood." *The Advocate*, March 28, 2000. http://www.advocate.com.html.stories/808/808_cvr_peirce.asp (accessed March 14, 2004).

Penley, Constance, and Sharon Willis. Introduction to *Male Trouble*, edited by Constance

Penley and Sharon Willis, i-xix. Minneapolis: University of Minnesota Press, 1993.

———, eds. *Male Trouble.* Minneapolis: University of Minnesota Press, 1993.

Pfeil, Fred. *White Guys: Studies in Postmodern Domination and Difference.* London: Verso, 1995.

Pidduck, Julianne. "Risk and Spectatorship." *Screen* 42, no. 1 (2001): 97-102.

Piper, Adrian. "Passing for White, Passing for Black." In *Critical White Studies: Looking Behind the Mirror,* edited by Richard Delgado and Jean Stefancic, 425-31. Philadelphia: Temple, 1997.

Plant, Sadie. "Beyond the Screens: Film, Cyberpunk and Cyberfeminism." *Variant* 14 (1993): 12-17.

———. "The Future Looms: Weaving Women and Cybernetics." In *Cyberspace/ Cyberbodies/Cyberpunk,* edited by Mike Featherstone and Roger Burrows, 45-63. London: Sage, 1995.

———. "On the Matrix: Cyberfeminist Simulations." In *The Cybercultures Reader,* edited by David Bell and Barbara M. Kennedy, 325-36. London: Routledge, 2000.

Polan, Dana. *Pulp Fiction.* BFI Modern Classics. London: BFI, 2003.

Powrie, Phil, Ann Davies, and Bruce Babington. "Introduction: Turning the Male Inside Out." In *The Trouble with Men: Masculinities in European and Hollywood Cinema,* edited by Phil Powrie, Ann Davies, and Bruce Babington, 1-15. London: Wallflower, 2004.

———, eds. *The Trouble with Men: Masculinities in European and Hollywood Cinema.* London: Wallflower, 2004.

Radstone, Susannah. "'Too Straight a Drive to the Tollbooth': Masculinity, Mortality and Al Pacino." In *Me Jane: Masculinity, Movies and Women,* edited by Pat Kirkham and Janet Thumin, 148-65. New York: St. Martin's, 1995.

Rank, Otto. *The Double: A Psychoanalytic Study.* Translated by Harry Tucker, Jr. London: Karnac, 1989.

Redmond, Sean. "The Whiteness of the Rings." In *The Persistence of Whiteness: Race and Contemporary Hollywood Cinema,* edited by Daniel Bernardi, 91-101. London: Routledge, 2008.

Rheingold, Harold. "A Slice of Life in My Virtual Community." In *High Noon on the Electronic Frontier: Conceptual Issues in Cyberspace,* edited by Peter Ludlow, 413-36. Cambridge, MA: MIT Press, 1996.

Rich, B. Ruby. "Dumb Lugs and Femme Fatales." *Sight and Sound,* November 1995, 6-10.

———. "Queer and Present Danger." *Sight and Sound,* March 2000, 22-25.

Riviere, Joan. "Womanliness as Masquerade." In *Formations of Fantasy,* edited by Victor Burgin, James Donald, and Cora Kaplan, 35-44. London: Methuen, 1986.

Robinson, Sally. *Marked Men: White Masculinity in Crisis.* New York: Columbia University Press, 2000.

Rodowick, D. N. "The Difficulty of Difference." *Wide Angle* 15 (1982): 4-15.

Roediger, David. *Colored White: Transcending the Racial Past.* Berkeley: University of California Press, 2002.

———. "Guineas, Wiggers, and the Drama of Racialized Culture." *American Literary History* 7, no. 4 (1995): 654-68.

———. *Towards the Abolition of Whiteness.* London: Verso, 1994.

———. *The Wages of Whiteness: Race and the Making of the American Working Class.* London: Verso, 1991.

Rogin, Michael. *Blackface, White Noise: Jewish Immigrants in the Hollywood Melting Pot*. Berkley: University of California Press, 1996.

——. "Blackface, White Noise: The Jewish Jazz Singer Finds His Voice." *Critical Inquiry* 18, no. 3 (1992): 417-53.

Romney, Jonathan. "Boxing Clever." *The New Statesman*, November 15, 1999. http://www.newstatesman.com/199911150043 (accessed May 30, 2000).

Rose, Jacqueline. *Sexuality in the Field of Vision*. London: Verso, 1986.

Rose, Tricia. *Black Noise: Rap Music and Black Culture in Contemporary America*. Hanover: Wesleyan University Press, 1994.

Ross, Andrew. *No Respect: Intellectuals and Popular Culture*. New York: Routledge, 1989.

Rowe, Kathleen. "Melodrama and Men in Post-Classical Romantic Comedy." In *Me Jane: Masculinity, Movies and Women*, edited by Pat Kirkham and Janet Thumin, 184-93. New York: St. Martin's, 1995.

Rutsky, R. L. "Being Keanu." In *The End of Cinema As We Know It: American Film in the Nineties*, edited by Jon Lewis, 185-94. London: Pluto, 2002.

Salih, Sara. *Judith Butler*. Routledge Critical Thinkers. New York: Routledge, 2002.

Salisbury, Mark. "Get out of My Face." *Empire*, July 1993, 74-78.

Sanchez, Tani Dianca. "Neo-abolitionists, Colorblind Epistemologies and Black Politics." In *The Persistence of Whiteness: Race and Contemporary Hollywood Cinema*, edited by Daniel Bernardi, 102-24. London: Routledge, 2008.

Sardar, Ziauddin. "alt.civilisations.faq: Cyberspace as the Darker Side of the West." In *The Cybercultures Reader*, edited by David Bell and Barbara M. Kennedy, 732-52. London: Routledge, 2000.

Sartelle, Joseph. "Dreams and Nightmares in the Hollywood Blockbuster." In *The Oxford History of World Cinema*, edited by Geoffrey Nowell-Smith, 516-26. Oxford: Oxford University Press, 1996.

Savran, David. *Taking It Like a Man: White Masculinity, Masochism, and Contemporary American Culture*. Princeton, NJ: Princeton University Press, 1998.

Sedgwick, Eve Kosofsky. *Between Men: English Literature and Male Homosocial Desire*. New York: Columbia University Press, 1985.

——. *Epistemology of the Closet*. Berkeley: University of California Press, 1990.

Segal, Lynn. *Slow Motion: Changing Masculinities, Changing Men*. Revised edition. London: Virago, 1997.

Seltzer, Mark. *Serial Killers: Death and Life in America's Wound Culture*. New York: Routledge, 1998.

Seshadri-Crooks, Kalpana. *Desiring Whiteness: A Lacanian Analysis of Race*. London: Routledge, 2000.

Sharrett, Christopher. Introduction to *Mythologies of Violence in Postmodern Media*, edited by Christopher Sharrett, 9-20. Detroit: Wayne State University Press, 1999.

Shohat, Ella, and Robert Stam. *Unthinking Eurocentricism: Multiculturalism and the Media*. London: Routledge, 1994.

Shome, Raka. "Whiteness and the Politics of Location: Postcolonial Reflections." In *Whiteness: The Communication of Social Identity*, edited by Thomas K. Nakayama and Judith N. Martin, 107-27. London: Sage, 1999.

Siegel, Carol. "Curing ~~Boys~~ Don't Cry: Brandon Teena's Stories." *Genders* 37 (2003). http://www.genders.org/g37/g37_siegel.html (accessed April 14, 2004).

Silverman, Kaja. *Male Subjectivity at the Margins*. New York: Routledge, 1992.

————. *The Threshold of the Visible World*. New York: Routledge, 1996.

Simpson, Mark. *Male Impersonators: Men Performing Masculinity*. London: Cassell, 1994.

Slotkin, Richard. *Regeneration through Violence: The Mythology of the American Frontier, 1600-1860*. New York: HarperPerennial, 1996.

Smelik, Anneke. "The Flight from Flesh: Virtual Reality in Science Fiction Films." http:// www.women.it/cyberarchive/files/smelik.htm (accessed September 10, 2002).

Smith, Gavin. "Inside Out." *Film Comment*, September/October 1999, 58-68.

————. "Momentum and Design." *Film Comment*, September/October 1995, 46-60.

————. "You Know You're in Good Hands." In *Quentin Tarantino: Interviews*, edited by Gerald Peary, 97-114. Jackson: University Press of Mississippi, 1998.

Smith, Murray. "Theses on the Philosophy of Hollywood History." In *Contemporary Hollywood Cinema*, edited by Steve Neale and Murray Smith, 3-20. London: Routledge, 1998.

Smith, Paul. *Discerning the Subject*. Minneapolis: University of Minnesota Press, 1988.

————. "Eastwood Bound." In *Constructing Masculinity*, edited by Maurice Berger, Brian Wallis, and Simon Watson, 76-97. New York: Routledge, 1995.

Snow, Tony. "Black Like Beckham." *Channel Four. Black and Asian History Map*. http://www.channel4.com/history/microsites/B/blackhistorymap/articles_02.ht ml (accessed October 1, 2004).

Sobchack, Vivian. *The Address of the Eye: A Phenomenology of Film Experience*. Princeton, NJ: Princeton University Press, 1992.

————. "Beating the Meat/Surviving the Text, or How to Get Out of this Century Alive." In *Cyberspace/Cyberbodies/Cyberpunk*, edited by Mike Featherstone and Roger Burrows, 205-41. London: Sage, 1995.

Spelman, Elizabeth V. "Woman as Body: Ancient and Contemporary Views." *Feminist Studies* 8, no. 1 (1982): 109-31.

Springer, Claudia. *Electronic Eros: Bodies and Desire in the Postindustrial Age*. Austin: University of Texas Press, 1996.

————. "Psycho-cybernetics in Films of the 1990s." In *Alien Zone II: The Spaces of Science Fiction Cinema*, edited by Annette Kuhn, 203-18. London: Verso, 1999.

Stacey, Jackie. "Desperately Seeking Difference." In *The Sexual Subject: A Screen Reader in Sexuality*, edited by Mandy Merck, 244-57. London: Routledge, 1992.

Staiger, Janet. "Taboos and Totems: Cultural Meanings of *The Silence of the Lambs*." In *Film Theory Goes to the Movies*, edited by Ava Preacher Collins, Jim Collins, and Hilary Radner, 142-54. New York: Routledge, 1993.

Stam, Robert, and Louise Spence. "Colonialism, Racism and Representation." *Screen* 24, no. 2 (1983): 2-20.

Stecopoulos, Harry, and Michael Uebel, eds. *Race and the Subject of Masculinities*. Durham, NC: Duke University Press, 1997.

Stoller, Robert. *Sex and Gender: On the Development of Masculinity and Femininity*. London: Hogarth/Institute of Psychoanalysis, 1968.

Stone, Allucquère Rosanne. "Will the Real Body Please Stand Up? Boundary Stories about Virtual Cultures." In *The Cybercultures Reader*, edited by David Bell and Barbara M. Kennedy, 504-28. London: Routledge, 2000.

Straayer, Chris. *Deviant Eyes, Deviant Bodies: Sexual Re-Orientation in Film and Video*. New York: Columbia University Press, 1996.

———. "Masculinity: Acting and Causality in *Boys Don't Cry*." Abstract for VI SAAS Conference, American Mirrors: (Self)Reflections and Self(Distortions), April 9-11, 2003. http://www.vc.ehu.es/castellano/paginas/otros/fiwsaas/program/pa/abst/pa041003cs.htm (accessed June 11, 2004).

"Strange Days Movie Notes." *Ralph Fiennes Interactive Fan Page*. http://ralphfiennes. hypermart.net/strangedays/RalphFiennesStrangeDaysNotes.htm (accessed September 11, 2002).

Svetkey, Benjamin. "Blood, Sweat, and Fears." *Entertainment Weekly*, October 15, 1999. http://www.edward-norton.org/fc/articles/bloodsweat.html (accessed March 30, 2000).

Tasker, Yvonne. *The Silence of the Lambs*. BFI Modern Classics. London: BFI, 2000.

———. *Spectacular Bodies: Gender, Genre and the Action Cinema*. London: Routledge, 1993.

———. *Working Girls: Gender and Sexuality in Popular Cinema*. London: Routledge, 1998.

Taubin, Amy. "The Men's Room." *Sight and Sound*, December 1992, 2-5.

Telotte, J. P. "The Tremulous Public Body: Robots, Change, and the Science Fiction Film." *Journal of Popular Film and TV* 19 (1991): 14-23.

Theweleit, Klaus. *Male Fantasies*. 2 Vols. Translated by Stephen Conway in collaboration with Erica Carter and Chris Turner. Cambridge: Polity, 1987.

Thompson, Margaret Drewall. "The Camp Face in Corporate America: Liberace and the Rockettes at Radio City Music Hall." In *The Politics and Poetics of Camp*, edited by Moe Meyer, 149-81. London: Routledge, 1993.

Thompson, Stacey. "Punk Cinema." *Cinema Journal* 43, no. 2 (2004): 47-66.

Tincknell, Estella, and Deborah Chambers. "Performing the Crisis: Fathering, Gender and Representation in Two 1990s Films." *Journal of Popular Film and Television* 29 (2002): 146-55.

Tinkcom, Matthew, and Amy Villarejo. Introduction to *Keyframes: Popular Cinema and Cultural Studies*, edited by Matthew Tinkcom and Amy Villarejo, 1-29. London: Routledge, 2001.

Traube, Elizabeth G. *Dreaming Identities: Class, Gender and Generation in 1980s Film*. Boulder, CO: Westview, 1992.

Tyler, Carol-Anne. "Boys Will Be Girls: The Politics of Gay Drag." In *Inside/Out: Lesbian Theories, Gay Theories*, edited by Diana Fuss, 32-70. New York: Routledge, 1991.

Vera, Hernan, and Andrew M. Gordon. *Screen Saviors: Hollywood Fictions of Whiteness*. New York: Rowman and Littlefield, 2003.

Wald, Gayle. *Crossing the Line: Racial Passing in Twentieth-Century U.S. Literature and Culture*. Durham, NC: Duke University Press, 2000.

Wellman, David. "Minstrel Shows, Affirmative Action Talk, and Angry White Men: Marking Racial Otherness in the 1990s." In *Displacing Whiteness: Essays in Social and Cultural Criticism*, edited by Ruth Frankenberg, 311-31. Durham, NC: Duke University Press, 1997.

White, Patricia. "Girls Still Cry." *Screen* 42, no. 2 (2001): 217-21.

Wiegman, Robyn. *American Anatomies: Theorizing Race and Gender*. Durham, NC: Duke University Press, 1995.

———. "Fielder and Sons." In *Race and the Subject of Masculinities*, edited by Harry Stecopoulos and Michael Uebel, 45-85. Durham, NC: Duke University Press, 1997.

———. "'My Name Is Forrest Gump': Whiteness Studies and the Paradox of Particularity." In *Multiculturalism, Postcoloniality, and Transnational Media*, edited by Ella Shohat and Robert Stam, 227-55. New Brunswick, NJ: Rutgers University Press, 2003.

———. "Unmaking: Men and Masculinity in Feminist Theory." In *Masculinity Studies and Feminist Theory: New Directions*, edited by Judith Kegan Gardiner, 31-59. New York: Columbia University Press, 2002.

Willemen, Paul. "Anthony Mann: Looking at the Male." *Framework* 15-17 (1981): 16-20.

Williams, Linda. *Playing the Race Card: Melodramas of Black and White From Uncle Tom to O.J. Simpson*. Princeton, NJ: Princeton University Press, 2001.

Willis, Sharon. "Disputed Territories: Masculinity and Social Space." In *Male Trouble*, edited by Constance Penley and Sharon Willis, 262-81. Minneapolis: University of Minnesota Press, 1993.

———. *High Contrast: Race and Gender in Contemporary Hollywood Film*. Durham, NC: Duke University Press, 1997.

Wilson, Anna. "National Uses for Bodies." Abstract. *The Flesh Made Text: Bodies, Theories, Cultures in the Post-Millennial .Era: Book of Abstracts*. Thessaloniki, Greece: Aristotle University of Thessaloniki, 2003. 205.

Wise, Damon. "Menace II Society." *Empire*, December 1999, 100-106.

Wolmark, Jenny. "Introduction and Overview." In *Cybersexualities: A Reader on Feminist Theory, Cyborgs and Cyberspace*, edited by Jenny Wolmark, 1-9. Edinburgh: Edinburgh University Press, 1999.

Woods, Paul A. *King Pulp: The Wild World of Quentin Tarantino*. London: Plexus, 1998.

Wray, Matthew, and Annalee Newitz. Introduction to *White Trash: Race and Class in America*, edited by Matthew Wray and Annalee Newitz, 1-12. New York: Routledge, 1997.

Wyatt, Justin. "The Formation of the 'Major Independent': Miramax, New Line and the New Hollywood." In *Contemporary Hollywood Cinema*, edited by Steve Neale and Murray Smith, 74-90. London: Routledge, 1998.

Yates, Candida. *Masculine Jealousy and Contemporary Cinema*. Houndmills, Basingstoke: Palgrave Macmillan, 2007.

Young, Elizabeth. "*The Silence of the Lambs* and the Flaying of Feminist Theory." *Camera Obscura: A Journal of Feminism and Film Theory* 27 (1991): 5-36.

Zilberg, Elana. "*Falling Down* in *El Norte*: A Cultural Politics and Spatial Poetics of the ReLatinization of Los Angeles." *Wide Angle* 20, no. 3 (1998): 182-209.

Žižek, Slavoj. *The Fright of Real Tears: Krzysztof Kieślowski between Theory and Post-Theory*. London: BFI, 2001.

———. *Looking Awry: An Introduction to Jacques Lacan through Popular Culture*. Cambridge, MA: MIT Press, 1991.

———. *The Metastases of Enjoyment: Six Essays on Woman and Causality*. London: Verso, 1994.

———. *The Ticklish Subject: The Absent Centre of Political Ontology*. London: Verso, 1999.

———. "Welcome to the Desert of the Real." *Re-Constructions: Reflections on Humanity and Media After Tragedy*. http://web.mit.edu/cms/reconstructions/interpretations/desertreal.html (accessed November 22, 2008).

Select Filmography

25th Hour (Touchstone Pictures), 2002, directed by Spike Lee; starring Edward Norton, Philip Seymour Hoffman, Barry Pepper, and Rosario Dawson.

8 Mile (Imagine Entertainment), 2002, directed by Curtis Hanson; starring Eminem, Kim Basinger, Mekhi Phifer, and Brittany Murphy.

Ali G Indahouse (FilmFour), 2002, directed by Mark Mylod; starring Sacha Baron Cohen and Martin Freeman.

American Psycho (Lions Gate Films), 2002, directed by Mary Harron; starring Christian Bale, Chloë Sevigny, Reese Witherspoon, and Jared Leto.

Bamboozled (New Line Cinema), 2000, directed by Spike Lee; starring Damon Wyans, Savion Glover, Jada Pinkett-Smith, Tommy Davidson, Michael Rapaport, and Thomas Jefferson Byrd.

Boys Don't Cry (Hart-Sharp Entertainment), 1999, directed by Kimberly Peirce; starring Hilary Swank, Chloë Sevigny, Peter Sarsgaard, and Brendan Sexton III.

Copycat (Regency Enterprises), 1995, directed by Jon Amiel; starring Sigourney Weaver, Holly Hunter, Dermot Mulroney, and William McNamara.

The Crying Game (Channel Four Films), 1992, directed by Neil Jordan; starring Stephen Rea, Jaye Davidson, Forrest Whitaker, and Miranda Richardson.

Disclosure (Warner Bros. Pictures), 1994, directed by Barry Levinson; starring Michael Douglas, Demi Moore, and Donald Sutherland.

Falling Down (Warner Bros. Pictures), 1993, directed by Joel Schumacher; starring Michael Douglas, Robert Duvall, and Barbara Hershey.

Fight Club (Fox 2000 Pictures), 1999, directed by David Fincher; starring Brad Pitt, Edward Norton, and Helena Bonham Carter.

Forrest Gump (Paramount Pictures), 1994, directed by Robert Zemeckis; starring Tom Hanks, Robyn Wright Penn, Gary Sinise, and Sally Field.

The Full Monty (Channel Four Films), 1997, directed by Peter Cattaneo; starring Robert Carlyle and Mark Addy.

Gladiator (DreamWorks SKG), 2000, directed by Ridley Scott; starring Russell Crowe, Joaquin Phoenix, and Oliver Reed.

He Was a Quiet Man (Quiet Man Productions), 2007, directed by Frank A. Cappello; starring Christian Slater, Elisha Cuthbert, and William H. Macy.

Jackie Brown (Miramax Films), 1997, directed by Quentin Tarantino; starring Pam Grier, Samuel L. Jackson, Robert Forster, Bridget Fonda, and Robert de Niro.

Kalifornia (PolyGram Filmed Entertainment), 1993, directed by Dominic Sena; starring Brad Pitt, Juliette Lewis, David Duchovny, and Michelle Forbes.

The Matrix (Warner Bros. Pictures), 1999, directed by Andy Wachowski and Larry Wachowski; starring Keanu Reeves, Laurence Fishburne, Carrie-Anne Moss, and Hugo Weaving.

Natural Born Killers (Warner Bros. Pictures), 1994, directed by Oliver Stone; starring Woody Harrelson, Juliette Lewis, Tom Sizemore, Rodney Dangerfield, Robert Downey, Jr., and Tommy Lee Jones.

Pulp Fiction (A Band Apart), 1994, directed by Quentin Tarantino; starring John Travolta, Samuel L. Jackson, Bruce Willis, Uma Thurman, and Ving Rhames.

The Real Blonde (Lakeshore Entertainment), 1997, directed by Tom DiCillo; starring Matthew Modine and Catherine Keener.

Regarding Henry (Paramount Pictures), 1991, directed by Mike Nichols; starring Harrison Ford, Annette Bening, and Bill Nunn.

Reservoir Dogs (Dog Eat Dog Productions Inc.), 1992, directed by Quentin Tarantino; starring Harvey Keitel, Tim Roth, Michael Madsen, Chris Penn, and Steve Buscemi.

Se7en (New Line Cinema), 1995, directed by David Fincher; starring Brad Pitt, Morgan Freeman, Kevin Spacey, and Gwyneth Paltrow.

The Silence of the Lambs (Orion Pictures Corporation), 1991, directed by Jonathan Demme; starring Jodie Foster, Anthony Hopkins, Scott Glenn, and Ted Levine.

Strange Days (Lightstorm Entertainment), 1995, directed by Kathryn Bigelow; starring Ralph Fiennes, Angela Bassett, Juliette Lewis, and Tom Sizemore.

Terminator 2: Judgment Day (Lightstorm Entertainment), 1991, directed by James Cameron; starring Arnold Schwarzenegger, Linda Hamilton, Edward Furlong, and Robert Patrick.

Troy (Warner Bros. Pictures), 2004, directed by Wolfgang Petersen; starring Brad Pitt, Eric Bana, and Orlando Bloom.

Index

ity of, 7, 15, 71, 138-39, 146, 150, 156, 217, 218, 236. *See also* homoerotic anxiety; homosocial bonds.

hip hop, 10, 13, 167-68, 178, 187-89, 192-93, 198n59. *See also* rap; "wiggers."

homoerotic anxiety, 87, 94, 99, 149.

homoerotic desire, 7, 15, 34, 68, 69, 71, 72, 75, 87-88, 149, 157, 163, 174, 175, 178, 181, 183, 190, 215-17, 235, 236. *See also* homosocial bonds.

homophobia, 27, 33, 34, 45, 47, 53n91, 99, 146, 149, 159, 178, 180, 181, 190, 192, 204, 210, 215-17, 221, 230, 252.

homosexuality, 2, 7, 27, 53, 72, 73, 87, 90, 144, 154, 176, 216, 230. *See also* homoerotic anxiety; homoerotic desire; homophobia; homosexuals.

homosexuals, 2, 14, 24, 25, 45, 53n91, 76, 95, 114n77, 152, 191, 216; as threats to straight white men, 14, 25, 53, 252.

homosocial bonds, 7, 42, 44, 60, 71, 76, 145, 146, 149, 157, 174, 175, 180, 216, 219, 236. *See also* homoerotic desire; heterosexuality.

hooks, bell, 8, 89, 110n5, 129, 138, 148, 149, 178, 214, 217, 222.

The Human Stain, 171-72.

Hutcheon, Linda, 78, 188, 209.

hypermasculinity, 3, 59, 65, 98-101, 105, 122.

hyperreality, 94, 118, 124, 228, 242, 245, 251.

hysteria, 67, 69; male, 14, 57, 58, 67, 69-72, 78.

identification, 5, 6-7, 57, 121, 243; cinematic; 9, 31, 34, 47, 74, 76, 86-88, 98, 110n5, 121, 212, 230, 237, 242; heterosexual, 15, 71, 138-39, 146, 150; male, 3, 66, 69, 70, 73, 80n44, 152.

identity critiques, 1, 13, 14, 57, 108, 117.

identity politics, 1, 2, 13, 15, 28, 29, 31, 35, 46, 57, 58, 184, 191, 228, 234, 251.

immigrants, 23, 32, 42, 48, 76.

immigration, 25, 27, 187.

impotence, 43, 97.

In the Valley of Elah, 253, 254.

infantilism (male), 44, 188, 220-22.

Irish-Americans, 48, 173, 205.

Italian-Americans, 183, 205, 206.

Jackie Brown, 179, 182, 204, 211, 212-13.

Jackson, Michael, 137-38.

Jameson, Fredric, 28, 128, 242.

Jeffords, Susan, 11, 57, 100, 105, 107, 108.

Jewish masculinity, 186-87.

Jordan, Neil, 149-50, 163n51.

Jumpin' Jack Flash, 142.

Kalifornia, 15, 232.

Kerouac, Jack, 175.

Kill Bill, 179, 194, 211.

King, Rodney, 26, 49, 120, 129n14, 171.

Klein, Calvin, 89-90.

Kristeva, Julia, 6, 71, 82n70, 130.

Lacan, Jacques, 5-6, 9, 96, 101, 111n6, 122, 147, 154, 155-56, 161, 170, 196n19, 217, 224n46.

Lacanian film theory, 6, 86.

The Last Seduction, 37, 38, 146, 147.

Latinos/as, 27, 32, 33, 47-48, 59.

The Lawnmower Man, 117-18.

Lee, Spike, 14, 46-48, 168, 182-85, 189.

Lehman, Peter, 12, 91, 96-97, 112n35.

lesbian and gay activism, 3, 25, 29, 46, 57, 161, 230.

lesbians, 46, 76, 148, 152, 155.

Lethal Weapon, 60, 73, 98-99, 102, 149, 214, 238-39, 240.

The Long Kiss Goodnight, 102, 104, 105.

The Lord of the Rings, 107-8, 254.

Los Angeles, 30, 31-32, 34, 48, 51n43, 119; 1992 uprisings in, 26.

Lott, Eric, 9, 48-49, 172, 173-74, 177, 178, 192, 194, 196n34.

M. Butterfly, 146, 148-49.

Madonna, 137.

Magnolia, 66-67, 71.

Mailer, Norman, 168, 175-76.

About the Author

Nicola Rehling received her PhD from Aristotle University of Thessaloniki, Greece, where she currently teaches courses on film and literature. She has also lectured in film studies at City College, Thessaloniki (Affiliated Institution of The University of Sheffield). She has published articles on popular cinema and modernist literature. Her current research projects include representations of Greek masculinities in popular film and cinematic representations of aging.